# Globalizing Justice

Combining deep moral argument with extensive factual inquiry, Richard Miller constructs a new account of international justice. Though a critic of demanding principles of kindness toward the global poor and an advocate of special concern for compatriots, he argues for standards of responsible conduct in transnational relations that create vast unmet obligations. Governments, firms and people in developed countries, above all the United States, by failing to live up to these responsibilities, take advantage of people in developing countries.

Miller's proposed standards of responsible conduct offer answers to such questions as: What must be done to avoid exploitation in transnational manufacturing? What framework for world trade and investment would be fair? What duties do we have to limit global warming? What responsibilities to help meet basic needs arise when foreign powers steer the course of development? What obligations are created by uses of violence to sustain American global power?

*Globalizing Justice* provides new philosophical foundations for political responsibility, a unified agenda of policies for responding to major global problems, a distinctive appraisal of 'the American empire' and realistic strategies for a global social movement that helps to move humanity toward genuine global cooperation.

# OXFORD
UNIVERSITY PRESS

Great Clarendon Street, Oxford OX2 6DP

Oxford University Press is a department of the University of Oxford.
It furthers the University's objective of excellence in research, scholarship,
and education by publishing worldwide in

Oxford New York

Auckland Cape Town Dar es Salaam Hong Kong Karachi
Kuala Lumpur Madrid Melbourne Mexico City Nairobi
New Delhi Shanghai Taipei Toronto

With offices in

Argentina Austria Brazil Chile Czech Republic France Greece
Guatemala Hungary Italy Japan Poland Portugal Singapore
South Korea Switzerland Thailand Turkey Ukraine Vietnam

Oxford is a registered trade mark of Oxford University Press
in the UK and in certain other countries

Published in the United States
by Oxford University Press Inc., New York

British Library Cataloguing in Publication Data

Data available

Library of Congress Control Number: 2009942572

Typeset by Laserwords Private Limited, Chennai, India
Printed in Great Britain
on acid-free paper by
Clays Ltd, St Ives plc

ISBN 978–0–19–958198–6 (hbk.)
    978–0–19–958199–3 (pbk.)

2

For
Peggy and Laura

# Acknowledgments

I HAVE been greatly helped by comments on work that led to this book, including insightful responses of Charles Beitz, Harry Brighouse, Robert Goodin, Daniel Koltonski, Mathias Risse, Carolina Sartorio, Henry Shue, Peter Singer, Kok-Chor Tan and anonymous readers for Oxford University Press. I am especially indebted to Richard Arneson for his incisive, constructive criticisms. I am deeply grateful to my wife, Peggy, for the patient, understanding support she has lovingly provided.

I have used parts of previously published work of mine, and would like to thank the publishers for permission. "Beneficence, Duty and Distance," *Philosophy & Public Affairs* 32 (2004): 357-83 is the source of much of Chapter 1, by permission of Blackwell Publishing. I also made use of passages from "Moral Closeness and World Community" in Deen Chatterjee, ed., *The Ethics of Assistance: Morality and the Distant Needy* (Cambridge: Cambridge University Press, 2004); "Unlearning American Patriotism," *Theory and Research in Education* 5 (2007): 7–21, by permission of Sage Publications; and "Global Power and Economic Justice," in Charles Beitz and Robert Goodin, eds., *Global Basic Rights* (Oxford: Oxford University Press, 2009). I am grateful to the National Endowment for the Humanities for a fellowship that supported work on this book in 2004.

# Contents

Introduction: International Justice and Transnational Power     1

1. Kindness and Its Limits     9

2. Compatriots and Foreigners     31

3. Globalization Moralized     58

4. Global Harm and Global Equity: The Case of Greenhouse Justice     84

5. Modern Empire     118

6. Empire and Obligation     147

7. Imperial Excess     181

8. Quasi-Cosmopolitanism     210

9. Global Social Democracy     238

*Notes*     261
*Bibliography*     321
*Index*     337

# Introduction: International Justice and Transnational Power

PEOPLE in developed countries have a vast, largely unmet responsibility to help people in developing countries. Their fulfillment of this political duty would produce great benefits for the global poor, but impose significant costs in developed countries.

This book is dedicated to justifying these claims in a distinctive way. The vast, unmet global responsibility is not a duty of kindness toward the needy. It is, primarily, a duty to avoid taking advantage of people in developing countries. Just as relationships to compatriots, friends and family give rise to distinctive duties of concern, the standards of due concern that must be met to properly value the interests and autonomy of people in developing countries, rather than taking advantage of them, depend on the nature of interactions with them. The crucial global interactions, in which power is currently massively abused, include transnational manufacturing, deliberations setting the institutional framework for world trade and finance, the global greenhouse effect and the effort to contain it, the shaping of development policies, and uses of violence in maintaining influence over developing countries. In repairing current defects in these transnational activities, we move toward global interactions of genuine cooperation based on mutual respect—an aspiration familiar from justice among compatriots, even if it leads to different standards of justice and very different institutions, on a global scale.

This inquiry into current abuses of transnational power reconciles the familiar cosmopolitan demand for massive help to the foreign poor with the patriot's insight that demanding political obligations reflect specific relationships. The study of the realities of international power becomes a basis for transnational moral standards, not a way of avoiding moral assessment. The account of how abuses of power create unmet responsibilities to help strengthens a vital social movement already under way, a global version of social democracy. Special concern for disadvantaged compatriots in developed countries is combined with demanding commitments to help the foreign poor, even in some cases in which these needs compete and even in times of domestic economic trouble: while charity begins at home, the main bases for transnational demands will be enduring imperatives to use power responsibly, not imperatives of charity.

Seeking to fulfill these promises, I will criticize prominent arguments of philosophers in the first two chapters and then engage in detailed examination of the interactions across borders that are the real basis for a vast, unmet transnational responsibility. Finally, the diagnosis of current moral disorders will be used to prescribe ultimate moral goals and current means of moving toward them. The rest of this introduction is a map of this long journey.

## Turning Toward Relationships

To justify resort to a wideranging survey of specific relations, I will first consider and reject two standard paths of philosophical inquiry into global justice. These approaches avoid reliance on all but the most obvious facts of transnational interaction in arguing for demanding duties of people in developed countries to help the global poor.

One is the path of general beneficence. Some philosophers have tried to base a demanding obligation to help poor people in developing countries on a general principle of responsiveness to neediness as such, regardless of relationship to the needy. They argue that virtually everyone would be led to this principle of beneficence by adequate reflection on the initially secure convictions that are the raw material for moral judgment. The power of their arguments—above all, Peter Singer's—keeps this position at the center of philosophical controversy over international responsibilities. But, I will argue, the proper outcome of reflective working up of moral common sense is too moderate and flexible to support extensive demands for aid to the global poor, independent of further relationships. A person is responsive enough to neediness as such when more underlying concern would risk worsening her life if she met her other responsibilities. Moreover, she is not obliged to devote her concerns to the neediest if other worthy causes are closer to her heart.

The second path—powerfully and diversely advocated by Charles Beitz, Thomas Pogge and Henry Shue, among others—takes a first turn into the sphere of transnational relations. A demanding transnational political duty of concern is based on aspects of the global scene that are, in part, relational, but utterly uncontroversial—not just the concentration of extreme neediness in developing countries, accompanied by much comfort and luxury in developed countries, but also the obvious fact of global economic interdependence, including the assertion of exclusive property rights. This perspective receives powerful support from a challenge to explain demanding political duties to help disadvantaged compatriots: if we have such duties, at least when transnational interactions are put to one side, what could their basis be other than the economic interdependence that now obviously links people throughout the world? In arguing that the second path is not sufficiently engaged in the specifics of transnational interactions, I will try to meet this challenge. Our political obligations to disadvantaged compatriots respond to specific forms of loyal participation, public provision and political coercion that bind compatriots but not mere partners in commerce. *If* the mere fact of global commerce were the only morally relevant link across borders, then these relationships would sustain a strong political duty of priority for compatriots: it would be wrong to support political measures advancing the interests of disadvantaged foreigners at significant cost to compatriots, even if the foreign poor are needier and more effectively helped. That "if" creates the agenda for the constructive project of this book. Transnational interactions might create vast, demanding duties to help the foreign poor, restricting means of helping disadvantaged compatriots. But the existence of such interactions has to be established through further empirical inquiry into current features of international life and reflection on their moral consequences.

## The Panoply of Relevant Interactions

Pursuing this method of inquiry, I will examine a series of ways in which conduct originating in developed countries affects lives in developing countries. The series will move from less to more intrusive forms, from specific commercial relations characteristic of globalization at one extreme to violent destruction inflicted across borders at the other.

*Exploitation in the Transnational Economy.* The first source of unmet responsibilities is a current feature of transnational production and exchange, giving substance to a charge of exploitation. People in developed countries take advantage of people in developing countries in deriving benefits from bargaining weakness due to desperate neediness. To express appreciation of the equal worth of people in developing countries and a proper valuing of their autonomy, people in developed countries must be willing to use the benefits to relieve the underlying desperate neediness.—Here, as in most of the other indictments, I will not claim that those who wrongfully take advantage impose poverty on the poor or typically make their lives worse than they would have been, claims of harm evoked by important arguments of Thomas Pogge's. So it will be crucial to show that someone can be wrongfully exploited when she is made better off.

*Inequity in International Trade Arrangements.*   In the second type of inter-action, governments reach agreements over the institutional framework of global commerce in ways that currently justify the charge of inequity. The governments of major developed countries, led by the United States, take advantage of bargaining weaknesses of the peoples of developing countries, often due to desperate neediness, to shape arrangements far more advantageous to developed countries than reasonable deliberations would sustain. This creates a duty of a citizen of one of these countries (especially pressing in the United States) to support new measures that reasonable deliberations would yield. — To specify this duty, I will describe how reasonableness is determined by responsibilities of participants, both international responsibilities of good faith and responsibilities toward compatriots. The combination of international good faith and domestic responsibility will turn out to require a large shift in current benefits and burdens in favor of people in developing countries, along with some significant losses to economically vulnerable people in developed countries.

*Negligence in Climate Harms.*   Recently, a different task of collective regulation has come to the fore, not the promotion of benefits of economic activity by mutually accepted constraints but the containment of climate harms inflicted as an unintended effect of economic activity. The American combination of contribution to the harm and reluctance to contribute to its remedy has been widely denounced. But there is little agreement on what standard of international equity should govern humanity's response to the greenhouse challenge and what rationale establishes the right current global goal in limiting future climate change.—I will defend a model of fair teamwork, as the equitable way of coping with the current tendency to cause unintended climate harm: people everywhere should seek an impartially acceptable allocation of sacrifices in a joint effort to keep global warming within bounds. This standard will turn out to strongly favor needy people in developing countries while probably imposing morally serious losses on significant numbers of people in developed countries. (The commitment to limit unintended harms that imposes these risks is entailed by the same values of free and equal citizenship as dictate concern for compatriots in developed countries.)

*Imperial Irresponsibility.*   In addition to describing what would be fair in specific agreements that advance global economic activity and contain its harmful side-effects, an account of global justice should identify moral responsibilities due to ways in which some governments exercise power over lives in foreign countries. This is the most direct analogue of the generation of responsibilities toward compatriots by sovereign domestic power. But the relevant facts and moral consequences are hard to describe in a post-colonial world in which transnational power is exercised without assertions of political authority. I will mainly investigate this source of duties to help through moral scrutiny of a pattern of domineering influence through which the United States takes advantage of other countries' difficulties in going against its will, a pattern worthy of the label "the American empire." While this imperial conduct will not create the same duties toward the disadvantaged as those that bind compatriots, it will turn out to create exceptionally demanding, largely unmet duties of concern. (Through alliance with the United States or similar independent initiatives, these responsibilities extend, to a lesser degree, to most developed countries.) In steering courses of development, often via international institutions, the United States acquires a residual responsibility to provide for basic needs. In propping up client regimes, the United States acquires a duty to make up for their moral failings. Finally, the violent destruction inflicted and sponsored by the United States generates large responsibilities. Extensive violent destruction in developing countries within the fairly recent past generates a correspondingly extensive duty of repair, even if this violence is not unjust. In addition, systematic tendencies toward injustice in this violence create a political duty of a U.S. citizen to take part in movements to reduce abuses of destructive power.

## Quasi-Cosmopolitanism

Each type of interaction in this survey generates an obligation to help that is limited in extent, stopping short of provision for important needs that people in developing countries cannot meet by their own efforts. Some of the obligations would not concentrate benefits on the world's neediest people. For these and other reasons, the relational perspective is apt to yield a total pattern of fulfilled obligations with different contours than the perspectives of impartial global concern that are generally labelled "cosmopolitan." And yet, these different perspectives give rise to similar strivings to help people in developing countries, within the bounds of political feasibility.

When moral demands due to all of these transnational interactions are combined with the real, if limited, demands of transnational beneficence, the outcome is a large moral responsibility to advance interests of needy people in all developing countries. This debt will not be paid, because of a disastrous irony: the transnational influence of developed countries that generates demanding responsibilities is guided by enduring interests and institutional tendencies that guarantee deep irresponsibility in dealings with vulnerable people in developing countries, especially among the most influential powers. Faced with the need to make progress against injustice, a responsible person gives priority to efforts that help more who suffer gravely from injustice over those that help fewer, to help for those who suffer more gravely and to efforts that do the most to lighten burdens. When these criteria conflict, choice behind a global "veil of ignorance" guaranteeing global impartiality will turn out to adjudicate the trade-offs. So, within the limits of political feasibility, people seeking to overcome current transnational irresponsibility should have the priorities of someone committed to globally impartial concern.

They should also, in a sense, be cosmopolitan in their political ideals. The ultimate positive goal implicit in the rejection of transnational relations of exploitation, inequity and negligent harm is a world in which mutual reliance across borders is genuinely cooperative, based on mutual trust among self-respectful participants. Domestic justice pursues the same general cooperative goal in relationships of different (but, often, analogous) kinds. So the ultimate goal of global justice will turn out to mirror the ultimate goal of domestic justice in this way: they are both goals of civic friendship, taking different forms appropriate to different circumstances.


## Global Social Democracy

Finding a sound argument that people in developed countries have vast unmet political responsibilities to help people in developing countries is one thing. Finding a method of persuasion that helps to promote fulfillment of these responsibilities is quite another. The political point of the arguments of this book might seem especially weak in the United States, where they ascribe the gravest unmet responsibilities. The thought that one's country has massively abused its international power and the admission that global justice may require serious losses among vulnerable compatriots are not apt to be very popular.

I will conclude by describing how the connections between power, moral responsibility and actual irresponsibility that dominate this book can be put to political use, especially in the United States. Arguments making those connections advance a crucial social movement that is already under way, a globalized form of social democracy that has a special potential to reduce transnational irresponsibility by changing strategic calculations that shape foreign policy. At least among Americans, commitment to this movement will turn out to be cosmopolitan in one further, painful respect. It makes American patriotism a moral burden. More positively put: in the United States and, perhaps, some other developed countries, future progress toward global civic friendship will turn out to be a prerequisite for secure, informed, responsible love of country.

## "Developing Countries"

My largest claims employ a category, developing countries, that requires a warning label. Following familiar usage, I use "developing countries" to refer to countries with a substantial proportion of inhabitants who are hard-pressed to meet urgent material needs and with a technology of production which has long, as a whole, been significantly behind the world's most advanced, and use "developed countries" to refer to those in which absolute destitution and backward technology are, at most, marginal exceptions. This standard usage requires a warning about diversity. There are great differences among developing countries. In 2005, one in six people in China lived below the World Bank's "dollar a day" poverty threshold, a third below the "two dollar a day" threshold, median annual individual consumption was about $1,200 at purchasing power parity, and 20 percent of young children were stunted by malnutrition. But national economic growth was stellar and supported by substantial investments in capital equipment and infrastructure, the scale of China's production, markets and military gave it a significant voice in international affairs, millions lived in urban enclaves of prosperity, and life expectancy at birth was 72 years. The situation was very different for people in the worst-off among sub-Saharan African countries—for example, Malawi, where, despite recent strong growth, median consumption was less than a third of China's, the per capita level of investment less than a tenth, the scale of the economy was globally negligible, and life expectancy was 48 years.[1]*

I hope to do justice to the differences among developing countries as well as their similarities. Detailed attention to specific features of transnational

---

* Numerals of this size will be used to indicate notes with substantive content. In bold face, they will refer to especially long and substantive notes. Small numerals (for example, "13") will refer to notes consisting solely of citations.

interactions will help to combat the illusion of uniformity among developing countries, and will yield moral standards that reflect their different capacities. Establishment of the quasi-cosmopolitan priorities will give proper standing to different needs for help throughout the range of developing countries. The rise of China, India and Brazil will turn out to make it all the more urgent to advance the cause of global social democracy.

In moving from moral flaws in the exercise of economic and political power to responsibilities for promoting much more help but less intrusion and, then, to a global social movement, the whole argument will rely on ever widening empirical inquiries. Before starting this exploration of global power, it is important to see whether it is needed to establish the most important duties of global justice. According to influential philosophical arguments, people in developed countries would be led by rational reflection on ordinary secure moral convictions to a demanding requirement of concern for the world's neediest, without reliance on any specific or controversial characterization of interactions with them. I will begin by explaining why this evasion of specific relationships in the foundations of international justice is misguided.

# 1

# Kindness and Its Limits

AN enduring argument of Peter Singer's is so central to philosophical controversies, so attractive in its moral premises and so radical in its demands that it is the natural benchmark for assessing the duty to help the global poor regardless of any special connection to them. He first presented it in 1972, in an article that began by describing the starvation and homelessness that were then ravaging East Bengal. If the argument is sound, there is no need to inquire into special relationships or shared histories to justify an extremely demanding answer to the question, "What advantages is a relatively affluent person in a developed country obliged to give up in the interests of poor people in developing countries?" Only that person's wealth, those people's poverty and the capacity to use the former to relieve the burdens of the latter come into play.

Singer is a utilitarian, committed to the doctrine that we always have a duty to make the choice by which we contribute as much as we can to over-all happiness. If he had argued for his conclusion from this stern philosophical premise, no one would have paid attention. Utilitarianism clearly gives rise to extraordinary demands. Few of us are drawn to a principle that obliges someone to sacrifice both her arms if this is the only way to save another from death by buzz saw, and, indeed, obliges surgeons secretly to harvest the organs of someone undergoing gall bladder surgery if the only other significant consequence is life for three children needing organ transplants. Singer's argument remains a vital presence because he seemed to describe a route by which virtually all of us, including people appalled by utilitarianism, would be forced by reflection on our own convictions and a plausible empirical hypothesis to embrace a radical moral imperative of global aid.

This project of deriving an extraordinary conclusion from ordinary views hinges on Singer's claim that the following principle is "surely undeniable," at least once we reflect on secure convictions concerning rescue.

The Principle of Sacrifice: "If it is in our power to prevent something very bad from happening, without thereby sacrificing anything else morally significant, we ought, morally, to do so."[1]

Combined with further premises, this principle leads to the demanding imperative to give which I will call "the radical conclusion":

Everyone has a duty not to spend money on luxuries or frills, and to use the savings due to abstinence to help those in dire need.

More precisely, the radical conclusion rules out spending money for the sake of enjoyed consumption on anything of a sort that is not needed to avoid deprivation.[2] For example, Singer condemns buying clothes "not to keep ourselves warm but to look 'well-dressed'" (p. 235) and insists that everyone who is not needy has a duty to donate until donating more would impoverish her or a dependent.[3]

The first of the two further, auxiliary premises needed to derive the radical conclusion is an uncontroversial assessment of importance: on any particular occasion, or small bunch of occasions, on which one has the opportunity to buy a luxury or frill, the choice, instead, to spend no more than what is needed to buy a plain, functional alternative is not a morally significant sacrifice. After all, no one outside of the inevitable minority of eccentrics would claim that I make a morally significant sacrifice if I buy a plain warm department store brand sweater for $22.95 instead of a stunning designer label sweater on sale for $49.95.

The other auxiliary is an empirical claim about current consequences of giving: because of the availability of international aid agencies, donating money saved by avoiding the purchase of a luxury or frill (perhaps combined with money saved on similar occasions in a small bunch) is always a way of preventing something very bad from happening. Suppose, for example, that donating the savings from buying the cheaper sweater to a UNICEF immunization campaign would prevent a child from being killed by the readily preventable infections that ravage children in the poorest countries. If I buy the designer label sweater instead, I violate the Principle of Sacrifice, doing wrong if that principle is right.

The empirical claim about the cost and impact of available aid might be challenged in several ways. While charity appeals tend to emphasize the cheapness of the resource used in the last link of international aid—a $25 dose of vaccine, say, or a few cents' worth of oral rehydration salts—this is the last stage in a process that is much more expensive, involving, at the very least, transportation, training and administration and sometimes the need to pay off the corrupt and replenish what they steal. The possible but avoidable calamities addressed by most humanitarian aid are not certain to occur in the absence of aid: about one in five Malians dies before the age of five, usually on account of readily treatable infections; so four out of five survive. Nor is it a sure thing that one's donation will increase humane interventions. For example, there is cause for concern that governments of poor countries reduce internally financed help to the vulnerable in response to external aid.

While these observations may be significant in other contexts, they seem lame excuses in the context of Singer's argument for a personal duty of aid. The combination of pro-rated overhead with the final link in aid to an imperiled foreigner typically adds up to no more than savings from a small bunch of abstentions from luxuries and frills, i.e., too small a bunch to constitute a morally significant sacrifice. (Taking the further expenses into account, Peter Unger has reported estimates that a $200 donation would provide a typical two-year-old in a poor country with adequate health care through the age of six, the end of the period of severe early vulnerability.)[4] In any case, our judgments that it was wrong to withhold aid often respond to the small burden of supplying one needed link in a larger aid process—the easy toss of a life-preserver, say, not the cost of building the jetty and installing life-preservers at regular intervals. While those helped by international aid are rarely doomed without it, moral requirements of preventing something very bad from happening do not limit prevention to the heading off of what was otherwise certain. One can, in the morally relevant sense, prevent a child from being mauled by leading him away from a snarling dog even if four in five children menaced by a snarling dog are not mauled. Finally, the worry about impact in recipient countries seems a reason to take care in choosing agencies, favoring those most effective in meeting desperate needs that local governments would not otherwise relieve, rather than a reason why one need not contribute. There is always some risk of doing no good on balance, but given the stipulated moral insignificance of the sacrifice, this seems as lame a reason not to help as the protest of someone who does not want to toss the life-preserver ornamenting his flagpole toward a drowning child: "Perhaps the waves will carry it away."

In any case, focussing the critique of Singer's argument on the premise of sufficient efficacy would by-pass an important, controversial moral thesis. This is the conditional claim that one has a duty to give up luxuries and frills and donate the savings whenever there are agencies that can use the donation to prevent something very bad from happening.

For all these reasons, I will adopt the simplifying assumption that buying the plain sweater means forgoing an opportunity to save a child's life in a poor country. When this assumption is combined with the other, moral premises, an upscale shopping mall becomes a place of dire moral danger.

Admittedly, once someone has seen its radical consequence, "the uncontroversial appearance" (p. 231) of the Principle of Sacrifice might disappear. But in Singer's view, it becomes undeniable, for virtually everyone, in light of adequate reflection on a revealing example. If Singer, rushing to a lecture, encounters a toddler drowning in a shallow pond, he has a duty to wade in and pull the child out so long as this only has a morally insignificant cost, such as muddied clothes and late arrival. But "if we accept any principle of impartiality, universality, equality, or whatever, we cannot discriminate against someone just because he is far away from us" (p. 232). So ordinary secure convictions concerning duties of nearby rescue seem to combine with ordinary deep convictions concerning moral equality to make the Principle of Sacrifice an accurate description of a duty to save those in peril, near or far.

Singer's reasoning is a paradigm of arguments for radical demands of beneficence that have flourished in recent decades, offered by Singer and his allies as entailing demanding aid for the world's neediest, in response to the distribution of needs, resources and capacities for transfer, in imperatives derived from ordinary moral convictions. But despite its continuing appeal, Singer's effort to derive the radical conclusion from rational reflection on ordinary morality and a plausible empirical claim misinterprets ordinary morality: it neglects the role of relationships to others, to oneself and to one's underlying goals in shaping the demands of equal respect for persons. Of course, it would be bizarre and appalling for anyone to deny that the importance of having that designer label sweater pales beside the importance of a child's going on to lead a healthy life. What makes the purchase not wrong, nonetheless, must be a general principle, a more permissive rival to the Principle of Sacrifice, which is justified by considerations other than the relative importance of the interests at stake on particular occasions of choice. After describing such a principle and defending it as an adequate expression of respect for persons, I will reconcile it with our secure convictions concerning duties of rescue, such as the conviction that Singer must save the drowning toddler. The outcome will not vindicate selfishness in a world of dire need, which is appalling to ordinary moral conscience. Even in the absence of special relationships, the well-off will have a duty, often neglected, to respond to neediness as such. However, relevant interaction with the needy will turn out to be a necessary ingredient in any genuinely demanding obligation to help the global poor.[5]

## The Principle of Sympathy

Like Singer's Principle of Sacrifice, the more moderate rival is meant to describe our duty to give to others apart from special relationships, circumstances and shared histories.

> The Principle of Sympathy: One's underlying disposition to respond to neediness as such ought to be sufficiently demanding that giving which would express greater underlying concern would impose a significant risk of worsening one's life, if one fulfilled all further responsibilities; and it need not be any more demanding than this.

Someone's choices or a pattern of choices on his part violate this principle if he would not so act if he had the attitude it dictates and were relevantly well-informed.

The "neediness" in question is the sort of deprivation that Singer labels "very bad." By "a significant risk of worsening one's life," I mean a nontrivial chance that one's life as a whole will be worse than it would otherwise be. The episodes that make a life worse than it would otherwise be need not extend through a long period of someone's life or impose grave burdens. Still, the fact that things could have gone better for me at a certain time or that my frustrated desire might have been satisfied does not entail that my life is worse than it would have been had things gone my way. When I eat in a restaurant and am not served as good a meal as might be served, I do not, by that token, have a worse life.[6]—Admittedly, some would respond to this example with a judgment that my life is worse, but only insignificantly. There is no need to pursue the disagreement, here. Someone drawn to this response can recalibrate the Principle of Sympathy and the rest of this chapter to fit this other appraisal: treat "significant risk of worsening one's life" as short for "significant risk of significantly worsening one's life."

By "underlying disposition to respond to others' neediness," I mean the responsiveness to others' neediness as a reason to help that would express the general importance one ascribes to relieving neediness—in other words, one's basic concern for others' neediness. This is the disposition that would figure in a judgment of one's character as kind or callous. Underlying dispositions, expressing basic concerns, need not, by themselves, entail any definite personal policy of specific conduct in response to specific circumstances. Thus, some are inclined to contribute to cancer research, while others, whose basic concern with human neediness is the same, are inclined to contribute to the relief of hunger. Still, basic concerns rationalize and are manifested in our personal policies, our specific determinations to act in certain ways.[7]

## A Moderate Duty

The Principle of Sacrifice only led to the radical conclusion in light of assessments of the moral significance of costs. Similarly, the impact of Sympathy on obligations to aid will depend on what counts as worsening someone's life. So long as these assessments are compatible with the judgments, on reflection, of most of us (as Singer's project requires), then Sympathy's constraint on spending-rather-than-donating is moderate: it is wrong to fill vast closets with designer clothes in a world in which many must dress in rags, but not wrong occasionally to purchase a designer label shirt which is especially stylish and, though not outlandishly expensive, more expensive than neat plain alternatives.

Additional responsiveness to others' neediness worsens someone's life if it deprives him of adequate resources to pursue, enjoyably and well, a worthwhile goal with which he intelligently identifies and from which he could not readily detach. By "a goal with which someone identifies," I mean a basic interest that gives point and value to specific choices and plans. Such a constituent of someone's personality might be part of her description of "the sort of person I am." Suppose her affirmation of a goal in such a self-portrayal would properly be unapologetic. Given her other goals and capacities, her attachment to this goal is an interest that enriches her life if she can pursue it well. Then it is, for that person, a worthwhile goal.

On certain puritanical conceptions of what goals are worthwhile, no goal requiring the occasional acquisition of a luxury or frill should be affirmed without apology. But these are minority doctrines, not elements of the ordinary moral thinking to which Singer appeals. In ordinary assessments, my worthwhile goals include the goal of presenting myself to others in a way that expresses my own aesthetic sense and engages in the fun of mutual aesthetic recognition. I need not apologize for being the sort of person who exercises his aesthetic sense and social interest in these ways. My life is enriched, not stultified, by this interest, given my other interests and capacities. And to pursue this goal enjoyably and well, I must occasionally purchase a luxury or frill, namely, some stylish clothing, rather than a less expensive, plain alternative. Similarly, I could not pursue, enjoyably and well, my worthwhile goal of eating in a way that explores a variety of interesting aesthetic and cultural possibilities if I never ate in nice restaurants; and I could not adequately fulfill my worthwhile goal of enjoying the capacity of great composers and performers to exploit nuances of timbre and texture to powerful aesthetic effect without buying more than minimal stereo equipment. So I do not violate Sympathy in occasionally purchasing these luxuries and frills.[8]

Granted, others' lives are illuminated, as least as brightly, by the pursuit of less expensive goals than my goals of expressing my aesthetic sense and interacting with others' in how I dress, savoring and exploring cuisines, and appreciating great musical achievements. Perhaps I could have identified with their less expensive goals, if helped to do so at an early age, so that these would have been the goals giving point and value to my choices. However, since the Principle of Sympathy regulates my duty of beneficence by what threatens to worsen my own life, the limits of my duty are set by the demands of the worthwhile goals with which I could now readily identify. For if someone cannot readily identify with less demanding goals, the possibility that they might have been his does not determine what would actually worsen his life. Many poor people in the United States would not be burdened by their poverty if, through some strenuous project of self-transformation, they had made their life-goals similar enough to well-adjusted hermit monks' and nuns'. This does not entail that their lives are not worse because of their poverty. One has a prerogative to refuse to do violence to who one is, radically changing one's worthwhile goals, rather as parents have a prerogative, within limits, to try to pass on their way of life to their children.

Even though Sympathy permits lots of nonaltruistic spending that Sacrifice would forbid, it still requires significant giving from most of the nonpoor. The underlying goals to which most of us who are not poor are securely attached leave room for this giving: we could pursue these goals enjoyably and well and fulfill our other responsibilities, while giving significant amounts to the needy. This is, then, our duty, according to Sympathy. Indeed, this principle preserves some of the critical edge of the radical conclusion, since people are prone to exaggerate risks of self-worsening. It is hard to avoid overrating what merely frustrates, blowing it up into something that worsens one's life. It is extremely difficult to avoid excessive anxieties about the future which make insignificant risks of self-worsening seem significant (say, overwrought fears of a future in which one will regret responsiveness to charities such as Oxfam). It is easy to convince oneself that one cannot readily detach from a goal which one could actually slough off with little effort, developing or strengthening cheaper interests instead. Because of these enduring pressures to misapply the Principle of Sympathy, it is a constant struggle to live up to its demands.

Because the Principle of Sympathy focusses on worsening rather than some absolute threshold, it might seem to generate the radical conclusion, in the end. After all, at any level of monthly giving above the level of material deprivation, if anyone asks herself, "Would giving a dollar more each month impose a significant risk of making my life worse than it would be if I did not give this little bit more?", the answer is "No." So her underlying responsiveness to neediness would seem to be less than the Principle of Sympathy demands, until she has brought herself to the margin of genuine material deprivation, which is all that the radical conclusion requires.[9]

On the face of it, this argument is an exasperating trick, like a child's recurrent objection, "You're being too strict. What difference will it make if I stay up ten minutes more?" The trick is the confusion of underlying dispositions with personal policies that might express them. In typical cases, how kind one is, how concerned one is for neediness as such, does not depend on whether one gives a dollar more or less a month. Underlying concern for neediness, at the level of what is ultimately important to a person, is not that fine-grained. By the same token, a situation in which greater underlying concern would impose a significant risk of worsening one's life will be a situation in which one could not have a policy of giving a *significantly* greater amount without imposing this risk.

What makes insistence on the coarse-grainedness of underlying attitudes seem, nonetheless, an inadequate response to the argument from the trivial burden of giving a little bit more is the naturalness of being drawn to more giving by the thought, "Giving even one more dollar a month would save innocent children from desperate peril," and the typical absurdity of reassuring oneself that one's unrevised practice is all right by the further thought, "But after all, underlying concern for neediness is not subject to such fine distinctions." This *is* an absurd response to nearly all actual nagging self-doubts, among affluent people, when they read appeals from Oxfam and other groups noting how much difference a small contribution would make. But nearly all of us affluent people are aware that substantially greater helping of the needy would not significantly risk worsening our lives—or, in any case, Oxfam appeals trigger such awareness. In this context, the thought based on the fact about a little bit more that ought to prompt more giving is: "I should be doing lots more, but temptations abound and worries about what I may need are hard to keep in perspective. Still, without struggle and anxiety, I could do this little bit of all that I should be doing, and it would still do good."

Suppose, in contrast, that someone can assure herself that her ongoing pattern of giving adequately expresses her underlying concern for neediness and that the significantly greater giving that would express greater underlying concern would impose a significant risk of worsening her life. After reading an Oxfam mailing describing the relief provided by a small donation beyond her pattern, she could, cogently, tell herself, "I could have arrived at a slightly larger aid budget, but this slight difference would not have made me someone with greater underlying concern for the needy. Underlying concern for the needy is not subject to such fine distinctions. Since I am sufficiently well-disposed in my underlying attitude toward the needy, I do not have to give a little bit more, through extra donations on this scale."[10]

## Grounding Sympathy in Respect

Ordinary morality is not just a collection of principles governing specific fields of conduct, such as responsiveness to neediness. In addition to our inclinations to affirm specific principles and judgments of particular cases, most of us are committed to vague yet comprehensive principles of moral duty. For example, in ordinary moral thinking, a choice is wrong if and only if it could not be made under the circumstances by someone displaying equal respect for all persons; equivalently, a choice is wrong if and only if it is incompatible with the ascription of equal worth to everyone's life. To this extent, ordinary morality is adamantly cosmopolitan, just as Singer and his allies insist. These are vague precepts, in need of further interpretation, like crucial precepts in most countries' constitutions, such as the guarantee of "equal protection of the laws" in the United States Constitution. Still, they are important constraints. Like a responsible Supreme Court Justice determining whether a law is constitutional, a morally responsible person will seek specific principles of obligation that satisfy demands imposed by the best interpretation of the general precepts, the one that best fits the most secure specific judgments.

The Principle of Sympathy is an adequate expression of the fundamental general perspective of moral equality. On the one hand, a person who would not display greater basic concern for neediness even if this imposed no significant risk of worsening his life and did not detract from his responsibilities treats others' lives as less important than his own. On the other hand, someone whose responsiveness to neediness as such is as limited as Sympathy permits can appreciate the equal worth of everyone's life and show equal respect for all. "I show appreciation of the equal worth of everyone's life through sensitivity to others' neediness as such, but stop short of a sensitivity that would impose a significant risk of worsening my life if I live up to my other responsibilities" is not an internally inconsistent self-portrayal.

Of course, these claims require further scrutiny in light of alternative interpretations of the fundamental moral perspective. If equal respect for all required equal concern for all, then the Principle of Sympathy would be much too permissive. I show much less concern for imperiled children in developing countries than for myself when I spend money on stylish clothes, nice restaurant meals and excellent stereo equipment that could be used to save a child from early death. But equal respect does not entail equal concern.

Because we are rightly wary of giving too much weight to our own interests (recall the worries about misapplying Sympathy), the difference between equal respect and equal concern is clearest when a valuable special relationship to another leads to special concern. I am not equally concerned for the girl who lives across the street and for my daughter; for example, I am not inclined to do as much for this neighbor when she is just as needy as my daughter, even if her parents have reached their limit. But I do not regard this neighbor's life as less valuable than the life of my daughter; my unequal concern reflects a proper valuing of my special relationship to my daughter, not unequal respect.

The moral appropriateness of special concern for a person in a valuable relationship (an important theme in Samuel Scheffler's work[11]) is not just a matter of the productive role of such partiality in impartial human betterment. Singer regards a particular attitude of unequal concern as a desirable feature of a person if it leads her more effectively to contribute to over-all wellbeing, the ultimate goal (in his view) of impartial concern.[12] This is consistent with his implicit rejection of the Principle of Sympathy: in a highly unequal world with effective international aid agencies, a major shift in someone's giving that would jeopardize relatively expensive, worthwhile goals with which she identifies might make a net contribution to wellbeing in spite of reduced zest in her activities. But in ordinary moral thinking, the compatibility of an attitude of unequal concern with equal respect for all does not depend on its effectiveness in making one a more abundant source of wellbeing. If my daughter became a salesperson and I faced the ghastly choice of saving one of two people from a burning building, her or a surgeon with exceptional life-saving skills, my attachment would be responsible for a choice that reduces my contribution to over-all wellbeing in the course of my life, but the choice would be compatible with equal respect for all. Nor does the compatibility with equal respect of an attitude of unequal concern depend on its being likely to maximize production of wellbeing in foreseeable circumstances (as opposed to such ghastly surprises as the forced choice in front of the burning building). Perhaps a doctor working in a chronically understaffed inner city emergency room would be apt to do more good in foreseeable circumstances if he weakened his attachment to his family, embracing a workaholic way of life in which saving lives is the central motivation. Still, he does not show that he regards the lives of people in the inner city as less valuable than others' if he sustains and expresses his attachment to his family by quitting to set up a suburban practice, when he sees that his family life is in jeopardy because he is returning home numb after long hours of life-saving work.

These judgments do not just reflect the fact that special relationships entailing special concern have independent value as components of wellbeing. Insistence that responses to special relationships be authorized, in the final analysis, from a perspective of impartial concern is misguided even if this point about well-being is accepted. The improvement in family life due to the physician's job-change will, presumably, be less than new deficits in family life due to worse medical care for parents brought to the emergency room. I do not express a proper valuing of my relationship to my child if I neglect her in order to increase over-all wellbeing by introducing nurturant parenthood into the lives of parents of two other children.

Neither is special concern in response to special relationships to be justified, in a rule-utilitarian way, by appeal to the over-all benefit of a system of social norms which enjoin or permit such concern. If the efficiency of raising children in group nurseries without the intense particular attachment of parental love were, in fact, a means of increasing total wellbeing, people could still rightly refuse to swallow a pill which allows them to blithely participate in the project, refusing because of their actual enmeshment in their children's lives or because of goals of parenting with which they actually identify. And similarly for children's loyalty to their parents, friends' mutual loyalties and other pills. In any case, the arbitrariness of confining utilitarianism to the level of social norms makes for bad justifications of atypical people's permissible partiality. The fact that the most beneficent system of norms for society as a whole permits special attention to family ties hardly explains why the emergency-room doctor does no wrong when he reduces wellbeing in response to his atypical opportunity to do good as a detached workaholic. Finally, a justification of partiality based on rule utilitarianism would rest the vindication of unequal concern on a doctrine that provides a notoriously defective account of inequality elsewhere. For rule utilitarianism clashes with secure judgments of what equal respect requires by endorsing social arrangements that severely oppress a few when this is a necessary side-effect of the most efficient means of producing over-all wellbeing—even slavery when this maximizes wellbeing by sustaining an especially productive division of labor.

In sum, if the comprehensive principles of moral obligation are interpreted in light of ordinary, secure convictions concerning partiality, the equal respect that determines moral duties is not itself an attitude of equal concern and does not require certification by a test of general benefit. But is the specific sort of unequal concern that Sympathy permits compatible with equal respect for all? The plausibility of this claim is strengthened by further scrutiny of valuable special relationships. In particular, the partiality toward one's child that is acceptable in parental nurturance combines unequal concern for persons with respect for all in a way that is analogous to the attitude toward oneself and others permitted by Sympathy.

Consider situations in which I could contribute resources to activities of my daughter which might, alternatively, help needier people to whom I have no valuable special relationship, to whom I have made no commitment, and whose needs I do not encounter in a special circumstance meriting special concern. It would be wrong for me invariably to devote the resources to my daughter in this kind of situation. This would involve my never giving to charity if I have a daughter (utterly different from my actual daughter) who always wants a new expensive trinket. But if greater responsiveness on my part to neediness as such were to pose a significant risk of worsening my daughter's life, then I do no wrong in failing to be more responsive.

The compatibility of such favoritism with equal respect is most vivid when doing less for a dependent child risks depriving her of access to extremely important capabilities. I do not manifest unequal respect or show that I attribute less worth to some lives than to others when I use money to pay for an excellent college education for my daughter, rather than not doing so and risking worsening her life; yet I know that the money I could save by insisting that she go to a much cheaper college that is not so good could be used by Oxfam to save many children from early death. But reasons for special concern need not be that strong to sustain a prerogative of favoritism. Suppose that my daughter has identified with the humble but worthwhile goal that I previously described of displaying her aesthetic sense and enjoyably interacting with others in the way she dresses. She can no more readily detach from this goal than most adults can. She has become her own person in this and other ways, although she will remain a financially dependent person for several crucial years, most of her childhood. Her life will be worse, in ordinary moral thinking, if I do not provide her with the means to pursue this humbler worthwhile goal enjoyably and well. Because of this, I do no wrong in providing a corresponding clothing allowance. Alternatively, by financing nothing more than neat, warm, plain clothing and donating the savings to an aid agency, I could prevent the early deaths of several other children. But my choice to make it possible for my child to exercise her sense of style as she grows up expresses an appropriate valuing of our special relationship, and not the horrendous view that her life is worth more than the life of a child in a village in Mali. (On the scale of early death, the badness of plain dressing for a typical child with that ordinary goal in dressing is not so different from the badness of going to a cheap mediocre college.)

The subject of Sympathy is a person's relationship to himself, as provider of his own resources. Of course, the sort of thing that a competent adult seeks, as a means of pursuing his goals, is, on the whole, very different from what a parent would provide to a dependent child. But in other ways, his relationship to himself is quite similar. He is his own most intimate dependent, profoundly reliant on his own efforts to provide needed resources and guidance, just as a child depends on a nurturant adult. And he has the primary responsibility for his life's going well, just as parents have the primary responsibility for their young children's lives. In ordinary moral thinking, there is a prerogative to express one's valuing of a parental relationship to one's child in special concern for her, so long as greater sensitivity to others' neediness as such would impose a significant risk of worsening her life. If so, it is hard to see why this same prerogative would not govern one's relationship to that other intimate dependent for whom one is responsible, oneself. Here, the avoidance of arbitrary distinctions, much emphasized by Singer and his allies as forcing the shift to radical beneficence, favors the relatively permissive Principle of Sympathy.


## Rejecting Singer's Principle

So far, commitment to the Principle of Sympathy seems compatible with equal respect. If so, the Principle of Sacrifice is too demanding to be a valid principle of moral obligation, a rule by which one must regulate one's choices to show equal respect for all. The crucial difference between the principles lies in what gets scrutinized by each: the impact, on particular occasions, of particular choices, or the impact of an underlying attitude on a life as a whole. On particular occasions on which donating the saving due to forbearance would prevent something very bad from happening, the Principle of Sacrifice only permits the more expensive purchase of a luxury or frill if choosing the cheaper plain alternative would constitute a morally significant sacrifice. There is no occasion or small bunch of occasions on which my declining an opportunity to buy a more luxurious item, buying a plain, cheaper one instead, constitutes a morally significant loss. After all, such a choice never makes my life worse; at most, it involves mere frustration. So, because of the opportunity presented by aid agencies, Sacrifice dictates abstinence. But what prohibits luxurious purchases on all particular occasions prohibits them, period. This would make it impossible for a typical, relatively affluent person to pursue, enjoyably and well, worthwhile goals to which he is securely attached, such as the goal in dressing that I described. So observance of Sacrifice would have an impact on someone's life as a whole in virtue of which it is to be rejected as too demanding, if Sympathy is right. No purchase prohibited by Singer's principle is morally significant, but the loss imposed by enduring commitment to the principle is, i.e., it is the sort of loss that can make it all right to embrace a less demanding commitment, instead. (Note the good fit between a principle scrutinizing the impact of underlying concerns and enduring commitments on a person's life and a morality based on an enduring, underlying attitude of equal respect, governing a morally responsible person's life.)

Of course, the thought that a donation could relieve desperate needs does, properly, lead people not to make a luxurious purchase on particular occasions, even when the purchase would advance a worthwhile goal. The Principle of Sympathy provides a basis for such reasoning, just as much as the Principle of Sacrifice. If a shopper is committed to Sympathy and inclined to purchase a shirt that is much more stylish but somewhat more expensive than a cheap but adequate alternative, the thought that donating the difference would relieve desperate needs might well prompt the question, "Would my life really be worse if I set tighter limits on my inclination to buy nice clothes?" His commitment to Sympathy, might, then, support a decision not to buy that particular luxury on that occasion, for one of the following reasons. Perhaps he realizes that the luxurious purchase would violate a personal policy that is his way of conforming to the demands of Sympathy, say, a policy of buying only occasionally and on sale. Then, he ought to stay the course unless other considerations intrude. (An occasional "just this once" purchase might be a means of pursuing the goal of avoiding rigid regimentation. But hasn't he been using this excuse rather often lately?) Or perhaps he realizes that the luxurious purchase would violate a personal policy that he should adopt as a way of resisting departures from Sympathy. Or he sees that he is simply spending more on nice clothes than he has to in order to avoid worsening his life. In each of these cases, in the absence of special considerations (say, a truly once-in-a-lifetime sale), he ought to implement the judgment of inadequate general sensitivity to others' needs through abstinence and donation now. The appalling ease with which one can submerge insight into one's deficient concern for neediness is a powerful reason to respond right away to the realization that one is moved by inclinations violating Sympathy

## Rescue and Distance

Within the circle of ordinary morality, this case for Sympathy is threatened by Singer's famous argument from the case of the drowning child. It is a secure conviction of virtually everyone that if Singer walks past a shallow pond on his way to give a lecture and sees a toddler drowning, he must wade in and save the child so long as he only incurs a morally insignificant loss, for example, muddied clothes. But by giving to international aid agencies, one can also rescue distant people from peril, for example, children in distant villages imperiled by lack of access to safe water and basic medical care. And someone's life is no less valuable because she is not near. So if we have a duty to prevent something very bad from happening to a nearby toddler at morally insignificant cost, it might seem that we have the same duty of aid to everyone in peril near or far, just as Sacrifice requires. Indeed, similar extrapolation to those near and far of plausible variants of Singer's example would impose even more serious demands than Sacrifice. If Bob is rushing to catch the only flight that will enable him to give the job talk that provides his one remaining realistic prospect of a career in philosophy before he must abandon this life goal, it seems that he must take the time to extract a toddler whom he encounters sinking into quicksand; he must do so even if he knows that he will miss the flight and may well have to lead a less satisfying life.[13]

If someone committed to moral equality had to be sensitive solely to the degree of neediness of others, the extent of her capacity to relieve it and the cost of the relief, when she chooses whether and how much to help those in need, then, there would be no way to resist the extrapolation of principles at least as demanding as Sacrifice from cases of obligatory rescue. But even when no special relationship or past interaction is in play (as in Singer's cases of the drowning toddler and imperiled children abroad), the requirement of sensitivity to neediness, capability and cost alone oversimplifies the demands of equal respect. Appreciation of the equal worth of everyone's life does entail a basic concern for neediness as such, a concern expressed in part by Sympathy. For someone who is faithful to this concern, a commitment to aid that does the most to help those in direst need is, as it were, the default personal policy: in allocating the demands of Sympathy; he only departs from it for adequate reasons. However, adequate reasons for departure do not have to appeal to costs or to any especially weighty consideration. The only large bequest in my stepfather's will was to help the blind. He was aware that the same donation to the fight against infectious disease in developing countries (the leading worldwide cause of death before the age of five) would have more effectively helped those in direst peril. But he gave to help the blind because his own vision problems made their plight especially poignant to him. In ordinary moral thinking, my stepfather's reason was good enough to reconcile his departure from the default policy with equal valuation of everyone's life. (In contrast, a rationale involving contempt for those whose needs he did not serve would have displayed unequal respect, even if the bequest helped those in need.)

Similarly, someone who appreciates the equal worth of everyone's life could be specially responsive to urgent needs encountered close at hand because close presence makes an urgent plight especially vivid and gripping to her. Her allocating aid on the basis of this reason no more expresses disvaluing of distant lives than my getting my car's brakes checked once a year expresses contempt for those whom my car approaches eleven months later.

Still, appreciation of the diversity of reasons that make special responsiveness all right is only the first step in meeting the challenge of the toddler judgments. More must be done to explain the duties toward the toddlers in a way that fits the case for Sympathy. In ordinary moral thinking, specific, potentially demanding responsiveness to imminent peril encountered close at hand is not just a personal policy compatible with equal respect for all. It is a requirement of equal respect. Yet the case for Sympathy depended on an interpretation of equal respect that might seem too permissive to reconcile with this requirement—indeed, too permissive in two different ways. First, the concern for neediness as such that equal respect requires was supposed to be an underlying disposition, regulated by its impact on one's life as a whole; the fact that one could relieve a dire burden on a particular occasion at no morally significant cost was not supposed to dictate aid on this occasion. Why, then, does equal respect require responsiveness to urgent peril of those encountered close at hand on the occasion of encounter? Second, equal respect was supposed to be compatible with unwillingness to display basic concern for neediness that would impose a significant risk of worsening one's life. Why, then, is Bob required to pull the toddler from the quicksand?

Suppose that someone who identifies the duty of general beneficence with Sympathy cannot explain why the duty to rescue someone in imminent peril close at hand is so much more urgent and more demanding than the duty of general beneficence that she acknowledges. Then, given the appeal of the toddler judgments, Sympathy is threatened. For (as Shelly Kagan has emphasized in similar contexts) we want our moral principles "to hang together, to be mutually supportive, to be jointly illuminated by the moral concepts to which we appeal."[14] In the absence of an explanation of the duties to rescue the toddlers that fits Sympathy as well, sterner principles of general beneficence, based on more stringent construals of equal respect, are waiting in the wings, to explain the toddler duties as specific consequences of their general demands.

This challenge to Sympathy can only be met by a suitable account of what is special about close encounters with people in urgent peril. The account must describe reasons shared by everyone who equally respects all which lead to a policy of special responsiveness to those encountered close by in urgent peril, responsiveness that can require aid as costly as Bob's. Yet these reasons must not undermine the claim that equal respect for all is displayed in responsiveness to neediness as such that is guided by Sympathy, with its moderate demands and primary attention to underlying attitudes.

In the normal background of human interaction, at least three mutually reinforcing considerations, shared by all who appreciate the equal worth of everyone's life, are compelling grounds for adopting a policy of special responsiveness to those in urgent peril who are near. First, any human who is, in other ways, disposed to display equal respect for all finds in herself a strong impulse to come to the aid of those whom she encounters in urgent peril close at hand. Assuming that she has no adequate reason to rein in this impulse as too demanding (an assumption that I will argue for later on), she ought to embrace it as a personal policy. Equal respect for all requires responsiveness to neediness that does not impose a serious risk of worsening one's life, and it is very hard to live up to this demand. It would be the height of arrogance to restrain a powerful impulse that helps to fulfill this imperative, if there is no reason to reject the impulse as excessively demanding.

In the second place, the prevalent special inclination to respond to nearby calamity with aid plays a distinctive coordinative role in advancing the general project of alleviating neediness that Sympathy imposes on us all: if people take on a special personal responsibility to aid someone in urgent peril encountered close at hand, then the probability of disastrous delay in meeting urgent needs is much less than it would be if no such specific allocation of responsibility were prevalent. For example, those in peril are less likely to drown or to bleed to death waiting for passersby to decide, "I'd better be the one."[15] An otherwise responsible person who lacks this special inclination to take responsibility takes advantage of others' having it, in advancing a cause he shares, while lacking an adequate reason to abstain. He is a parasite in the shared cause of Sympathy.

Finally, the expectation that others who encounter us would help us if we needed to be rescued from imminent peril makes us much less alone, much more at home in our social world. Even if I were guaranteed not to need help in emergencies from mere passersby—say, because official emergency services were so wonderfully effective—I would be profoundly deprived of fellowship if those whom I encountered typically had no such inclination to help me if need be. (We find it chilling if someone "looks straight through us"—even if we know this person is intensely active in relieving neediness worldwide.) So deep social interests of any self-respecting person are served by the prevalent inclination to help those encountered in distress; if she does not share it, she takes advantage of others' good will, not joining in a stance whose prevalence vitally concerns her, while lacking an adequate reason to abstain.

The second worry, about the potential extent of the demands of rescue, must now be faced. The reasons for responding to nearby perils on the occasion of encounter will only make a specific policy of special responsiveness compelling for all if no one who respects all can reject the policy as too demanding. If equal respect requires responsiveness to nearby perils as demanding as Bob must display, it might seem that the ethics of rescue conflicts with Sympathy. After all, Bob puts his career in jeopardy, while Sympathy does not require basic concern that imposes a significant risk of worsening one's life.—However, there is no conflict if burdens are appropriately assessed.

The right perspective for assessment is clearest once one appreciates the inherent connection of obligations on a particular occasion with an underlying moral code, regulating responses to occasions as they arise. In asking whether a choice would be morally wrong, one faces a question of principle: in order to show respect for all, would one have to commit oneself to some system of principles prohibiting it, as a moral code to be generally observed? If so, the choice is wrong, and the requirement to avoid it (for example, not to neglect the imperiled stranger one encounters) is a moral duty. This alternative description of moral wrongness emerges from reflection on the precept that conduct is not wrong just in case it expresses respect for all. Respect for all is an enduring personality trait, to be specified by describing enduring commitments that guide particular choices in particular circumstances. If one respects all, one will commit oneself to ultimate principles of moral obligation that are the same as those incumbent on others. After all, the denial that one is on a par with others to this extent expresses contempt ("I don't have to observe the standards that bind the likes of you") or condescension ("I am made of finer moral stuff and do wrong unless I follow a higher standard"). In assessing the demands of a system of rules binding all, one ought to take account of benefits of others' compliance, to avoid contemptuous dismissal of their contributions.[16]

If the toddler judgments are right, then no one who respects all could reject a principle along the following lines:

> The Principle of Nearby Rescue: One has a duty to rescue someone encountered closeby who is in imminent peril of severe harm and whom

one can help to rescue with means at hand, if the sacrifice of rescue does not itself involve a grave risk of harm of similar seriousness or of serious physical harm, and does not involve wrongdoing.

The worry is that the arguments for Sympathy create a need to amend Nearby Rescue with the following proviso, which wrongly exempts Bob: "unless rescue imposes a significant risk of worsening one's life." However, this worry reflects a misconstrual of the deliberations over costs that ought to guide the acceptance or rejection of a moral code. These deliberations involve individuals' reflections on expected costs to them of general observance of alternative codes—deliberations *ex ante*, in philosophers' jargon, i.e., before encounter with the particular circumstances that dictate particular choices. Unfortunately for Bob, a moral principle that he could not reject in the relevant *ex ante* deliberations has come due in circumstances that were not to be expected.

When the object of rejection or acceptance is proposed terms for a particular joint project in which two negotiators might voluntarily engage, each party's particular current circumstances determine what terms she could refuse, while respecting her co-deliberant (refusing "for now, because of the fix I am in," as she might add). But we are trying to determine what personal concerns are an acceptable basis for rejecting or accepting a moral code which would be in the background of responses to particular current circumstances; this is the sort of enduring commitment that a person of moral integrity brings into interactions with others, as they arise. Here, greater abstraction from current particular circumstances is appropriate. The rejection of a proposed moral principle as too demanding should be tied to the assessment of likely costs and benefits in light of the background of resources and underlying goals with which the agent approaches particular circumstances and the *ex ante* probabilities of the various particular circumstances in which the sharing of the proposed commitment would affect her life. Decisions made behind a veil of ignorance blocking all awareness of personal resources and concerns would abstract even more strenuously from actual circumstances. But the requirement of this much abstraction would impose principles of moral obligation which can, in fact, be rejected, without unequal respect, if previous arguments are right. The intermediate level of abstraction further specifies the morally decisive deliberations.

In the relevant *ex ante* reflections, Bob would note that the Principle of Nearby Rescue may require him to give up a great deal. But the chance of his being called on, through encounter with someone in imminent severe peril, is quite small. The costs of his monitoring his circumstances and conduct to insure commitment to the Principle of Nearby Rescue are exceptionally small, adding nothing significant to his normal attention to his immediate environment. Moreover, from the appropriate *ex ante* perspective, Bob must consider the possible consequences for him of general acceptance or nonacceptance of the Principle of Nearby Rescue if he should be the one in dire straits: in such circumstances, he obviously has much to gain from a demanding general commitment that binds people close by, the people who, in general, most readily notice such peril and initiate aid.

The result of these facts in the background of the relevant *ex ante* assessment will be a no more than trivial net risk that his life will be worsened by participation in general acceptance of the Principle of Nearby Rescue. Thus, in the relevant assessment of moral codes, Bob could not reject the principle as excessively burdensome while treating others' lives as no less valuable than his own.

Bob could be any of us. Facts about everyone's capacities and potential needs make the expected net costs of the Principle of Nearby Rescue no more than trivial, from everyone's relevant *ex ante* perspective.[17] So, given the reasons for special attentiveness to closeness that were previously rehearsed, someone who equally values everyone's life must adopt this principle, as a basis for responding to neediness close at hand. From the relevant perspective, it meets the same test of demandingness that made Sympathy the right principle to govern general beneficence: it does not impose a significant risk of worsening one's life.

Like virtually any definite principle of obligation, Nearby Rescue presupposes normal background circumstances of human interaction. A radical change in this background could qualitatively change *ex ante* expectations of the costs and benefits of adherence to Nearby Rescue. These departures would deprive Nearby Rescue of moral force, in ways that fit the explanation of Bob's duty. If encounters with those in imminent peril were as common as encounters with those in serious financial need or those in non-imminent physical peril, the expected net burden of rescue could be substantial. Similarly, the monitoring of what is nearby would be burdensome and would not be very useful for nearby victims in a future society in which people lead their lives with eyes fixed on computer screens and keyboards grafted onto their bodies, with only the most awkward and peripheral awareness of their immediate noncomputer environments. Just as the explanation of Bob's duty would lead one to expect, potential rescuers in these different background circumstances do not seem to be bound by the most demanding constraints of Nearby Rescue, even though they would still be bound by Sympathy. In general, Nearby Rescue is a principle binding people who are embodied, aware, capable and emotionally sensitive in the actual human way.

## Kindness Only Goes So Far

The moral demands of sensitivity to neediness, apart from special relationships, have turned out to be limited in three respects, which could have an enormous impact on transnational duties to people in developing countries. First, the total amount of sacrifice required to live up to the Principle of Sympathy is much less than what the Principle of Sacrifice requires. Second, although Sympathy requires substantial responsiveness to neediness by a relatively well-off person in a developed country, he has a prerogative to honor worthy causes that are especially important to him in allocating this aid. In practice, this prerogative of departure from the default position of doing the most for the neediest severely limits duties of people in developed countries to help the poor in developing countries. For the worthwhile causes closest to people's hearts are apt to be local. In the United States, for example, only about 4 percent of donations to tax-exempt nonprofit organizations go to those whose primary interest is international, including organizations concerned with international security, foreign affairs and cultural exchange rather than development and humanitarian assistance.[18] Finally, the concern for neediness that Sympathy requires is limited by responsibilities to others due to specific interactions with them, including responsibilities to be specially concerned for those to whom one stands in valuable special relationships. The reduction of resources that may properly be used to relieve neediness, as such, because of duties that bind one, for example, to friends, children or promisees, increases the impact on one's life of giving up the remaining resources. So less must be done to satisfy Sympathy.

These features of Sympathy block the route to a vast unmet duty to help poor foreigners in developing countries that Sacrifice would have opened. Although developing countries are the home of virtually all who suffer from grave unmet needs that could be relieved at small expense, this fact will not create a demanding duty to aid in the absence of specific interactions creating ties of obligation. If there is a way to establish the vast unmet duty, the goal will have to be reached via those special ties.

The first step in exploring this possibility is to look at rival claims about the interactions generating political duties to help disadvantaged compatriots. Most people think that these duties are generated by relationships that do not extend to foreigners, as well. Partly on this basis, they would condemn political choices that neglect compatriots with significant needs in order to help foreigners with more serious needs. However, an important trend among philosophers argues from political duties to compatriots to a demanding political duty to help the foreign poor. Agreeing with most people that we have demanding duties to help disadvantaged compatriots if further obligations to foreigners are put to one side, these philosophers claim that those responsibilities within borders are due to economic interdependence, a tie that now binds people throughout the world. This would open a new path to demanding transnational obligation, an alternative to the blocked path of general beneficence.

In the next chapter, I will reject the cosmopolitan extrapolation, arguing that demanding duties to help disadvantaged compatriots are not based on mere economic interdependence, but derive from political ties within sovereign borders. If people in developed countries have demanding political duties to help disadvantaged foreigners, even at the cost of doing less for disadvantaged compatriots, this obligation derives from features of transnational activity going beyond the mere fact of commerce. This outcome will set the agenda for the rest of this book, in which I will base a vast, demanding, unmet responsibility on empirically controversial descriptions of ways in which people, firms and governments in developed countries now take advantage of people in developing countries.

# 2

# Compatriots and Foreigners

WHEN people in developed countries resist claims that they are bound by a demanding duty to help the disadvantaged worldwide, most have to rely on their belief that there is a distinctive duty to help disadvantaged compatriots. Otherwise, their substantial political concerns for compatriots would extrapolate to the world at large. For example, if citizens of the United States were to learn that there are places in their own country where children must pick over garbage in the town dump to stay alive rather than going to school, or die because their parents cannot afford 15 dollars' worth of medicine, most would be outraged, and insist that something be done to change this appalling situation. If local solutions were not feasible, because these children lived in towns and states that were too poor, most would accept a demanding federal responsibility to use tax-revenues to keep compatriots from falling to such depths. Yet, while virtually everyone in the United States is aware that millions of children live in such depths in developing countries too poor to rescue them by local means, relatively few protest their government's neglect of these foreign children's needs. (In 2006, U.S. official development assistance was $76 per U.S. resident.[1])

An important current trend in discussions of international justice argues that political duties to help the disadvantaged should, in fact, be extrapolated from one's compatriots to the world at large. In this cosmopolitan perspective, what gives rise to our potentially demanding duty to help the disadvantaged within our countries' borders also links us to disadvantaged people throughout the world. Demanding political duties to help disadvantaged compatriots are said to be duties of fairness toward associates in economic interdependence; the principles that would shape duties toward disadvantaged compatriots in an economically self-contained political society have, thus, been spread worldwide by global commerce.

This cosmopolitan view of economic justice—advanced, for example, by Charles Beitz, Thomas Pogge (in his earlier writings) and Darrel Moellendorf—differs from the appeal to general beneficence of Peter Singer and his allies. The extrapolation appeals to a feature of transnational interactions, not to the mere coexistence of wealth inside the borders, dire need outside and a capacity to use the one to relieve the other. Also, the duty that is extrapolated is political. It involves support for measures, ultimately enforced by political coercion, that fairly allocate responsibilities to rectify unjust disadvantages (perhaps through taxes, perhaps through other means). Unlike the Principle of Sacrifice, the political duty does not require individuals, acting on their own, to make up for the consequences of others' failures to do their part.[2]

Still, despite these differences, the global extrapolation appeals to a characterization of global realities that is one easy step beyond the elementary facts of global wealth and poverty: the obvious mere fact of extensive and important global commerce, asserted without commitment to any further feature of interactions across borders. And it poses a challenge to normal political partiality toward compatriots that parallels the challenge to self-concern posed by the Principle of Sacrifice. Given the global distribution of dire needs and of resources to relieve them, citizens of the high income countries in which one-sixth of the world's people live might have to make a large sacrifice of current advantages, engaging in comparatively little relief of compatriots' burdens, in arrangements that implement concern for the world's most disadvantaged that generalizes the duty of concern for one's most disadvantaged compatriots. For Gross National Income in high income countries was $34,933 per capita at purchasing power parity in 2006, consumption expenditure was about $21,700 per capita, while the most disadvantaged live in the rest of the world, where per capita Gross National Income was $4,436, per capita consumption expenditure about $2,900. In the global income distribution, there is hardly any middle class.[3]

Because so many people outside the high income countries are very poor, even conservatives' commitment to help the truly deserving to escape from dire poverty might, once globalized, require an enormous sacrifice for foreigners. In 2005, about 2.6 billion, 40 percent of the world's people, lived on less than $2.00 a day, the median official national poverty line among developing countries, most living on less than $1.25 a day, the average poverty line of the fifteen poorest countries.[4] However, the leading arguments for global political extrapolation take a much more egalitarian stance as their startingpoint in domestic justice, leading to an even more demanding political duty when it is extrapolated worldwide.

The leading extrapolators all begin with John Rawls' view of justice within borders. Rawls' domestic standard of justice prescribes three ranked political goals, the lower ranked to be pursued so far as the higher endeavors allow: the securing of civil liberties and political rights; then, the promotion of fair equality of opportunity; then (the so-called "difference principle") the maximization of the typical economic lifetime expectations of the most disadvantaged. Rawls' most distinctive basis for this conception of domestic justice is the claim that it is justified because it is the standard every fellow citizen would choose, as the standard for all to uphold, in a hypothetical situation, "the original position," in which each seeks to advance her life-goals behind a veil of ignorance of her advantages and disadvantages and the specific content of those goals.[5]

Rawls' original position, meant to establish the terms of justice among fellow members of a society under one sovereign government, solely involved the choice of a standard for judging measures of one's own government in light of consequences for members of one's own society, a choice made in ignorance of one's actual situation in that society. The extrapolators insist that the terms of justice toward everyone in the worldwide system of interdependence are determined by the choice of a standard for all to uphold everywhere made in light of consequences for people throughout the world and in ignorance of one's actual situation in the world. In effect, one seeks the standard one would choose in ignorance of whether one is the child of a landless farmworker in Burkina Faso or of an investment banker in Switzerland. Concern for one's life-prospects if one turned out to be among the worst-off globally would lead, they think, to the choice of global analogues of Rawls' egalitarian domestic economic principles, which, by analogous moral reasoning, should serve as standards we all apply in promoting just institutions.

In opposition to the global extrapolation, I will argue that the mere fact of economic interdependence does not sustain a demanding duty to help the disadvantaged. One has demanding duties to help disadvantaged compatriots, perhaps duties as demanding as Rawls claimed, but they are due to further facts of interaction, primarily facts of political interaction. Because of the basis for political duties to disadvantaged compatriots, familiar beliefs about the political priority of compatriots' needs have a certain conditional validity. *If* economic interdependence is the only relevant transnational tie, then one has a duty to prefer a set of policies doing significantly more for disadvantaged compatriots to a set of policies doing significantly less which does much more to relieve much more serious needs of disadvantaged foreigners. *If* economic interdependence is the only relevant transnational tie, this priority of attention might well justify an aid budget mostly devoted to disadvantaged compatriots in developed countries, such as the United States, in which many people have serious needs that it is costly to relieve, despite very high average income on a world scale. In our actual global situation, it is still possible to establish a vast unmet transnational responsibility and to reverse the priorities for compatriots, but only because of the moral importance of ties less obvious than economic interdependence.

## The Basic Challenge

When one reflects on situations in which economic interdependence is not accompanied by political ties, the claim that this connection by itself generates demanding duties toward the most disadvantaged economic associates is not initially plausible. The peoples of Bronze Age Europe were tightly bound by their ties of commerce. These peoples had to be interdependent, since bronze is an alloy of copper and tin, which were not evenly dispersed throughout their lands. But the economic interdependence of Bronze Age tribes does not seem to ground a demanding duty of Hibernians to help Britons if Britons' life-prospects were the worst among the Bronze Age economic associates and if the Hibernians could have improved them. By the same token, constancy in economic association seems compatible with large changes in political duties of concern. When the typically poor people of Norway ceased, in 1814, to be politically united with prosperous Denmark and were politically united with the typically poor people of Sweden, instead, constancy in abundant ties of Scandinavian economic association seems to have been accompanied by a fundamental shift in the location of political duties to support measures helping the poor of Norway.

Seeking further support for the duty to help disadvantaged associates in economic interdependence, cosmopolitan extrapolators sometimes note that the disadvantages that are their topic are undeserved. This is said to generate a demanding political duty to relieve disadvantage. For example, Darrel Moellendorf insists on a political duty to support measures bringing about a world in which "a child born in rural Mozambique would be as likely to become an investment banker as the child of a Swiss banker," and explains the basis for this principle of equal opportunity in these terms: "The underlying idea is that one cannot claim to deserve things such as place of birth and education, race, or parents' privilege. Hence, these things should not be the basis of a distribution."[6]

Although Moellendorf presents this argument in an account of duties among economic associates, it seems quite arbitrary to limit the underlying demand to people bound by economic interdependence. If the undeserved difference is enough to generate the duty to the child of the Mozambican farmworker, why wouldn't it generate similar duties among Robinson Crusoes such as Milton

Friedman first described and Robert Nozick made famous among philosophers? Living alone on islands on an archipelago in which large differences in fertility are undeserved disadvantages or advantages for each, they communicate via shortwave radios left behind by downed and rescued aircraft pilots and discover the archipelagan distribution of brute luck.[7] If the undeserved advantage of Matilde in Switzerland as compared to Agostinho in Mozambique is the sort of superiority that entails a duty to eliminate the disadvantage, then, presumably, the Crusoes have similar duties: if possible, the better-off Crusoes should float tools, yams and dried fish to the worst-off Crusoe on the archipelago to make the life prospects of the worst-off as good as possible. But this moral demand is quite implausible, especially in light of the arguments against the Principle of Sacrifice.

Granted, if Agostinho and Matilde were engaged in principled deliberations over global political arrangements, Agostinho would advance a morally relevant reason favoring his rejection of a proposed arrangement in observing that his lifetime expectations would be much less than Matilde's because of undeserved differences. But the loss of benefits depending on undeserved advantages can also be a serious reason to reject proposed arrangements. For example, Matilde would advance a morally relevant reason favoring her rejection of Moellendorf's global principle in noting, "This would force me to give up resources which I want to employ in making good use of my undeserved advantages, pursuing worthwhile personal goals."[8] What is not deserved is not, just by that token, illegitimately obtained or wrongly used. That the loss to Matilde from implementing the global egalitarian principle would be less than the gain to Agostinho does not make her rejection unreasonable. The absolute extent of her loss (after she has fulfilled her other responsibilities) is relevant, as in the case of Sympathy. If Matilde sought Agostinho's loyal commitment to her political order, she should support measures to relieve his disadvantages. But she does not ask this of Agostinho in a context of mere economic interdependence.[9]

Despite these liabilities, the cosmopolitan extrapolation poses a strong challenge to those who affirm demanding political duties to disadvantaged compatriots but resist their global extrapolation on account of economic interdependence. The extrapolators have an explanation of why the duties to compatriots would be demanding if the international situation were irrelevant: the duties would be duties of fairness to them as associates in economic interdependence. Given a shared deep commitment to the existence of demanding duties to disadvantaged compatriots if foreign responsibilities are put to one side, their opponents ought to accept this explanation if it is the best available, tolerating further, less plausible consequences. But then, in light of actual global interdependence, the refusal to acknowledge the same basic demanding duties to the disadvantaged in the world at large will be exposed as lethal arbitrariness, like the negligence characteristic of deeply racist societies. The basic challenge is to find a satisfactory basis for the demanding duties one would have to disadvantaged compatriots if the rest of the world were morally irrelevant that does not bind all economic associates when global interdependence is taken into account.

## False Starts

I will respond to this challenge in the rest of this chapter. To establish the difficulty of this task and the most promising way to meet the challenge, it is useful to first consider some tempting but inadequate responses.

One is an appeal to the role of shared institutions and understandings in facilitating help for the needy. As Robert Goodin has emphasized, on account of those institutions and understandings, the provision of aid to compatriots is less burdened by costs of transfer, waste and mistakes than aid to foreigners.[10] But with the demise of Sacrifice and other demanding duties of general beneficence, these superior facilities will not explain why there is a demanding duty to help compatriots, in the first place. Moreover, even in pursuit of beneficence, the difference in facilities would be very far from ruling out priority for foreigners who suffer from greater disadvantages than compatriots. As Goodin acknowledges, if desperate needs in poor foreign countries can be relieved at little expense at the site of suffering, there can be more relief, on balance, for the same expense as aid to compatriots, despite the special costs of reaching across borders.[11]

Alternatively, a distinctive political duty of concern for compatriots might be grounded on an obligation to support mutually beneficial arrangements. As Richard Dagger emphasizes, tax-financed giving to compatriots is more apt than tax-financed giving to foreigners to be part of an arrangement in which, over the long run, the contribution of each is compensated by benefits in return.[12] For example, those who pay taxes to provide assistance to compatriots in need may eventually need help from the same program of assistance. In any case, such schemes provide those who give with benefits, in return, of social harmony and heightened productivity, returning such benefits more reliably and efficiently than foreign aid. But this rationale does not support the full extent of people's duties to disadvantaged compatriots. Those who contribute more to social output can have a duty to make sacrifices to help those who contribute less when the lesser contribution is due to unchosen disadvantages. An American would hardly take on the standard commitment to compatriots if she regarded the news that some Americans have spent their childhoods picking garbage rather than going to school as having little impact on her political duty to help them because she thinks children who have been so neglected will not become productive enough to return the costs of investing in their redemption. Nor would a conscientious compatriot neglect an orphaned compatriot with spina bifida, doomed not to compensate for contributions.

The appeals to ease of provision and to mutual benefit both value ties among compatriots purely instrumentally, as means of creating further, independent outcomes, the ones of genuine moral importance. Alternatively, one might insist that special concern for compatriots is needed to properly value one's relationship to them, rather as a special disposition to help a friend in need properly values the friendship. I will be defending a version of this view, in which the compatriot relationship is identified with certain political ties. But first, it is useful to consider the outlook of nationalism, which insists on the duty to properly value certain cultural and historical ties. David Miller's insistence on the moral importance of nationality is a distinguished philosophical expression of this politically powerful view. In Miller's favored sense, compatriots are fellow members of a nationality, a group sharing a distinctive way of life with a distinctive history, most of whom identify with this history, seek to insure the continued flourishing of their group and its culture into the indefinite future, and want other members to share the same project. A further feature of nationality, in Miller's conception, is the shared view of a territory as the group's homeland and an aspiration to sovereignty for this homeland. When this aspiration is realized, then, in his view, co-nationals properly use their state to advance the project of being a flourishing nationality, relieving disadvantages among co-nationals.[13]

Miller is right to take shared nationality to be an appropriate basis for deep commitments, as shared skin color and a shared taste in clothes are not. Co-participation in an ongoing project of cultivating a shared way of life inherited from past generations and passing it along to generations to come is worthy of a central place in someone's personal goals. As part of this intelligible commitment, someone will have a special concern for those who share that way of life, both because the flourishing of the group is part of her project and because co-participation generates special loyalties. But whether there is a duty to take on this nationalist goal and whether it ought to guide political choices to use the state to help the disadvantaged are other matters. A patron's contribution to productions of promising young playwrights' plays advances a worthy cause, but he has no duty to contribute. I have a duty to show special concern for my daughter in private choices concerning young people's education, but this same partiality should not guide my political choices: in school board elections I would be deeply wrong to vote against the slate favoring more help to disadvantaged children because this might hurt my daughter's prospects—say, by increasing competition for admission to the best colleges from bright poor children in my town.

Admittedly, when the struggle against attacks on a nationality is the only political process with which nationals can self-respectfully identify, then the commitment is cultural and political at once, and, arguably, one that all members of the embattled nationality ought to share—regardless of whether the nationality is represented by a state. This is, presumably, many Kurds' view of the Kurdish cause, even if they take attacks on their nationality to be confined to Kurdish culture and culturally-identified Kurds. However, our central topic (and Miller's) is choice among laws and policies to be enacted by a state in which one nationality is an unthreatened majority. As Miller recognizes, many people outside of the majority nationality also make their homes in such territories. If, in accord with his nationalism, people in the dominant nationality used the state as a vehicle of special concern for co-nationals' disadvantages, they would show inadequate regard for these non-co-nationals in their political choices.

For example, most citizens of Norway are also members of a Norwegian nationality (in Miller's sense), descended from Vikings. But Norwegian Lapps are not. Neither are immigrants who make their home in Norway.[14] If a national health service clinic were to require a Lapp in Spitsbergen or a Filipino citizen of Norway in Oslo to pay a fee, unlike the Norwegians descended from the Vikings, virtually all Norwegians would be appalled. And rightly so—cultural-historical nationality isn't the right basis for denying to some of the disadvantaged in the territory aid that is given to others. No doubt, the presence of excluded minorities would interfere with peace and order in Norway, in ways that inhibit the project of cultivating and passing along the culture inherited from the Vikings. But someone born into that culture who only supports inclusion for that instrumental reason shows inadequate respect for those who are also at home in Norway.

If "compatriot" means fellow member of a nationality in David Miller's sense, then a special political concern for disadvantaged compatriots in choices of important shared domestic institutions would improperly value the special tie, just as nepotism improperly promotes a legitimate special concern. Too partial to be a source of justice within borders, this preference will hardly justify neglect of needs in the world at large.

## Ties of Modern Citizenship

If there is a demanding special duty to help disadvantaged compatriots that binds people in developed countries, it is multiply political. First, it is a duty regulating political choices to support laws and policies, not private choices of whom to aid. (In responding to a plea for donations from the Save the Children Foundation, one can check a "United States only" box, a "Where the need is greatest" box, a "Latin America only" box, and so forth. Only a patriotic nut would insist that an American does wrong in checking any box except the first.) Second, the duty toward the disadvantaged has turned out to be a duty to relieve disadvantages of all who make their home in the territory of one's government, not just of fellow members of one's nationality. Finally, the duty of special concern for compatriots (in this political sense, which I will adopt from now on) does not just reflect the usefulness of the shared sovereign state as a tool—i.e., a tool for producing further benefits in a territory or an independently desirable pattern of benefits and contributions. Just as the proper valuing of one's relationship to a friend entails special concern when he is in need, special political concern can be part of properly valuing one's relationship to those governed by the same sovereign state. How can ties binding compatriots acquire this moral power?

The special relevance of the shared sovereign government makes it tempting to derive demanding responsibilities to compatriots from participation in their political coercion. After all, coercion is the essential business of a sovereign state. In order to be the sovereign government of a territory, an organization must have sufficient control over the use of force within the borders, force used to impose laws and policies. The simplest derivation of demanding duties of concern from the compatriot tie would insist that political coercion disrespects disadvantaged compatriots unless it is accompanied by those concerns.

But this derivation is too quick. Political coercion can be part of a variety of sets of governmental activities. These sets do not all generate demanding duties of concern for the disadvantaged who are under their sway. This is especially clear in the case of minimal sets. Seeking protection from bandits and from cheaters on market days, farming households might establish a government in their territory confined to simple police functions, which requires nothing from those in the territory besides payment of taxes needed to finance these functions, honest discharge of official tasks, and respect for decisions that apply laws very close to everyone's precepts for honest dealing. This would hardly create a demanding duty to help the least-advantaged households, going beyond the Principle of Sympathy and its specifications, such as Nearby Rescue. Told that their support for the police force that protects their granary entails a further, demanding duty to transfer grain to the less fortunate, a well-off family can rightly reply that they merely protect people in their efforts to make good use of what resources they have. Nothing in the fable so far—for example, no mention of exploited hired hands—undermines this reply.

Because of the dependence of political duties of concern for compatriots on the nature of their shared political life, I will concentrate on one central case, the exercise of the functions characteristic of government in modern developed countries. Indeed, simplifying a bit more, I will assume that these functions are all exercised by the central, sovereign government. I will argue that the shared political life in which these activities are pursued makes it incumbent on a politically active citizen to be guided by considerations of loyalty, public provision, imposed disadvantage and trusteeship that create a demanding duty of concern for disadvantaged compatriots, as strong, egalitarian and wideranging as the global extrapolators could plausibly assume.

There are sovereign governments that differ from this central case. Far from denying that these differences are relevant to political duties of concern, my argument about the central case will entail their relevance, and not just in such minimal arrangements as the farmers' republic. For example, this argument will imply that in a highly federal arrangement, duties of concern for those within the federal borders may well be predominantly duties to fellow citizens of one's canton. However, if the analysis of the central case is right, alternative political arrangements within sovereign borders create weaker ties of concern among compatriots without generating strong transnational ties, or are divided in ways that attach demanding obligations to special sub-classes of compatriots (for example, to fellow cantoners) rather than to humanity at large.


## Justified Functionings

The shared political life whose consequences I will explore responds to the diverse, complex, changing, unavoidably contentious functionings of the state in developed countries. Prior to investigating the moral consequences of this state activity, the modern state's engagement in such functions must be morally justified, on a basis that does not create a further duty to extend these activities to other territories in which people could benefit from them. One can create a broad enough justification by exploiting a grain of truth in the argument from mutual benefit. In modern circumstances, every compatriot's rational self-interest supports an extensive set of governmental tasks, shaping compatriots' prospects of self-advancement in profoundly important ways.

To begin with, everyone has an interest in reliable enforcement of property rights more specific, wideranging and socially productive than protections that are licensed by reflection on right and wrong in individual transactions scrutinized in isolation from institutional consequences. May all members of certain collectives rightly disown personal responsibility for its debts? How extensively, how far into the future and under how much duress of dire alternatives may people commit themselves to provide services to others in agreements that they are obliged to fulfill? Under what conditions is a contract to provide skilled services marred by inadequate information about competence on the part of the buyer? Under what circumstances does someone's assertion of exclusive control over land or raw materials give rise to a right, and how extensive, permanent and transferable are these rights? Conscientious people can agree to tentative partial answers to these questions in some specific cases, without further assessment of the consequences of legally enforcing this or that norm. However, this would be an utterly inadequate scaffolding for modern economic activity, too fragmentary and too insensitive to social consequences. It is in the interest of all for there to be politically enforced regulations, definite and comprehensive, distinguishing a limited liability corporation from a partnership of deadbeats, valid labor contracts from agreements to enter into slavery, adequately credentialed professionals from poseurs, and valid rights to land or raw materials from mere land grabs. Inevitably, informed and conscientious judgments will favor incompatible legal resolutions of these questions, and the body of laws chosen will benefit some more than others, as compared with reasonable alternatives. The basic, enduring shape of this body of law—which has to be basically enduring for the economy to prosper—will play an important role in sustaining the repertoire of positions for which people may strive. These positions—such as executive, wage-earner, professional, venture capitalist, rentier—will be associated with distinctive responsibilities and powers and with typical rewards reflecting consequent bargaining power.

At least as important and more demanding of funding by taxation is the provision of facilities that everyone has reason to want the state to supply. Public control over violent enforcement is the classic case, both because of the dangers of feuding among private enforcers (Locke) and the dangers of inadequate private defensive efforts (Hobbes). But in modern circumstances, the sphere within which public provision avoids disasters of bad coordination and inadequate provision is vastly greater, extending throughout the vital infrastructure of the economy. The expected pay-off of investment in constructing any underpinning for production, communication or exchange, whether road, airport or e-mail-capable computer, depends on the extent of facilities with which it is expected to connect. At least in early stages of a type of infrastructure, its provision requires substantial sums which are entirely lost if the project fails. So, recurrently, everyone's legitimate self-advancement is facilitated by tax-financed aid for projects that would otherwise be too expensive or risky. Even after a type of infrastructure is well-established, public goods problems often make government-enforced public support the only adequate basis for maintaining it. No one has an interest in a road system burdened by tollbooths at every corner or firefighting agencies committed to letting the houses of nonsubscribers burn even if the ignition of subscribers' houses is the inevitable accompaniment; yet without these disastrous restrictions on access, the option of freeriding will make private payment an inadequate source of funding.

Similar rationales entail extensive public financing of the start-up and maintenance of educational facilities. Parents do not have an adequate incentive to finance their children's education in productive skills unless there is sufficient education of others' children in related skills to create adequate demand in an enduring segment of the labor market. In any case, too few parents may have the personal means to obtain education for their children that would sustain a thriving economy, especially when new skills will be needed. Yet speculations about the future trajectory of national development will not motivate enough private subsidies for the education that national prosperity requires—both because of the uncertainty of the speculations and because a well-educated workforce will be a public good, beneficial to all employers, subsidizers or not.

Finally, private commerce is deeply public in its financial underpinnings in every modern society. To mitigate the costs of a business cycle driven by uncoordinated private investment, fiscal and monetary policies are used to manipulate financial opportunities. Whatever the blunders of particular governments, no one's prospects would be better if commerce in her territory had to cope with boom, bust, and inadequate liquidity in the absence of government facilities and ultimate government management. So everyone has reason to support his government's engagement in a project whose aim is economic prosperity as such for people in its territory, not just the facilitation of this or that aspect of economic life.

Libertarian defenders of capitalism say that they advocate the Nightwatchman State, implying that defense against burglars is the epitome of the state's legitimate functions. But this restriction would be the death of modern capitalism. Everyone in a modern capitalist economy has a vital interest in state involvement, often with prolific public funding, in a variety of further very unnightwatchmanlike functions. But the fact that a public role for government is in the interest of all does not entail that any particular script is equally in everyone's interest. Which policy is to be implemented is inevitably controversial among informed and conscientious compatriots. A defensible response to a specific question of public policy is typically an action that makes some lives worse than they would be through inaction and many lives worse than they would be in alternative responses. For example, an extensive program of highway construction helps trucking and hurts railroads. An investment boom sustained by easy credit and reduced government borrowing may help well-situated compatriots while doing little, nothing or even worse than nothing for those who lack skills, resources and geographic luck that fit new employment patterns. Given the inevitable, important and contentious differences in the impact of legitimate state functions on compatriots' lives, self-respectful loyalty to the shared political order will have to be based on trust that shared concern for one another's wellbeing underlies particular political choices.

## Civic Duties to Poor Compatriots

The diverse and vitally important roles of a modern state in creating and shaping opportunities for those who live in its sovereign territory generate a rich array of political duties toward disadvantaged compatriots. These include duties of civic friendship (i.e., loyalty to those who are expected loyally to support shared institutions), fair provision of benefits, mitigation of socially created disadvantage, and trusteeship over the territory in which wideranging, exclusive sovereign power is asserted. I will describe these sources of special responsibility to compatriots in turn, arguing that they justify the patriotic priority that the global extrapolators reject.[15]

*Civic friendship.* In taking part in governance of a territory, each ought to value others' willing support for the shared political institutions. Like the proper valuing of friendship, this is primarily a response to aspects of one's own relationships, not a commitment to maximize the prevalence of a good in the world at large: I do not express the proper valuing of friendship by deserting my friend as part of a strategy of introducing friendship into the lives of two lonely people.[16]

In general, if one is joined with others in an important project depending on potentially demanding loyalty of co-participants, one ought to value their loyalty to the project by showing special loyalty to them, displayed in special concern for their needs. Although special concern for loyal co-participants responds to their role in a project one would not willingly do without, it is not simply a consequence of gratitude (which others' cultivation of a shared national heritage might evoke) and is not necessarily required for proportionate benefit (Dagger's basis for patriotic concern). A music lover can be grateful for the pleasure of hearing Maurizio Pollini without having any duty of loyalty to him. Loyalty, rather than fairness, can dictate help for the friend who has been unable to do as much to help in times of need or who simply has had no call to help.

This duty of interpersonal loyalty, which derives from shared participation in a relationship, takes the relationship as its proper vehicle of concern and is limited by the importance of the relationship and the extent of its potential demands. Consider the duty of the healthy members of a philosophy department to give a colleague a break if her voice has begun to weaken from Parkinson's disease and she can no longer teach the sort of large service course, which no one wants to teach, that is part of everyone's expected mix of courses. It would be quite wrong for the healthy colleagues to say, "We are glad that you have been loyal to the department. But our sharing this loyalty is enough, without our being loyal to you." Everyone in the department has a duty to support a departmental decision in favor of special concern. But if the majority of one's colleagues were to vote for callous disloyalty in the crucial department meeting, one would have no duty to use one's own salary to reduce the harm. Without a restriction to aid via the joint project, a requirement of aid to loyal joint participants makes each of us, as potential benefactor, too vulnerable to others' disloyalty.

In addition to the special role of the joint project as a vehicle of help, the extent of the help that is a duty of loyalty and the nature of the needs addressed depend on the joint task. How much provision for needy participants a duty of mutual loyalty entails depends on the importance of the project to all concerned, how demanding the needed institutional loyalties are and how effective the cooperative project is as a means of helping the needy. What ought to be provided in time of need depends on the normal point of the shared activity (so that, among close friends, duties of emotional support tend to be clearer and more extensive than duties of financial aid). These connections between duties and the projects that create them are needed to ration the demands of loyalty, since mutual loyalty in one project is bound to compete with the demands of mutual loyalty in other projects, with other special responsibilities and with legitimate self-concern. Since the nuclear family is the vehicle of profoundly important activities, potentially demands a great deal to sustain effective cooperation in its important tasks, is a relatively effective means of aid and pursues goods of many kinds, it would be ludicrous to take duties of concern for one's colleagues to be as extensive and demanding as duties of concern for members of one's family.

According to these precepts of loyalty, special concern for loyal participants in the political project of joint governance ought to be expressed in choices concerning the use of the shared political facilities—just the doubly political duty that emerged from initial reflections on obligations to disadvantaged compatriots. These precepts also imply that the strength of a duty to help disadvantaged compatriots will depend on the nature of the shared political arrangement. In the farmers' republic, the scope and demands of the shared political arrangement would be quite small. So would be each household's consequent responsibility to show loyalty to others through help in time of need. But the tasks of the modern state that everyone has reason to endorse are profoundly important. Their stable and effective pursuit on a basis of willing cooperation requires trusting expectations that current neglect will be made good, resistance to pervasive temptations to shirk responsibilities and to exert pressure through fearsome coalitions rather than engaging in principled compromise, and, in grave crises, a willingness to dedicate one's prosperity and safety to the defense of the shared political order.

While political conduct is not uniformly guided by these cooperative commitments in any country, in many, including all developed countries, conduct comes close enough that a citizen ought to treat compatriots as loyal in this way, in political choices outside the sphere specifically devoted to coping with crime and other civic deviance. Just as one should extend suffrage to all who meet simple, basic standards of competence and responsibility, despite one's awareness that some will abuse their right to vote, a citizen of such a country shows a proper valuing of willing cooperation by this civic assumption of loyalty, avoiding betrayal and encouraging trust. This treatment of one's compatriots as loyal co-participants in demanding, wideranging, centrally important political activity entails a political duty of loyalty to them that is correspondingly extensive in the sacrifices it requires to help civic friends in need.[17]

Beyond the borders of developed countries there are even needier people. Many of them are not treated by their own compatriots with the concern that would express an adequate aspiration to base political life on willing cooperation. Those in developed countries who value civic friendship ought to do something to help people to achieve it in other countries where the cultivation of civic friendship is especially urgent yet arduous. But the thought that they should therefore neglect seriously needy compatriots to help yet needier foreigners is of a piece with the view that someone properly values friendship in deserting a friend to befriend two friendless people.

Given the terms on which loyalty is rightly rationed, the mere fact of global economic interdependence will not override the demands of political loyalty to compatriots, even when accompanied by the current global distribution of neediness and resources. International commerce can be extremely important, but even in countries in which it is, local economic relations have primary importance, since they are the basis for making good use of international opportunities. While commerce merits commitment to co-participants, this commitment is mainly a matter of honesty in fulfilling specific and limited promises; even duties to help, for example, the duty to give a customary commercial associate going through a rough patch extra time to repay a loan, are oriented toward the goal of making good on commercial engagements made in good faith. The preferred vehicle for expressing loyalty to the relationship, among responsible co-participants, is the commercial relationship, not a government. Further special features of a commercial relationship—for example, the special dangers of exploitation which will be explored in the next chapter—can establish further duties. But the mere fact of global economic interdependence and severe foreign neediness is not enough to override the political duty of loyalty to needy compatriots. That would be like neglecting serious needs of a family member to express one's departmental loyalty to a colleague with more serious needs.

*Fair provision.*   The requirement that the benefits of the modern state's many economic tasks be fairly allocated forges a second link between mutual respect and special concern for disadvantaged compatriots. Citizens advance prosperity in their sovereign territory through public and publicly funded facilities and public management whose privatization would be in no one's interest. But the fact that these public functions are in everyone's interest does not determine the extent to which different compatriots' interests are served when these functions are discharged. In the ongoing process of public provision, fairness requires priority for the disadvantaged, i.e., more ought to be done to lift more burdensome disadvantages, while letting the numbers count if helping many more with significant needs requires doing less for the needier. For example, in steering the economy, government should try to shape the pace and nature of economic development in a way that advances the prosperity of the most disadvantaged. So the enormous growth of U.S. national income in the last quarter of the twentieth century, which did essentially nothing for the poor and mostly benefited those who were not deprived to begin with, should be deemed a failure, unless no feasible alternatives would have done more for the disadvantaged. When highways are built, special attention should be paid to communities in which people are burdened on account of isolation or highway congestion. Taxes should, over-all, impose lighter burdens on those who are needier to begin with. If a politically active citizen does not show such special concern, in seeking to promote economic success by coercively enforced measures, she shows inadequate appreciation of the equal value of the lives of all whose prospects of success she seeks to shape by public provision.

In response, it might be objected that the right rule is "You get what you pay for," in public provision as well as private transactions: public provision aims at a distribution of benefits in proportion to taxes. Those in an isolated, impoverished community will be disappointed if they cannot get the highway that would end the poverty that makes a corresponding tax payment unaffordable. But, in this view, there is no reason to provide the highway unless further effects can be expected to provide more munificent taxpayers with further, compensating benefits. From this perspective, bearing up under the disappointment and loyally supporting the political order would be an expression of self-respect. Alternatively, the right rule might be described as "Get from society in proportion to what you contribute to the social product," taking all economic and fiscal activities as determining the net contribution and benefits from economic activity and the government as determining the net receipts. This rule will be extremely disappointing to many disadvantaged people, whose inferior skills and unfortunate local situations make them less productive than their compatriots. But, it will be said, loyal support for public provision on this basis is a self-respectful commitment not to be a parasite.

What these and similar objections to priority for the disadvantaged ignore is the role of public provision in creating the greater prosperity of those who are well-off. What government provides makes modern prosperity possible. This does not entail that all benefits from successful individual self-advancement are there for the taking, to help the disadvantaged. Any defensible political arrangement will protect many benefits of self-advancement depending on unearned opportunities, as legitimate entitlements. Otherwise, autonomous activity, through which people constructively implement their own freely chosen goals, will lack sufficient point and value. But in the ongoing public enterprise of provision, those who have already benefited more cannot rightly claim more provision than others on the basis of those prior benefits. Those who got the first helpings should be willing to go to the back of the line. And the situation of greater benefit from past provision does typically separate the well-off from the disadvantaged in developed countries. The prosperity of the well-off derived, to a large extent, from their having benefited richly from public provisions of opportunities that the disadvantaged could not take abundant advantage of, through no fault of their own.

Indeed, in addition to multiple material benefits derived from public provision of infrastructure, education, research, and fiscal steering of the economy, those at the upper ranks of the basic modern hierarchy of economic roles benefit from public provision of the hierarchy itself. With managers and highly skilled professionals on top, unskilled manual workers on the bottom, this is a hierarchy of responsibility, authority and capacity to engage in valued and valuable work in which occupancy of a higher rung itself makes someone much better-off. This hierarchy is due to a legal setting established by the modern state going far beyond the dictates of natural rights. The setting can be part of a larger legal complex more or less beneficial to those at the lower rungs. If voices from the top were to complain of inadequate public attention to their needs, the right response would generally be, "Sitting where you are is already benefit enough."

Of course, a destitute farming family in the Angolan countryside, separated from the nearest market town by atrocious roads and bereft of any modern medical care, is radically unprovided for. But this atrocious circumstance plus the mere fact of international commerce produces no political duty of, say, a U.S. citizen to support aid to avoid unfairness in public provision. At least under the assumption of mere economic interdependence, the Americans and Angolans are not linked by a joint project of provision by a coercive authority. To suppose that there is a duty to set up a wideranging joint authority of this kind is to assume what the global extrapolators are trying to prove.

*Creating and mitigating disadvantage.*    In devising laws that shape the prospects for wellbeing in their territory, a citizenry ought to dismiss certain options as inherently unacceptable—for example, a political order that permits slavery or that forbids the practice of certain religions. Because nurturance within families must be permitted, a legitimate political order will be accompanied by lesser life prospects of success for some than for others. However, the ruling out of inherently unacceptable types of interference leaves a broad range of legitimate arrangements, to be judged in light of further consequences for people's prospects. The difficulties of the least advantaged may vary a great deal, depending on political choice among these options. For example, if there is only a low safety net for those who lose in capitalist competition, if public education in poor neighborhoods is ineffective and the goal of economic policy is high growth through rapid private exploitation of opportunities for profit, then the children of those who do not succeed may be more burdened by their disadvantages than the disadvantaged are in alternative legitimate arrangements.

In responding to such possibilities in their political choices, citizens have a duty to show special concern for social disadvantages among compatriots, i.e., for significantly greater difficulties in getting ahead that are due to social circumstances that could legitimately be changed rather than to choices for which those with greater difficulties are rightly held responsible. In assessing a choice that shapes life-prospects of their compatriots, they must show appreciation of the equal value of the lives of those on whom they might impose inferior prospects. To treat compatriots as equals in this way, citizens must take the reduction of social disadvantage to be a reason to change from one to another imposed alternative, a reason that is stronger the more burdensome the disadvantages endured by those who endure the most.

This concern for social disadvantage does not extend to all disadvantages and does not dictate doing whatever is feasible and compatible with background rights to reduce burdens of social disadvantage. Some compatriots may suffer from calamities of bad health with no relevant social component. These may be of political concern—say, on account of duties of civic loyalty or the duties of trusteeship that I will describe later. But the concern will not derive from the social imposition of disadvantage. To properly value self-reliance and avoid infantilization, citizens should be reluctant to single out compatriots for help on grounds of social disadvantage if they are not young. Moreover, excessive interference with people's uses of their advantages may fail to properly value autonomy, the capacity (as Joseph Raz aptly puts it) to be part-author of one's own life.[18] Still, putting to one side hard questions about how to specify and remedy social disadvantage, it matters a great deal to political choice if there is a duty among compatriots to seek acceptable ways to reduce significant inequalities in life-chances, given equal willingness to try, due to growing up in different social circumstances. For example, in the United States, when people are ranked by family income, adjusted for age differences and family size, over a third of those who grew up in the bottom tenth remain there and over a half rise no more than one tenth, while 30% of those born in the top tenth stay there and 1.5% end up in the bottom tenth. On average, 60% of the difference in long-term earnings among fathers is preserved among sons, in a process in which transmission of whatever IQ measures plays only a minor role.[19]

Although they move social policy in the same general direction, the argument from fair provision and the argument about social disadvantage are not the same. The first insists that facilities provide benefits on the right basis, but makes no further distinctive claim about institutional goals. The current argument asserts that institutions must mitigate the burdens of the most disadvantaged.

A variety of political perspectives claim to show due concern for disadvantage in choices among basic social arrangements. Each makes its alleviation an important reason for political change, the more so the more burdensome the disadvantage. Some claim that disadvantage is given its due, in assessing alternative arrangements in light of their impact on life-prospects, when average utility is promoted, since the promotion of average utility counts a bit of illfare or welfare as equally important no matter whose it is. But among other liabilities, this perspective permits the choice of an arrangement that is extremely burdensome for a few simply because this is an inevitable side-effect of maximizing the average by affording small benefits to enough more. Such procedures may express an equal valuing of equally valuable bits of utility, but they do not seem to treat compatriots as equals. For example, a citizen does not seem to treat homeless compatriots as equals in supporting a standard of justice in which homelessness is not to be eliminated just because consequent fiscal problems would impose a loss on enough non-destitute people on the order of having a normal-screen rather than a wide-screen television set.

Among those who seek more protection for disadvantaged compatriots than a utilitarian standard would provide, there is a further, important disagreement. Some would take the guarantee of a decent minimum, meager but compatible with basic human dignity, to be the crucial nonutilitarian precondition for mutually respectful citizenship: disadvantage receives its due in a commitment to raise everyone to this threshold and to maximize average utility so far as this endeavor permits. Others claim that this criterion is not responsive enough to the claims of the least advantaged, which retain special force even if all are above the threshold. They impose a demand along the lines of Rawls' "difference principle," insisting that the life-prospects associated with the worst-off social position be as great as they can be if civil and political liberties are respected.[20]

This disagreement has special standing in the debate over patriotic priority. For the global extrapolators reach out, in particular, to those who regard the difference principle as right so far as relationships among compatriots are concerned. It might seem that the choice of this principle rather than the less egalitarian alternative must be based on some general duty to transcend undeserved disadvantages. But such a duty would presumably require support for a global difference principle.

In fact, those who reject readily globalized rationales for Rawls' egalitarianism need not abandon his standard of domestic economic justice. Rather, they should take his own advice to heart. He ultimately characterized the difference principle as "worth studying . . . [having] many desirable features . . . [favored] by the balance of reasons . . . but certainly less clear and decisive" in its superiority to the requirement of a decent minimum than his conception of justice is to purely utilitarian alternatives.[21] Nonetheless, confronting the requirement of the decent minimum, he argued that the difference principle ought to be upheld by fellow members of a society, as the basis for a political life in which "the least advantaged feel that they are part of political society, and view the public culture with its ideals and principles as of significance to themselves."[22] Without such a shared commitment, the least disadvantaged may owe acquiescence to their society. In return for being guaranteed conditions of minimal decency along with civil liberties and political rights, while having their welfare count in the impartial pursuit of maximum average utility, they may be expected not to be "bitter . . . [not] to reject society's conception of justice and see themselves as oppressed."[23] But in pursuing justice, one must seek the basis for something more, a political life in which we do not "grow distant from political society and retreat into our social world" but rather "affirm the principles of justice in our thought and conduct over a complete life. . . . We hope that even the situation of the least advantaged does not prevent them from being drawn into the public world and seeing themselves as full members of it."[24] Rawls thought that only a public commitment to the difference principle would satisfy this aspiration, sustaining a political life in which the least advantaged, "once they understand society's ideals and principles . . . recognize how the greater advantages achieved by others work to their good."[25]

These brief, poignant remarks evoke the forms of thought and conduct that distinguish full loyalty to shared political arrangements from mere obedience. The fully loyal citizen identifies with the continuance of the basic features of her political institutions, including the standards of justice dominating political discourse, as an important feature of her own good. She commits herself to principled compromise in the interpretation of the shared standards of justice as the basis for resolving inevitable political disagreements, even if those with her interests could get their way more effectively through disruption or threats. She regards demanding sacrifices to help defend her political order from internal crises or external enemies as proper grounds for self-esteem. Suppose that the shared standard of justice that is the basis for political persuasion among fellow citizens only requires that the worst-off be at a threshold of minimal decency, even if their life-prospects are significantly worse than others' and the worst-off under alternative arrangements could have significantly better prospects. It is part of the basic political order that the worst-off at this threshold will be told, "You are living in conditions of basic dignity, so your situation merits no special concern." Given the profound and extensive shaping of everyone's life-prospects by the modern state, could everyone in this worst-off situation (not just saintly types) be wholeheartedly loyal to the political order that leaves them at the threshold? Rawls' plausible response seems to be: "Not if they take their lives to be as valuable as others'." On the other hand, if the worst-off are told, as an expression of the general political commitment to justice, "We have done all that can be done without creating an arrangement under which the worst-off are at least as badly off as you," then the public political interest in their prospects does seem enough to reconcile wholehearted loyalty with self-respect.

Among the various ways in which citizens might respond to complaints about burdensome disadvantages that they impose, the difference principle, in Rawls' ultimate view, has the distinctive virtue of sustaining an especially valuable form of shared political life. This rationale for choosing it does not entail that all disadvantages everywhere must be reduced by transfers from the advantaged, regardless of their role in creating them. Similarly, in determining what shared political arrangements would sustain self-respectful, wholehearted loyalty, the original position is useful as a device for identifying what each would support if each sought a basis for shared self-respectful loyalty to the political order among all fellow citizens. Such uses in further specifying political attitudes do not express a fundamental general commitment to impartial concern, a sort of Utilitarianism Lite. Rawls himself ascribes such limited and context-specific value to his device in his own ultimate appraisal.[26]

In general, the sources of the political duty to reduce social disadvantage are not spread worldwide by mere economic interdependence. In global circumstances of mere commerce, while the citizens of a developed country impose shared political arrangements on one another, they do not seek to impose political arrangements shaping life prospects in foreign countries, as well. So their failure to respond to complaints of burdensome social disadvantage, beyond doing what Sympathy requires, is not a failure to respect disadvantaged foreigners. The foreign complaints are properly addressed within the foreign borders.

Still, even in global circumstances of mere commerce, political coercion has an impact on foreigners' lives. Commerce, after all, involves transfers of property. As Henry Shue has emphasized, in arguing for a potentially demanding transnational duty of concern, property involves exclusive control which must be coercively protected to be effective.[27] So mere engagement in commerce will include support of coercive prevention of worse-off foreigners' coming and taking. However, in a world in which the mere fact of commerce is the only relevant feature of transnational interactions, compatriots may treat their advantages as compared to worse-off foreigners as mere differences in luck, which they did not impose. So their duties of concern are limited by Sympathy. They may rightly refuse to adopt a policy giving foreigners control over gains from uses of their luck which merit no moral criticism, in order to avoid a significant risk of worsening their lives while taking account of other responsibilities and commitments. Their use of coercion to protect against the worsening of their lives by protecting their property is justified as defense of this prerogative, without further correction of foreign disadvantages.

In support of a potentially stringent requirement of transnational aid, which might even require sacrifice of all cultural enrichment in order to meet subsistence needs among the global poor, Shue notes that someone in dire need might do no wrong in coming and taking from those who are not similarly deprived.[28] But the permissibility of intrusion (as a last resort, when it does not excessively risk violence) does not exclude the permissibility of protection. The defense of a standard of living above the level of subsistence from outsiders who need to take resources for their own subsistence can be permissible, even if the attempt to take is not to be condemned. For example, one need not condemn the practice of a pastoral people of raiding more prosperous agrarian peoples in hard times, when one judges it all right for the agrarian peoples to try to protect their standard of living.

Matters are different if foreigners are prevented from coming, not to take, but to get ahead by offering what others value. Unless it has a further justification, such prevention thwarts, rather than protecting, efforts to get ahead by making legitimate use of one's luck. It would be quibbling to rule out such exclusion as irrelevant to the cases at hand on the grounds that it is not part of the mere fact of commerce. The exclusion is a characteristic exercise of authority of any modern state, occurring at, not beyond, its borders.

However, even if the citizenry of a developed country have a duty of justice to open its borders to those who seek to make use of economic opportunities, this responsibility would fall far short of their duty to relieve socially imposed disadvantages of compatriots. As compared with the strong determination of structures of advantage and disadvantage within a country by the laws of that country, immigration restrictions play a relatively minor role, eliminating some means of getting ahead that appropriately equipped people in developing countries sometimes employ, usually with great reluctance.[29] Moreover, each developed country should be regarded as responsible for no more than a proportionate share of the impact of excluding the global poor from developed countries as a whole. In contrast, each citizenry of a developed country bears exclusive political responsibility for disadvantages imposed among compatriots.

In any case, the assumption that relevant transnational interactions consist of the mere fact of commerce makes immigration restrictions relatively easy to justify.[30] At the point at which policies further opening the borders would pose a significant risk of worsening the lives of those who are now compatriots, the current citizenry may express their responsibilities to one another by refusing to open the borders more. "This will hurt those for whom we are responsible, and we have no responsibility for the disadvantages you seek to remedy" would be reason enough.—In contrast, if the restriction to mere commerce is suspended, further interactions (such as those described in later chapters) can make the exclusion of would-be immigrants from developing countries an unjust denial of responsibility in which passports are moral analogues of the passbooks by which South Africa, under apartheid, regulated the movement of people assigned to allegedly independent Bantustans.

*Territorial trusteeship.*   Special political responsibility for one sort of disadvantaged compatriot remains to be explained, namely, the responsibility to take care of those so profoundly disabled from the start that they are not expected to be loyal participants in the local political process. Loyalty must be extended to people who loyally uphold shared institutions, but those who cannot take part in such activity, such as people born paralyzed by spina bifida, are not obviously owed this duty of civic friendship. Providing very little to those who play no role in public provision or social cooperation is not obviously unfair. In any case, providing just a little to a helpless person can be of enormous benefit to him, putting in question the duty to provide more. Further reflection on socially imposed disadvantages is unlikely to account for the political obligation to these severely disabled compatriots, since they may be victims of natural calamities that would be severe misfortunes in any social setting.

The ordinary view of patriotic priority extends to these helpless compatriots. There is supposed to be a political duty to relieve their burdens, even if their fate is not involved in the personal goals of another, able-bodied compatriot, say, a parent; in the circumstances of mere global economic interdependence, it is supposed to be wrong to significantly reduce this provision in order to do even more good for similarly helpless foreigners. But these helpless compatriots are no more engaged in the civic life of their country than those foreigners. Unless more is done to ground a special, prior obligation to them, this part of the thesis of priority will be exposed as morally arbitrary. The political obligation to help them will have to be based on the seriousness of their needs and the absence of other means of relieving them, a rationale that will generate demanding duties toward the foreign poor, apart from any further interactions.

In seeking a relevant special responsibility toward the most severely disabled compatriots, one might begin with a second look at the demands of civic friendship. Obviously, an active compatriot's duty of concern for an orphan with spina bifida will not respond to this severely afflicted compatriot's actual engagement in sustaining their shared institutions. Still, both the able and the severely afflicted compatriot fall within the scope of an obligation to do what one can loyally to sustain the shared political institutions. If you are born in the territory of a government worthy of loyalty, then you have a duty loyally to uphold the shared political order if you can, unless you emigrate. If people did not generally recognize this duty, governments could not be stable and effective vehicles of justice.

In light of this principle, someone born with a severe disability, such as the paralysis of spina bifida, has the same duty as any compatriot loyally to participate if she can—but she cannot. She is like an utterly impoverished parent who has any parent's duty to do the best he can to guard his child's health, but who can do nothing to discharge this duty, since he cannot afford the only medicine that could help his child. So, if the concern that *active* participants in a worthwhile political project have a right to expect from each other is concern for each as someone doing what she can to discharge a duty to participate, it would be arbitrary of them not to show the same concern for congenitally severely disabled compatriots, who are also doing the best they can, viz., nothing, to discharge the same duty. And in fact, doing what one can to discharge the conditional duty of loyalty *is* the basis on which active participants properly expect concern.

The mutual loyalty that responsible active participants seek involves using their common project to express special concern for one another. It is a matter of solidarity, like friendship, not reciprocity in matching contributions with benefits. Because concern for persons, not benefits, is in question, the well-wishing that active participants seek must not be contingent on the good fortune of being able to meet the ability-condition. Imposing this condition for aid, in this context, would show that one was not concerned for the other, but only for the pay-off of her participation. Even if I am never disabled until death suddenly strikes me down in vigorous old age, my compatriots have never been concerned for me if they would have told me, if I were disabled, "You are not useful to us and resources for insurance were equally distributed, so your distress is no concern of ours."

It follows that if I withhold special concern from those who are bound to a common political project by the same duty of loyalty as me, withholding it because they are physically unable to follow through, I do not have an attitude of concern toward them that I ought to expect toward me on the part of those who share my duties of loyalty. So, in withholding this special concern, I would be making an arbitrary distinction, discriminating in a way that violates moral integrity. But I make no arbitrary distinction in withholding the same concern from similarly needy foreigners who, similarly, do not and cannot participate in my political project. For the shared special concern that I ought to seek and offer among compatriots reflects the sharing of a duty of loyal participation which foreigners do not share.

Still, this extension of what actively loyal compatriots owe to each other seems too indirect to explain the immediate grip of the thought, "It is our responsibility to take care of helpless people within the borders." Moreover, this compelling thought extends care to those who are not obliged to do what they can to support a shared political order. For example, a potentially demanding political duty to take care of victims of severe misfortune extends into an enclave, like those sometimes provided to indigenous peoples, within which people are largely left free to regulate their own lives, on the basis of their own traditions and deliberations, without any expectation of larger loyalties. Those who take part in the political life of the state exercising ultimate sovereign authority have a duty to provide for basic needs for health care and subsistence that the enclave-dwellers cannot meet internally.

Although this duty to be provider of last resort for basic needs does not respond to active engagement by the beneficiaries in the same political process as the benefactors, it does reflect political activity on the part of the benefactors, singling the beneficiaries out from similarly needy people in the world at large. It is a responsibility of territorial trusteeship.

The assertion of wideranging exclusive ultimate authority to set the terms of self-advancement throughout a territory is accompanied by this responsibility. Such ultimate authority is compatible with granting considerable scope to local rule in an enclave. The authority is maintained, for example, if the grant is revocable, it is understood that it will be revoked if vital extra-enclave interests, as assessed by the sovereign government, are in play, and relationships of the enclave with the world outside the sovereign borders are strictly regulated. (The limited over-all authority claimed by the farmers' republic and the tenuous sovereignty of medieval polities such as the Holy Roman Empire are other matters. They generate different and lesser duties of trusteeship.)

This sort of wideranging exclusive prerogative is not responsibly asserted unless a corresponding duty of trusteeship is accepted. If I stake a claim to some land in a wilderness, asserting a prerogative to deny others uninvited entry and to use the land as I think best, I acquire a special obligation to take care of life within my territory: I must help people in dire peril within its bounds (even uninvited hikers and poachers) and prevent non-human life from languishing. Negligence, here, gives rise to a just charge not of unfairness but of being unworthy of the exclusive prerogative I assert.

The connection between control and trusteeship is quite general, not a strictly territorial matter. Another example is the special responsibility of owners of works of art not to let them decay. To be worthy of the exclusive control one asserts, one must accept a responsibility to take care of what is valuable in what one seeks to control. Other considerations reinforce the connection between control and trusteeship. In pursuit of interactions based on mutual respect, someone asserting control must hope for willing acceptance of it by those subject to it. But it would be arrogant to aspire to such acceptance by those whose wellbeing is under one's control without any commitment to take care. The connection between control and trusteeship also has support in a consequence of breaking it: the laxer moral code in which there is no such source of special responsibility would not restrain the strong in expanding their dominion without regard for the interests of the weak.

Helpless, suffering people within the borders are a special responsibility, not because of political participation one invites from them but because of political authority in which one takes part. If there are no relevant transnational interactions apart from mere commerce, there is no corresponding international duty of trusteeship.

Political relationships based on a shared sovereign home territory have turned out to generate demanding political duties of special concern for compatriots. In contrast, the mere fact of international commerce generates, at most, extremely limited political duties to help disadvantaged foreigners, even if they are much needier. To find vast unmet transnational political obligations of people in developed countries, commanding resources that might otherwise be used to relieve compatriots' needs, we need to enter the real world. Here, transnational interaction is not just commercial and morally relevant features of commercial interaction go very far beyond the mere fact of interdependent production and mutually beneficial exchange. The next chapter will start on the new path, by describing how global commercial interactions currently take advantage of people in developing countries, giving rise to demanding duties toward them, to avoid and repair this irresponsibility.

# 3

# Globalization Moralized

IN every era, the bare statement that countries are economically interdependent, engage in commerce and protect property has left out facts with a vital bearing on international justice. Paradigmatically, commerce in slaves was not mere commerce: the slave trade and slavery were wrong, everyone had a duty to help end these wrongs, and no one had a just complaint against losing the right to own humans. However, if one rejects the moral perspectives that I have criticized in the previous chapters, it is by no means clear how current international arrangements are to be judged. Ours *is* an era in which abject suffering, on the one hand, and resources for relieving it, on the other, are concentrated in different countries. For example, in 2006, 37 percent of the world's people lived in countries with per capita Gross National Income of less than $905 (the World Bank's "low income" threshold), where one in nine people died before the age of five, usually of readily treatable infectious diseases, and health expenditures averaged about $27 per person. In contrast, 16 percent of the world's people lived in countries with per capita income greater than $11,116 (the "high income" threshold), where the before five death rate was a sixteenth as great (0.7%) and health expenditures averaged about $3,979 per person.[1] Everyone ought to be appalled by the fact that so many suffer in a world in which such suffering is not inevitable. But the mere fact that abject suffering and resources that could relieve it are concentrated in different countries, linked by commerce, and that the global affluent could give up resources to relieve the dire burdens does not entail a substantial duty to help, given the personal prerogatives and patriotic responsibilities that have emerged in the last two chapters. What could entail such a duty is the need to live up to responsibilities due to further transnational interactions, analogues of the responsibility to end the slave trade, free the slaves and provide them with the means to an adequate life in freedom. Are there analogous responsibilities now? What must be done to live up to them?

This chapter will begin this inquiry, by scrutinizing processes and institutions that sustain and regulate globalization, i.e., the dramatically increased economic integration into worldwide market processes at all levels of production, exchange and finance of developing as well as developed countries starting in the last quarter of the twentieth century. I will argue that individuals, firms and governments in developed countries currently take advantage of people in developing countries in both the process of production, exchange and finance and the institutional framework that regulates it, and that they have a duty to give up consequent benefits, promoting the interests of the global poor.

The flawed processes will be normal and pervasive features of globalization, not the inevitable isolated wrongs. However, this critique will not condemn globalization as a whole, insisting that the world would be better off without it. Export-led growth, which contributes to and depends on globalization, has been the only path by which developing countries have substantially reduced poverty. Through this escape route, the number of people living in abysmal poverty has declined by hundreds of millions since 1980 (almost entirely in East and South Asia, and mostly in China).[2]

Neither will the critique support the accusation made in Thomas Pogge's incisive, influential writings that most people in developed countries violate "a negative responsibility based on the fact that we participate in, and profit from, the unjust and coercive imposition of severe poverty . . . a negative responsibility according to which most of us do not merely let people starve, but also participate actively in starving them."[3] If people in developed countries met the responsibilities that I will describe, then there would be a large reduction of suffering among the global poor. But the irresponsibilities that I will emphasize in this chapter consist of making improper use of the desperate neediness of people in developing countries, not imposing it on them. This might be called "harming" in the broad usage in which someone is harmed if he suffers a loss because someone else is irresponsible. But this usage fits the negligent failure to fulfill "positive responsibilities," such as a negligent passerby's harming Singer's toddler by failing to rescue. The standards that I will use in criticizing aspects of globalization will not derive from a duty not to make someone worse off than if one had done nothing, acting like the villain who tosses a toddler into deep waters. Nothing is gained by calling these responsibilities "negative" rather than "positive." Rather, they are relational responsibilities, responsibilities toward others derived from specific types of interactions with them, as compatriots' political duties of concern were derived from their interactions in the last chapter.[4]

## The Moral Flaw: Taking Advantage

According to the critique I will present, affluent people in developed countries have duties to respond to globalization with measures that would strengthen developing economies because otherwise they take advantage of people in developing countries. A person takes advantage of someone if he derives a benefit from her difficulty in advancing her interests in interactions in which both participate, in a process that shows inadequate regard for the equal moral importance of her interests and her capacity for choice. In the case of globalization, the central difficulties are bargaining weaknesses due to desperate neediness.

Using someone's weakness to get one's way always stands in need of justification, to reconcile it with respect for the weaker person. In such conduct, rather than basing participation on willing cooperation, one overrides the will of another, who is forced to defer by her circumstances. Rather than allowing her an equal capacity to assert her interests, one makes use of her inferior capacity in order to extract benefits from her that advance one's own goals. In the absence of further justification, such conduct fails to express an appreciation of the equal worth of others, and, instead, uses them as means, human tools subordinate to one's purposes.

However, there are justifications that reconcile the use of others' weaknesses with respect for them, so that taking advantage of someone's weakness does not involve taking advantage of him. These justifications involve excessive costs to stronger parties of avoiding the use of weakness, in the case at hand or relevantly similar cases in general, excessive costs to the weaker parties or those at least as needy, and the need to take advantage of weakness to correct for the shortsightedness, moral insensitivity or outright injustice of other parties. In assessing processes characteristic of globalization, it will be important to consider whether justifications of these kinds are available, so that the underlying reason to condemn, the fact that agents based in developed countries make use of bargaining weakness in developing countries, is not decisive. However, one purported justification for using others' weakness is so familiar in debates over globalization that it ought to be debunked at the outset. The fact that the weaker party is better off than she would have been in the absence of interaction with the stronger party is quite insufficient to show that the stronger party did not wrong her by taking advantage of her. That is why the criticism of globalizing agents for taking advantage of people in developing countries is quite compatible with the view that those with a just complaint against their activity are better off for contact with them.

Suppose that I am lost in a desert, about to die of thirst, when a man on a camel appears out of the shimmering haze and convinces me that he will lead me to a well next to his home, if I agree to be his servant for life, making the beds and cleaning the toilets of his palace. He assures me that once I accompany him to the oasis, I will not be able to survive without continually exchanging my services for sustenance. I would agree, and would be better off on account of my encounter with him. But he does wrong in exacting the bargain. He has taken advantage of me, benefitting from my inferior capacity to pursue my interests in our interaction due to the urgency of my need, doing so in conduct that displays an inadequate appreciation of my equal moral worth. This is not to say that it would have been all right for him to have turned away on catching sight of me, leaving me in the lurch. If he does, he does not take advantage of me. But there are other ways of doing wrong. By leaving me in the lurch, he violates the duty of nearby rescue. There would be no objection to his asking for some payment for his services. Perhaps he makes a living by rescuing lost travelers. But the right response for him is to extract less than the most the other would provide if noninteraction were the only alternative, pursuing an outcome that the other would accept if bargaining power were not crippled by urgency.

If one puts aside the question of whether a prohibitive law would be desirable, a modern capitalist society is also a setting for clear examples of taking advantage of weakness that wrongs while bettering. The dentist who triples his normal fee for a procedure when someone from another town walks into his office driven by excruciating pain and the billionaire seeking land for a third summer home who extracts every dollar he can gain from a poor farmer's desperation to sell are so far beyond the justifications for using another's weakness that their conduct is clearly to be condemned as wrong. That nonworsening is not decisive is also strongly confirmed by judgments of other processes of taking advantage, turning on other weaknesses. A militarily brilliant despot who extracts harsh tribute to sustain a luxurious court does wrong in benefitting from the weakness of his subjects, even if in his absence they would suffer a worse fate of chaotic anarchy. A Victorian husband who relies on sexist discrimination in opportunities for employment and terms of divorce to insure his wife's self-abnegating deference does wrong even if in his absence her life would be worse. In all of these interactions, stronger parties make some contribution to the lives of weaker parties. Yet the benefits of the interaction to the stronger parties also derive, in significant part, not from contribution to the others but from the others' difficulties in advancing their interests by means of the interaction. This is why the mutually beneficial interaction is appropriately condemned as unfair, in the absence of further justification.

In emphasizing wrongdoing in which the weaker party is not made worse off, I do not mean to set aside the badness of the situation of people in developing countries as irrelevant to the critique of globalization. To the contrary, when a person takes advantage of another's weakness in an economic interaction that does not worsen her, the further, moral judgment that he takes advantage of *her* typically depends on the badness of the outcome for her. It is usually hard to tell whether one is taking advantage of another's weak capacity to advance her interests through bargaining or simply taking part in a normal and legitimate process of advancing one's personal goals. So the burdensomeness of monitoring whether one benefits from others' bargaining weakness and the risks of serious loss as a result of needless scruples are apt to be excessive unless attention is restricted to cases in which the other party's fate is bad. In addition, in market interactions, there is a danger that excessive restraint in profit-seeking will destroy efficiency and economic expansion which the weak need, a danger not apt to be worth its risks when outcomes would otherwise be good for both the strong and weak (as opposed to being bad but better than the fate that was avoided).

To avoid these dangers, one should adopt this working assumption in the moral scrutiny of globalization: no one takes advantage of another in an interaction involving no force or deception by either party in which both parties do better and neither ends up badly. Even though the critique of globalization is not based on worsening, it is important that billions of participants in global interactions end up very badly indeed.

In this critique, I will locate major unmet transnational responsibilities in two aspects of globalization. The first corresponds to the familiar charge that transnational corporations exploit. In transnational processes of production, trade and investment, people in developed countries currently take advantage of bargaining weaknesses of individuals desperately seeking work in developing countries, in ways that show inadequate appreciation of their interests and capacities for choice. Responding to this moral flaw, a citizen of a developed country ought to use benefits derived from this use of weakness to relieve the underlying neediness. The other aspect corresponds to familiar charges of inequity in the institutional framework that regulates world trade and finance. The multinational arrangements that sustain globalization depend on tainted deliberations in which the governments of developed countries take advantage of the weak capacity to resist their threats of governments of developing countries. Citizens of developed countries should support arrangements that would be the outcome of responsible deliberations based on relevant shared values, a shift that would entail giving up large current advantages to promote the interests of people in developing countries.

## Exploitation

The most striking feature of globalization is the vast expansion of exports to developed countries of goods and profits due to manufacturing in developing countries, often through local employment by transnational firms based in developed countries, often through their contracts with local suppliers, and always facilitated by transnational firms' engagement in building up the infrastructure of developing countries. In 2000, the current dollar value of manufactured goods imported from low and middle income countries by high income OECD countries was 3.7 times the current dollar value in 1990, as compared to a ratio of 1.7 in the values of total high income country imports in those years. Those imports from low and middle income countries had risen to 16% of high income country merchandise imports, from 7% in 1990.[5] By 2005, the proportion had further increased to 21%.[6] Opportunities to profit from this expansion are a major source of the growth of foreign direct investment in developing countries: from 1990 to 2005, foreign direct investment in low and middle income countries grew elevenfold (nearly thirteenfold in lower middle income countries), as compared to a fourfold increase in high income countries.[7] These steep increases significantly depend on taking advantage of poor people in developing countries, a defect generating duties of repair.

The great expansion of exports and investments involving manufacturing in developing countries reflects the cheapness of the wages and working conditions that are accepted by competent, hardworking people there. At the turn of the twentieth century, hourly labor costs in manufacturing were a tenth of U.S. costs in Malaysia, a thirtieth in Thailand, a sixtieth in China and India.[8] As fans of globalization remind us, people seek work in the sweatshops of globalizing firms because the alternatives are even worse: grinding rural poverty, horrors of unemployment, or lower wages and harsher working conditions in local firms producing for local markets. These hard facts of life in developing countries benefit globalizing firms. Typical jobseekers in such a market are in no position to hold out for terms of employment that sustain a life fully worthy of human dignity. They would not respect themselves and their dependents if they jeopardized their chances of escaping worse misery by holding out for nonmisery. They compete with others driven by similarly desperate needs—directly in the local labor market and indirectly with desperately poor people abroad to whom direct investment could shift in pursuit of cheaper labor inputs. Transnational firms are subject to competitive pressure as well, but it is less intense. The capacity to establish and coordinate production and sales on a worldwide scale, efficiently and reliably, is limited to relatively few firms, while the global reservoirs of desperate job-seekers are vast.

This is not to say that the special difficulty of using labor for profit in a developing country plays no independent role in explaining lower wages in developing countries. Supplies and repairs may be less prompt and reliable; advanced and efficient techniques may not fit local skills; international coordination and shipment to distant markets have costs, even in the era of globalization, and may be hampered by problems of communication and tenuous networks of acquaintance; burdensome regulations and corruption may add to costs. If such difficulties were the whole story, then the inequalities in the price paid for labor would correspond to equality in the ratio between the price of labor and the value it adds. But there are stark international inequalities of the second kind, as well, which explain the steep increase in the flow of manufactured goods from developing countries. According to an extensive survey by the World Bank of labor costs in manufacturing per worker per year and value added in manufacturing per worker per year at the end of the twentieth century, the ratio of labor cost to value added in the United States was .36—i.e., it took $.36 in wages and benefits to add a dollar of value. The ratio was significantly less in a number of countries playing a large role in U.S. imports and investments, for example, .19 in Thailand, .23 in the Philippines, .25 in China, .27 in Malaysia and .29 in Mexico.[9] Moreover, these ratios for manufacturing as a whole substantially underestimate the special productivity of transnational investment in manufacturing in developing countries and the savings due to importing manufactured goods from developing countries; for globalized manufacturing favors especially labor intensive processes that do not depend on elaborate and advanced local technology, such as stitching garments, assembling components and milling textiles. For an assessment of the productivity of globalized manufacturing, we should turn to the experts, executives in charge of making profits. That elevenfold increase in foreign direct investment reflected appreciation of exceptional revenue-productivity of labor which transnational employers use in developing countries, not the view that low wages barely balance the difficulties of production.

Because they flee from worse alternatives, those who are employed in the burgeoning export sector accept, even actively seek, work that is stultifying, without anyone's forcing them to accept these terms of employment. In this sense, they voluntarily consent to these terms. (In another usage, which can be revealing, their agreement is not fully voluntary, since it is forced on them by their circumstances. For present purposes, I will put this more demanding construal to one side.) In the course of an eminent book-length defense of globalization, Jagdish Bhagwati insists that this voluntary acceptance blocks the charge that the employer exploits. For example, he emphasizes the role of voluntary consent to very long hours, among workers whose hourly wages are very low, in his gloss on this *New York Times* report on women who had fled dire rural poverty to work in a leather-stitching operation in southern China:

We chatted with several women as their fingers flew over their work.

"I start at about 6.30 after breakfast, and go on until 7 p.m.," explained one shy teenage girl. "We break for lunch and I take half an hour off then."

"You do this six days a week?"

"Oh no. Every day."

"Seven days a week?"

"Yes." She laughed at our surprise. "But then I take a week or two off at Chinese New Year to go back to my village."

The others we talked to all seemed to regard it as a plus that the factory allowed them to work long hours.[10]

Bhagwati says, of the workers in this factory, "[L]ike many of us who work long hours, they are not being exploited; they drive themselves."[11] Assimilation of the worklife of that child to the worklife of a University Professor at Columbia must be unintended, but it *is* clear from the *Times* report that the workers have made their labor contract voluntarily, i.e., without anyone's forcing them to do so. So the same example shows that such voluntary engagement is compatible with exploitation in one usage: deriving benefits from the bargaining weakness of another, which leads her to enter arrangements involving drudgery or penury that are not fully worthy of human dignity. Presumably, in his denial of exploitation, Bhagwati has another usage in mind, even more morally loaded. The assertion of exploitation, in this usage, alleges that a process of exploiting someone in the first sense derives benefits in a way that is incompatible with adequate appreciation of the moral worth of her interests and of her capacity for choice. Exploitation in the first sense is a matter of taking advantage of someone's bargaining weakness; exploitation in the second sense involves something more, taking advantage of a person by taking advantage of her bargaining weakness. Strictly speaking, only the second usage condemns. But it is also quite compatible with voluntary acceptance. The wanderer saved in the desert voluntarily agreed to be exploited, in the second sense as well as the first.

Do transnational corporations exploit workers in developing countries in the second sense, as well as the first? Sometimes, they do, creating a duty to improve wages and working conditions to avoid the wrongdoing of exploitation in the second sense ("immoral exploitation" as one might call it). Even when they do not, this is not, by any means, the end of the significance of exploitation in the first sense ("mere exploitation" as one might call it) for the critique of globalization. Mere exploitation at the point of production gives rise to a series of moral demands, moving from initiatives by the employing firm at the site of production, to regulation by the government of the country where production takes place, to collective negotiations of governments over the international framework of globalization, to a political duty of people in developed countries to relieve desperate neediness in developing countries.

Exploitation in the first sense is a prima facie reason for ascribing exploitation in the second sense. To derive benefits from another's bargaining weakness through an arrangement that is stultifying is only compatible with adequate respect for her interests and capacity for choice on account of special, exculpatory reasons. Voluntary consent by the employee and her improvement as compared with opportunities available from other sources have turned out to be insufficient reasons. But others might work. In particular, costs of avoiding mere exploitation can be reasons why it is not immoral.

Of course, no grave loss is entailed by any particular decision by a transnational manufacturer to avoid taking advantage of someone's bargaining weakness, by hiring her on terms that she would rightly regard as satisfactory rather than merely better than extremely bad alternatives. However, duties of responsible participation in transactions, like duties of beneficence, are determined by principles to be assessed in light of the impact of enduring conformity on people's lives, not just in light of the impact of conformity on particular occasions. And a moral principle requiring individual firms, on their own initiative, to avoid benefitting from bargaining weaknesses in employing people in stultifying work arrangements would have excessive costs, both for firms that seek to fulfill this obligation and for potential employees.

In the management of an investment, it is none too easy to draw the line between benefits of bargaining weakness and compensation for special difficulties of production in developing countries. The burdens of scrupulous self-monitoring are heavy, and, at best, would produce extremely fallible assessments. If a firm were to avoid all significant risks of taking advantage of bargaining weakness, it would have to withdraw from developing countries or so severely jeopardize its profit margin that its operations in developing countries are apt to fail. This would only make life worse for jobseekers in developing countries. If a firm is much more scrupulous than most who would seek to engage in the same type of production in the same labor market, i.e., if it tolerates much greater risks to revenue to avoid taking advantage of bargaining weaknesses, then less scrupulous rivals will expand at its expense. Again, needy people in developing countries lose, as well as the scrupulous self-monitor.

More moderate self-monitoring avoids these costs. A conscientious manager should ask herself whether she really has reason to believe that net revenues will be jeopardized if she finds arrangements that are easier on workers or pay more, and should try to improve benefits if the answer is "No." As in the case of Sympathy, undue anxieties will make this a hard principle to live up to. So it ought to be affirmed and promoted, for example, by the pressures epitomized in organized consumer boycotts, and the humane managers who live up to the principle ought to be admired. No one is reasonable to reject a moral code that requires at least this much. Exploitation that could be mitigated by such conscientious management is immoral and should be changed at the firm's own initiative, in the interest of those who are exploited. The leather goods factory in China might or might not pass this moral test. One doesn't know enough to tell, from the evidence Bhagwati provides.

In addition, sometimes and to some extent, morally relevant costs to individual firms and actual and potential employees of avoiding mere exploitation can be eliminated by government imposition of minimum labor standards. By imposing such measures, the government of a developing country takes over burdensome responsibilities for monitoring and information-gathering and protects firms from loss due to competition from sub-minimal operations within the borders. If the line is properly drawn, the dangers to vulnerable people in the country of driving out employers by raising costs will be sufficiently contained. Those dangers can be further reduced by international coordination of labor standards. Such political measures change the terms of moral judgment. If labor standards eliminating relevant costs of reducing mere exploitation are in place, then exploitation that once was mere becomes immoral, a violation of duties to actual and potential employees, not just duties to obey the law.

The great limit to this remedy is a risk of disaster for the vulnerable when minimal standards are imposed. The higher the minimum, the greater the danger that the needy will be hurt by stunted growth of economic opportunities. Faced with the new balance sheets, firms may take their business elsewhere, perhaps to developed countries, which are still the predominant sites for production. These dangers are greatest in the countries where needs are greatest, because these are the countries in which local infrastructure, skills and supplies are least inviting and structural unemployment is most burdensome and pervasive.

Still, mere exploitation can generate important duties to give up benefits even when there is no duty to employ on different terms or to institute laws setting higher minimum terms of employment. For a great many beneficiaries of globalized manufacturing are simply people living in developed countries who buy goods more cheaply or derive more income from their investments because of the bargaining weaknesses of needy people in developing countries. The net benefit is especially significant for relatively affluent people in developed countries: their compatriots who are not well-off derive little or no income from investments[12] and may suffer, on account of globalization, from the loss of manufacturing jobs and from downward pressure on wages and working conditions in jobs that remain.

Of course, if relatively affluent people in developed countries were to abstain from buying products of mere exploitation and investing in firms that merely exploit, the loss would be devastating to the desperately needy people who are the proper objects of concern. On the other hand, if a relatively affluent person making a purchase or investment were constantly to assess the extent of the benefit from bargaining weakness and seek means of transferring it back to the exploited, this individual self-monitoring and transfer would interfere with normal life, while holding little promise of accurate reallocation. But these are not the only options. The affluent can support measures by their government that relieve the desperate needs underlying bargaining weakness in developing countries when those measures reduce gains that they would otherwise derive from that bargaining weakness. In this way, they can honor the autonomy of people in developing countries and the equal worth of their interests, without taking on undue burdens or undermining people in developing countries by leaving them in the lurch. In the buying and investing that generates their benefits from mere exploitation, these affluent people play an active role in taking advantage of bargaining weakness, a process that is fueled by what they provide. They take advantage of others, disregarding their autonomy, if they refuse to let the benefits be used to relieve the plight they exploit.

Aid deploying the benefits of foreign bargaining weakness would appropriately be used to reduce the burdens of both those who are currently exploited and those who are especially vulnerable to exploitation, including people living in other countries. For, as a consequence of globalization, the existence of large numbers of people in desperate material circumstances in distant places can increase the bargaining weakness of people who seek to sell their labor. "If we have to pay this higher wage, we will move production elsewhere" is a more serious threat the greater the distant desperation.

Granted, relatively affluent people in developed countries may have compatriots who could use benefits of transnational exploitation to escape from poverty, even if the poverty is less dire than that of destitute people in developing countries. They have special responsibilities to help these poor compatriots, on account of distinctive relationships to them. (In addition to the relationships emphasized in the last chapter, exploitation within borders creates duties to avoid taking advantage.) However, obligations to be a responsible party to civic and economic interactions within borders are not to be fulfilled by conveying fruits of irresponsibility in interaction across borders. I do not live up to my responsibility to interact with some in a way that expresses appreciation of their equal worth by interacting with others in a way that shows disregard of their equal worth. Indeed, this abuse of others dishonors my relationship. Thomas Scanlon offers the apt, ghastly observation that someone does not properly value friendship if he says, "Because of our friendship, I would be glad to steal someone's kidney if you need one."[13] A well-off person in a developed country makes a similar mistake in saying, "I am such a good compatriot that I exploit the desperately poor in foreign countries to relieve disadvantages among my compatriots."

While the value of manufactures exported from developing to developed countries is one-sixth of developing countries' Gross National Income, foreign aid is about 1 percent.[14] So the use of benefits of taking advantage of people in transnational manufacturing might, by itself, exceed current foreign aid. Still, these benefits are severely limited by difficulties of profitable production in developing countries. When market outcomes reflect differences in the desirability of what people offer, rather than differences in pressure from need or competition, no one's autonomy is disvalued, even if many are disappointed. Manufacturing in developing countries does, on the whole, offer less in the way of skill, technology, reliability and easy transition to lucrative sales. (If this weren't so, they would be developed countries.) This limit to the argument from exploitation is especially stringent at the sites of the greatest need.

The limited scope of the responsibility to avoid immoral exploitation makes it important to scrutinize a different aspect of globalization, where the imprint of superior power is very large, more easily discerned, and subject to potentially demanding prohibitions of political injustice. This is the political process in which governments of developed and developing countries have agreed to the institutional framework on which globalization relies.[15]

## Inequitable Frameworks

Globalization is not just a matter of interactions among firms, workers and consumers. It has required coordinated activities among governments, in which they commit themselves to enduring constraints on their legitimate sovereign prerogatives in joint decisions that provide a suitable framework for the deepening integration of developed and developing economies. More specifically, it has required the coordinated reduction of barriers to international trade in goods and services and to international flows of capital epitomized by the arrangements negotiated in the Uruguay Round, administered by the World Trade Organization.

This trade and investment framework has been shaped by threats of exclusion or discrimination, through which major developed countries take advantage of the especially urgent need of developing countries for access to developed countries' markets. In the Uruguay Round negotiations, from 1981 to 1994, the United States frequently used threats of devastating trade discrimination—for example, U.S. Trade Representative Carla Hills' flamboyant warning that if others held out the U.S. would start "trade wars over all sorts of silly things,"[16] or Secretary of State James Baker's more measured but no less ominous intimation, "we hope that this follow-up liberalization will occur in the Uruguay Round. If not, we might be willing to explore a 'market liberalization club' approach, through minilateral arrangements or a series of bilateral agreements."[17] The resulting regime has been sustained by similar bullying. For example, after a coalition of developing countries united in insistence on an end to rich-country farm subsidies in the Cancun WTO conference of 2003, Robert Zoellick, the U.S. Trade Representative (who was to become President of the World Bank four years later), noted that "the transformation of the WTO into a forum for the politics of protest . . . dismayed" the United States, and announced an American commitment "in our hemisphere, and with sub-regions or individual countries . . . to move towards free trade with can-do countries" excluding the "won't do" countries that had held out for an end to the subsidies.[18] As intended, the threat led countries such as Costa Rica, highly dependent on access to U.S. markets and without good alternatives, to cave in and leave the coalition.

Presumably, the bullying trade representatives believe that if they did not use fear to steer the negotiations, interest groups seeking protection from market forces, including political elites and their clients in many developing countries, would, instead, carry the day, making matters worse for all. Even if this is true, developed countries wrong the global poor, taking advantage of them, if the outcome seriously departs from what could result from reasonable deliberations, i.e., negotiations in which the mutually respectful offering and assessment of reasons for alternative proposals leads to the willing acceptance of a shared commitment by all. If a trade regime essentially depends on concessions that responsible representatives of some countries could only make under pressure of need, rather than in mutual accommodation to relevant justifications, then it is a means by which the strong take advantage of the weak. Thus, an account of reasonable deliberations over a trade and investment framework is the proper basis for assessing the justice of the current arrangements. (The claim that the mutually respectful alternative to stability through rational accommodation to bullying is principled compromise through reasonable deliberations is familiar, in political philosophy, as the core of John Rawls' political liberalism. But he said hardly anything about the constraints of reasonableness in deliberations among governments concerning shared institutions.[19])

In developing an account of reasonable deliberations over a trade and investment regime, it is important to distinguish deliberations with a goal of justice internal to the regime from deliberations with external goals. In reasonable deliberations internal to the regime, proposed permissions, prohibitions and injunctions concerning regulation of transnational trade and investment are justified to others in light of their consequences and their coherence; the representatives initially assess consequences and scrutinize for arbitrary discrimination in light of the interests of those they represent and, then, taking one another's initial assessments into account, seek fairness in the permissions, prohibitions and injunctions; but they do not, and do not expect others, to judge measures by their tendency to advance a further collective goal. There is nothing wrong with such further instrumental use, as when the Montreal Accord stipulated that trade sanctions could be used, as a last resort, to punish those violating an agreement to eliminate chlorofluorocarbon use in order to heal the ozone layer. Once the responsibility to pursue the further goal has been established, the justification for the use of the trade framework is relatively straightforward, a matter of reflection on the feasibility, effectiveness and side-effects of alternative means. In light of subsequent reflection on further goals of justice, I will make a case for such uses in Chapter 8. But the derivation of transnational responsibilities from globalization itself involves the internal assessment of the framework that has sustained it, to see what distinctive demands of justice emerge.

Simplifying further to cope with this daunting task, I will concentrate on joint agreements not to impose trade restrictions (including restrictions on transnational investment and transnational flows of services), among governments that already accept one another as co-participants in setting the terms of such an agreement. The implications will be clear, in broad outline, for terms on which new members should be allowed to join regulative institutions and for joint arrangements, now epitomized by the IMF, to preserve liquidity and avoid destructive instability in currency rates and investment flows.

In general, willing acceptance of a joint binding commitment is the outcome of reasonable deliberations among countries' representatives if and only if everyone involved fulfills all responsibilities in these negotiations. These responsibilities are of three, interacting kinds. First, the representatives must fulfill their responsibilities of good faith toward one another. This responsibility involves two duties of reciprocity. On the one hand, each must seek an arrangement that all representatives can responsibly willingly accept, provided that all the others have the corresponding commitment. On the other hand, the representatives must observe reciprocity in their reasoning, backing their own proposals with morally relevant reasons and giving weight, in proportion to seriousness, to relevantly similar reasons offered by others, so that the importance of a consideration is assessed by its strength rather than the identity of those affected by it. Second, the representatives must fulfill their responsibilities to those they represent, so that they only accept outcomes that they can justify to the people of their country in terms that these people can accept while regarding their interests and autonomy as no less important than others'. Third, the people of each country must live up to their responsibilities. For example, they have a duty to live up to their demanding political responsibilities to compatriots. This is a duty to foreigners, as well, since it is violated when the citizens of one country insist on arrangements that shift what are properly their own burdens of responsibility onto foreign shoulders.

Each sort of responsibility helps to give content to the others. For example, what kinds of reasons are morally relevant in deliberations among the negotiators is partly determined by the considerations that a representative must offer as objections in order to deserve her citzenry's confidence. Conversely, a government should appeal to constraints of good faith in negotiations with other governments when it justifies an arrangement to those it represents.

All of these responsibilities are relevant to virtually any important moral question about a trade regime. However, one aspect of reciprocity, the responsibility of each party to seek an outcome that all could responsibly justify to their responsible citizenries, plays the leading role in assessing alternatives in light of their over-all impact in each country. The requirements to show reciprocity in reasoning and bear the burdens of domestic justice play the leading role when protection of especially vulnerable groups in a country is advanced as a reason for modifying an accord that would fairly promote the prosperity of each citizenry as a whole.

To begin describing the basic shape of trade justice: a trade regime that all responsible representatives can willingly accept must be justifiable to each citizenry as advancing their good on the whole. More precisely, this must be

possible if trade-external considerations are put to one side and relevant adjust-
ments have been made for past departures from reasonableness. In accepting
the regime, a government binds itself not to exercise legitimate prerogatives
in excluding and regulating trade and investment. Except as a reflection of
trade-external commitments or correction of past unreasonableness, the report,
"We willingly agreed to set aside your prerogatives in an arrangement that does
you no good," is an admission of irresponsibility on the part of the negotiating
team to the citizenry they represent.

Past unreasonableness creates an exception because of the duty to accept
a change for the worse that only subtracts benefits due to relevantly recent
departures from responsibilities of the government and its citizens. While this
duty to rectify will not reach indefinitely far back, it will certainly extend to
previous phases of an ongoing process of negotiation which are sufficiently
recent that failure to make good would make a party unworthy of trust. The
constraints taken on at the end of the Uruguay Round, which occurred in
the current generation, continue to shape lives in developing countries, in
an ongoing process of bullying. (The furors of the subsequent Doha Round
can create an illusion of developed-country impotence. However, the Doha
Round is supposed to be "the Development Round," attending to developing
countries' needs neglected in Uruguay Round arrangements that will otherwise
remain in place. Impasse sustains, rather than negating, developed countries'
dominance. For example, negotiations sustained this dominance when, at an
advanced phase of the Doha Round, the United States made an offer to cap
its production-related agricultural subsidies at a level twice their actual size
provided that developing countries ended protections for their farmers, and
negotiations collapsed because India and other developing countries rejected
the deal.[20]) If they acted responsibly, developed countries would support the
erasure of benefits from unreasonableness in the Uruguay Round as correction
of a mistake and only seek benefit over and above the corrected baseline.
Thus, the requirement of benefit for each citizenry as a whole can only be
implemented by consulting the further standards of responsibility that I have
yet to present.

The requirement of some benefit for each citizenry (relative to a suitably
corrected baseline) attends to the interests of the most prosperous parties
as well as the poorest. However, so long as this requirement is met, the
vulnerabilities of a poor country should have special standing, even if it is
not one of the poorest. Suppose that a responsible representative is faced
with a proposed regime in which suffering among the people she represents
is extensive and plausibly foreseen to be substantially greater than in an
alternative providing her country with greater trade access to other countries,

permitting wider recourse by her government to measures it regards as useful means of overcoming economic burdens, or providing more resources for alleviating harms of disruption from imposed trade policies. As a responsible representative of her citizenry, she must count this as a serious reason not willingly to accept the proposal. International reciprocity of reasons must also be observed. So the representative must take account of similar concerns to avoid suffering among their people on the part of other representatives, giving them weight appropriate to the seriousness of the concern. As a result of this combination of national and transnational responsibilities, the basic tendency of reasonable trade deliberations will be a trade regime whose allocation of openness to goods, exemptions from constraints and mitigation of burdens of disruption due to trade most favors the countries where there is the most need for growth through trade, for policy instruments for development and for mitigation of disruption and other burdens of exposure to global markets. In short, in the absence of serious reasons to the contrary, the poor will be favored—for reasons of justice, not beneficence.

Conflicting considerations of need and vulnerability can make this standard hard to apply. For example, an alternative that would facilitate a great many escapes from destitution in China might disrupt more urgently needed development among far fewer, much poorer people in Southeast Asia and sub-Saharan Africa. Here, asking what pattern one would prefer behind a veil of ignorance is a helpful device for taking proper account of the seriousness of the competing concerns. Even though there is no duty to implement a comprehensive global standard of justice that one would choose behind a veil of ignorance of where one lives, the veil of ignorance device is useful at specific junctures of responsible global decisionmaking at which the impact of specific kinds of choices on certain interests of participants is impartially assessed, as one aspect of the justification that respects the interests and autonomy of all.

It might seem that any departure from a pattern of utter openness of developed countries to goods from developing countries is precluded, as irresponsible, by these considerations. After all, the inhibition of export-led growth in developing countries condemns people to recurrent fatigue, constant threats of bad health, and constraining isolation. Even in China, already the site of stupendous export-led growth, over 100 million people were undernourished, in the first years of the twenty-first century, over 200 million lived on less than $1.25 a day, there were a mere 1.5 physicians per thousand people, highly concentrated in urban areas, and those in the countryside had to make do with a highly inferior share of transportation resources that involved 24 motor vehicles per 1,000 Chinese in 2005.[21] The cost of thwarted escape from such destitution is much more serious than the worst suffering imposed in developed countries by uninhibited entry of goods from developing countries, namely, the displacement of middle-aged workers in industries that cannot compete. So long as people in a developed country benefit as a whole from a trade regime, it might seem impossible to justify protection in the name of these lesser burdens.—But "impossible" is an exaggeration. In principle, representatives of developing countries might have to acknowledge special domestic responsibilities of governments of developed countries as providing sufficiently strong reasons to justify protection that departs from the basic pattern favoring the global poor. However, this will be extremely difficult, when deliberations are guided by good faith and the duty not to shift burdens of domestic justice onto foreign shoulders.

Governments of developed countries have special responsibilities to their especially vulnerable citizens. Faced with a free-trade agreement that would improve economic life in the United States on the whole but devastate industrial cities in the Midwest, the United States government might, in principle, be reasonable in seeking more protection, even at the cost of slowing the escape from dire poverty in China and Brazil. If the government were to tell Americans whose morally serious interests were in jeopardy, "We agreed to let in these goods to enable needier people abroad to escape from poverty," those at risk in the Midwest have a morally relevant response: "You should treat our interests with special concern, rather than absorbing them in impartial global concern for suffering due to trade arrangements as soon as over-all national benefit is achieved." (That they have a legitimate fear of serious harm, not just a desire for greater benefits, is important. The representative of a developed country would not be irresponsible in telling the citizenry, "We could have held out for an even better deal, but this would have required other countries to accept substantial suffering that this agreement avoids.")

However, developed countries and their citizens must live up to all their political responsibilities in reasonable deliberations. Duties of good faith among representatives make it hard for governments of developed countries responsibly to maintain that imports from developing countries are to be inhibited to protect vulnerable people within their borders. In pressing for liberalization in the world at large, developed countries propose that considerable disruption is worth the gains in developing countries. It would show bad faith not to swallow the same medicine at home. In addition, what counts as a gain in productivity and growth that justifies displacement through *domestic* policies should count as adequate in judging the domestic effects of international trade policies as well. Developed countries, especially the United States, are, domestically, receptive to "creative destruction" through displacement.

The gate through which reasonable developed-country protection must squeeze is further narrowed by responsibilities of fellow citizens toward one another. Suffering due to economic displacement that would not be endured if the local safety net were as high as domestic justice requires provides no reason for a responsible citizen to support constraints on imports from developing countries. This irresponsibly shifts burdens of domestic justice onto foreign shoulders. Similarly, when domestic burdens of displacement could be avoided by precautions that do not burden other countries, it would be irresponsible to insist that foreigners bear the burden of inadequate precaution. Having agreed to phase out textile import quotas directed at developing countries over a ten-year period, the United States waited until the last year to end quotas in the important categories. As expected, a flood of Chinese imports unleashed a storm of demands for "anti-dumping" sanctions (including sanctions licensed by a special clause forced on China as a condition for WTO entry). New trade restraints were established as a consequence. These barriers were expressions of unreasonableness. It was the responsibility of the United States to reduce burdens of displacement through gradual liberalization and retraining, which would have occurred in a period of general prosperity.

When people in a developed country protest harms of liberalization—say, job loss from the influx of cheap Chinese goods into the United States—the most familiar rebuttal is the standard economist's, that the vast majority in the developed country will benefit from the efficiencies of freer trade. True though this may be, the concentration of serious losses in a small group, not well-off to begin with and not well-equipped for recovery, can be a more serious moral concern than the proliferation of gains. Another response, common among philosophers, is the cosmopolitan reminder that the harms to disadvantaged compatriots are a side-effect of means to escape abject poverty among much more disadvantaged people elsewhere. The weakness of the political duty of impartial global concern makes this a weak response, even if true. But reflection on reasonableness in deliberations over the global trade framework suggests a response that almost always works. Almost always, a citizen of the developed country should regard domestic measures as the right means of reducing the harms of liberalization, on pain of shifting domestic injustice onto foreign shoulders, and should regard complaints to other countries based on those harms as showing bad faith, given her government's support for shared terms requiring people in developing countries to tolerate harms of the same kind that are at least as serious. For example, on these grounds, it will generally turn out to be wrong of the U.S. to block arrangements opening U.S. markets to goods from relatively strong developing economies—not because no serious domestic harm results, not because harms to Americans should have no special political standing among Americans, but because this would be an irresponsible use of the trade framework.

In broadest outline, the pattern of trade justice is openness of richer economies to imports from poorer economies and exemption of developing countries from prohibitions and injunctions that would conflict with their governments' informed concern for development and stability. While departures from this pattern are justifiable in principle as protecting especially vulnerable people in developed countries, they are strongly constrained by the responsibility to take account of similar reasons from representatives of developing countries and by the primary responsibility of citizens of developed countries for their vulnerable fellow citizens. Reasonable deliberations that only pursued trade-internal responsibilities would seek the maximum expansion of world trade compatible with these demands of fairness.

## A Shortfall in Equity

The WTO, like the GATT regimes that it transformed, is officially committed to the pursuit of reciprocal reductions in barriers to free trade, modified as needed to guard against severe disruption of economic life in member countries and to respect the special needs and vulnerabilities of developing countries. Far from indicting this broad official commitment, the criterion of reasonable deliberations confirms and specifies it. Similarly, reasonable deliberations over the institutional framework for international finance and payments would support the IMF's official general commitment to combine a goal of facilitating monetary measures needed to sustain international trade and investment with special concern for damage from disruptive fluctuations and currency and fiscal crises, which especially afflicts the people of developing countries. The current epidemic of inequity in the global frameworks for trade and finance is a pervasive failure actually to implement such general commitments in specific measures that reasonable deliberations could justify.

An assessment of this shortfall cannot be certain and precise, since estimates depend on controversial empirical claims. Still, there is little room for doubt that the outcome of reasonable deliberations would be very different from the current outcome of bullying.

*Distorting the basic shape.* Current arrangements drastically depart from the general rule of openness by richer countries to imports from poorer countries. In 2000, developing countries' exports faced trade barriers in high-income countries that were, on average, three times higher (value-weighted) than the barriers faced by other high income countries. The barriers that the United States imposed on goods from the least developed countries were ten times higher than the barriers faced by high income country exporters.[22] Indeed, the poorest countries lost out on balance in the Uruguay Round on account of barriers to their exports and requirements of bureaucratic procedures and patent constraints. The most widely cited estimate of the initial impact on the poorest countries is a net loss of $600 million a year among the forty-eight poorest.[23] If developed countries' tariffs on imports from developing countries were eliminated, benefits to developing countries of this improved access might well exceed $100 billion a year.[24] There is little reason to suppose that significant rich-country restriction of this access could be justified without violations of reciprocity in reasons.

*Non-reciprocal reasoning.* Violation of reciprocity is a basis for the most pervasive criticisms of the trade regime, objections to rich-country agricultural subsidies. In 2005, the governments of developed countries gave subsidies to their farms (often inefficient farms owned by rich people) of $280 billion, a sum equalling a third of the value of these countries' farm product and substantially exceeding the total GDP of the fifty poorest countries, where one in eight people lived.[25] These subsidies shield rich-country farms from the pressures of market competition on which the governments of rich countries generally insist in trade negotiations. Granted, a country could reasonably resist abandonment of its farm subsidies by appealing to considerations of cultural continuity, national independence in provision of vital needs or stability in families' economic lives. But whatever the role of thriving farms in continuity, independence and stability in developed countries, they are much more important to continuity, independence and stability in developing countries. And extensive farm subsidies in developed countries destroy farming life in developing countries, undermining all of these values, by choking off opportunities to compete in world markets. Because of subsidies to U.S. cotton farming which amounted to $3.9 billion in 2001, the United States, the world's largest cotton exporter, doubled exports in a three-year period of slumping prices, from 1998 to 2001. The cost to people in poor countries of the skewing of competition by U.S. cotton subsidies was about $300 million a year in Africa alone.[26]

A much more important departure from reciprocity in reasoning is promotion by developed countries of measures enhancing the transnational flow of all factors of production except for one that holds special promise of benefitting people in developing countries while promoting efficiency worldwide—human labor. On conservative assumptions, if developed countries were just to allow a 3 percent expansion of their workforces by workers from developing countries, without serious bias against the unskilled, there would be an annual gain to people now living in those countries of over $100 billion.[27] Both increased remittances from migrants (which are already three times as great as foreign aid) and reduction of oversupply of labor at home would be sources of relief. At present, a 10 percent per capita increase in remittances to people in a developing country from relatives working abroad is on average independently associated with about a 3 percent decline in the proportion whose income is below $1 a day.[28]

*Unequal burdens.*    The turn toward reasonableness that I have described so far would reduce burdens on developing countries of protection by developed countries. However, mandated liberalization imposes its own burdens, whose special severity in developing countries requires special help in mitigation, if the joint commitment to greater openness is to be fair. A developing country's entry into the world of globalization is often grim, as vulnerable firms, shops, farms and whole sectors of the economy succumb to more effective outside competitors. Even countries that benefit over the long run, in the average year often bob like a cork in the ocean of global investments, subject to the exuberance and panic of investors in developed countries responding to strange and distant prospects. So affluent people in developed countries, whose goods are cheaper and investments more lucrative on account of liberalization, benefit from the special fortitude of people in developing countries. This is an inequitable way of sharing the burdens of liberalization, regardless of whether it violates reciprocity in reasoning.

Developed countries' support for safety nets to help vulnerable people in developing countries cope with disproportionate burdens of disruption from liberalization has been late and little. Eventually, "IMF riots," disruptive demonstrations at sites of major trade negotiations and learned critiques aroused international concern about burdens of liberalization and the increased reliance on market forces that accompanied it. In response, "social funds" to cushion the transition were set up in developing countries, typically with a substantial proportion of their funding from abroad. In a 2004 study, Giovanni Cornia and Sanjay Reddy reported that these funds, on average, disbursed only $18 per poor person per year. Among the social funds that were mostly externally financed, annual expenditure averaged less than $8 per poor person. (Mexico's program, by far the most generous, was entirely locally funded.) In five of the twelve countries for which figures were available, social expenditure as a proportion of GDP was less during the period of social funds than in the two years before their start. Most increases were around 1 percent of GDP.[29] This meager response in expenditures partly reflected a direct conflict between trade liberalization and government spending. In many developing countries, tariffs and other taxes on trade, which are much easier to collect than taxes of other kinds, have been a substantial component of revenue, much more important than in developed countries. For example, in 1990, in the midst of structural adjustment and toward the end of the Uruguay Round, they were a quarter of government revenues in sub-Saharan Africa and in the Philippines.[30]

*Blocked options for development.* While much more could be done to mitigate the human costs of trade liberalization, they can hardly be eliminated. This makes it all the more important to consider whether the current extent of mandated liberalization of developing economies deprives them of policy options that informed and responsible governments would seek to preserve.

No country has ever successfully developed without relying on measures to manage damage and increase advantages from world trade that are banned by rules that were instituted by the Uruguay Round, through dire threats overcoming heated resistance.[31] In 1960–78, the heyday of those currently banned measures (such as export subsidies and high tariff walls protecting vulnerable economic sectors), population-weighted average annual growth of per capita GDP was 2.8% among Latin American countries; in 1978–98, when such state-direction was replaced by direction by world markets, first through structural adjustment conditions imposed, on U.S. initiative, by the IMF and World Bank, then through the trade, investment and property rights regime administered by the WTO, growth declined to 0.8%. The comparable figures for Asia are a decline from 4.0% to 3.6%, for Africa, a decline from 1.5% to 0.1%.[32] According to Rodriguez and Rodrik's incisive analysis of the major international studies of the relationship between economic growth and policy-induced liberalization in the last quarter of the twentieth century, the causal contribution of trade liberalization to economic growth in developing countries was, on average, nil—despite the tumultuous instability that liberalization policies introduced into millions of lives.[33]

Given the state of the evidence and the profound importance of the outcome for the peoples of developing countries, responsible governments of developing countries in the current world trade regime have reason to complain of being prevented from using plausible development strategies, which may be the best in their situations. Any major strategy for development is a gamble.[34] Those whose futures will be shaped by the gamble ought to have the main voice in choosing which bet to place. Since the right package of policies is extremely hard to discover and almost certainly varies from region to region and time to time, the exclusion of a wide range of plausible strategies also has a familiar epistemic cost of regimentation: it eliminates needed experimentation. The prohibition of these development strategies was, at the very least, an objectionable constraint, and may have been a disaster.

## A Response to Inequity (and Its Limits)

Support for the global framework that I have criticized cannot be justified by appeal to the limits of beneficence. For the criticism is not that the framework violates a responsibility to help; rather, it violates a responsibility not to take advantage of others' weaknesses in arrangements in which they are required to give up legitimate prerogatives. Neither is support for this framework justified by duties of patriotic concern within developed countries. Political loyalty to my poor compatriots in the South Bronx is properly expressed by transfers of gains from legitimate projects of better-off Americans, but not by providing benefits from bullying people in Malawi. Indeed, the arguments for patriotic concern themselves entail the duty to aspire to the replacement of international bullying by international reasonableness. If fellow citizens must seek terms of joint governance that could reflect their reasonable deliberations, not just rational accommodation to the domestic balance of power, participants in a multigovernmental enterprise must similarly seek joint arrangements that reasonably reconcile their legitimate interests, rather than simply reflecting the rational need of the weak to acquiesce to the threat influence of the strong.

In addition to the duty to restore responsibility to the institutional framework for globalization, there is a duty to make up for previous political irresponsibility, at least in the recent past. Merely freeing developing countries from obstacles to commerce and development and letting them shape their own trade, finance and investment policies would be as irresponsible as freeing the slaves at the end of the U.S. Civil War without further help to cope with challenges slavery had created. In the Philippines, the elimination of tariffs on corn in the 1990s, to accommodate the WTO, led to the loss of hundreds of thousands of agricultural jobs among people who, despite their poverty, had been able to meet basic needs and sustain family, social and cultural relationships on the basis of self-reliant work.[35] It is too late to put a safety net under them and pointless to try to restore the sundered agrarian relationships. But it would be irresponsible for citizens of developed countries, whose governments control the dominant institutions, to wash their hands of the matter, rather than making up for the imposition of liberalization without an adequate safety net. In a joint enterprise, those who have imposed inequitable arrangements in the recent past have a duty to compensate for the toll and a duty to mitigate ongoing consequences of the inequity after it has ended.

The duty to avoid taking advantage of people in developing countries has turned out to require large changes in the trade regime that sustains globalization, promising large reductions of suffering, and a major effort to make good on past inequity. The international framework facilitating the flow of funds and the viability of currencies that centers on the IMF is subject to analogous criticisms. Reciprocity seems to be violated by IMF responses to currency and debt crises in developing countries that give creditors in the economic elites of developed countries comfortable escapes from the consequences of their economic choices but impose the discipline of the marketplace on people in those countries through painful austerity and widespread bankruptcies.[36] Recurrent proposals that the IMF create extensive Special Drawing Rights on members' currencies to replace reliance on holdings in dollars as the bulwark against currency crises in developing countries would reduce the borrowing costs of governments of developing countries and eliminate ties to U.S. fiscal policies that are an enduring source of instability. By eliminating a global need to maintain stocks of U.S. Treasury bills, the proposals would also deprive the United States of a global source of low-cost loans even from the poorest countries. Reasonable deliberations would seem to support these measures, to reduce the heaviest burdens in the joint project of maintaining global liquidity, but U.S. power has sustained the status quo.[37]

Nonetheless, the responsible setting of the trade and financial frameworks would be of limited use to needy people in developing countries. Unfair burdening of their efforts to escape from poverty by other governments' barriers to their exports or policy constraints imposed on their own governments would end. The burdens of disruption from liberalization would be reduced. But difficulties, within their borders, in meeting needs would continue. Facing no trade barriers in developed countries, no prohibition, under the WTO, of any responsible policy option, gentler integration into world markets and no unjustifiable discrimination in resources offered by the IMF, many people would still be unable to escape destitution. The primary problem of not having enough to offer in commerce would not be solved. So it is important to see how far unmet transnational responsibilities to foreigners in developing countries extend beyond bargaining in global production and exchange and the establishment of the institutional framework for global commerce.

One further powerful source of unmet responsibilities is a globally dangerous consequence of economic activity, the burgeoning emission of greenhouse gases. It will be the topic of the next chapter. The other major source is the exercise of transnational power, which extends far beyond negotiations setting the framework for global commerce. Chapter 5 will begin the exploration of this source, emphasizing a currently preeminent paradigm, the transnational power of the United States.

# 4

# Global Harm and Global Equity: The Case of Greenhouse Justice

In the last chapter, unmet transnational responsibilities were derived from conduct in which some take advantage of others, without necessarily worsening those they wrong. This chapter will derive further unmet responsibilities to help people in developing countries from a different sphere: the requirement of due concern for unintended harmful side-effects of conduct which may, itself, be morally flawless.

Due concern for unintended harmful effects of our actions is a routine and deeply important duty. Crossing a street would be a perilous adventure if people did not take due care. In limiting harmful side-effects of our conduct, we express a proper valuing of trust. Without the expectation of such concern, wariness is the appropriate interpersonal attitude, and others' success merits anxiety about their heightened influence over our shared environment, natural, economic and social. Even someone with the resources to be successfully wary and to ward off others' harms ought to be repelled by this prospect, to aspire to mutual trust instead, and to express this aspiration in a special commitment to take due care.

While this aspect of moral responsibility is routine, its dictates depend on diverse considerations whose implications vary from case to case. For one thing, our duties to avoid and repair unintended harms due to our own conduct are limited by others' responsibilities to avoid being victims. I have done nothing wrong if I bump into my neighbor because he has rushed onto the sidewalk without looking to see who is coming. (In contrast, if I intentionally push him, I do wrong and am responsible for the consequences even if he thoughtlessly missed an opportunity to dodge my push.) Also, due concern for our unintended harms is sensitive to the costs of desisting. In a dry region, a farming family is justified in making use of water in ways that will, inevitably, make matters worse for others. Granted, one should seek a mutually acceptable way of overcoming conflicts of interests in which one's self-advancement has harmful side-effects. But what terms ought to be accepted is far from clear: contributions to harmful processes, costs of desisting, advantages derived from others' harm, and others' responsibility for their victimhood all seem relevant considerations and are frequently in conflict. For example, those who contribute more to a water shortage may also need water more (say, for irrigation), and will bear disproportionate costs of proportionate reduction of use.

For these and other reasons, the dictates of due concern over transnational consequences of an unobjectionable economic activity will depend, in complex ways, on the specific character of the interaction. Because of these complexities, I will devote this chapter to the detailed study of one such process, the production of harmful climate change by the release of greenhouse gases, above all, carbon dioxide, in virtually all economic activities. This emphasis corresponds to the especially large impact of this process on duties of people in developed countries to give up advantages to help people in developing countries. As in the study of trade agreements in the previous chapter, the goal will be the discovery of underlying moral principles for meeting responsibilities generated by this particular human interaction. The possibility of using greenhouse regimes to satisfy moral obligations external to the greenhouse interaction will be put to one side, until the summary of transnational responsibilities in Chapter 8.

## Questions of Greenhouse Justice

By thickening an atmospheric blanket of gases in which carbon dioxide is the most important ingredient, business-as-usual in economic activity poses a worldwide danger of grave harms, through consequences of increased warmth. The contribution of this process to duties of people in developed countries to help people in developing countries depends on the answers to two questions: what allocation of tasks is equitable in seeking to limit harms of global warming, and what goal of limitation is adequate, fulfilling the collective responsibility of humanity to limit the harm we jointly cause? If people in developed countries do less than their fair share in reducing the global harm, they owe it to people in developing countries to do more. What they are obliged to do in their fair share depends on the limit that ought to be sought in humanity's project of climate control.

In addition to the division of moral questions into adequacy and equity, the terminology of the greenhouse literature divides responses to the greenhouse challenge into mitigation, i.e., reduction of emissions and their climate consequences, and adaptation, i.e., improved coping with the residual climate consequences. In principle, there could be mitigation without emissions reduction, through direct intervention in climatic processes, for example, the sprinkling of particles in the atmosphere to reflect back sunlight and cool the earth's surface. But there is a broad consensus that these interventions would be gravely risky, at best unfortunate last resorts in response to inadequate emissions reduction. While adaptation will be vitally important, developing countries have limited capacities to adapt and aid flows have limited efficacy in improving those capacities. So controversy over what developed countries should do to help developing countries in response to the greenhouse challenge has centered on the question of what allocation of emissions reductions is fair in an adequate mitigation regime. I will follow this emphasis and ultimately defend it. However, the moral principles that emerge for assessing proposed greenhouse regimes will also be suitable for judging proposals with varying degrees of emphasis on adaptation.

While the central, unavoidable questions, adequacy and equity, are distinct, they are also interdependent. If adequate containment is demanding, this creates a need to develop a standard of equity fit for assessing serious conflicts of interest. Conversely, a limit on climate change may have to be relaxed if it creates unacceptable burdens even in an equitable allocation of tasks.

As it happens, a global standard of adequacy has been affirmed (in the abstract) by a multigovernmental group with some power: in 1996, the governing Council of the European Union declared that "global average temperatures should not exceed 2 degrees [Celsius = 3.6 degrees Fahrenheit] above pre-industrial level"—a position that the EU has periodically reasserted.[1] Six years before, the Advisory Group on Greenhouse Gases of the World Meteorological Association and United Nations Environmental Program had argued for this upper limit.[2] A petition by 215 climate scientists pled for it at the Bali conference of 2007 that set the stage for negotiations over a post-Kyoto greenhouse regime.[3] To cope with the interactions between the two moral aspects of the greenhouse, I will start out by assuming this goal, argue for a standard of equity and then circle back to vindicate the goal of Two Degrees, helped by a conception of our shared duty to seek an adequate limit that will emerge from arguments about equity. The outcome will be a requirement of fair global teamwork in pursuit of a daunting goal, a requirement that imposes significant risks of sacrifice on many people in developed countries, while advancing interests of the global poor.

Because standards of adequacy and equity and the assessment of their consequences depend on the actual nature of the greenhouse challenge, these judgments must respond to a vast body of evidence, which currently creates wide margins of uncertainty on some important points. I will largely rely on the most authoritative recent summary of this evidence, the 2007 assessment report of the Intergovernmental Panel on Climate Change, and studies that significantly contributed to its findings. There will no doubt be major changes in the future, but as we shall see, the best evidence now is that a long wait for definitive evidence before taking decisive action would be a profoundly irresponsible bet.

## Equity: Some Proposals

Equity is a topic of heated public controversy over what to do in response to the greenhouse effect. (Equity, not junk science, was George W. Bush's reason for refusing—in agreement with a 95–0 vote of the U.S. Senate—to accept even the utterly inadequate constraints of the Kyoto Protocol. He rejected an arrangement that "exempts 80% of the world, including major population centers such as China and India . . . "[4]) In this clamor, many proposals have inherent appeal, as morally appropriate responses to the greenhouse challenge. One is a mandate of cheap rescue. People in developed countries are said to have the opportunity to keep the world below the threshold of inadequacy without morally significant risks to their compatriots, in a regime that imposes no burdensome restrictions on people in developing countries imperiled by climate change; since they can rescue without sacrifice, they should. On less optimistic assessments of the needed effort, fairness requires the justification of significant imposed burdens. This might be seen as a matter of fair teamwork, an impartially acceptable allocation of sacrifices in the work that is required to achieve the shared goal. Alternatively, special concern for poverty is sometimes treated as an independent requirement of climate equity. Often, equity is judged by some version of the precept, "Polluter pays." The fair division of tasks can also be seen as the fair bargain in light of the benefits and burdens of alternative climate regimes.

My proposal is that only the teamwork approach to equity deserves fundamental status. What is right in some of the other approaches derives from consideration of the impartially acceptable allocation of sacrifices on the greenhouse team. Greater costs of emission constraint, lesser per capita emissions and greater climate harms will all turn out to play important roles, all heavily favoring developing countries. However, they play their proper roles by contributing to the burdens that are to be impartially allocated.


## Costs of Rescue

The search for climate equity should begin with detailed scrutiny of the standard we all want to be applicable, cheap rescue. If, as Al Gore conveniently implies in *An Inconvenient Truth*, no one in a developed country would have to bear significant costs in the implementation of an adequate regime that does not burden people in developing countries at all, then this virtually cost-free rescue is the way to go. Responsible people in developed countries would be glad to provide such cheap relief from dire dangers to people with so much else to worry about. But the Two Degree standard of adequacy threatens greater expense than this comforting argument admits. If our shared duty is to keep below Two Degrees, tasks ought to be allocated in light of a significant risk of serious consequent losses due to economic disruption for many people in developed countries.

Given the range of currently plausible estimates of the sensitivity of climate to greenhouse gases, the stabilization of atmospheric greenhouse gases at the carbon dioxide equivalent of 450 parts per million by volume by 2150 has an even chance of keeping temperature increase, at equilibrium, within Two Degrees; a seven in ten likelihood of avoiding excess would require reduction to 400, while 500 would pose a seven in ten likelihood of breaching the limit.[5] These temperature equilibria would be reached after the end of this century. However, irreducible physical constraints and the avoidance of severe economic risks require a mid-twenty-second-century stabilization target at least as low as 450 ppm to avoid probable breaching of Two Degrees within this century.

When the Fourth Assessment Report of the IPCC appeared in 2007, the concentration of greenhouse gases was already at a carbon dioxide equivalent of about 450 ppm.[6] The increase over the pre-industrial level was already 0.8°.[7] On account of delayed processes of ocean warming, global mean temperature would have increased about a half degree more by the end of the century, even if concentration were immediately stabilized at 450 ppm.[8] And immediate stabilization is not an option, if widespread industrial shutdown is to be avoided. Overwhelming the processes of terrestrial and ocean-based absorption that kept atmospheric concentrations of greenhouse gases stable prior to the industrial revolution, the annual addition to the atmospheric stock of greenhouse gases has amounted, in recent decades, to about half the year's emissions from the use of fossil fuels. From 1965 to 1975, average annual carbon dioxide emissions were about 45% less than the 2004 level, while atmospheric concentration increased by about 1 part per million per year.[9] Because of the contribution of flow to stock, an emissions trajectory that achieves a mid-twenty-second-century stabilization target of 450 ppm while avoiding widespread economic shutdown must start out by overshooting the concentration target. This overshoot boosts near-term temperature increase. When the economic constraint is added to the physical constraints, trajectories stabilizing at 450 ppm, which have an even chance of avoiding Two Degrees at ultimate equilibrium, also have a mere even chance of keeping below this temperature limit in the twenty-first century.[10]

Because emission reductions achieving the 450 ppm target (much less 400) are so daunting, they have not been much studied. Indeed, when the Fourth Assessment Report was issued, the only detailed studies considering how and at what cost reductions in the full range of greenhouse gases could achieve this target were by a team at the Netherlands Environmental Assessment Agency who use the label "FAIR" for their model, as in "Framework to Assess International Regimes for differentiation of commitment." (Other work of broadly similar ambitions reached compatible conclusions.[11]) Sensitive to the need to avoid global economic shutdown in a world in which factories last for decades (over thirty years in the case of electric plants),[12] the FAIR team, in a 2007 proposal, postpone decline in the global emissions total until 2015. Then, their mitigation project requires a decline of 50% in the global total in the next thirty-five years, 60% per capita. At the end of the century, emissions are to be 30% of the 2000 total (20% per capita), a quarter of the 2015 peak, and a seventh of the emissions expected on the mid-level Business As Usual scenario they employ.[13] The late century drop, which makes the initial permissiveness feasible, crucially depends on carbon dioxide capture technology "which still has to be proven in large scale application," the uncertain availability of aquifers for carbon dioxide storage, and uses of crop-based fuels whose energy potential is profoundly uncertain.[14] Other studies of stringent targets were even more indulgent of optimistic technological speculations, such as the creation of a huge global carbon dioxide vacuum cleaner combining vast plantations, biofuels derived from them, and sequestration of the emissions from their use.[15]

What would be the costs of this commitment? Detailed studies of stringent, long-term emissions trajectories do not currently answer this question. Instead, they estimate how much the value of goods and services would be reduced by a process that substituted the most efficient allocation of energy sources fitting the mitigation trajectory for energy use without mitigation measures, making the substitution infallibly and without any further economic disturbance. This would, in effect, be a magic version of cap and trade, in which emission permits adding up to the permitted current total are exchanged through an auction among perfectly informed and rational transactors confident of compliance with all commitments. In the FAIR team's study, these annual costs would ascend, from 2015 to 2040, from a 0.3% to a 2% reduction of the Business As Usual baseline Gross World Product and then decline, after 2050, to 0.8% at the end of the century.[16] In the idealized auction through which they determine direct abatement costs to people in particular countries and regions, FAIR's preferred system for allocating permits strongly favors countries with low per capita GDP and low per capita emissions, so that the distribution of idealized direct abatement costs approximates the accommodation that Cheap Rescue envisions.[17] For example, in the United States, an allocation that is 30% below the Business As Usual baseline for emissions in 2020 would be associated with idealized direct abatement costs amounting to 0.5% of baseline GDP, and these annual costs would rise to 2.5% of GDP in 2050 when the allocation would be 90% below baseline emissions; in China, idealized direct abatement costs of 0.25% of GDP in 2020 would rise to 1% in 2050.[18]

The difference between magical least-cost reallocation and feasible efficiency, the indirect costs of macroeconomic disruption and the use of alternative, plausible Business As Usual scenarios would greatly increase these costs. Even in accommodation to the pathetically undemanding limits proposed in the Kyoto Protocol, direct abatement costs without trade in allocations would have been much greater than those from least-cost reduction through idealized global exchanges, about five times greater in the United States.[19] But in actual permit markets, the uncertainties of trading and problems of monitoring and enforcement can be expected to yield fuel allocations that are much less efficient than the ideal, if emissions are to be kept in bounds.[20] (Alternatively, in a carbon tax regime, optimal efficiency requires an internationally uniform tax, effectively imposed. If developing countries were spared, this would more than double direct abatement costs in the near term.[21]) In assessing the prospect of U.S. participation in Kyoto, the U.S. Energy Information Agency estimated costs of macroeconomic disturbance due to inflation and plant shut-downs to be more than four times the direct abatement costs, even assuming a domestic permit auction and revenues recycled through payroll tax reduction.[22] In addition to these disturbances, global cap and trade would trigger reverberations in world trade and finance from vast transfers of dollars. The FAIR team takes two-thirds of U.S. emissions to be covered by emissions trading in 2050.[23] (Transfers of carbon tax revenues from developed to developing countries in a globally comprehensive carbon tax regime would have similar consequences.) Among mid-range Business As Usual scenarios, the IPCC tends to treat A1B, a higher per capita growth and carbon dioxide emissions scenario than the FAIR team's B2, as the paradigm intermediate case.[24] A shift in scenarios would increase by three-fourths the percentage of Gross World Product lost in idealized direct abatement costs,[25] with greater developed country costs and cuts, by FAIR's equity rules.

Granted, more GDP per capita is not associated with more happiness on average in developed countries. The tendency at a given time of those with much more than the average to report more happiness, those with much less to report less, seems to reflect comparison with how others are doing within their society and goal-setting calibrated to the societal average, rather than the noncomparative need to have more, which does shape trends in developing countries.[26] However, the disturbances in the pace and structure of the economy in developed countries, especially the United States, would put many people at risk of serious losses of disruption, which exact distinctive costs. For a middle-aged production worker in the United States, losing a job is typically a serious loss, an interruption, not infrequently a long one, in employment, which often ends the prospect of a successful lifetime economic trajectory that had been a focus of plans, hopes and self-esteem.[27] Retraining programs do not seem to help much in developed countries now,[28] and might well do worse in the face of rapid technological change with unpredictable winners and losers.

Perhaps the reasons to worry about job loss, economic displacement and insecurity are false alarms. Above all, the cautious optimism about the pace of technological innovation and its impact on investment that underlies the FAIR team's cost estimates may be overly cautious. But similarly, the imposition of stringent emissions constraints to keep below Two Degrees might respond to a false alarm based on a misestimate of the future trajectory of economic activity. Indeed, one of the IPCC's scenarios of Business As Usual in the twenty-first century has a significant chance of keeping below Two Degrees without any greenhouse-specific intervention.[29] In response to both sorts of possibility of false alarm, a failure to take risks of over-optimism seriously is a failure to take the potential victims seriously.

Admittedly, risks of burden from commitment to the Two Degree target to people in developed countries, including the United States, are accompanied by possibilities of prevention of climate harms that people in those countries would otherwise endure. For example, commitment to Two Degrees, as compared to less stringent targets, might significantly reduce harms in the United States in this century from the drying of the Southwest. An assessment of proposed climate regimes should certainly respond to these possible benefits of mitigation. However, while needed climate measures will have to be adopted and imposed by national governments, the morally relevant burdens are, in the final analysis, burdens of individuals. What answers to the self-interest of a drought-fearing resident of Phoenix may not answer to the self-interest of an industrial worker in Chicago, whose serious losses should not be ignored. In any case, when an imposed policy inflicts important harms on some while also producing separate benefits at least as important for them, they ought to be offered a justification for accepting this arrangement rather than others inflicting less harm. They should not be told that they have no complaint. This room for complaint will turn out to be crucial to fair provision for developing countries.

The quick moral fix that I have called "Cheap Rescue" treats burdens of adequate mitigation as nothing, in claiming that people in developed countries would take on no burden to speak of in taking up the whole global burden of keeping warming within Two Degrees. Evidence that this claim is false absolves no one of responsibility. It simply moves the search for climate equity into a sphere in which the imposition of morally serious costs must be justified. Here, a model of fair teamwork ought to guide us.

## The Model of Teamwork

The emissions involved in anyone's own activity as consumer and producer would not, by themselves, cause climate harms. Indeed, the greenhouse gas emissions from activity in one country, even the United States or China, are not harmful by themselves. Greenhouse harm is a collective effect of our individually innocent pursuits taken together, generating a shared duty of containment. Because forbearance from those pursuits can constitute an important loss, we owe it to one another to work out a shared standard for the fair division of burdens in pursuit of the common goal.

Suppose we humans have a shared duty to pursue a certain goal of containment, say, of avoiding the Two Degree increase. As responsible people sharing a duty to reach this goal, we should all be equally willing to sacrifice to reach it. Unwillingness to sacrifice would be irresponsible, a lack of commitment to a goal one has a duty to help pursue. But if one has to do more to make up for others' lesser commitment to the shared goal, then they are behaving parasitically. If everyone pursuing the goal were fully responsible, no one would have to make up for others' lesser commitment. So insistence on equal willingness to make sacrifices needed to reach the goal would emerge from responsible deliberations, as a basis for equity.

This equal commitment need not lead to an overriding preference for schemes imposing equal sacrifices. There might be an adequate greenhouse regime in which people make unequal sacrifices and the greatest is less than in any other adequate regime. For example, the concentration of burdens of mitigation on people in developed countries might be an especially powerful driver of decarbonizing technological change that rapidly diffuses throughout the world, accompanied by an investment-driven economic boom. To insist that everyone, instead, bear equal, heavier burdens would be sadism, not fairness. But one shouldn't be obsessed with minimizing the gravest costs, when this would impose somewhat lesser but serious sacrifices on a great many more. If utmost squalor in Saudi Arabia is the worst loss under an adequate regime in which hundreds of millions in India, Brazil and China can emerge from lesser but severe poverty, then a poor Brazilian does not show less than equal willingness to sacrifice for the common goal in preferring this regime to an alternative in which many more suffer the lesser loss of continued poverty while a few are saved from a greater loss of pauperization.[30]

In these and other cases, an unequal set of sacrifices would be the preference of someone choosing among available loss sets behind a veil of ignorance, seeking to advance her interests but ignorant of which loss would be hers. These are impartial choices of who is to sacrifice what, so they express equal willingness to sacrifice.

Once the question of adequacy is settled, does greenhouse equity require anything more than the commitment to an impartially acceptable set of loss outcomes, which expresses everyone's equal willingness to make sacrifices for the shared goal? It does not. Other considerations, which I will survey, are initially attractive. But their proper role in greenhouse equity can be ascribed through a proper understanding of equal willingness to make sacrifices.

## The Relevance of Poverty

It might seem that this claim of completeness requires neglect of obviously relevant considerations of neediness. Even if greenhouse-external goals of poverty reduction are put to one side, a climate regime that is insensitive to the special needs of the world's poor seems grossly inequitable. The model of teamwork does not deny this. To the contrary, the special needs are robustly relevant to the model because of the difference they make to sacrifices in pursuit of the shared goal.

The postponement of the ending of suffering from the nonfulfillment of acute need is a serious sacrifice. For example, in China, hundreds of millions suffer from the destitution described in the previous chapter, including inadequate nutrition, inadequate health care, geographic isolation, and drudgery yielding meager subsistence. In 2005, one in three people in China lived on less than $2.00 a day.[31] Emissions constraints that block or substantially postpone escapes from such destitution would impose a much more serious sacrifice than constraints producing the economic disruptions in developed countries that we have considered. The cost is more serious even if the constraints on developing countries only reduce the rate of increase in per capita emissions while the constraints on developed countries impose a large per capita decline. While the job loss of a middle-aged production worker in a carboniferous industry in the United States is apt to be a serious matter, this disruption is not at all as bad as enduring lifelong fatigue, isolation and insecurity. And escapes from destitution in developing countries *are* closely tied to greenhouse gas emissions. Growth in GDP per capita has been by far the biggest contributor to the stupendous growth in Chinese carbon dioxide, eight times more important, in the last decade of the twentieth century, than the next most important factor, population growth. (There was a large decrease in energy used per unit of GDP.[32])

Fair teamwork, then, requires special permissiveness toward emissions that are needed by the global poor to escape to a better life—extending the special attention to "subsistence emissions" that Henry Shue incisively urged at the start of greenhouse concerns.[33] However, sacrifices required of team-members in developed countries will still be significant, and could make one greenhouse regime (say, with more gradual mandated emissions reductions) more equitable than another. Simply to dismiss the concerns about disruption of people in developed countries, as if their worry about losing a job had no more moral standing than a worry about postponing the advent of the next electronic gadget, is to dismiss those people.

Combined with currently warranted expectations about Business As Usual, these considerations of fair sacrifice suggest the broad shape of an equitable regime for avoiding Two Degrees. The warranted expectation at present is that there must be some constraint on emissions from developing countries to keep under Two Degrees. On a mid-range scenario of Business As Usual, developing countries will start to exceed the *global* carbon dioxide budget compatible with the 450 ppm stabilization target by around 2035.[34] A greenhouse regime that accepts hard facts of adequacy while respecting equity will probably slow escapes from destitution in slowing the growth of emissions in the developing world. But it will be much sterner (in emissions terms, not in terms of sacrifice) in developed countries, cutting emissions sooner and more steeply to minimize the burden of thwarted escape among the climate team. In the least developed countries, where any additional economic burdens threaten to tilt lives toward death or misery, undue sacrifices would be avoided by limiting change to "win/win" arrangements that make emissions less than they would be without threatening the pace of growth. Although it correlates with benevolence, this attention to poverty is a dictate of fair teamwork in the joint task of controlling climate change.

## "Polluter Pays"?

The most familiar standards of greenhouse equity are versions or variations of the theme "Polluter pays." Since disincentives to emit are essential to any satisfactory greenhouse regime, policies imposing costs on emitters will certainly play a role. But the proposed standards are addressed to a more fundamental level of moral assessment. A standard of proportionality between emissions and emission constraints is offered as an independent, basic criterion of justice in the imposition of constraints.—In fact, these standards are either morally distorting or aspects of the more fundamental rule of impartially acceptable burdens on the climate team. Independent reliance on "Polluter pays" as a fundamental standard of greenhouse equity introduces undue recrimination into the quest for climate justice, as independent reliance on considerations of poverty creates unmerited ascriptions of benevolence.

Sometimes a duty of people in developed countries to virtually monopolize emissions constraints is based on a duty to accept constraints on emissions from one's country in proportion to the contribution of emissions from this site to cumulative emissions in the history of humanity so far. But this seems an unreasonable response to pre-1990 emissions. It is hard to see why people living in developed countries now bear a responsibility to sacrifice their interests on account of past activities of people within the borders, mostly long-dead, which were not inherently illegitimate and whose harmful side-effects could not have been foreseen.[35]

What about emissions after about 1990, when there began to be substantial evidence of harmful consequences? These past emissions will have a special role to play in any sound moral assessment of current proposals. If a country would have exercised more restraint post-1990 under all morally satisfactory greenhouse regimes, then its citizens have a political duty to compensate others, by accepting more stringent constraints now, in order to avoid transferring burdens of their government's irresponsibility onto foreign shoulders. But this instruction to compensate for recent negligence does not tell us what standard of negligence to apply.

Alternatively, a forward-looking variant of "Polluter pays" might require people to reduce their emissions, once the greenhouse harms are foreseeable, in proportion to what they would emit in the absence of constraint, to the extent required for adequate reduction over-all. But if everyone's emissions are compatible with equal willingness to sacrifice in pursuit of an adequate climate goal, no one would seem to merit any further burden. And this requirement would be burdensome. A reduction of emissions in the near future would impose a significant sacrifice, involving postponed fulfillment of basic needs, on billions of poor people in developing countries.

To avoid unfairness due to proportionate reductions, those who emphasize emissions differences as the basis for greenhouse equity toward people in developing countries increasingly appeal to a right to equal per capita emissions.[36] According to this sophisticated variant of "Polluter pays," people whose emissions exceed the global average have, just by that token, a duty to compensate for taking more than is rightfully theirs. — On closer examination, what is valid in the claim of an equal right to emit either is not helpful or derives from the commitment to impartially acceptable sacrifices on the greenhouse team.

Obviously, people in developed countries are in no position to respond to greenhouse proposals by complaining of violation of a moral right to higher emissions than others'. The much greater emissions associated with the activities of a Swiss banker's child as compared with an Angolan farmer's child are, like so many other differences between them, consequences of her making use of greater opportunities and resources that she does not deserve. But the nonexistence of the right to emit more does not entail that it is wrong to emit more. What is undeserved is not, by that token, unjustly obtained or wrongly used. The banker's child can accept that the permissibility of her emissions is not based on a right to emit more than others while denying that there is anything wrong with her using her undeserved superior life situation to pursue worthwhile goals in processes that do emit more.

In comparing typical Swiss and Angolans, the model of fair teamwork has already provided a powerful reason to favor the latter, based on gravity of burden of reduction, not amount of emission, and will provide more. The test of independent reliance on equal per capita emissions rights would be cases in which greater gravity of burden of reduction and lesser emissions single out different emitters. The impartial allocation of burdens takes account of the greater winter impact of emissions reductions suffered by more emissive Swedish Sven as compared to Italian Stefano. If, independent of impartial allocation of burdens, Stefano has an emissions right equal to Sven's, then Sven's emitting more in keeping warm could make him liable for compensation of Stefano, even if the difference generates no unfair burdens. This is vindictiveness, not fairness.

Still, there is something valid in insistence on equal emissions rights. When policies constraining emissions are assessed, regimes under which some people would emit much more than others stand in need of a justification explaining why that feature is morally acceptable under the circumstances. "Swedes need more emissive activity to keep from freezing in the winter" could be part of an adequate justification. "Don't worry about these big inequalities. That is mere emissions-envy" is morally idiotic. What considerations internal to the greenhouse problem and the struggle to contain it might explain this moral pressure?

The right explanation derives from the limits of the atmospheric sink. A joint commitment to keep below a threshold of danger is a joint commitment to keep a single shared atmosphere into which everyone's emissions mix below a dangerous level of saturation. If the Two Degree standard (or any plausible standard) specifies adequacy, then the responsible pursuit of equity must be governed by a daunting assumption: keeping below the threshold requires a downward trend in global emissions, starting soon, to a global level substantially below Business As Usual, with a sharp decline in worldwide per capita emissions. In this process, more emissions for some entail a corresponding increase in constraint on others, reducing opportunities to make use of nature. Even if people in developing countries are currently exempted from constraints, greater global emissions now entail a sharper subsequent decline in the global carbon budget, so that developing countries, where benefits from emissive activities are especially likely to meet important needs, will be subject to stronger constraints later. The reduction of opportunities is a burden, part of the burdening whose allocation must be impartially acceptable, if cooperation in containing climate dangers is to be fair. By the same token, if per capita emissions in one country are greater than those in another, this will, all else being equal, give rise to an unfair allocation of burdens, i.e., of opportunities reduced in pursuit of climate safety.

At the level of policy, the right response might or might not include the assignment of an equal per capita allotment of tradeable permits adding up to the global sum in the current phase of the agreed emissions trajectory. (Equal per capita untradeable allotments make no sense. Bangladesh had per capita carbon dioxide emissions of 0.2 tons in 2004, China 3.9, the United States 20.6, and the global average was 4.5. Per capita equality of permitted emissions would have entailed great loss and waste.[37]) The appropriateness of this form of cap and trade partly depends on the much-debated comparison of permit auctions with carbon taxes as means of mitigation. For example, the permit total can be directly constrained by the desired global maximum emission, but the uncertainty and volatility of the permit price may reduce incentives for desirable technological innovation.

What *is* required is a pattern of "Contract and Converge," a strong correlation of decline in global emissions with convergence on rough equality among countries in per capita emissions. As time goes on, the capacity of people in currently developing countries to make productive use of fossil fuels grows, while the total global emissions budget must shrink in pursuit of an adequate global climate goal. So, in an adequate climate regime, there is an increasing tendency for inequality in per capita emissions to reflect imposed inferiority in opportunity to make use of nature. Since the inferiority would be imposed on those with greater need to spew carbon dioxide, failure to aim for rough convergence is incompatible with mutual respect among members of the climate control team.

## Irrelevant Bargains and Greenhouse Duties

Finally, the model of fair teamwork contrasts with an alternative standard of fairness in meeting the greenhouse challenge, insistence on a fair deal, identified with equality of net benefit from mitigation.[38] This alternative would place heavy burdens of mitigation on the global poor. Because of the special benefits of containing global warming to poor people in developing countries, a regime imposing large sacrifices in forgone development opportunities could still afford them net benefits at least as great as the net benefits of people in developed countries.

Keeping to the Two Degree threshold will disproportionately benefit poor people in developing countries, to an extent that is well-correlated with the depth of their poverty. In part, this is an outcome of the terrain in which people live. For example, huge numbers of people in east and south Asia live in coastal lowlands especially affected by rising sea levels. The melting of glaciers is especially important for the water needs of people in India and South America. Mostly, the greater impact reflects, not mere terrain, but the economic, social and political situations of people in developing countries, engaged in ways of life more sensitive to climate change with fewer resources for adjustment. More severe storms and drier droughts, the most likely important near-term consequences of Business As Usual, are the bane of farmers and a special burden for rural communities. In developing countries of Africa and Asia, about two-thirds of the population live outside of urban areas and agriculture contributes about a sixth of GDP, as compared to a fifth living rurally and a 2 percent contribution in developed countries.[39] The United States government can readily provide better levees and sea-walls, even where it does not. Bangladesh, Burma, India, Pakistan and Sri Lanka cannot so readily cope with the prospect that additional tens of millions of people on their coasts will be severely burdened by floods in the second half of the present century, if warming is not kept within Two Degrees and additional flood protection is not provided.[40]

As a consequence of the inequality in benefits from constraints, net benefits from an adequate climate change regime could be equal, worldwide, even if poor people in developing countries suffered substantial losses in retarded development due to stringent constraints on their countries' emissions. In such a greenhouse regime, people in India and Bangladesh could be required to pay for a reduced risk of suffering climate harms through an increased risk of postponement of development that fulfills basic needs. While they only come out a bit ahead of the game, the same is true of people in the United States. The Americans expect to bear lighter burdens due to mitigation, but they gain less by way of reduced dangers of loss from global warming. Those who need more insurance give up more for insurance. What is unfair about that? Contemplating a regime that will impose serious risks of disruption on him in order to seriously reduce risks of devastating flood and deadly disease for Bangladeshis forty years from now, a West Virginian coal miner would be a creep to say, "I just don't care what happens in Bangladesh." But if he is inclined to say, "Given the costs to me and the benefits to them and their children, people in Bangladesh should be willing to give up a lot for the extra safety," this is an initially plausible appeal to equity.

In assessing the fairness of alternative contractual arrangements, someone's complaint about having to spend more can certainly be countered by the observation that he is getting more. But such reasoning about fair sacrifice can be horribly out of place in other contexts. Rationing was important for the British war effort in World War II, and it was important that the rationing scheme be fair. The suggestion that British Jews accept shorter rations because they had more to lose from British defeat would have been absurd and appalling. Everyone's commitment to the system of constraints was properly based on an interest in the continued freedom of all, not on his or her own interests together with a desire to be fair. An effective response to the coal miner's complaint against departure from equal net benefit should, similarly, appeal to the moral foundations of the duty to limit greenhouse warming. Here, the investigation of equity requires inquiry into the grounds for upholding a standard of adequacy.

A reminder of the duty of concern for those in need will not be an effective response, given the limits of Sympathy. The coal miner is not refusing to lift a finger to prevent dire harm in Bangladesh. Rather, he is not willing to impose on himself a significant risk of a worse life. If he has a strong conservationist commitment to protect the global environment from deterioration, then he might count the protection of the Bangladeshi environment as a gain from his own point of view, that makes up for his material sacrifice. But presumably, he has no such strong commitment. In any case, those who seek to impose emissions constraints in his political society should seek justifications that are acceptable to everyone committed to values of free and equal citizenship. Not to seek such a justification for important political impositions shows intolerant disrespect of fellow citizens who are willing participants in civic cooperation. One can find such a justification of commitments to contain greenhouse harms in familiar political considerations of trust and trusteeship. Identification with a demanding goal of reducing greenhouse emissions expresses ordinary political commitments in response to an extraordinary crisis.

The central morally relevant fact that the coalminer's complaint ignores is his contribution, along with his fellow citizens', to the climate danger faced by Bangladeshis. Insistence on equality of net benefit in containing harmful effects of activities in which all participate, but to a greater or a lesser extent, is, in effect, insistence that pollutee pays: in international cooperation to reduce harm, citizenries whose activity makes a disproportionate contribution to harm would bear lower costs on account of the additional need for relief that they have created. Acquiescence in this standard of equality would be rational for those facing calamity if they had no better option. Indeed, this standard provides an equal, rational incentive to all to accept a mitigation regime. But by rewarding the infliction of suffering that others could not willingly accept, this standard of equality violates the valuing of trust expressed in the political interactions of responsible compatriots.

In seeking fellow citizens' agreement to arrangements advancing wellbeing within the borders, a responsible person seeks measures that all can willingly accept while affirming their equal worth, rather than arrangements to which those vulnerable to others would acquiesce as the price to be paid for dissuading others from exploiting their vulnerability. The strong, who could extract a better deal—whether through armed might or membership in stable, dominant electoral coalitions—will, if responsible, prefer to forgo the concessions they could exact, in order to base political stability on mutual trust rather than asymmetric fear. Otherwise, like tyrants, they base rule on the exploitation of vulnerability. In coping with the greenhouse challenge, a preference for the model of teamwork over the standard of equal net benefit expresses the same valuing of trust. In a greenhouse regime, as in the domestic system of institutions, the strong should treat gains from others' vulnerability as a cost they seek to avoid, in pursuit of genuine cooperation.

The rejection of the standard of equal net benefit is also required for coherence with the ordinary political value of trusteeship—without any need to rely on special environmentalist or religious values. Special concern for helpless compatriots partly depends on a duty of territorial trusteeship: the assertion of exclusive ultimate control over a territory is irresponsible without acceptance of an obligation as ultimate protector of those in the territory from threats of grave loss. If the exclusion of outsiders from sovereign prerogatives is only responsible on this condition, sovereignty will also be irresponsible in the absence of concern for gravely harmful effects on outsiders of processes starting within the borders. In the one case as in the other, the trustees' concern should extend to side-effects—paradigmatically, harms of environmental pollution—as well as intentionally inflicted harms.

The goals that underlie ordinary political responsibilities do not just explain why those less vulnerable to greenhouse harms should not insist on extra insurance charges to those more vulnerable. They create a further reason to favor them, on grounds of equity. Within borders, responsible citizens must be especially attentive to the interests of compatriots whose life prospects are inferior under the laws that shape terms of self-advancement in the territory. Those who support these laws do wrong unless they have an adequate answer to the reasonable complaints of those burdened by the inferior prospects they help to create. They must show equal regard for the interests of the disadvantaged despite conduct that imposes disadvantage. Suppose that a mitigation regime is instituted under which some are asked to put up with especially severe, unmitigated burdens from others' emissions. Like those asked to put up with social disadvantages, they are treated unjustly, unless their complaint of greater burden is answerable in terms that show equal regard for their interests.

Such residual climate harm is, in fact, an inevitable outcome of the greenhouse effect, generating further duties of equity. The Two Degree threshold does not, by any means, mark the onset of severe greenhouse harms, which occur throughout the warming process. For example, the increase through the first decade of the twenty-first century, of about $0.8°$, is very likely to have caused drought and desertification in northern Africa, while shrinkage of Andean glaciers is expected to cause water shortages in Peru not much later, when $1°$ is reached. Someone has serious reason to object to an arrangement under which she will suffer disproportionate greenhouse harm.

Such a complaint must not be regarded as decisive. Feasible mitigation arrangements inevitably involve greater climate harms for some than others, and efforts to reduce such inequalities can have morally prohibitive costs. The just solution is to take account of the unmitigated climate impact on each member of the climate team of emissions under others' control in assessing the fairness of sacrifices under a proposed greenhouse regime.

These residual climate harms are independent of the reduction of opportunities for growth through emissions constraints or through the filling of the atmospheric sink. So the pursuit of the impartially preferable allocation of burdens must, independently, take account of the human costs of the residual climate change. This adds the requirement of help to developing countries in coping with climate change to the other demands of climate justice.

In principle, foreign aid sent to developing countries to help in such adaptation to climate change could significantly lighten developed countries' responsibilities to reduce emissions, by using economic returns from emissive activity in developed countries to reduce the worst climate harms. So could foreign aid to help developing countries adopt less emissive technologies. In fact, foreign aid for these purposes should supplement, not displace, emphasis on emissions reduction in developed countries. The use of foreign aid to meet the greenhouse challenge would share liabilities with the long-proclaimed goal of using aid to improve economic growth. Both endeavors must cope with grave difficulties in fitting new projects and technologies to the local environment and to local social, political and economic processes. No doubt, the interests of the most powerful developed countries shape foreign aid in ways that add to these difficulties. Citizens of these countries should imagine better behavior by their governments, in framing an ideal aspiration. But they will do people in developing countries no favors in ignoring limitations due to processes in developing countries that severely diminish the benefits of aid—limitations of governmental capacity and integrity, which are sometimes made worse by large aid flows. (These constraints will be described in more detail in Chapter 8.) Foreign funds for projects whose benefits are hard to estimate and monitor are especially ripe for diversion to nurture local client-networks and especially likely to serve as substitutes for more effective, demanding efforts by the local government. The history of Kyoto's Clean Development Mechanism, in which recipients and donors are rewarded on the basis of inevitably speculative reckonings of reductions of emissions from business as usual, already provides abundant evidence of limits to the usefulness of foreign aid.[41]

These are not reasons for abandonment of foreign aid for climate goals, which will probably reduce burdens in recipients while creating no comparable burdens in donor countries. They are reasons not to rely on this alternative as a basis for avoiding stringent enforced emissions reductions in developed countries. Avoiding intermediaries who interfere with help through foreign aid, the reduction of greenhouse gas concentration through developed country mitigation directly benefits those most at risk in developing countries. With climate harms prevented, the farmers of Ethiopia and the urban poor of Shanghai can cash in their improved opportunities on their own. In addition, the foreign aid process would be too slow to cope adequately with rapidly mounting devastation from rapidly escalating temperature. This danger plays an important role in setting the target of climate control, resolving the question of adequacy, to which I will now turn.

## Adequacy, Trust and Constrained Impartiality

Political duties to take on burdens to reduce climate dangers to others have turned out to derive from ordinary political duties of trust: the duty to base joint commitments on mutually respectful trust and the duty of trusteeship over a sovereign territory.[42] These duties of trust are not just important in establishing the equitable division of labor in humanity's common task of limiting the greenhouse effect. They also determine adequacy in the common climate goals that should be our shared aim. Within provisos that the greenhouse process can be expected to satisfy, duties of cooperation and due care make impartial acceptability of burdens—both burdens imposed by climate policies and unmitigated climate burdens—the criterion of greenhouse justice as a whole, including both equity and adequacy.

First, to properly value trustworthy cooperation, citizenries responding to the greenhouse challenge must be willing to impose significant burdens on compatriots in the interest of global climate safety. So long as every citizenry benefits as a whole from an international greenhouse agreement, reasonable deliberations would reduce the heaviest burdens worldwide due to unmitigated climate harms and restricted opportunities, impartially assessing the seriousness of each global set of burdens. Otherwise, as we saw in connection with trade deliberations, representatives could not act responsibly, protecting vital interests of those they represent while recognizing the force of similar reasons advanced by others. As in the case of trade deliberations, some citizens will suffer special losses of economic displacement in countries that benefit as a whole. But significant exemption from emissions constraint on these grounds would defeat the global response if parity of reasoning is observed among all parties.

Since commitment to the joint climate goal (say, keeping below Two Degrees), the division of tasks, and capacities for adaptation all, interdependent-ly, determine the allocation of burdens, the primary topic of moral judgment should be whole greenhouse regimes, i.e., total packages of mitigation and adaptation goals and divisions of responsibilities, for people throughout the world. The distinction between adequacy of goals and equity in their pursuit corresponds to different policies and different motivations for perseverance, but the same demand for impartial acceptability regulates the two standard topics of greenhouse justice.

This argument from the morality of trustworthy cooperation to impartial acceptability starts with the proviso that the ultimate agreement benefit each party, over-all and on balance, as compared to nonagreement. Greenhouse negotiations meet or, in any case, closely approximate this condition, so long as they adhere to the rule of impartial acceptability. Developing countries, with their special climate vulnerabilities, will benefit if burdens of thwarted development are taken into account. Given their greater technological cap- acities, greater wealth and the climate dangers of Business As Usual to their people, developed countries can take on disproportionate burdens of emissions reduction in an arrangement that is beneficial to their people as a whole. Even if the resulting trajectory of GDP, total or per capita, in developed countries, were to lag substantially behind Business As Usual, no great burden would be imposed. Over time, growth in GDP does not significantly contribute to happiness in developed countries. On the other hand, environmental degradation remains a source of unhappiness—so that, as economists say, the relative price of environmental goods increases.

Granted, a severe, prolonged downturn produced by the pursuit of an extremely stringent climate goal might give rise to harms in a developed country on the scale of the climate losses avoided there. But global economic interdependence would spread such harms to developing countries, thwarting escapes from destitution and efforts to adapt to unavoidable climate change. These special economic dangers of extremely stringent targets are as serious as the reductions in climate danger that they are expected to add to the protections of less stringent targets. So a regime of impartially acceptable burdens would not require them: no citizenry has an interest in a mitigation-induced economic crash. In general, the proviso of net benefit over-all in each country will be satisfied if impartial acceptability is pursued.

In the second place, in addition to trustworthy cooperation, due care is an alternative route from ordinary political values to greenhouse justice. Suppose that Canadians could expect to benefit, as a whole, from Business As Usual, through better harvests in the prairie provinces and the opening of the Northwest Passage. This consideration would violate the proviso about expected benefit. But it would not be an adequate reason to refuse to take on a fair share of a global effort to reduce the global emissions that threaten grave damage in the world outside of Canada. Such a refusal would fail to show due care in a party to a gravely harmful process.

Further reflection on the goals of due care leads, once again, to the criterion of impartial acceptability of burdens. The goals of due care in climate policy are not limited to reduction of the harmful side-effects of greenhouse gas emissions. In the effort to mitigate the harms that they jointly create, those whose business-as-usual would harm must also take account of harmful side-effects of cures that they adopt. Concerned to reduce both unmitigated harms and thwarted opportunities due to mitigation, we joint producers of climate harms should give priority to the gravest combined burdens of climate danger and climate mitigation that people suffer, to grave burdens that more people suffer and to grave burdens that are readily relieved. In order to resolve trade-offs among these dimensions of responsible mitigation, we ought to consult the familiar impartial perspective of choice among allocations of burdens that is made in ignorance of one's actual situation.

Might this much impartiality demand too much of a participant? This is a pressing question, because of limits to the risks that people are obliged to impose on themselves to avoid unintended harm to others. Soldiers have a duty to avoid unintended harm to civilians at some cost to their safety, but not at all costs. In a poignant example of Michael Walzer's, British soldiers clearing cellars of enemy troops in French villages during World War I recognized a duty to take on some additional risks by giving warning before they threw grenades down coal chutes, so that villagers huddled in those cellars could announce their presence and escape harm.[43] Still, in a pitched house-to-house battle, announcing one's presence and giving civilians time to escape while the enemy responds to the announcement might be too much to ask. Similarly, if the Canadian economy were so rigidly tied to a promiscuously emissive smelting process that an impartially acceptable greenhouse regime would impoverish Canada, this seems a plausible reason for Canadians to reject it.

There is, at present, no well-established comprehensive, reasonably precise description of when costly forbearance from conduct with harmful side-effects is morally required. The establishment of such a standard would have to settle questions about the difference between intentional and unintended harm that are among the most obscure and contested in ethics, and provide a principled solution to a problem that theorists of justice in war have tried to solve for a long time, a reasonably precise prescription of adequate care to avoid causing civilian deaths. Just as a commitment to Christian stewardship is a sectarian basis for mandating a greenhouse regime, to be avoided if possible, so, at present, is any precise and general specification of due care. Nonetheless, limited, uncontroversial convictions combine with the nature of the global greenhouse and the global economy to make an impartially acceptable allocation of greenhouse burdens the means of fulfilling everyone's duty of due climatic care.

Uncontroversially, those taking part in an activity giving rise to grave harms must make a good-faith effort to reduce those harms. Just how much self-imposed risk is required for good faith is not clear. But some significant risk must be taken on. To adequately value civilians' lives, the soldiers clearing the cellars had to increase their own peril. A citizenry who are good-faith participants in the project of reducing the climate harms they would otherwise help to cause have to be willing to impose costs appropriate to the pursuit in good faith of an important civic project. These normal civic costs are at least as great as the significant risks of disruption in developed countries that are part of an effort to pursue a climate target such as Two Degrees/450 ppm. After all, railroad workers are rightly told that their job security may be sacrificed to advance national prosperity by constructing a highway system. So workers in emissive industries may certainly be told that their security may be sacrificed in the project of avoiding grave climate harms.

The duty to accept risks of harms to one's own in the cause of avoiding grave risks to others is especially compelling when there are alternative, plausible scenarios in which one's own will not suffer harm, indeed, may well benefit from the project of protecting others. These are typical alternative expectations for large emissions reductions in developed countries. Within the realm of plausible hypotheses about technological change and economic responses to new costs, a greenhouse regime aiming to keep below Two Degrees might have significant economic costs, or might, on the other hand, stimulate investment-led growth in pursuit of new technology. Until targets become extremely stringent, there are, as usual, economists on all sides.[44]

Admittedly, a cautious application of the duty of due care, restricted to moderate costs of care, will not establish a duty to participate in a regime imposing a requirement of emissions reduction which carries a substantial risk of pervasive, severe losses for the people of one's country. But the severity of such losses will be taken into account in finding a regime that is impartially acceptable in light of all of its burdens. From this perspective, pervasive, severe economic losses to the people of a country from imposed emissions reductions will be avoided unless the imposition on this and relevantly similar countries is needed to avoid worse consequences in the rest of the world.[45] So emissions reductions that would be economically devastating for a country whose relevant emissions, together with those of relevantly similar countries, are not a grave climate danger will not be imposed. If wellbeing in Cambodia is rigidly tied to methane-promiscuous rice-paddy agriculture, there is insufficient reason to devastate the Cambodian economy by methane restrictions. Similarly, in the fantasy of Canadian smelting, Canadians might have grounds for insisting on special treatment—though such a rigid, vital, special tie to a distinctively emissive process of production is not characteristic of any advanced economy, for fundamental economic reasons.

In contrast, all else being equal, the global climate damage avoided by economically devastating emissions reductions imposed on the leading per capita emitters might justify the imposition, in an impartial allocation of burdens. But all else is not equal: economic interdependence would extend the economic losses to the world at large. Because of the consequent severe harms to the global poor, such a regime could be rejected from an impartial perspective. Granted, there may be some countries, such as Saudi Arabia, with economies so rigidly tied to the sale of fossil fuels that their people would suffer severe pervasive losses in an impartially acceptable greenhouse regime. But the people of these countries can hardly require foreigners to depart from dictates of due care constraining their own economic activity to make purchases catering to the special needs of fossil-fuel sellers. The most that they should require is choice of a greenhouse regime from an impartial perspective in which their losses are taken into account.

Evidently, any citizenry worthy of trust will seek a package of global climate policies that is impartially acceptable to every person. This is the perspective for equity in pursuit of the global climate goal whose consequences were explored in previous sections. The remaining question is one of adequacy, how low to go in the global goal that is pursued.

## Costs and Gains: Toward Two Degrees

The most important precept guiding pursuit of an answer very broadly resembles the standard economists' prescription of policies equating marginal costs with marginal benefits. In choosing among long-term global emissions reduction projects, one should choose lower and lower targets until the costs of more stringent targets are not worth the gains. Here, worth is to be determined from the appropriate impartial perspective. There ought to be no assumption that numerical measures of aggregate gains and losses are relevant and accurate, that preferences in markets measure relevant worth, or that gains and losses due to small increases determine whether further stringency is worth it. The commonsense precept of rational choice only motivates standard marginalist techniques of cost–benefit analysis in special cases, without requiring them in the project of containing global warming.

The basic pattern of costs in emissions-reduction regimes is substantial increase as targets shift from low to very low, rapidly accelerating as the physical limit to temperature containment is approached. Small reductions in business-as-usual emissions are not just cost-free but cost-saving. The incentives to reduce—whether taxes, the need to buy permits or subsidies—lead to energy-efficient choices that more than pay for themselves, choices which sufficiently active, farsighted economizers would have made anyway. We procrastinators finally weatherize our houses. Further near-term reductions can make use of readily available technologies whose use can be substantially expanded at some but not much cost. But as near-term reduction goals become more ambitious, they start to encounter harder constraints. The needed additional inputs, equipment and infrastructure become difficult and costly to obtain and deploy, or generate harms of their own. For example, fewer windy prairies are available for wind-turbines; biofuel crops intrude more and more on food crops, significantly reducing the terrestrial carbon sink through deforestation and burdening the global poor through increased food prices; additional accessible uranium ore becomes low-grade and in need of more emissive processing, while controls over dangers of nuclear proliferation are strained. Losses from emissions reduction start to become substantial, and they substantially increase with yet more stringent goals.[46] Moreover, increasingly stringent targets require more and more constraint on developing countries, whose business-as-usual emissions become more quickly and greatly in excess of the target-compatible global emissions budget.[47]

Eventually, further pressure toward near-term emissions reduction reaches an economic cliff at which further substantial reduction would trigger widespread shut-downs of factories and energy plants with dire macroeconomic consequences. The FAIR team's estimates suggest that this cliff would probably be reached in the course of pursuing a mid-twenty-second-century stabilization target around 425 ppm.[48]

Of course, technological progress will push the frontier of economic stress and the economic cliff farther and farther back, as time goes by, until they finally disappear and energy production is carbon-free. But a good-faith effort to contain global warming within a fairly low limit—even Two and a Half Degrees, much less Two—cannot tolerate postponement of reduction from Business As Usual or a long postponement of absolute reduction. Continuing flow adds to the atmospheric stock that generates increased temperature, soon guaranteeing the breaching of the temperature limit. The lower the low target, the sooner steep reduction must begin—and so, the more poor people in developing countries will be affected by thwarted development and the less effective will be the available means of making production less emissive.

On the other side of the ledger, the gains in climate safety associated with costs of policies striving for emissions reduction will depend on the impact of emissions on atmospheric concentration, the impact of concentration on warming and the harms generated by this warming. In over-all assessments of these physical linkages, the 2007 IPCC report confined itself to mechanisms that were already well-established and securely within the reach of computational capacity. Given the IPCC's mid-range guesses, emissions reductions with low costs in disruption and inefficiency are certainly worth the gains in climate safety. The mid-range IPCC Business As Usual scenarios are associated with best estimates of temperature increase averaging somewhat above Three Degrees by 2100.[49] Trajectories that would lower such increase by a significant fraction of a degree without economic stress seem feasible. For example, the FAIR team estimate that a trajectory stabilizing at 650 ppm would lower the increase at 2100 by 0.7° without significant costs.[50] By the end of this century, reductions in warming on this scale are apt to save at least a few million people from coastal flooding even if flood protection increases in line with income and only sea level change is taken into account.[51] The increase in severity of storms that theory dictates (since vapor from warming powers storms) would add many millions more to those saved from harm. These differences are smaller than the impact of enhanced flood protection. But there is no reason to suppose that economic loss would interfere with such adaptation in an equitable regime imposing such a mild global constraint on emissions. Similarly, moderate regimes would, on balance, reduce the tendency of new rain patterns to create additional breeding grounds for malaria-bearing mosquitos, without canceling the health gains through interference with economic capacities to drain the pools, acquire impregnated mosquito nets and provide effective anti-malarial therapies.

However, as goals of climate control become more ambitious, the risks of increased economic harm, including lost ability to adapt to climate change, become more substantial, especially when macroeconomic reverberations are taken into account. As these dangers from extra mitigation increase, mid-range estimates of climate harms show a steep decline in incremental gains in safety.[52] Even studies as fiercely opposed in tone and methodology as Nicholas Stern's and William Nordhaus' locate the turning point at which the expected climate gains are not worth their costs significantly above Two Degrees.[53]

## Two Degrees and Catastrophe

If harms through the mid-twenty-second century are in question, the case for a good-faith commitment now to a climate project aiming at Two Degrees depends on possibilities that are increasingly significant but not, as yet, predicted as likely to occur. Possible interactions between atmosphere, land and ocean that would speed the increase in the atmospheric stock of greenhouse gases are especially troubling. In the IPCC's 2007 report, the diverse models based on the best-established of these couplings produced a broad range of concentration outcomes, which would sustain differences in estimates of temperature increase in the range of $2°$ by 2100.[54] Other processes, which might reduce terrestrial absorption of carbon dioxide or even convert the land surface from a sink to a source, were put to one side, as insufficiently studied, and have become bases for deeper concern through subsequent inquiries. Limitations in nitrogen and minerals needed for plant growth seem to severely inhibit plant uptake of additional carbon dioxide in response to increased concentration of carbon dioxide—by a factor of 3.8 in this century, according to one study.[55] Wildfire, which already contributes a third of the carbon due to fossil fuel emissions, can be expected to increase substantially on account of drying from greater warmth, though the specific global balance between effects of drying from warmth and wetting from rain is unclear.[56] The thawing of permafrost might give rise to emissions equivalent to a sixth of current fossil fuel emissions.[57]

Because of the live possibility that mid-range expectations of concentration are much too low, climate policies that would, on mid-range expectations, keep substantially below Two and a Half Degrees throughout this century could, in fact, be necessary to avoid the harms characteristic of Three Degrees and higher. Ordinarily, the right response to such possibilities is to wait and see and correct if necessary. But robust estimates of complex natural feedbacks take a long time to establish. So does the negotiation of new, more restrictive global emissions policies, which have to set demanding mandates for the intermediate future if they are to quicken the pace of technological innovation. Waiting for new evidence, new policies and new conduct means accepting an increase in the atmospheric stock of greenhouse gases that makes it impossible to avoid the harms that new evidence might establish.

A live possibility of steady increase in temperature to Three Degrees is troubling enough. Increase to Three Degrees would add about a billion to the number of people at risk of water shortage at Two Degrees, and would involve a global decline in cereal yields, especially steep in the tropics.[58] According to one influential extrapolation of current sensitivities to habitat change, about a third of current species would be committed to extinction once Three Degrees is reached.[59] In addition, there are live possibilities of rapid, large-scale harmful responses to initial increases well below Three Degrees, too rapid for adaptation by vulnerable people. In principle, positive feedback between warming and the degradation of tropical forests or the permafrost could produce a surge of global warming in a few decades.[60] Even if warming keeps substantially below Three Degrees, some observations and theories of melting, run-offs, and the interaction between changes in sea-borne ice shelves and ground-based ice sheets suggest that global warming might induce rapid shrinkage of the Greenland Ice Sheet, the Antarctic Ice Sheet, or both, leading to a rapid rise in sea level. While this concern is not a firm dire prediction, it is within the range of past changes. At the end of the last ice age, polar warming on the scale produced by Two and a Half Degrees (which will be higher in high latitudes) led to deglaciation producing a rise in sea level of about a meter in a century.[61] Such a steep increase now would flood coastal regions where hundreds of millions live.[62]

Given these live possibilities, a refusal to adopt climate policies just because their likely costs exceed their likely benefits in prevention of climate danger is as foolish as a refusal to pay for a year's health insurance just because one is unlikely to have a serious illness that year. Still, the search for greater climate safety is burdened by deep uncertainty as to how much greater safety is purchased through a more costly climate policy. Rival models of the coupling between atmosphere, land and ocean that entail very different relationships between emissions and concentration fit current evidence equally well. The warming that might trigger rapid, irreversible widespread harm might occur above the limit that would be sought in any case on the basis of likely climate harms and mitigation costs, below the limit that the planet is already destined to reach, or somewhere in between. These potentially disastrous processes are sensitive to temperature, but current evidence does not sustain an estimate of the threshold of too hot.

In the face of these uncertainties, someone impartially concerned with human burdens, both climatic and economic, would purchase safety from the dire climatic possibilities through mitigation policies that she does not expect, on balance, to impose widespread severe human costs through economic losses. Currently, a good-faith effort to keep increase below Two Degrees meets this standard of moderation. On some views of technological progress and investment, it will impose no net economic cost. On other views it will, but these hypotheses are not much more likely to be valid and the expected, moderate costs are within the normal range of burdens created in pursuit of important civic goals. The pressures to decarbonize that implement the aspiration to Two Degrees are unlikely to push the world economy over the cliff of widespread shut-down. In any case, a safeguard such as a maximum emissions permit price could serve as a fence against this calamity, without destroying incentives that are, on current evidence, likely to be enough to keep within Two Degrees.

A good-faith effort to keep substantially below Two Degrees is another matter. Adherence to the emissions regimes with about an even chance of keeping increase that low is more likely than not to cause widespread significant economic harm, and has a substantial likelihood of pushing the world economy over the cliff. Safety valves avoiding these dangers cannot be attached in a good-faith effort to keep substantially below Two Degrees: only the secure fear of severe penalties for over-emission is likely to be enough to motivate the needed technological changes.

Imposing risks that are severe, likely and widespread is not justifiable as a speculative means of avoiding speculative widespread calamities. Evidence available at the outset of negotiations over a successor to the Kyoto accord makes a target of Two Degrees about right.

Of course, the difference between $2.0^{\circ}$ C over pre-industrial, $1.9^{\circ}$ C or $2.1^{\circ}$ C has no special moral standing, any more than whole numbers and the Celsius scale have special moral standing. But a standard of adequacy is not just a basis for assigning a grade of "Satisfactory." It is a shared goal to which responsible people throughout the world would hold themselves and others in the face of inevitable scientific controversies, shifts in technologies and burdens, grounds for suspicion and temptations to bad faith. A single shared numerical commitment that is simple in the most common scale of measurement has obvious advantages in this stressful coordination of the greenhouse team. This function singles out Two Degrees within the approximate region.

## The Horizon of the Grandchildren

The final ingredient in a case for Two Degrees is an appropriate perspective on time. Because of the endurance of greenhouse gases in the atmosphere and the high level of atmospheric concentration already reached, steep reduction of emissions will have to start soon in a good-faith effort to keep below Two Degrees. This will risk losses from economic dislocation and slowdown, starting soon. In contrast, the climate harms whose prevention has figured in the case for Two Degrees would become a serious global burden decades from now, with the main onslaught starting toward the end of the century. So a case for Two Degrees must give adequate standing to climate harms that will not be endured in the lifetimes of many people who are asked to agree to emissions reductions that may impose significant costs on them.

The valuing of trust that underlies our current political duty to limit the greenhouse effect entails an interest in others' interests sustaining this concern for the future. One seeks to be worthy of the trust of those with whom one interacts when one takes responsibility for harms stemming from what one controls, avoids exploitation of others' vulnerability in setting terms for joint activity, and promotes shared constraints on self-advancement that all who take on the constraints can self-respectfully uphold. Trust is an attitude among contemporaries, who rely on appropriate mutual concern for one another's interests. But this is not to say that a trustworthy climate choice only attends to the immediate impact of the conduct in question. The relevant interests include contemporaries' interests in meeting their own needs later in their lives, as well as now, and also their interests in nurturance, such as the interest in bringing up children who can themselves successfully meet their own needs, in turn. A similar interest in the next generation and their interests should be presupposed in the childless, in the search for terms fit to guide political interaction among those seeking justice. Someone who does not care how institutions in his society will affect people in the younger generation after he is dead does not care about the justice of those institutions. Given the centrality of these nurturant interests, climate impacts through the start of the next century—in the lifetimes of children of children alive today—will be a vital concern, which can only be expressed responsibly through an effort to keep increase from crossing a threshold of about Two Degrees.

This case for Two Degrees as a goal of people who want to live together with others responsibly does not attend to dangers to people who will live in the remote future. The presumed eventual love of people who are young now for their eventual grandchildren might extend the temporal horizon a bit, but only within the next century. Does this limited time horizon, implicit in ordinary political duties, make a difference to greenhouse obligations? In particular, what kind of evidence now concerning the remote future might create a duty to impose even steeper emissions reductions, aiming for a limit significantly lower than Two Degrees, despite the substantial risk of severe additional economic costs?

At a minimum, a substantial body of evidence would have to establish a significant probability that a much more burdensome project than Two Degrees, plunging many people now into destitution and stripping them of means to cope with climate change, is necessary and sufficient to prevent a highly distinctive sort of calamity: much more extensive climate suffering, at least as acute for individual victims, in the remote future, through an irreversible process with a long time delay. Each feature of this grim possibility is essential to the deeper demand (though perhaps their combination is not sufficient.) One is not obliged to create a substantial probability of dire loss to oneself and those one loves in order to avoid a speculative danger to others. Dire losses need not be imposed to avoid side-effects on others that are much less significant for each person affected—say, many billions of larger bills for air conditioning. Because of the irreducible uncertainty of the remote future, the enormous compounded future benefits forgone through the imposed economic loss, and the inevitable risk in forgoing resources which would have helped to cope with the many needs of the vulnerable human species, the future extra climate harms had better be much more widespread than the current economic burdens of avoiding them, not just individually grave. The many billions living between now and a remote effect will have their own responsibilities to prevent harm and, presumably, much greater material resources than humanity's now; so the triggering of a process insensitive to future intervention, rendering these responsibilities irrelevant, must be part of the case for the deeper demand.

Currently, no dire prospect fits this demanding prescription. There is substantial evidence that global warming at a threshold somewhere between Two and Four and a Half Degrees would trigger a gradual meltdown of the Greenland Ice Sheet, unstoppable by any currently foreseeable means, that would add about 1.7 meters to sea level in three centuries, 7 meters in three thousand years.[63] Since the FAIR team's overshoot trajectory to 450 ppm has an even chance of exceeding Two Degrees, a much more demanding project would reduce this risk. But the extent to which the likely severe burdens now would reduce risks of triggering the meltdown is quite uncertain, as are the material and cultural capacities of people born centuries or millennia from now to cope with the threat of gradual meltdown. Some other possible outcomes of increase significantly lower than Two Degrees would certainly overwhelm future capacities. For example, such warming in the near future might, conceivably, slowly and irreversibly penetrate to the ocean depths, releasing a vastly lethal melt of frozen methane hydrate millennia from now. But these are, at present, mere speculations.

The failure to act now to head off possibilities of vast harm in the future at severe but lesser current cost now might seem incompatible with appreciation of the equal value of people's lives whenever they are born. But in fact, it expresses an attitude toward choices and their possible effects that would be endorsed from a generationally impartial perspective. "Act in ways that are likely to inflict grave widespread harm on oneself, those one cares about and those alive to whom one bears special responsibility when there is a speculative possibility that this is necessary to avoid much greater harm in the remote future" is not a principle that one has a compelling reason to embrace when one puts knowledge of one's own position in world history to one side. Speculative possibilities are too easy to come by.

Far from weakening the case for low targets, this refusal to base severe sacrifice in the near future on speculations about vast harm in the distant future strengthens it. For the harms that warming substantially above Two Degrees would inflict through the start of the next century might be needed to prevent much graver, more extensive harms, by preventing ice ages in the remote future. Ice ages, which last tens of thousands of years, seem to be triggered by a decline of northern summer temperatures below a threshold value allowing for sufficient long-term accumulation of snow and ice. The lowering seems to have depended, in the past, on variations in the earth's orbit. While the next ice age-threatening orbital situation, three thousand years from now, seems to be a bit above the threshold, this prediction is uncertain. Emissions that will burden people in the near future with warming significantly above Two Degrees might well provide crucial protection. At the next point of orbital jeopardy, fifty thousand years from now, the warming that near-term-destructive emissions would provide seems likely to be crucial to avoiding an ice age.[64] Of course, we do not have substantial evidence of how much protection from the dangerous natural process will be purchased through near-term climate suffering or of what the situations or psychologies of people born thousands of years from now will be. Perhaps they will have adequate means of regulating nature or will not be affected very much by a mile-high ice sheet over the latitude of what is now called "Chicago." But the same can be said of the threat of yards of water, due to a melted ice sheet, over what is now called "lower Manhattan," centuries from now.

The duty to limit global warming to no more than Two Degrees depends on special attention to harm within a limited time horizon. The proper valuing of trust has a limited horizon that extends far enough.

## The Greenhouse Effect and Transnational Justice

The values of trust that generate political duties of concern for compatriots have turned out also to generate a demanding political duty of people in developed countries to choose climate policies that help needy people in developing countries. The equitable pursuit of an adequate limit to global warming would impose significant risks of economic disruption on people in developed countries while reducing climatic harms to which people in developing countries are especially liable and minimizing obstacles to the development they need.

There is very little chance that the demands of adequacy and equity will be met. In the United States, fear of economic displacement, alarm at the prospect of new taxes, the relatively small scale of near-term risks of local climate damage, the influence of firms helped by continued use of fossil fuels, and resistance to measures that would speed the overtaking of the U.S. by China will have an impact on choices shaping the global greenhouse regime quite out of proportion to moral reasons for limiting Americans' role in meeting the greenhouse challenge. The political leadership of China, depending on continued rapid economic growth for continued deference, can hardly be expected to make large concessions to compensate for American reluctance. Meanwhile, the atmospheric concentration of greenhouse gases grows, making the target of Two Degrees even more arduous.

Soon, the target will no longer be attainable at acceptable cost to the global poor. But its moral significance will not end. The harm due to the failure to achieve it will generate a moral debt of repair, especially large for countries whose departure from greenhouse justice was especially grave and whose resources for compensation are especially great. For example, the United States will have the leading moral debt on account of irresponsible emissions. Every year of departure from adequacy and equity adds to this duty of repair, as surely as it increases atmospheric concentration.

Harmful side-effects of economic activity have turned out to add a great deal to the responsibilities to help people in developing countries generated by transnational manufacturing and the institutional framework of world trade. However, the morality of political concern for compatriots that emerged in Chapter 2 suggests that there may be another, exceptionally powerful source. Political duties to help compatriots in a modern society reflect the shaping of people's self-advancement within the borders by a sovereign government; distinctive forms of concern must be shown in order to make this process of power justifiable to those whose lives are shaped. This suggests that transnational political power can generate its own demanding responsibilities.

The first step in exploring the consequent responsibilities is clarification of currently important relations of transnational power. In Chapter 2, domestic political duties of concern for the disadvantaged depended on specific features of the civic interaction of compatriots. While these can significantly differ in different political societies, relatively uncontroversial characterizations of civic interaction in stable modern societies were the basis for establishing the currently most important duties. There is much less agreement about how to characterize transnational relationships of power.

Here, the distinctive transnational power of the United States has special importance. It is especially important for the world at large since it has the greatest influence and, hence, presumably, generates the weightiest responsi-bilities. Obviously, citizens of the United States have a morally urgent concern to understand this transnational power and identify the political responsibilities it creates. The proper characterization of American global power also promises to clarify the responsibilities of people in other developed countries, since their governments are part of coalitions led by the United States and, in several cases, independently exert similar though lesser power.

I believe that American global power is accurately characterized, in a way that illuminates all of these responsibilities, dangers, and challenges, through a specification of the metaphor "the American empire." Because of its importance to the rest of this book, I will devote the next chapter to developing and defending this characterization. Then, I will argue that the exercise of American imperial power has created extensive, unmet imperial responsibilities toward people in developing countries.

# 5

# Modern Empire

THE exercise of power by governments is the most obvious source of political responsibilities. But ways in which the transnational powers of governments generate transnational responsibilities are currently hard to discern. In our post-colonial era, the systematic influence of great powers crosses borders unaccompanied by appeals to political allegiance or legitimate authority. This silence does not eliminate responsibilities to those whose lives are shaped. In Stendhal's novel, the Prince of Parma, the odious Ranuccio-Ernesto, dispenses with such appeals, in the frank use of power to sustain a life of luxury at his court, yet no reader supposes that the Prince fulfills his political duty of concern. Still, in the international setting, the absence of an established political practice of justifying the transnational exercise of power to its targets makes the description of responsibilities of power an unfamiliar task.

In mapping this terrain, I will concentrate on the currently most important system of transnational influence by a government, what is sometimes labeled "the American empire." This chapter will begin the exploration by presenting a construal of "the American empire," defending it as an accurate description of current realities, and offering an account of the major mechanisms sustaining this network of influence. Then, in Chapters 6 and 7, I will describe duties of Americans toward people in developing countries that are generated by the American empire, along with duties of citizens of other developed countries due to analogous relationships. In Chapter 6, I will try to show that the transnational influence of the American empire generates vast responsibilities, even if exercises of American imperial power are not themselves unjust. Respect for the autonomy of those subjected to imperial power will turn out to generate a demanding residual responsibility to provide for basic needs. The destruction inflicted by the American empire will turn out to generate a demanding duty of repair. Finally, in Chapter 7, I will argue that the American empire has enduring tendencies toward injustice, including widespread unjust violence, that create a distinctive duty of an American citizen to hem in imperial excesses.

Of course, any global role worthy of the metaphorical label "the American empire" will eventually come to an end, as every literal empire has. But the existence and the moral implications of this role are of long-term interest. For one thing, despite recurrent crises and surges of self-doubt, the bases of American power are robust. In 2006, United States Gross Domestic Product, as a proportion of Gross World Product, was slightly higher than in 1980 or 1970 (27% as compared to 25% and 26%.)[1] Over the decades, the qualitative change in power has been a gain along the military dimension, the shift to post-Cold War military preeminence. In 2007, the U.S. military budget was 45% of the global total, nine times the budget of the largest non-allied country, China.[2]

In any case, the decline of American imperial power will not signal the decline of its moral significance. The history of past empires prompts great moral anxiety about ways in which declining empires use military power to stave off their displacement—anxieties that Chapter 7 will reinforce. Also, unmet obligations of empire will be enduring moral debts once power has faded, or so I will argue in Chapter 6.

Finally, once the nature and moral implications of American imperial power are understood, they will illuminate responsibilities among other powers and at other times. Among other powers, alliance with the United States and engagement in similar domination have analogous moral consequences. When the American empire has disappeared, it is likely that another country or bloc will exercise similar sway. In the exploration of the morality of power, the United States serves as a paradigm of the most important type of transnational power that has succeeded literal empire.

## Construing "the American Empire"

The label "the American empire" is now in common use, even in the United States. People use the term to describe a system of oppressive power that they condemn, or simply a fact that must, for better or worse, be taken into account, or (lately) a source of humane benefit worth strengthening and defending.[3] Most discussions using the term seem to have a common subject matter. But sometimes it is hard to separate productive disagreement from mere verbal differences. So an investigation of how moral responsibilities are created by interactions constituting the American empire had better begin with clarification of the term.

One cannot hope to capture all usages of "the American empire" in a single specification, and one should not try. Like all spontaneous metaphorical growths, this efflorescence is unruly. For current purposes of moral inquiry, one should seek a usage that is definite enough to make such questions as whether the American empire should be ended, hemmed in or promoted revealing and answerable, and that is close enough to characteristics of at least one paradigmatic literal empire that the extended usage is not inevitably misleading. (For the usage that I will describe, the largest and best-investigated of recent literal empires, the British Empire, can play this role.) Within these limits, one should be as ecumenical as possible, to avoid ruling out, by mere stipulation, features of interest to people engaged in productive disputes over "the benefits and dangers of the American empire." If some who say, "There is an American empire" regard some American superiority of power as crucial to its existence and if virtually all who say, "There is an American empire" regard it as an enduring characteristic of the United States, this superiority should be associated with the phrase, so that "the American empire" labels the whole package of these superiorities. This usage is most apt to reveal the extent to which global American power creates distinctive responsibilities.

In this ecumenical conception, the American empire involves three kinds of transnational influence emanating from the United States: the influence of prerogatives, the influence of threat power, and the exercise of destructive power. "Domineering influence" would be an apt generic label for the three types of influence that I will describe: their direction is determined by the interests of the United States as perceived by the United States government or politically influential American groups, and they change lives outside the United States through processes that do not depend on willing support by the foreigners who are affected. In contrast, if the United States were to influence lives in other countries simply through persuasion, the attractiveness of American institutions and the superiority of American made or designed commodities, virtually no one would speak of an "American empire." In broad outline, the ecumenical version of the claim "There is an American empire" will be: the United States has substantial domineering influence based on each of the three types of power in every region of the world, to a far greater degree worldwide than any other country, and the United States uses its domineering influence to shape lives in many developing countries, profoundly, pervasively and with greater force than any other foreign power.

## Prerogatives

By America's "prerogatives," the basis for the first element in the triad of domineering influences, I mean America's capacity to pursue interests in ways that give rise to costs to others on account of the importance of the United States in joint arrangements depending on shared norms and answering to shared needs. In this sense, the bearer of a prerogative has importance that forces others to give way. The prime examples have been U.S. prerogatives due to the role of the dollar and American financial instruments in the international system of finance and payments. In this system, the dollar has been the dominant basis for stating and settling monetary obligations in international transactions and is the preeminent ingredient in the reserve holdings through which governments seek to avoid destructive changes in the value of their home currencies.

That the dollar should play this role is a reflection of the global importance the American economy has had and of widely shared needs for fluency and security in commercial transactions. International transactions are less complicated and risks of currency fluctuations are less serious if there is a widely shared monetary basis for commitments and payments, even among parties who are outside the home of the currency. For this reason, about 60% of U.S. currency is held outside the United States, and, in 2004, the dollar was involved in 89% of all foreign currency trades.[4] To damp fluctuations in the value of their currency and prevent outbreaks of self-confirming fear of a major devaluation, governments concentrate reserves in holdings denominated in the most important currency worldwide. At the start of 2008, 63% of foreign exchange reserves were held in dollars, the norm for the previous four decades, higher than in 1965 (56%) or in 1982 (58%), at the beginning of the surge of globalization.[5] Even if the economic superiority that gave rise to the preeminence of a currency fades, convenience and fears of instability will sustain it for a long time, as the pound sterling long maintained preeminence despite the relative decline of Britain.

There is an additional reliable foreign need for dollars because the United States tends to be the safest harbor for international financial investments. This is only relative safety. No internationally important financial market offering substantial returns is safe from outbreaks of disorder. But while U.S. markets are fairly safe from foreign financial problems, there is no foreign shelter from major storms that start in U.S. markets. They quickly spread worldwide, driven by the global importance of the U.S. economy, investments from abroad that the trade and reserve uses of dollars guarantee, and the great and growing enmeshment of U.S. financial and insurance firms in foreign financial affairs. (For example, three-quarters of the $441 billion of credit-default swaps which led to the near-collapse of AIG was held by European banks.[6])

Because of the global role of the dollar, the United States has been able to finance vast budget and trade deficits year after year, relying on the global function of U.S. Treasury bills in foreign exchange reserves and the continued in-flow of investment funds seeking a relatively safe haven. Indeed, foreign investors now hold about two-fifths of the federal debt in private hands.[7] In 2006, they had claims on U.S. assets with market value over $16 trillion, greater than that year's Gross Domestic Product.[8] Even though America's unique borrowing prerogative is due to shared interests in a reserve currency and safe haven, America's routine exercise of this prerogative to sustain budget and trade deficits makes investment funds harder to obtain in other countries. The borrowing prerogative finances foreign policy initiatives that are by no means guaranteed to serve the interests of other countries.

In addition, because of the economic importance of the United States and the special role it creates for U.S. currency and finance, particular monetary and fiscal policies that the United States government adopts, from time to time, to cope with problems for the United States often create severe costs for other countries. For example, when the Federal Reserve tamed U.S. inflation by tight money policies, starting in the fall of 1979, the eventual, predictable side-effects on developing countries were disastrous. Previously, because of historically low real interest rates on dollar-denominated loans, aggressive selling of loans to governments of developing countries by U.S. banks, and exuberant promotion of large development projects involving U.S. firms, the flow of loans to developing countries, mostly dollar-denominated and frequently tied to Federal Reserve bank rates, had surged, growing nearly tenfold, in constant dollars, from 1970 to 1979 (when this net flow was ten times the level of foreign aid.)[9] As the Federal Reserve's anti-inflationary policies took hold, the appreciation of the dollar, rise in interest rates and reduction in worldwide demand precipitated debt crises and sharp economic contraction in many developing countries.[10] The share of developing countries in world trade declined from 28% in 1980 to 19% in 1986.[11] In Latin America, especially hard hit by the crisis, a 1960–78 average growth rate in per capita GDP of 2.9% was followed by a 1978–98 rate of 0.9%.[12]

In another set of policies and consequences, in the 1990s, the U.S. government's tendency to favor depreciation of the dollar reduced the real burden of U.S. indebtedness to foreigners, while the government's promotion of measures encouraging fluent transnational capital flows benefitted U.S. financial institutions, contributing to a growing surplus in the financial services sector that was virtually unique in the over-all U.S. trade balance. The depreciation and the volatile transnational flows did not destabilize the U.S. economy, because of U.S. financial prerogatives. But the policies sustained by those prerogatives exacted a large cost in depreciated returns for U.S. creditors such as Japan and contributed to severe instability in the East Asian financial crisis.[13]

American superiority has given rise to prerogatives in other spheres as well. For example, in the Western military alliance, other countries had to defer to U.S. strategic initiatives because the U.S. military contribution was much more important and the strength of the alliance depended on a unified command. Much more generally, the special importance of the United States in the world economy and the global flow of information creates what might be called "coordination prerogatives," in which the efficient matching of what is offered to what is needed on a global scale makes resources, activities and attitudes adapt to American initiatives and needs. World culture is powerfully affected by American prerogatives due to the growth of English as a global language, the importance of internationally recognized sources of credentials, formal and informal, certifying expertise in areas where the U.S. plays the leading role, the need for fluent transnational collaboration in globalized production and exchange in which U.S. firms and U.S.-dominated institutions play the leading roles, and a vast U.S. labor market which is relatively open to foreigners who provide their services very cheaply or offer scarce skills. The consequent U.S.-oriented needs of foreigners for affiliation, recognition and at least partial integration create a global network of elites at home with the practices, culture, language and personnel of American business, government and science, and give American universities a special capacity to set the agenda in global intellectual work. These global needs to defer to processes, practices and institutions in the United States also provide American employers with access to global reserves of labor who are especially responsive to U.S. employment opportunities, especially apt to spend time in the United States and likely to be bound to the United States by family ties.

Like the U.S. currency and financial prerogatives, these coordination prerogatives can have ramifications that do not serve the interests of foreigners, even though the prerogatives are based on shared needs. For example, it may not serve the interests of most people in a developing country when, as a consequence of these prerogatives, the local way of life merges with American culture and local elites increasingly affiliate with a U.S.-centered network of managers, entrepreneurs and bureaucrats.

In every important sphere of international activity, American prerogatives invest American choices, including choices of the United States government, with an impact on lives in foreign countries that does not depend on whether the governments or most of the people in those countries regard the effects as in their interests. In every important sphere, the United States has much more of this domineering influence based on prerogatives than any other country.

## The Influence of Threat Power

The influence of America's prerogatives is so vast that it might be taken to be sufficient to constitute imperial sway. But most would take the label "American empire" only to be fully apt on the basis of an analogy with sovereign domestic political power, whose core, Hobbes saw, is "a common power holding all in awe." The analogy rests on what I will call "the influence of threat power": the United States influences lives elsewhere because people have reason to fear what the U.S. will do if it does not get its way, in American conduct partly motivated by an interest in maintaining such fears. In contrast, mere prerogative does not depend on American choices, actual or foreseen, to instill fear in order to influence conduct, even though U.S. prerogatives typically make it more costly to pursue policies opposed to U.S. interests. (Of course, prerogative vastly facilitates influence by threats, a theme to which I will return.)

On every issue, everywhere, the United States can make trouble. The United States must sometimes exercise its power and actually make trouble to preserve the credibility of its threats. But the shaping of global conduct by the influence of threat power usually vastly exceeds its shaping by the carrying out of threats. Indeed, the shaping of lives by U.S. threat power is more extensive than the carrying out of U.S. threats by three orders of magnitude. First, American threats are generally sufficiently credible to shape events without actually being implemented. Second, expectations that a departure from U.S. interests would lead the United States to instill rational fear to motivate deference often prevents departure without the need for the United States to express a specific threat. Third, the enduring threat power of the United States can shape structures of incentives within which choices usually conform to U.S. interests without intimidation by threats, express or implied. The process of bullying that we have already considered in which the United States influences other countries' policies concerning trade, finance and property rights illustrates all three possibilities of vast influence by threat power without actual exertion.

In the Uruguay Round, the United States often voiced threats, of exclusion from favorable regional arrangements, punitive trade sanctions, concessions to the protectionism of special U.S. interests or a general retreat into "bilateral or minilateral arrangements." Several of these threats resulted in ultimatums with firm dates attached. But virtually none of them had to be implemented to steer the negotiations toward essentially the outcome the U.S. sought, in the face of strenuous opposition from many developing countries and stubborn reluctance of nations in the EU to change their Common Agricultural Policy.[14]

In addition, while the United States explicitly resorted to threats in exemplary disputes with the most powerful representatives of competing interests, analogous fears did their work elsewhere without the issuance of specifically targeted threats. Countries in sub-Saharan Africa were profoundly dissatisfied with the treatment of agricultural subsidies. In an organization officially working by consensus, countries as small and poor as Burkina Faso could, in principle, have obstructed the final accord. But there was no need to issue an explicit threat to such a country of grave consequences in withdrawn aid and blocked trade to insure that fears of these consequences would be influential.

Finally, once the new trade regime was established, commercial activity adapted to it, so that departures from norms initially imposed by threats against heated resistance became undesirable, threats to one side. The WTO regime in trade, investment and financial services, established through the aggressive splitting of resistant groups of developing countries, made it illegal to follow South Korea's path to development, through similar export subsidies, sheltering of infant industries, governmental steering of investment funds and requirements of local reinvestment of profits. Now, in countries such as Thailand, where this liberalization has given foreign firms and banks a leading role in major sectors of finance and production, these tactics would, in any case, be recipes for disaster, quite apart from the fear of U.S. retaliation, whether through the WTO or independent of it. Similarly, in India, the skills, plans, and research and development commitments of software firms now presuppose friendly relations with firms in the U.S. computer industry which insist on conformity to U.S. patents and copyrights. So the WTO requirement of respect for these extremely long-term rights, first established with robust American threatening of India and Brazil, has largely become a matter of mere self-interest.

Granted, if the current effect of past threatening or fear is purely a residue of the distant past, like the current consequences of eighteenth-century British imperialism in the middle latitudes of North America, it is a bad guide to responsibility and a farfetched analogue to literally imperial practices. To avoid these distortions, U.S. threat influence should count as shaping lives in a country only if there is an ongoing process in which American threat influence originally affected the terms of self-advancement and now waits in the wings, to exercise significant influence, directed (depending on U.S. interests) at maintaining those terms in the face of challenge or changing them in light of new circumstances despite local resistance. Similarly, in many territories of the British Empire that were subject to indirect rule, people's lives were normally almost entirely regulated by their own customary laws, applied in "native courts," with ultimate recourse to their own traditional leadership. Still, indirect rule was rule by Britain, even when and where the only current political activity was the indigenous political elite's. For actual exercise of British power, which had shaped the local terms of self-advancement to suit Britain's interests, continued to wait in the wings to maintain or change these terms, as Britain's interests dictated.

The threats that the critique of globalization described are economic, matters of economic disorder or reduced economic opportunities. However, the most fearsome threat is physical violence. The importance of threats of this sort is also far, far greater than the frequency of their implementation would suggest. Indeed, this aspect of power provides the prime example in the twentieth century of the regulation of international life by unimplemented threats: through threats of nuclear annihilation that were never implemented and rarely even expressed, the United States and the Soviet Union each largely succeeded in keeping the other from intruding on the spheres of influence of most concern. The basic integrity of these spheres was also testimony to the strong influence of credible but unimplemented threats of violent intervention in case of local departures from the interests of a foreign power. In Eastern Europe, for example, Soviet armed intervention was rare and not very lethal, yet adequate to sustain dominance for decades. In Central America and the Caribbean, the encouragement and arming of repression in Guatemala and of right-wing insurgency in Nicaragua, the launching of the Bay of Pigs landing, the reversal by U.S. troops of Bosch's election in the Dominican Republic and their overthrow of regimes in Panama and Grenada had a dissuasive impact on those who might have taken part in leftist nationalist movements that extended far beyond the times and places of these exercises of destructive power.

## Destructive Power

Conquest and violent repression have been part of the conduct of every literal empire. Some would take such activity to be essential to appropriate nonliteral application of the term. For example, in seeking to distinguish empire (in a broad sense, requiring no assertion of political authority) from mere constraint due to another country's superiority, Michael Doyle makes it a criterion that "the metropole . . . employ force successfully against resistance."[15] The corresponding element in the triad of American domineering influence is the exercise of destructive power—more precisely, its exercise in processes other than defense against an armed attack on the United States, actual or imminent, and without an invitation representing the desires of the people of the territory affected, as a whole. (These qualifications will be left implicit, from now on.)

The exercise of destructive power makes threats credible, and does more besides. It also serves as a means of increasing the influence of threat power by destroying resources on which others' contrary threat power depends and serves as part of a process of forcibly gaining resources at others' expense. For example, the overthrow of Saddam Hussein was an exercise of destructive power expected to serve all three goals: heightening fears of costs imposed by the United States on governments inclined to oppose American interests, destroying contrary threat power in an important region, and gaining increased access to oil reserves, markets and investment opportunities.

Both to capture common usage and to establish the moral significance of "the American empire," one should include violence by foreign groups which rely on U.S. support, along with the violent actions of U.S. armed forces, as exercises of destructive power that are part of American imperial power. Sometimes, these foreign groups (such as the contras of Nicaragua and the mujaheddin of Afghanistan) direct their violence at regimes the U.S. opposes. Sometimes, they are armed forces of governments using violence to end local resistance (for example, the Israel Defense Force in Palestinian territories or Turkish forces using U.S. equipment to crush a Kurdish insurgency).

In an assessment of domineering influence that is to guide the assignment of transnational responsibilities, the impact of U.S. destructive power should not be limited to destruction that serves U.S. interests and is currently inflicted or sponsored by the United States. Violence that is a foreseeable consequence of an exercise of U.S. destructive power should be included in its impact even if U.S. interests would be served by less destruction. To detonate the means of influence is to be responsible for the damage to those put in jeopardy. For example, the arming of the mujaheddin of Afghanistan, the invasion of Iraq, and the installation of Mobutu, Reza Pahlevi and the Guatemalan junta that replaced the Arbenz regime were intrusions guaranteeing destruction that was not limited to what the United States wanted to destroy.

In addition, the terms of life in a territory should count as currently shaped by the destructive power of the United States after U.S. sponsorship of violence is over, if U.S. destructive power set the terms and U.S. domineering influence is waiting in the wings to respond to serious departures from U.S. interests. Having installed a regime that violently ends a popularly supported threat to U.S. interests, the United States may eventually withdraw military assistance and criticize its abuses. Still, the United States has exercised destructive power to push the country in its current direction in one of those crises that determine the routine features of national life. If the United States stands ready to use threat influence, destructive power or its prerogatives to push again if its interests dictate, then the terms of self-advancement in this country (for example, Guatemala or the Congo/Zaire) are shaped by U.S. destructive power. The drama of domineering influence can be a matter of hard pushes to change trajectories, rather than constant pulls on puppet strings.

The United States has exercised destructive power abroad much more extensively than any other country since the end of World War II, continually adding to a vast toll of death and devastation in far-flung countries. At any given time, there have been few sites of violence, but this has been true of literal empires for periods of similar length. An empire, like a national government, is struggling for its very existence when it exercises destructive power far and wide. It is a sign of strength, not weakness, if the exercise of destructive power is rare, directed at establishing structures of peaceful incentives that are normally self-maintaining and at sustaining these structures in the face of exceptional challenges.

## Territorial Dominion

Everyone accepts that the three forms of influence that I have described add up to worldwide influence on the part of the United States far exceeding that of any other nation. Each form is powerful and extensive. Indeed, U.S. prerogatives and U.S. threat power significantly influence conduct in every country. And each form of power reinforces the others. For example, U.S. borrowing prerogatives sustain the fiscal deficits produced by exercises of destructive power, as in Vietnam and Iraq. Measures that would reduce prerogatives based on the role of the dollar are blocked by the influence of American threat power, which has, for example, rendered moot the recurrent proposals that the IMF grant developing countries special drawing rights to mixtures of major currencies that would reduce the need for holdings in U.S. Treasury bills. If the exercise of destructive power did not provide evidence of American readiness to carry out threats, the influence of threat power would wane since this influence is due to expectations.

However, the strength and pervasiveness of this package of powers is not all that is conveyed by talk of an American empire. Those who use the phrase usually mean to evoke, not just pervasive global superiorities, but also special relationships of dominance over specific territories, the characteristic feature of literal empires.[16] Of course, with a few possible marginal exceptions, such as

Guam, territorial dominance by the United States does not include the assertion of political authority over officially subordinate territories that played a major role in literal empires. Still, the ascription of territorial dominance is meant to convey more than the presence of significant American threat influence and the significant impact of American prerogatives. These are features of U.S.–French and U.S.–Chinese relations, but those who seek an analogue to literal empires' dominance of colonies would hardly include France and China in the territorial empire of the United States.

For territorial domination to be ascribed, America's domineering influence ought to be deep and utterly asymmetrical. Governments routinely take account of one another's threat influence and capacities to destroy in their foreign policies. Subordination penetrates further. In countries subordinate to the United States, such as Guatemala and the Philippines, the terms of life within the borders have been affected in profoundly important ways, in the face of local resistance, by the threat influence or destructive power of the United States and the mobilization of American prerogatives to strengthen the hold of local elites. The United States continues to have significant power to shore up or change these features of the local framework, in the face of resistance, as its strong interests dictate. While the need to give way in the face of U.S. power has had this profound impact in an ongoing process, the United States is hardly affected at all by the need to propitiate these countries.[17] In contrast, the imposition of terms of life in France and China through the domineering influence of the United States has been limited, and influence is mutual, despite American superiority. U.S. policies in Africa and U.S. initiatives in international trade liberalization have adjusted to costs that France would exact. U.S. policy toward Taiwan and Southeast Asia is affected by the need to avoid provoking China, while the need to encourage vast Chinese holdings in U.S. financial instruments has provided a serious reason against depreciations of the dollar that might otherwise be advantageous to the United States.

Where there is deep, asymmetric domineering influence from abroad in which the United States plays a role, something more must be included to justify the attribution of territorial domination to the United States: U.S. initiatives that are independent of the other foreign powers' must be especially important in the shaping of the local terms of life. (Otherwise, one should simply speak of domination by the North, by developed countries, or the like.) A usefully ecumenical understanding of "the American empire" would count two different processes by which U.S. initiatives exert this special influence as forms of American territorial domination. One is the exercise of special influence by the United States over the territory through direct unilateral action, the characteristic vehicle of literal imperial influence, in the past. The other is domination at one remove through preeminent American domineering influence over multilateral institutions, such as the World Bank and IMF, which use prerogatives and threats in turn to shape lives in the dominated territory, according to policies and preferences shaped by U.S. initiatives.

Territorial domination by the United States takes the traditional form when the unilateral exercise of American prerogatives and threat influence has a much greater impact on local political and economic choices than any other foreign government's, deeply and asymmetrically shaping the local terms of life. Guatemala, the Philippines, Egypt and Ethiopia are part of this unilateral American empire, but Senegal is not, since the independent influence of France is very great as well.

The uniquely strong influence of one government acting independently of others almost always characterized territorial subordination in literal empires. Dual authority threatened chaotic dual allegiance in the face of competing interests, so it was only asserted in rare and short-lived episodes, such as the brief Anglo-French suzerainty in Egypt. The unique authority of a single metropole would have been undermined by powerful outside influence from another source. However, when political authority is not a vehicle of domineering influence, new prospects of domination by multilateral means emerge.

Through unique domineering influence over multilateral institutions, especially the World Bank, the IMF and the trade regime now administered by the WTO, the United States has played the leading role in reshaping the political and economic structures of developing countries, overcoming inertia and, sometimes, outright resistance by other major developed countries. Having promoted these structures, the United States continues to play the leading role in defending or changing them, using these institutions, as U.S. interests dictate. But other developed countries are free to take advantage of the new opportunities opened up by this global process, playing a comparable role in many places. American steering of the terms of structural adjustment and world trade accords has had a deep impact on Senegal and the Dominican Republic, even though the current role of the United States in local economic and political life has not superseded the role of France in the one case and is challenged by Spain's in the other.

Because it has a special tendency to give rise to international rivalry and is sometimes sustained by sponsorship of client regimes, direct, unilateral domination merits special attention, as a special source of responsibility and danger. But the special role of the United States in steering multilateral processes that affect the course of development of the vast majority of developing countries is a form of dominance that may give rise to special American responsibilities, as well. In an ecumenical construal of "the American empire," meant to illuminate responsibilities due to American power, it is best to acknowledge both roles as establishing imperial dominance over other countries.

In addition to including both direct and indirect forms of American influence, the ecumenical construal of territorial domination is permissive in another way. It requires deep, asymmetric domineering influence, but not influence that is so restrictive that the United States nearly always gets what it wants in the decisions of the local government. Granted, if such stringent constraint on local politics were part of the metropole's relation to imperial territories in all literal empires, then it might be appropriate to condemn a metaphorical usage of "empire" as farfetched and misleading because it requires substantially less. This seems to be Michael Walzer's basis for condemning talk of an American empire: "[I]mperialism is a system of political rule—not necessarily direct rule, but rule in some strong sense: an imperial power gets what it wants from the governments it creates, or supports, or patronizes. . . . Less than two years after 9/11, on the eve of a major war, we could not count on such states as Mexico and Chile [in U.N. Security Council deliberations]—well, what kind of an empire is that?"[18] However, this requirement rests on a caricature of literal empire.

For example, in the British Empire, Britain did not by any means always get what it wanted. On account of Francophone resistance, London could not rally Canada to full-fledged participation in the Boer War, the great crisis of empire at the turn of the century, and had to be satisfied with two contingents of volunteers sent without Canadian parliamentary approval.[19] In general, Canada engaged in ruthless departures from the free trade that London wanted for the British Empire—and got away with this, decade after decade, because of the need to avoid offense that would drive Canada into the orbit of the United States. Britain was similarly concessive toward Australia and New Zealand, to sustain allegiance over vast distances. In the case of India, the interests of British manufacturers had to be balanced against the need to maintain support among Indian elites, a process in which British manufacturers frequently lost out.[20] After Britain's military occupation of Egypt in 1882, the country was clearly part of the empire, in fact if not in name. But the Khedive was left free to pursue territorial ambitions in adjacent territories, leading to the independent military expedition that ultimately triggered the disaster of Khartoum.[21]

Nineteenth-century British practice also included relationships of unofficial territorial dominance, closely resembling those that bind countries to the

United States today, which contemporary observers, like modern historians, freely characterized as imperial. It was clear to commentators on South America after the wars of independence from Spain that Britain had soon made Argentina, Brazil and Chile into "quasi-colonies . . . without the expense of their maintenance as such," as an American diplomat in Brazil sourly put it 1843.[22] This territorial domination consisted of ready acceptance by locally dominant Anglophile elites of the trade liberalization Britain advocated and the loans London banks offered, consequent British dominance of profitable foreign trade, and imposition of austerity and liberalization measures in response to debt crises. The latter measures were demanded by and often administered by London banks, with only very rare and transitory resort to gunboats to enforce loan obligations. (The gunboats themselves were rarely means of terrorizing a population or physically threatening the dominant elite. They were means of securing control over customs collection, the major source of government revenue.) No one would have supposed that Britain always got what it wanted in these quasi-colonies. For example, Britain long pressed for the abolition of slavery in Brazil—an appealing goal economically as well as morally, in order to end the self-sufficiency of slave-based plantations—without getting what it wanted.

Granted, Walzer's comment points to a real danger: it is important not to assimilate U.S. influence to caricatures of literal empire which do ascribe stringent control. But it is also important to recognize differences in degree of stringency of domineering influence, from territory to territory, among both literal and figurative imperial territories. Britain's domineering influence over India, Egypt and Canada differed significantly in 1900, yet all were counted as part of the British empire—even though domineering influence was limited in all three cases and did not always reflect the degree of legal subordination (least in Egypt, which was, nonetheless, more dominated than Canada). If Guatemala has been like the Raj, Mexico has been like the White Dominions.

## The Fact of Empire and Its Mechanisms

Because of its tendency to provoke nationalist outrage, territorial domination is an attention-grabbing aspect of empire. But facts of territorial domination hardly exhaust the facts of power conveyed by the phrase "the American empire." Indeed, for some who use the term, the uniquely pervasive domineering influence of the United States would merit the label even if it nowhere congealed into territorial domination. The territorial and the nonterritorial aspects of American power coexist and reinforce each other. The ecumenical construal incorporates both. The thesis that there is an American empire is to be associated with the following four claims, jointly describing what the fact of empire involves:

1. Lives everywhere are significantly affected by domineering influence based in the United States.
2. U.S. power, worldwide, in each dimension of domineering influence is much greater than power based in any other country.
3. International institutions and practices that deeply affect lives throughout the world are largely molded by U.S. interests, on account of the three, mutually reinforcing, types of domineering influence.
4. The terms of life in many developing countries are deeply shaped by U.S. domineering influence, including threat influence or destructive power, in an utterly asymmetric process, in which the influence of the U.S. is much more important than rival foreign influences—i.e., much more important in steering the over-all course of development, and, often, much more important, as well, in shaping current political and economic choices.

That there is an American empire in this sense is widely acknowledged, on the basis of evidence that I have begun to present, which will become abundant by the end of this book. However, an account of the nature of the American empire should supplement the claim that it exists with a description of how it exists. In particular, there is a need for more specific descriptions of the major processes of domineering influence that sustain territorial domination where they are sufficiently powerful, asymmetrical and exclusive. For one thing, the survey of mechanisms plays an essential role in establishing the existence of extensive territorial domination over countries which, nonetheless, have the appurtenances of sovereignty and do not always act as the United States wishes. An unstructured collection of narratives of destruction and threat-and-compliance is not enough. In the second place, in a relational account of moral obligations, the responsibilities entailed by domineering influence will depend on its vehicles, not just its impact. Finally, the study of mechanisms of domineering influence that can congeal into territorial domination will help to assess the responsibilities of countries less globally domineering than the United States and help to assess responsibilities generated when those same mechanisms are not so strong, asymmetrical or exclusive.

## Indirect Financial Rule

The domineering influence that the United States exerts on developing countries through domination of multinational institutions is especially far-reaching.
Yet it is an unfamiliar topic for reflections on political responsibility: in its
traditional concern with how a state regulates life within its territory, political
philosophy scrutinizes forms of influence with very different vehicles, structures and scopes. Because of its important impact and normative unfamiliarity,
this mechanism merits detailed attention.

I have already described how the United States has used its threat influence
to shape the virtually worldwide trade regime administered by the WTO,
transforming patterns of ownership and ways of life in developing countries.
The IMF and the World Bank have been at least as important as vehicles
of American domineering influence. Housed in adjacent buildings in Washington, D.C., with the same governments as members, a joint Development
Committee, an annual joint meeting and frequent collaboration among their
staffs, the IMF and World Bank are dominated by the United States in the same
ways. In both institutions, voting and veto procedures are visible emblems of
this dominance. Votes are weighted by contributions, giving the United States
many more votes than any other country and giving an absolute majority of
votes to a tiny coalition of developed countries centered on the United States.
As the size of the U.S. vote has declined over the decades, the supermajorities
required for major policy changes have been adjusted so that the U.S. remains
the one country with veto power. For example, in the early 1970s, as the U.S.
share in the IMF declined toward the 20% threshold that had been required
for veto of "special decisions," the United States strenuously resisted Japanese
and European proposals to take on larger shares, but finally accepted a decline
in its share to 19%—accompanied by the lowering of the veto threshold to
15%.[23] In 2008, the United States had 16.77 % of the votes, nearly three times
the share of the next highest country, Japan. These two countries along with
Germany, France and the United Kingdom are the permanent participants in
a twenty-four-member Executive Board, managing the daily business of the
IMF, in which the other members possess the weighted votes of groups they
represent. The big five had 38% of the IMF votes. Together with Belgium,
Canada, Italy, the Netherlands and Switzerland, they had most of the votes
among the 184 members. Italy had more votes than India, while Italy and
Finland could outvote China.[24]

Although the possibility of U.S. veto helps to restrict the agenda of policymaking in both institutions, fears due to U.S. financial resources are more influential in most decisionmaking. The IMF relies on the United States to contribute additional dollars to IMF reserves as world liquidity requirements increase. The World Bank's access to U.S. capital markets is subject to U.S. approval. When, for example, the Bank sought to raise new capital in 1984, a U.S. Treasury official told the Bank's Vice President that failure to accommodate U.S. emphasis on private funding of the energy sector in developing countries had led to the government's "reviewing whether the Bank should continue to have access to the U.S. capital markets." The concerns were accommodated.[25] In 1991, the U.S. used its threat of veto over a proposed increase in World Bank capitalization in order to increase emphasis on loans to private enterprises, in the face of general resistance by other members.[26]

The Bank's program of low-interest, deferred-payment loans, the International Development Association, which is its primary means of helping developing countries, would be crippled if the United States did not periodically contribute to its replenishment. The World Bank's authorized history of its first fifty years notes that the IDA was itself created as a U.S.-led response to growing support for a U.N. fund, the Special United Nations Fund for Economic Development, that would have been more difficult to control. "Failing to make SUNFED disappear, the United States had decided to try cooptation. Richard Demuth [a World Bank liaison to the U.S. Treasury] reporting to Bank colleagues explained that IDA was . . . 'a desire to assuage Congress' and 'to keep off SUNFED.' "[27] In a nice illustration of consequent influence, the Bank's history reports elsewhere that "[a]s President McNamara was boarding an airplane in 1979 he was told that if he did not promise then and there that there would be no lending to Vietnam, during the period of the replenishment, the IDA 6 bill faced imminent defeat. He authorized the sending of an immediate letter to the Congress so stating."[28]

The most important vehicle and sign of U.S. influence is the routine role of U.S. policymaking elites in World Bank and IMF decisionmaking. The quasi-official rule that the Bank's President must be a U.S. citizen nominated by the U.S. government provides the most visible aspect of this involvement. Routine interactions between these institutions and the U.S. Treasury are a less visible yet vital linkage. In a study of the World Bank informed by basic sympathy with U.S. objectives, Catherine Gwin observes that "the United States is the only country that carries out detailed reviews of every bank proposal and the only one to maintain constant contact with the Bank through government officials, in addition to its representative to the board. Often, the

United States will question a prospective loan early in the preparation process, And during final deliberation of a loan proposal by the Bank's executive board, it will make comments designed to draw attention to general matters of concern in order to influence future lending."[29]

Similarly, at the IMF, the initiative of the U.S. Treasury in major bailouts is so great that negotiations with the latter are the quick route to rescue by the former. The East Asian financial crisis that broke out in 1997 led South Korea to send an envoy on a mission of utmost urgency to work out an IMF rescue. "I didn't bother going to the I.M.F.," the envoy subsequently recalled. ' "I called Mr. Summers' office at the Treasury from my home in Seoul, flew to Washington and went directly there. I knew this was how this would get done."[30] In 2001, in constructing an IMF response to the disastrous end of an IMF-imposed currency regime in Argentina, the Treasury functioned again as the IMF's front bench. "It is not unusual," noted a *New York Times* report, "for the United States, the largest single shareholder in the fund, to play an important role in shaping a package of aid to a large developing country. But . . . the administration's role was especially intricate in this case, with many late-night sessions in Treasury offices rather than at I.M.F. headquarters nearby."[31]

This potent influence has been used by the United States to shape the conduct of international financial institutions that, in turn, powerfully influence the terms of life in developing countries. On the whole, the choice of recipients of aid has helped countries favored by the United States and held back countries and courses of development that the U.S. strongly disfavors. For example, accommodating the United States and overriding resistance from other members, the World Bank refused loans to Allende's Chile, Vietnam and Sandinista Nicaragua. Yet it provided loans to Somoza's Nicaragua, Marcos's Philippines and Mobutu's Zaire. In Loan Committee meetings, such anxieties as the concern that a Bank project would largely benefit the Somoza family were met by such tranquilizing rejoinders as, "The problem of the land holding and Somoza ownership is an unfortunate one but it is one that we have been aware of from the very start and I think it is too late to raise the question now." Anxieties about trends threatening U.S. power had a very different impact, as in the non-agronomic comments that accompanied the granting of farm credit to Ecuador in 1961: "Ecuador would seem to be the next country on the list to go 'Fidelista,' " "[W]e might consider more IDA money because of these political risks."[32]

"Structural adjustment" is the paradigmatic use of international institutions to shape lives in developing countries. It has mobilized the Bank and the Fund in threatening, energetic, far-flung and coordinated efforts to impose requirements of large-scale changes in policy as a condition for loans.

Conditionality has long been a distinctive concern of the United States, implemented through threat influence. When the International Monetary Fund was created, all participants except the United States rejected the imposition of policy changes on countries in crisis as a condition for access to needed currency; modifications of domestic policies were to be "at the discretion of the affected governments," as Keynes put it.[33] Although this "automaticity" was initially prescribed by the IMF's *Articles of Agreement*, U.S. representatives used their powers to block drawings from the Fund until automaticity was replaced by conditionality.[34] In the early 1980s, in the course of a debt crisis in developing countries triggered by U.S. Federal Reserve interest policies, conditionality took a distinctive form, which pervaded the developing world and has persisted since. The IMF and World Bank imposed "structural adjustment" conditions including fiscal austerity (with consequent reduction of social expenditures), privatization, and liberalization of foreign trade and finance—large-scale policy shifts meant to open a country to what President Reagan described, at their 1983 joint meeting, as "the magic of the marketplace."[35]

The loans are often urgently needed. Once granted, the conditions are backed by the threat that a bad report from the IMF or the Bank (which typically work as partners in structural adjustment) will dry up private credit. This instrument of threat influence was installed and maintained by the familiar processes of U.S. institutional domination. At the start of the Reagan administration, the World Bank's authorized history reports, the Treasury Department "commissioned a study to determine whether the bank had 'socialistic' tendencies and held back on replenishments for the International Development Association . . . "[36] Reagan's advocacy of the magic of the marketplace in 1983 was combined with thinly veiled threats that U.S. participation in replenishments would depend on the Bank's receptivity to this magic. Within the Bank, this stance was vigorously advanced by a new chief economist, appointed by the new bank president, the former chief executive of a major U.S. commercial bank. In crafting the World Bank response to the debt crisis in developing countries, U.S. involvement was so intense that Paul Volcker, the Federal Reserve chair at the time, later said that the Federal Reserve and U.S. Treasury "directed" the Bank's loans.[37] Throughout the 1980s, in exchange for its approval of replenishments of International Development Association funds, the U.S. forced more extensive use of conditionality to deepen the role of unrestricted markets in debtor nations.[38]

In 1983 alone, fifty-two countries were subject to IMF structural adjustment conditions.[39] The average Latin American country was subject to six IMF or

World Bank adjustment programs in the course of the 1980s, while sub-Saharan African countries averaged seven.[40] In the 1990s, financial crises which were stirred up in part by the capital market liberalization that the Fund and Bank encouraged provided further impetus for structural adjustment, with conditions sometimes especially far-removed from the emergencies that prompted them. Thus, when volatile transnational capital flows converted the bursting of a real estate bubble in Thailand into the East Asia Crisis in 1997, loans to rescue South Korea's well-managed economy from a transient liquidity crisis were conditioned on the elimination of import restrictions and the opening of the Korean financial sector to foreign banks; the change was as well-connected with long-sought goals of the U.S. financial community as it was ill-connected with the task of containing volatility.[41]

In the course of the 1990s, the IMF and the World Bank retreated from use of the phrase "structural adjustment." For example, the IMF retired "Enhanced Structural Adjustment Facility" in favor of "Poverty Reduction and Growth Facility." The development of a Poverty Reduction Strategy Paper for a low income country in local deliberations, led by the World Bank and the IMF, among the government, donors and NGOs, was presented as a basis for "country ownership" in debt relief and development assistance in general. In allocating concessional loans, the Bank consulted a multidimensional index, the Country Policy Institutional Assessment. But the reality has remained much the same.

While much of the Country Policy Institutional Assessment favors character-istics that obviously improve wellbeing, such as less corruption, the "Structural Policies" cluster essentially monitors compliance with the enduring prescrip-tion of a shift from state-directed development to development by global markets, and it is by far the most important in practice. In a 2005 study for the Bank, Harold Bedoya found that 45 percent of all legally binding loan con-ditions focussed on structural-policies conditions, as compared to 25 percent in the next most important cluster, the good government ratings in "public sector management." (This emphasis was not a lesson from what worked. The independent correlation of structural conditions with growth was trivial and negative.[42]) Eric Neumayer's study of factors contributing to lending under the CPIA regime found that, when other factors such as depth of poverty were controlled for, there was a (statistically insignificant) *negative* correlation of low corruption and of the rule of law with receipt of a loan; what helped was "low regulatory burden."[43]

Similarly, structural policies conditions remain an integral part of IMF practice. In 2002, the IMF adopted generic guidelines favoring "parsimony," "criticality" and "streamlining" in setting these conditions. A 2005 review found that the average number of structural conditions in Fund-supported programs had, nonetheless, increased, from seventeen in 2002 to eighteen in 2004, as compared with ten in 1995.[44] The process of developing a Poverty Reduction Strategy Paper (PRSP) requires initial acceptance of a framework unilaterally imposed by the IMF, a gateway that comprised over thirty non-negotiable conditions en route to Tanzania's PRSP in 2001.[45]

Significantly affecting the vast majority of developing countries, structural adjustment has been the most far-flung coordinated project of large-scale policy transformation in human history. It has changed the contract between governments and citizens in developing countries from a state commitment to manage development to a state commitment to give the lead to global private enterprise. The role of international trade and capital flows in setting the pace and shape of economic change has been substantially enhanced. While economic displacement has created extensive needs for help, social expenditures as a proportion of GDP have normally been reduced, often sharply.[46]

Market pressures toward efficiency, innovation and expanded production are supposed to more than make up for the human costs of structural adjustment. This always speculative hope endures in the highest echelons of the Bank and the IMF, but it does not reflect experience so far. In the most extensive controlled comparison of IMF-adjusted with relevantly similar non-adjusted countries, Adam Przeworski and James Vreeland estimated that being under an IMF structural adjustment program lowered annual growth by 1.53 percentage points, on average. Countries did not tend to grow faster after structural adjustment programs than relevantly similar countries that never entered. Countries did not tend to grow faster after leaving the programs than they had before entering.[47] Nor are these failings problems of noncompliance. In a study of IMF programs in ninety-eight countries, Axel Dreher estimated that acceptance of an IMF program tended to lower growth by about 1.5 percentage points under full compliance.[48] In a World Bank study based on controlled comparison in a vast data base, William Easterly concluded that IMF and World Bank adjustment loan programs tend to reduce the rate at which growth alleviates poverty, with this consequence: "the effect of the actual adjustment loans on the number of poor was a net increase of 14 million [in the number falling below the threshold of $2 a day]."[49]

These projects to reshape the economies of developing countries were not sought or welcomed by the peoples of those countries as a whole. Indeed, about half of the countries subjected to structural adjustment programs have been the scene of large and tumultuous "IMF riots" protesting the imposed austerities.[50] The benefits of structural adjustment to the peoples who undergo it are, to put it mildly, unclear. On the other hand, the geopolitical interests of the U.S. government and the economic interests of leading U.S. firms are clearly served by policies that open markets in developing countries to foreign goods, displace local authorities and firms from the commanding heights of the economy, integrate local finance with the global system of banking and investment, privatize communications and transportation and open them to foreign investment, and displace participants in farming and small business into the labor force for transnational manufacturing. Structural adjustment is an exercise of the domineering influence of the United States by multinational means.

The multilateralism of the World Bank and the IMF makes them forums for objections and resistance to U.S. initiatives, which produce compromises and occasional U.S. defeats. But rather than serving as a second-best substitute for direct U.S. involvement, these multilateral institutions are a major advance in promoting U.S. interests, given the fact that the general direction of their influence (though not each decision) is what the U.S. wants. The inevitable resentment of poor debtors toward creditors who impose stringent conditions tends to be directed at an international bureaucracy, rather than the United States or U.S. banks. As David Beim, Executive Vice President of the U.S. Export–Import Bank, noted in a prescient 1977 discussion of the over-extension of credit by U.S. commercial banks to developing countries, "The real risk in LDC [less developed country] lending is not that the countries will walk away from the banks, but rather that they will draw the banks too deeply into their own internal affairs, making them a target of resentment over conservative economic policies . . . Some local politicians may like having a lightning rod to draw off the adverse reaction of the people. But this carries a clear political risk to the banks and to the United States generally."[51] In addition to moving the lightning rod elsewhere, there is a further, crasser advantage, noted in the Reagan administration's synoptic 1981 assessment of U.S. participation in multilateral development banks: "Because of the resource leveraging nature of the multilateral assistance program . . . the United States should be able to carry on its foreign policy objectives through the MDBs [multilateral development banks] at a lower over-all cost to the United States taxpayer than if an equivalent amount of funds were to be appropriated by the U.S."[52]

In practice, IMF and World Bank decisions reflect international cooperation of two kinds. First, other major developed countries usually agree with the broad drift of U.S. initiatives, which open developing countries to trade and capital flows and protect foreign creditors' interests when those countries are in crisis. The United States has always pushed faster, more extensively and more deeply in using the international financial institutions to inculcate the magic of the marketplace. Still, the other leading developed countries play a real, if secondary role. This is important at the stage of moral assessment, since it leads to shared responsibility.

In the second place, structural adjustment is often a covertly cooperative venture linking governments and economic elites of developed countries and the government and economic elites of the country subject to the conditions. While fear of dire alternatives may drive an unwilling government to accept structural adjustment as a way out of a crisis, a government and its supportive elites may, alternatively, welcome the occasion to institute measures with severe costs to many of its citizens while proclaiming that these measures are imposed from outside and must be observed on pain of devastating losses of access to foreign credit. As Joseph Stiglitz noted after his work in the Washington development community as Chief Economist at the World Bank, "The IMF interacts with a country's finance ministry, which all too often largely reflects the interests of that country's financial community, or more broad elites."[53]

Here, too, there is shared agency which generates shared responsibility—shared by the local government and outside powers. The fears of consequences on which local elites rely are fears created by the United States and institutions it dominates. The local government's willing, if tacit, invitation does not cancel outside responsibility for the consequences, since the responsibilities of the outside powers are responsibilities toward the people of the developing country, not to their government (except in so far as it represents the common good and general will of its people).

This sort of mingled agency of outside powers and local elites is familiar from the history of literal empire. Fears of what Her Majesty's army would otherwise do often overcame resistance of chiefs and emirs in the march of the British Empire through Africa and the Middle East. But possible British repression sometimes, alternatively, served as a resource of chiefs and emirs whose situation would be more secure and luxurious under imperial sponsorship, as agents of "indirect rule," than as rulers free and remote from British power. The fact that they invited the Empire in did not free Britain from responsibilities.

## Violent Molding and Military Sponsorship

Other mechanisms shaping life in developing countries by-pass management by multinational institutions. For example, the terms of life in developing countries are often shaped by U.S. destructive power. This activity is most dramatic when it plays a crucial role in overturning a regime whose end is perceived as important to the United States, as in Iran, Guatemala, Nicaragua, Afghanistan and Iraq. In addition, regardless of the origins of the local regime, the general direction of policies in a territory is often connected with U.S. interests by the regime's dependence on U.S. military support.

The Middle East is one prominent site of military patronage. The House of Saud has played the leading role worldwide in containing oil price surges and expanding production and has provided preferential terms to American oil companies, in exchange for support for its tenuous rule, renowned for repression, bigotry and the taking of national wealth for princely luxury. The largest arms supplier to Saudi Arabia, the United States had military sales of over $115 billion (in contemporary dollars) to the Saudi regime in the second half of the twentieth century.[54] This exchange of arms for oil created a military force that is at once highly advanced and highly dependent on U.S.–Saudi military cooperation. As the U.S. State Department put it, in 2004, "a long-standing security relationship continues to be important in U.S.–Saudi relations. A U.S. military training mission established at Dharan in 1953 provides training and support in the use of weapons and other security-related services to the Saudi armed forces. . . . The U.S. Army Corps of Engineers has had a long-term role in military and construction activities in the Kingdom."[55]

In the last quarter of the twentieth century, Israel was by far the largest recipient of U.S. military aid, often receiving over 40% of total military aid, 51% in 1999. Egypt was second largest, receiving 35% in 1999.[56] These levels of aid continued or increased in the first decade of the new century, with some changes in rank in some years due to massive military aid to Poland and the sponsorship of new regimes in Iraq and Afghanistan. In 2005, the proportions of total military aid of the leading recipients were 30% to Israel, 18% to Egypt, 17% to Iraq.[57] U.S. military aid provides the Israeli government with an essential ingredient in maintaining either sovereignty or much-resented oversight over territory in which most people are Arab.[58] In return for massive support, the United States has an utterly secure military and diplomatic ally in the Middle East, in a relationship that provides powerful assurance of loyalty to other clients throughout the world and reinforces awareness of defeats for the Arab nationalism that was once the major threat to U.S. interests in the region. In Egypt, this aid helps to sustain a beleaguered autocracy that is the leading Arab advocate of U.S. interests in the Middle East.

Because military sponsorship gives the United States a central role in a local regime's survival, it might seem that military sponsorship establishes an especially tight connection between local decisions and U.S. interests. This is by no means always the case. Expensive, visible, infuriating to opponents of the client and of American domination, creating risks of embarrassing defeat or direct engagement of U.S. forces, military sponsorship is a sign that the U.S. perceives its interests to be vital where its influence would be tenuous without the collaboration of the sponsored regime. The sponsored may be able to use the vital U.S. needs as protection for their own agendas, which may not closely conform to the wishes of the sponsor. Although his political survival had depended on an invasion of U.S. Marines, Balaguer sometimes imposed personal control over the Dominican economy at the cost of inefficiency in international transactions and fought off rivals with terror and corruption that endangered stability. The cables from Saigon in the *Pentagon Papers* are full of complaints about the military juntas' pursuit of personal interests in the face of U.S. pressures toward reform.

In any case, there are limits to what a regime can do to achieve the preferred American outcome in the case at hand without a larger loss of influence that would serve neither's interest. In 1973, when a U.S. military airlift restored Israel's military prospects in the October War, Saudi Arabia seems to have responded to calls for an Arab oil embargo reluctantly, to moderating effect and without expectations of the large price increase that was the actual outcome.[59] If, in addition, Saudi Arabia had utterly refused to participate in the embargo, the short-term reduction in the effectiveness of the boycott might well have been outweighed by the long-term loss of moderating influence.

Despite these departures, military sponsorship is a means by which the United States can keep the general course of government in a territory within bounds that would otherwise be transgressed. Although the sponsored regime is profoundly responsible for the consequences of its rule, so is the outside sponsor: without internal acquiescence depending on the outside support, the regime might not otherwise stay in power.

## Aid Dependence

Dependence on U.S. economic aid, without the mediation of multilateral institutions, is a further mechanism of domineering influence over developing countries, which can contribute to outright territorial domination by the United States. If distinctive U.S. interests in the domestic and foreign policies of recipients did not guide the allocation of aid and the fear of aid reduction did not serve as a means of influencing those policies, then aid dependence would be an unfortunate effect of poverty, not a vehicle of domineering influence. In fact, in apportioning aid, the United States exercises a prerogative of a very rich country to promote policies and alliances that suit its interests, independent of the interests of peoples of needy countries. In especially aid-dependent countries, U.S. aid serves as a vehicle of threat-influence and, sometimes, regime-elimination, through feared prospects and dramatically disruptive effects of aid reduction.

The emphases of U.S. giving track U.S. strategic needs, as perceived by those in charge of the protection of American domineering influence, with speed and precision. In 1999, Israel was the largest recipient of U.S. economic aid, even though Israel (i.e., Israel proper, excluding the West Bank and Gaza) is a high income country, with per capita GNI at purchasing power parity in the top fifth of the 207 countries ranked by the World Bank. The genuinely impoverished West Bank and Gaza received 7% of Israel's stipend. Israel was closely followed by Egypt, a corrupt autocracy ranked "lower middle-income" by the World Bank. In 2001, these countries were overtaken by Colombia (ranked eighty-eighth out of 208 countries in per capita Gross National Income at purchasing power parity), cementing support from a new Colombian administration adjacent to the most defiant regime in an increasingly unfriendly region. In 2003, other events had produced a different ranking, in descending order: Iraq (first by far), tiny but utterly strategic and potentially unstable Jordan, Afghanistan, and Colombia, which received more than five times the aid of the Democratic Republic of the Congo, a more populous country, recovering from a devastating war, in which per capita income is a tenth of Colombia's at purchasing power parity. Those four countries alone received a third of U.S. economic aid, and were followed by others of significant strategic interest.[60]

Even in the disbursement of aid classified as "development assistance," the U.S. does not favor low income countries. In 2006, only 32% of U.S. bilateral development assistance went to low income countries, in which 37% of the world's people lived.[61] Further reflecting the force of distinctive U.S. interests in U.S. development aid, about 70% of U.S. bilateral development aid commitments are tied to the purchase of goods and services from the United States. In addition to the U.S.-destined revenue they yield, these are ties that help to bind economies to U.S.-based firms, business practices and investment objectives.[62]

Where aid dependence is sufficiently deep, continued approval by the United States can become a condition for political viability. Haiti is a vivid illustration. In the face of Aristide's resistance to IMF/World Bank prescriptions he had promised to accept, together with political malfeasance that was trivial on the scale of repressive and corrupt regimes to which the U.S. willingly contributes,

U.S. aid dropped from $158 million in 1995, the first year of Aristide's U.S.-backed restoration, to an average of $99 million in 1996–9, and then steeply decreased again, while World Bank and IMF provisions dwindled. In 2003, the U.S. entirely stopped giving aid directly to Aristide's regime, giving a total, through nongovernmental organizations, which was 28% lower than the 1995–9 average, 55% lower than in 1995. Haiti's aid dependency in 1995, measured by the ratio of aid to Gross National Income, had been 28%, one of the highest ratios in the world.[63] So the withdrawal of aid played an important role in enabling leaders of the death squads of the prior regime to reenter Haiti and depose a popularly elected president, whose continued broad and militant support required periodic violent suppression for the next two years. At this point, another member of Aristide's political party, a former President who was more respectful of U.S. power and amenable to U.S. demands, was elected Haitian president. According to "political observers" as reported in the *New York Times*, he had been "sought out by the United States and governments leading the United Nations Stabilization Mission struggling to restore order."[64]

## Trade Dependence

Most U.S. trade is with rich countries, whose internal markets, alternative partners and technological and commercial facilities give them substantial power to respond to U.S. threats in the jostling of international negotiations. Matters are very different for a small and poor country, deeply dependent on U.S. markets, oriented toward U.S. direct investments, and sensitive to U.S. favor or disfavor in trade agreements and allegations of unfair trade practices.

For example, costs of U.S. displeasure which are created by trade dependence, rather than aid dependence, are a major influence in Central America. With the occasional exception of Panama, no Central American country gets most of its development assistance from the United States; routinely, several receive more from at least one other country, often more than one. Yet, with the exception of Panama, these countries are vitally and especially dependent on trade with the United States. In 2006, the ratio of exports to the United States to Gross National Income was 18% in Costa Rica, 29% in Nicaragua and 42% in Honduras.[65] U.S. threats of exclusion from favored access extended to trade competitors have a powerful impact on such trade dependents. After a group of developing countries, insisting on reduction of developed countries' farm subsidies, rejected the sort of trade-liberalization that the U.S. sought at the 2003 WTO conference at Cancun, the threat of exclusion from the

Central American Free Trade Association successfully pried Central American countries from the coalition. In 2005, when the largest party in the Nicaraguan parliament had allied with the Sandinista party in an effort to unseat the Nicaraguan president, the U.S. Deputy Secretary of State, soon to become President of the World Bank, flew down to Managua. There was no point in threatening to reduce U.S. aid, since this constituted a seventh of total aid, a fifth of bilateral aid, about $20 per Nicaraguan. But exports to the United States constituted 24% of Nicaragua's GNI.[66] The Deputy Secretary of State "warned business leaders . . . that they should not continue supporting the political parties that are trying to unseat Nicaragua's president if they hoped to continue doing business with the United States. 'Your opportunities will be lost,' Mr. Zoellick said he told the businessmen."[67]

On the ecumenical construal, the claim that there is an American empire seems accurate. This enduring system of transnational political power involves diverse forms of domineering influence with enormous impact on foreigners' lives, exercised in ways that are hard to reconcile with respect for their autonomy. Just as the reconciliation of diverse domestic relationships of power with respect for autonomy entails concerns for disadvantaged compatriots, the transnational system, presumably, gives rise to political duties to help disadvantaged foreigners. But the transnational relationships of the American empire are not the same as those within the United States, so one would expect the transnational duties to differ as well. What measures helping disadvantaged people in developing countries must a citizen of the United States support to live up to her responsibilities in the American empire? What measures must citizens of other developed countries support to live up to their responsibilities as citizens of countries that collaborate with the American empire and, sometimes, pursue similar, independent, lesser paths of power? In light of the survey of imperial relationships in this chapter, the next one will seek to identify these imperial responsibilities.

# 6

# Empire and Obligation

THE subject, the American empire, is usually addressed in arguments over whether the world would be better for its absence. I will eventually enter this debate, at the end of the next chapter. But a rush to enter it would by-pass a central question of transnational responsibility: how does the existence of this power structure, which shows no immediate prospect of ending, affect the political responsibilities of citizens of the United States and allied developed countries to people in developing countries? In Chapter 2, political responsibilities among compatriots turned out to depend on the ways in which they help to shape one another's lives by taking part in their shared government. The ways in which the United States, in basic alliance with other developed countries, exercises domineering influence over developing countries could also create transnational responsibilities to help these foreigners. I will argue that major, unmet imperial responsibilities are in fact created by imperial power.

## No Short Cut

It might seem that a demanding imperial duty of concern extending to most developing countries is easily established, in light of the domineering influence described in the last chapter. Directly or by steering multilateral processes, the United States has shaped the terms of self-advancement in most developing countries. So (it might seem) the political responsibilities to the disadvantaged that would bind a U.S. citizen to her fellow citizens in the absence of this network of domineering influence must be extended to all those who are part of it. Granted, within the network, as within borders, participants should insist that the disadvantaged fulfill their own responsibilities to try to get ahead. Also, the political obligation to help disadvantaged foreigners will hardly be limited to Americans: citizens of all developed countries that take part in the transnational shaping of lives should help in proportion to their countries' resources and initiatives in influence. Still, the disproportionate resources and initiative of the United States would give it by far the largest share of a responsibility to uphold a standard of justice extending throughout the American empire that would only bind fellow Americans if power did not reach beyond borders. For example, if citizens of the United States would have a duty to insure that the life-prospects of their most disadvantaged compatriots are as good as possible if power did not reach beyond borders, then they would have the largest share of a duty to maximize the life-prospects of the most disadvantaged throughout the territory of the American empire.

This argument is too quick. Morally speaking, the American empire is not the United States writ large—not if Chapter 2 adequately described the origins of political duties among fellow citizens. The extent and nature of duties of Americans to one another reflect deep dependence of the prospering of each on the laws and policies of their shared government, the impact of those laws and policies on differences in life-prospects, the demanding loyalty toward the shared political order expected of all and normally displayed, and the exclusive ultimate political control that the citizenry exercise over life within their sovereign borders. The same commonalities do not bind all fellow subjects of the American empire. A responsible American citizen does not seek loyal support of American institutions from Guatemalans. Prosperous people in the United States and prosperous people in Guatemala largely depend on very different public facilities for their success. Differences in life-prospects in Guatemala are largely due to Guatemalan social and political arrangements; and nothing in the survey of mechanisms of imperial influence showed that the typical vast differences between Guatemalan and American life-prospects are largely due to imperial dominion. Whatever the extent of American influence on Guatemalan life, Guatemala is not within the borders of exclusive sovereign control by the United States. In sum, no quick extrapolation will establish the nature and extent of transnational responsibilities due to the American empire.

Rather than seeking such a short cut, this chapter will draw on and add to the portrayal of empire in the previous chapter to describe how important, largely unmet responsibilities to help people in developing countries arise from three specific processes of imperial power: the shaping of the course of development through structural adjustment and similar uses of economic needs, the propping up of repressive client regimes, and the exercise of destructive power, both direct and sponsored. The first process generates a demanding residual responsibility to meet basic needs, the second, a duty to promote prosperity in subordinate territories that extends beyond basic needs, the third, a vast duty of repair.

Severe though they may be, criticisms of the United States for failing to live up to these responsibilities do not amount to the indictment that leads many to wish for the disappearance of the American empire, the charge that governance of the empire has enduring tendencies to inflict unjustified harm including a vast toll of unjust violence. The next chapter will assess this indictment, the wish for an end of empire that it naturally prompts, and the responsibilities its truth would create. The conclusions will be that the charge is true, that it does not support a wish for the disappearance of the American empire, but, instead, that it contributes to a distinctive civic responsibility to hem in immoral excesses of empire.

## Steering Development

Sometimes acting directly, often acting through international financial institutions, the United States, in recent decades, has steered the course of development in most developing countries in its favored direction: away from state-directed development, toward privatization, fiscal austerity, openness to the free flow of goods and investments across borders, and treatment of transnational firms on a par with local enterprises. The most visible steering device has been structural adjustment, i.e., the stipulation of movement in this direction, by the IMF and the World Bank, as a condition for aid and below-market-rate loans needed to emerge from currency or fiscal crises. But this device has worked in tandem with others that also produce development policies preferred by the United States, but not by the people as a whole of a developing country, through the setting of conditions, stated or implicit, on help in meeting desperate needs. For example, structural adjustment moved in parallel with the manipulation of pressing needs for market access in the Uruguay Round, described in Chapter 3. It has been accompanied by the conditioning of U.S. foreign aid to poor countries on movement in the same direction of market penetration—conditioning that is sometimes informal or implicit, sometimes officially stipulated, as in the use of Heritage Foundation rankings of trade policies in selection for aid through the Millenium Challenge Account. In this section, "structural adjustment" will refer to the whole bundle of mutually reinforcing manipulations of need in which structural adjustment proper has been the most prominent strand.

Widespread steering of development by the manipulation of need did not begin around 1980. In prior decades, U.S. foreign aid—funds, technical assistance and, in the early years, vast flows of food aid—laid the groundwork for development through transnational manufacturing, by discouraging nationalist courses of development, promoting appropriate infrastructures (despite much waste), and eroding traditional agrarian economies.[1] Indeed, there are important antecedents to structural adjustment in the collaborations between the British government, London banks and local elites that shaped the course of development in South America in the nineteenth century.[2] Concentration on structural adjustment provides a template for the responsibilities created by a variety of devices by which empires, metaphorical and literal, without threatening or deploying violence, shape frameworks of self-advancement of those struggling to escape from destitution.

In exploring the moral implications of structural adjustment, I will initially simplify complex causal processes in two ways. In reality, many developed countries and organizations play active roles in this process. It helps to start out by adopting the simplifying fiction that a single outside agent steers development through this vehicle: the United States, often acting through international institutions. Once the consequent simple responsibility is identified, it will be easy enough to end the fiction and divide the actual shared responsibility among the multiple agents.

In the second place, I will initially put to one side the active political roles of internal agents in limiting, altering, or crucially supplementing the impact of structural adjustment on development policies. In effect, I will assume that the policy framework for development is unwillingly adopted by the local government solely because of conditions attached to external offers that the government could not responsibly refuse because of the urgency of local needs. Later, when the impact of local political agency is taken into account, it will generate extremely important local responsibilities—but without alteration of the fundamental principles of responsibility of structural adjusters.

On a maximal assessment that I have already questioned, structural adjustment (in this simplified version) would create a responsibility of U.S. citizens to treat the disadvantaged in affected countries on a par with disadvantaged compatriots. On a minimal assessment, the consequent responsibility is merely a duty to follow through on commitments to aid, loan or give access to markets if the stipulated conditions are met. I will defend a demanding assessment between these extremes.

Recognition of duties to take care in guiding others' choices when the stakes for them are high is enough to establish more than the minimal demand. The only appropriate goals of the structural adjuster in setting policy conditions are goals of economic improvement. As means to any other end, the conditions would be inappropriate impositions on others' choices of how to conduct their affairs, like a mortgage lender's insistence that houses be painted in his favorite colors. In stipulating ways of pursuing these vital goals, the adjuster had better have good evidence that the prescription will work. Because of the decision to attach the condition to the offer, the economic patient has (we are supposing) no responsible choice except to take the prescribed path, and lives are in jeopardy if the prescription is misguided. If the prescription was based on unwarranted confidence, a wrong of negligence has been committed and the consequent harms should be made good, just as a doctor should make good her negligence, however beneficent her intentions may have been. If failure reveals, after the fact, that the intervention was misguided, there is a duty to renew the offered aid on appropriately altered terms. This is what we must do to be worthy of others' trust when their lives depend on our guidance.

These precepts, familiar from all professions in which vital interventions are made in others' lives, connect structural adjustment with substantial duties. While the duty of nonabandonment in case of bad advice has been fulfilled by structural adjusters, previous chapters sketched a case that they have been pervasively negligent. Restraint in imposing prescriptions of submission to market forces has not kept pace with evidence undermining warranted confidence in their efficacy. Indeed, given the repeated failures of the expert consensus in the past, insistence on uniform compliance with the Washington Consensus was negligent at the start of structural adjustment.

However, the avoidance of negligent intervention is hardly the limit of political duties of concern. On account of our joint impact on one another as compatriots, we have duties to help one another, not just duties to be careful if we choose to help. While structural adjustment does not extrapolate the same duties throughout the territorial empire of the United States, it, too, makes efforts to help nonoptional. In shifting courses of development through structural adjustment, the United States has acquired a residual responsibility to provide for basic needs, to the extent that these needs cannot be met by a good faith effort of the citizenries whose framework for self-advancement has been changed.

By "basic needs," I mean those whose fulfillment is normally a prerequisite for any satisfactory life even when people exercise self-discipline in adjusting their life-goals to their resources. Nonfulfillment of basic needs has special political ramifications. If someone cannot meet her basic needs through her own efforts and the help of others exercising their apolitical responsibilities, and if the government claims extensive prerogatives to set terms of self-advancement in the territory, then her acceptance of her government rightly depends on its commitment to help her meet her basic needs. If it does not help her (in ways compatible with her exercise of her own responsibilities) and if those at least as badly off as her would not be neglected if she were helped, then this neglect of her needs justifies her withholding willing support for her government. She would not take her own needs seriously if she committed herself to a political order claiming extensive authority with so little commitment to assuring her the means to live a satisfactory life through her own efforts. By the same token, a government can only act responsibly in shaping the terms of self-advancement in a territory if it gives priority to the fulfillment of basic needs that people in the territory cannot fulfill on their own.

With widely varying degrees of honesty and competence, the governments of developing countries provide facilities and enforce policies that are supposed to relieve the economic disadvantages that thwart the basic needs of many of their citizens. In structural adjustment, an external agent—the United States, in our simplification—uses urgent basic needs to produce a shift in these political measures, transforming the nature and prospects of self-advancement. Before, let's say, farmers sold to the marketing board, the poor bought subsidized food, and farms and businesses were protected from foreign competition by tariff barriers, requirements of domestic ownership and the preferences of local banks and credit agencies. Now, perhaps for better, perhaps for worse, self-advancement is determined by heightened market-based risks, opportunities and pressures for change, disrupting the previous network of relationships and quickening the previous pace of life.

By imposing a new direction on the national project of better meeting basic needs, the United States takes on a responsibility to help in the project. This is the sort of political project—wide-ranging and unavoidable in impact, extending far beyond uncontroversial protections of pre-political rights—that is only rightly imposed if it merits the willing support of all. A lack of commitment to meet basic needs among those whose lives will be shaped makes the project unworthy of support. Before, the responsibility to engage in this effort to meet basic needs was the local government's. Now that the United States has used fear of dire consequences to get its preferred direction imposed, it shares this responsibility.

The responsibility to help of the United States is especially demanding if the local government is at least as competent in choosing the right course of development and more representative of local preferences. The government was compelled to accept policy conditions it would otherwise reject by its responsibility to its citizenry to get help in meeting urgent needs. By stipulating these conditions, the United States has arrogantly taken over the proper prerogative of those who will live with the consequences of the development policies that it has imposed. It has ignored the morally crucial difference between its citizenry and the citizens of another country. The proper indemnity for this usurpation is an effort to insure the successful escape from destitution to which their own government was rightly committed. Having treated those foreigners as if they really were its own citizens, the United States should, if need be, devote its own resources to their success in development.

Given the repeated failures of the consensus guiding external agents in shaping the course of development and the remoteness of those agents from local political processes, these constraints of competence and representativeness are not very demanding. But suppose that they are not met. Still, considerable American resources must be devoted to helping those who must live with the new course of development.

If the government that is the target of structural adjustment is sufficiently incompetent and unrepresentative, then its need for economic survival can be manipulated without disrespect for the value of choice. What counts is the capacity for choice of those who are thwarted by this government, not the effort to dominate of the local elite. Still, in seeking to have its preferred course of development imposed, the United States must take care that this course deserves the willing support of those on whom it is imposed. Otherwise, the American empire is tyranny at arm's length. That structural adjustment improves on what a predatory government would do otherwise is not good enough. Subjects of a predatory tyrant may be very glad that he has deposed his much more predatory uncle and accept that no other currently available source of stable political order is at all as good. What the nephew does is, still, politically irresponsible. Without defensive comparisons with the local government, the United States must respond to locals' complaints that their basic needs will go unmet despite their own best efforts if the new course is successfully imposed.

It might seem that the adjuster can meet such complaints by noting that it (in the final analysis, its taxpayers) gave something in exchange for a commitment to meet the conditions. Aid was given, or a loan was made at below the market rate. However, this reply neglects the moral implications of the broad and deep impact of the conditions. That an agent has set the framework in which others pursue their vital and legitimate interests is a moral reason for him to insure that their basic needs are met, even if an offer was the means of framework-setting.

For example, in pre-modern circumstances, the last resort of someone who is bereft of resources may be a well-off person's kind offer to receive him into his household as a servant. That this is a kind offer, by someone who does not need a servant, does not negate the obligation to provide decent working conditions, meeting basic needs, even if doing less would have made the offer sufficiently attractive. In a modern setting, the inevitability, for nearly all employees, of living in an environment set by some employer or other for much of one's life generates an obligation of employers to provide a decent working environment. "This is better than starving" is not an adequate response to workers' complaints. Similarly, when the structural adjuster tries to get a framework for self-advancement imposed on a whole society, this ought to be accompanied by a commitment to satisfaction of basic needs so long as people must live with the consequences of the imposition. In all of these cases, setting the framework for people's pursuit of the goals with which they identify creates a special responsibility to insure that it is a basis for leading a satisfactory life. The framework setter who does not recognize the responsibility does not adequately value the capacity for choice of a person who is forced (at least, forced by her circumstances) to accept the framework.

Granted, a responsibility to help meet basic needs within the scope of a framework may have to be reduced in light of the burdens that would be imposed on the framework-setter. The kindly grandee is not required to sacrifice his prosperity because he has decided to share it. Capitalist employers have a right to make a profit, including fair wages for managerial work. Still, the vast gains to the United States from the structural adjustment process constitute a fund for sustaining basic needs that must be exhausted before the plea "This is too much to ask of us" can be entertained as a limit to responsibilities acquired in the process.

American steering of the course of development is a powerful means of enhancing advantages to people in the United States of economic activity in developing countries. Extremes of openness to markets have greatly increased the investment and trade opportunities of American firms and greatly helped American consumers, while often creating disruption without commensurate gains in developing countries. By removing local political elites from the commanding heights of the economy, the economic shift has also advanced the interests of the U.S. government in political influence over strategic places. Grants and below-market-rate loans were important instruments in this transformation because markets did not adequately stimulate large, long-term structural changes, not because the process of change was a matter of self-sacrificing beneficence. Accordingly, a grant or loan that is a lever for structural adjustment should be seen as an incident in a process in which the United States benefits from its capacity to get its way on account of others' weakness. Those who extract benefit from control over others' terms of self-advancement should not be ceded anything more than a fair wage for their efforts by those whose lives they shape. Otherwise they treat the weaker parties as assets, rather than persons. In retaining vast benefits from its practice of imposing a course of development, rather than promoting more successful satisfaction of basic needs, the United States imitates a tyrant whose rule is both a stay against chaos *and* a means of extracting tribute to sustain his court.

Thus, whether or not it is an arrogant usurpation, structural adjustment generates a strong responsibility of concern. However, this responsibility has distinct limits. The concern it dictates is a residual concern to help those seeking fulfillment of basic needs once due weight has been given to their self-reliance.

The concern is residual because the acceptance that must be sought by the responsible structural adjuster is acceptance compatible with self-respect. Self-respecting people in a sovereign country prefer self-reliance, both individual and collective, to outside help. They want to be able to take pride in their own accomplishments. They favor collective efforts that express the proper valuing of ongoing relationships by displaying special concern corresponding to the inherent value of interpersonal ties. These ties largely bind within borders and do not include subordination to the American empire. Self-respect includes a strong preference for reciprocity, the ultimate, wholehearted return of important benefits. Such reciprocity is sustained by ongoing projects of willing cooperation within developing countries, not by processes of foreign help.

The proper appreciation of self-reliance does not require rejecting all help. The point of self-reliance is to live a life that is truly one's own, in which self-fulfillment derives from engagement in one's own meaningful life-projects. (In Joseph Raz's poignant example, a woman on a desert island who must invest all her energy and attention in staying out of the clutches of a voracious beast does not live a life that is truly her own, even if she cleverly, continually escapes its clutches.[3]) Unable to obtain, on one's own, sufficient resources for living a life that is truly one's own, one shows that one cares about self-reliance by accepting aid and then making good use of it. Those within one's circles of mutual obligation are the first resort for this help, but further outside aid is acceptable, if needed. So help by the structural adjuster should serve this residual interest, preferably providing resources by which people in a developing country can go on to help one another to help themselves.

In addition to its residual role, engagement in structural adjustment only creates a responsibility to attend to basic needs, not to all of the many things that people need in order to pursue valuable goals. The duress that the United States exploits is urgency in meeting basic needs, compelling wants that people cannot reasonably be expected to end by adjusting their desires to their resources. If, on the other hand, the United States provides for other worthy wants, such as higher education and attractive public buildings, it is fulfilling desires that people in a poor country could, alternatively, have put to one side in light of their resources. Not to hold them responsible for choosing to pursue these goals is to fail to honor self-reliance. To treat the United States as controlling them in providing for these wants is to infantilize them. In addition, basic needs are the needs that are served by the projects of development that the United States seeks to redirect. So the justification for the redirection ought to involve promotion of these specific interests. Finally, respect for local cultural autonomy favors concentration on basic needs for subsistence, health care and security when an outside power seeks to determine local policies. These needs are regarded as urgent in any culture. If the outside power, in addition, chooses among future national trajectories according to criteria other than the satisfaction of basic needs, there is a danger that the measures will distort the local process of determination of culture and institutions in favor of one faction or the outside power's culture.

While the restriction to basic needs prevents the generation of excessive demands, its stringency should not be exaggerated. These needs will include needs for subsistence, basic health care and physical security. But they will not be satisfied by mere physical survival, since mere survival for oneself and one's dependents is not the point of a meaningful life. In addition, basic needs for security and stability require widespread support for shared political institutions, and this support requires attention to interests of people throughout society on the basis of some defensible interpretation of the common good. So basic needs in a poor society will not be satisfied at the price of wholesale neglect of those who seek improvement beyond the basics. The further price would be conflict, disorder and pervasive insecurity. The American empire would not be absolved of responsibilities if the people of the Philippines had the means of eliminating Filipino destitution by measures that left nearly all Filipinos just a bit above destitution.

Still, people can lead lives truly their own when they lack access to a flourishing national university, live in small quarters, and have possessions much sparser than nearly all Americans'. To deny that someone in Mali could live a satisfactory life as a result of an intelligent choice to become a farmer, craftsman or shopkeeper with an income that is a small fraction of the American average is inaccurate and insulting. The overcoming of such limits is not, as such, a goal of the acquired responsibility for development.

It is time to cancel the simplifying assumption that there is just one ultimately independent exerter of domineering influence through structural adjustment, the United States. In the institutions that have served as the chief administrators of this domineering influence, the World Bank and the IMF, the U.S. is the leader in a dominant coalition of developed countries, not the sole independent force. While the U.S. has inveigled France, Germany and Japan into following its initiative in major shifts, they are not, by any means, client regimes, and are not under dire threats that absolve them of responsibility. Also, unilateral mechanisms of domineering influence of the American empire are paralleled by independent mechanisms of influence of other great powers, such as France's uses of economic dependence in Francophone Africa, which can work to similar effect, to a lesser degree.

How should the efforts of dominators be compared, to determine whether they are doing their fair shares in developing countries? Two dimensions of comparison are especially important. One is effective initiative, the extent to which the distinctive energy and the distinctive wishes of one of these governments determine terms of self-advancement in developing countries. The greater the vigor with which one party pursues activities that threaten to disvalue the autonomy of another, the greater its contributions should be to further activities that promote the weaker party's autonomy. At the same time, fairness requires attention to burdensomeness to the citizens of each domineering government. Among those joined in an activity generating further responsibilities, some have reason to complain if the burdens of meeting the responsibilities fall more heavily on them than on others. (Within borders, this might be a complaint of disproportionate tax burdens.) If the United States were a poor but militarily powerful country, taking the lead in shaping lives abroad but unable to meet joint responsibilities without special pain, then it might be difficult to take account of both dimensions of comparison in assessing the current American share. But in fact, the standard of burden and the standard of leadership roughly coincide. The leader in taking advantage of difficulties in resisting its will does least, in proportion to its own resources, to relieve basic needs. So the United States bears the greatest share of unmet responsibilities due to the steering of the course of development.

In addition to acknowledging the complexity of outside agency in structural adjustment, the other simplifying assumption, of passive accommodation by insiders, should, finally, be cancelled. Political agency within targets of structural adjustment generates important political responsibilities. While the vast majority of developing countries have been moved farther and faster from state-directed development into market-driven development by structural adjustment than they would have on their own, none has been a passive receiver of Washingtonian prescriptions. Usually, significant portions of the population support the prescribed changes. Sometimes, movement in this direction is supported by the government, as in Mexico (even though the government may try to deflect resentment by tying the change to demands of outside institutions). Conversely, conditions are sometimes softened in response to official objections or angry riots, frequently are not fully complied with, or are partly reversed when the crisis has passed. In any case, governments can make good or bad use of the imposed framework. The IMF never requires a ruling political party to treat privatization as a private sale of the nicest state assets to its best placed members, however often this happens. In these and other ways, development is a joint project of insiders and outsiders.

To see how agency within developing countries affects transnational political duties in developed countries, one has to distinguish among a variety of claims about responsibilities for development. Otherwise, large claims of external responsibility will obscure profoundly important internal responsibilities.

In the first place, the effort that the government and citizens of a developing country ought to make in overcoming local destitution is demanding, and this demanding duty is not in the least reduced by structural adjustment. Whatever the framework for development and regardless of whether it is externally imposed, the government and citizens should strive to make good use of it.

Second, a local government's conduct in setting development policies is always a source of liability to blame. But this need not reduce the responsibility to help of an outside participant. For example, a government that willingly accepts and implements loan conditions that it ought to have resisted, relying on desperate needs for outside help to produce reluctant acquiescence of the citizenry as a whole, is blameworthy. But its collaboration does not reduce the structural adjuster's responsibility.

Third, whether or not the policies guiding development are wholly externally imposed, the external duty to help will be restricted by the value of self-reliance. The proper valuing of self-reliance will include reasonable demands on the political as well as the personal efforts of people in developing countries to meet their own needs. But it would not honor self-reliance to withhold assistance because hard-pressed people have not jeopardized their basic needs through political activity that invites grave losses through repression or corruption, channels scarce energies into almost certainly doomed causes, or makes unreciprocated concessions to people in other social groups or social positions that are apt to create severe disadvantages.

In addition to these moral considerations, local accountability and civic participation are practically important. Locals know what they need, whom to trust and whom to distrust better than outsiders, and local governments have deeper reasons to be responsive to their demands than foreign ones. So improvement through local initiatives is the favored process in development. What weakens it by weakening local demands for accountability may well make matters worse. These may be reasons not to engage in transnational conduct that, at first glance, seems beneficial. But they are not reasons for outsiders not to do what would help in meeting basic needs. They are reasons why excessive intervention by outsiders would not help.

In all of these ways, the impact of local initiative is vitally important, morally and practically. However, it does not cancel the transnational duty that emerged before, the residual duty of structural adjusters to help provide for basic needs. Instead, the importance of local initiative guides the implementation of this duty, and creates parallel responsibilities of local governments that will reduce the residue if these duties are discharged. In part, the enduring responsibility of the outside agents reflects their superior resources. Above all, it reflects their intrusion. Structural adjustment (in the broad sense that I have stipulated for present purposes) is a frank effort to transform the course of development, which has resulted in substantial changes in most developing countries, continues to be pressed where these changes are incomplete, and expands the resources of developed countries. The refusal to use these gains to help those whose basic needs are at stake (with due regard for self-reliance) disowns the responsibility created by this special intrusiveness. If, to reduce their residual responsibility, the structural adjusters were to tell the local poor, "This help is too much to ask of us, since we did not create all of your burdens," the poor could aptly reply, "No one forced you to intervene in our lives." If the structural adjusters were to propose, "Your governments are to blame for not doing better," those who must live with the jointly set course of development can rightly respond, "We blame them, but not to much purpose. If you do not use your resources to help us help ourselves, we will blame you, too."

## Client Regimes

When the United States uses the urgency of basic needs to alter policies meant to fulfill basic needs, it acquires a responsibility limited to those needs. This connection suggests that direct collaboration in more extensive coercion might create a political duty of concern extending beyond basic needs in an imperial territory. In fact, an outside power does have this further responsibility toward people living under its client regimes, i.e., repressive, allied governments substantially depending on support from the outside power for survival.

A great deal of the Middle East and Africa is governed by client regimes of the United States (for example, in recent years, Egypt, Ethiopia, Israel in its governance of the Palestinian territories, Somalia, and Iraq) or by regimes that are, at the very least, profoundly shaped by recent clientelism and hopes for future propping up as needed—for example, the Democratic Republic of the Congo. (Other powers, such as France, also have clients, such as Chad and the Côte d'Ivoire, incurring similar responsibilities.) In the Congo, the Israel-occupied territories and Somalia, life-prospects are probably worse than they would have been in the absence of transnational clientelism, generating a duty to make good on the patron's part. (The client regime, of course, has a duty to improve its governance, but its failure in no way reduces the patron's responsibility to compensate for sponsorship of a burdensome political order.) In other cases, such as Egypt and Ethiopia, life-prospects might well be worse if the client regime were not propped up. But the avoidance of worsening is not the limit of the patron's moral liability.

As guarantor of the Mubarak regime, the United States has a duty to treat deficiencies in the regime's exercise of political responsibility as failings that it shares. Even if it has blocked the political autonomy of Egyptians for adequate reasons of regional stability, it can only honor the thwarted desire for autonomy if it advances local aspirations insofar as they are compatible with these security interests. Like the occupying power after a just war, the right standard is not, "What would make this country better off than it would otherwise be?" (not very demanding in the case of defeated Germany), but "What would a just government accomplish in advancing the interests of the people of this country?" Perhaps if the United States did not guarantee the Mubarak regime, Egyptians would convert brutal and corrupt decrepitude to fratricidal devastation. This no more justifies America's failure to promote goals of responsible governance in Egypt than my lawyer would be justified in appropriating funds that I gave to his care by the secure knowledge that I will otherwise waste them on a stupid investment. Having used its resources to insure that Egyptians have the government that the United States wants regardless of whether this regime suits their wishes, the United States must, within the limits posed by values of self-reliance, insure that the situation of Egyptians comes as close to the outcome of responsible government as circumstances allow.

The expertise, resources and entrepreneurship of the Egyptian people are, presumably, capable of sustaining prosperity beyond basic needs, under responsible governance. So the duty to promote a simulacrum of life under a responsible Egyptian government has this broader reach. The reasons for restriction to basic needs in the case of structural adjustment do not apply. Sponsorship of outright coercion, not manipulation of basic needs, is the vehicle for thwarting Egyptians' aspirations to autonomy. (Reduced though it was by Iraq expenditures, U.S. military aid to Egypt in 2005 amounted to more than half of Egypt's huge military budget, sustaining armed forces that comprise 3.5% of the labor force of a country at peace with all of its neighbors. Of total U.S. aid 86% was military.[4]) Rather than just steering development policies, the United States props up a regime exercising the full range of political prerogatives, with a pervasive impact on Egyptian life and culture. So it cannot appeal to the limited scope of its intrusion.

Nonetheless, the United States would not be guided by the same goals for Egyptians as for Americans, in living up to its responsibilities as patron. What a responsible Egyptian government would do would still be limited by Egyptian resources. Of course, those limitations themselves have a history, including Britain's brutal imposition of a parasitic protectorate in the late nineteenth century. But U.S. citizens today can refuse to take responsibility for burdens due to past empires. The burdens of the current American empire are another matter.

## Imperial Repair

The shaping of a course of development and support for a regime are, broadly speaking, constructive activities. However, empire also involves destruction. American imperial destruction is an extremely powerful source of unmet responsibilities.

For more than fifty years, under every presidential administration, seeking to protect or extend American influence in developing countries, the United States government has directly engaged in, intentionally prompted or crucially sustained processes of devastating destruction, claiming many innocent victims, without the consent of the people as a whole in the affected territories. This might be the start of an indictment of the United States for engaging in unjustified destruction, an indictment which will be a central topic in the next chapter. However, a verdict on that charge is not essential for establishing an important moral consequence: even if its deployment of destructive power has been justified, the United States has a duty of aid reflecting the scale of the damage.

If a political authority has a practice of using violence in ways that devastate people who are not engaged in an unjust attack, it owes a justification for this practice to the innocents it puts in grave jeopardy. An adequate justification must reconcile the practice with respect for those who are endangered. Otherwise, those who are put in jeopardy by the practice may be rational to submit, but this will be nothing more than rational acquiescence in unjust disregard, like the acquiescence of powerless minorities resigned to unjust neglect by their compatriots.

The total practice involving violence is what must be justified, and violence without due repair may be unacceptable even if the violence is not unacceptable in itself. If the United States government had to use heavy artillery and thousand pound bombs to root out bandit gangs entrenched in small towns in Wyoming, the devastated townspeople would be owed help in rebuilding, even if the bombardments were a justifiable last resort. Perhaps I am justified in unilaterally deciding to flood my neighbor's field to stop an advancing forest fire, even though this measure endangers his house and his family: there is a much graver risk that the fire will consume my family and there is no time to consult him. Still, I owe him a serious effort to repair or compensate for damage from my flood. Without the commitment to repair or compensate, I do not properly value the capacity for choice of the person whose life I may change without his having any choice in the matter.

Like my response to the threat of fire, the American exercise of destructive power in developing countries has not reflected informed, morally authoritative consent of those affected. To respect the capacity for choice of those they endanger, Americans must support a commitment, on the part of their government, to repair or compensate for the damage their government inflicts. At least when a government has the abundant resources of the United States, the refusal to make good for harm inflicted on innocent, unconsenting victims would express a failure to appreciate the equal value of their lives.

Because it is backward looking, the duty to make amends for violent intrusion has to be further specified by considering the moral impact of the passage of time. Initially, when a government has incurred a liability to make good for damage, its citizenry have a responsibility to pay the moral debt, as part of their duty to use their political power justly. But the initial injustice of a failure to make good can fade and finally disappear over time, cancelling the moral debt. Although the people of Spain regard the monarchy of Ferdinand and Isabella as having been the government of their country, they are not under an obligation to compensate contemporary Jews or Muslims for the unjust expulsion of their families in 1492. A moral code in which political debts of justice endured as long as polities endure would eventually enslave people to choices in the distant past over which they had no control. It would also base current claims for compensation on tenuous speculations concerning the current burdens of injuries in the distant past, injuries that have often shaped proud legacies and become part of secure and valuable cultural identities.

On the other hand, it seems wrong to let someone escape moral obligations simply by postponing fulfillment long enough. At least if an appropriate complaint has been lodged—as it is, loudly and bitterly, in the political cases that concern us—stalling seems to increase irresponsibility, not end it.

Moreover, the proviso that the duty to repair fades away over time threatens to create a perverse incentive to negligence by assuring the reckless that the case for remedy will eventually go stale. Finally, if the destruction is part of a continuing practice, considerations of trust provide reasons not to let duties of repair fade quickly. A practice of foreign policy is wrong if it makes a country untrustworthy. Those who have reason to believe that a foreign power will tell them, "Let's let bygones be bygones," when it has not lived up to its responsibilities have reason not to trust the power.[5]

A moral statute of limitations of about two generations on the transnational duty of repair seems a reasonable accommodation of both sorts of concerns, the worries about premature dismissal and the concern not to be mired in the past. In important international agreements with one another, citizenries hope to shape a shared sphere of conduct a generation or two into the future. A desire to shape conduct even further into the future would strain the limits of foresight and exceed the generational limit of the active concern that people may presuppose in one another, namely, concern for one's own and the next generation. To be worthy of trust in a commitment extending this far into the future, a citizenry must have an ongoing commitment to make good on responsibilities that far into the past, one that will not be exhausted before the future limit is reached.

In addition, the two-generation rule tends to give standing to complaints without expressing a poisonous attachment to victimhood. In insisting on compensation for what one's parents suffered one acts as the custodian of their just grievances, asserting a healthy identification with them. But in the next generation, if there has been no further, ongoing injustice, continued complaint begins to express an identity as a victim. Seizing on speculations about how much better off one would have been threatens to become more important than seeking recognition of what one has accomplished.

Finally, on the perpetrators' side of injury, the thought that civic responsibility for negligence will disappear over the course of a generation is a strong incentive for stalling and weakens concern to prevent harm by one's government. But not many people would be similarly moved by the thought that two generations of neglect will eventually wash out the stain. People are rarely motivated by such distant chances of relief.

It might be thought that this norm is too lax. Legal statutes of limitation, after all, respond to the gravity of crimes and, in the case of the worst—above all, murder—impose no limits on prosecution. However, reasoning about temporal limits to the legal prosecution of persons is governed by different considerations from reasoning about the temporal limits of citizens' moral responsibilities for past harms inflicted by their political society.

The legal limits keep the authorities from being over-burdened and make it easier for people to become nonfurtive active participants in society if they abstain from further crimes long enough. These considerations are more compelling the less serious the past crime. While they can justify temporal limits to legal liability, they do not resolve questions of moral responsibility and moral debt. One normally respects another person's agency by continuing to hold him morally responsible for harms for which he was once responsible. Occasionally, people undergo a wholesale transformation of personality that brings into question the presupposition of continuing moral accountability. But this is too uncommon and too hard to securely ascertain to be a basis for legal immunity. "He is not really the same person" is a rare, troubling reason to reduce punishment, which does not figure in the rationale for the basic norms of legal liability.

In contrast, in judging citizens' current responsibility to make good on harms by their country's government well before their birth, the central, uncontroversial fact is personal non-participation in inflicting the relevant harms. People have, nonetheless, responsibilities as citizens, as current joint representatives of the political society that once committed the harms. In this representative role, they should certainly acknowledge grave harms inflicted, no matter how long ago. But the question at hand is whether they are obliged to take on a potentially burdensome responsibility to make good past damage. This political responsibility of collectives ought to be determined by considering the prerequisites for mutually respectful interactions among citizenries now, the inquiry which, I have argued, makes something like a two generation cut-off appropriate.

In this collective political responsibility, as in individual legal liability, the gravity of harms is a relevant consideration. One doesn't want delving into relatively minor past harms, of the sort that are bound to occur in the absence of a just world government, to make bickering the hallmark of international relations. In both realms, then, there ought to be recognition of duties to make amends that extend farther back the more serious the past wrong. But the further claim of unending responsibility for grave collective wrongs would make too much of this resemblance. The basic presupposition that individuals are morally responsible for their earlier wrongs whenever committed is not paralleled by a basic principle that a political society is responsible for its earlier wrongs whenever committed. In the collective realm, moral integrity is not denied when all liability for burdensome amends, even for the gravest wrongs, is allowed to fade entirely.

Can an agent make good damage that includes death, injury and illness through uninvited intrusion? In a very real and poignant sense, this is impossible.

One cannot bring back the dead or make wrecked lives as good as they would have been. Still, having initiated, sponsored or intentionally stirred up destruction in a country without the invitation of its people as a whole, the United States can make amends to that people, even if it cannot raise the dead. It can use its vast resources to effect an improvement of wellbeing among that people as substantial as the harm that was caused, giving priority to feasible restoration of what was destroyed.

The narratives that follow are a partial accounting of this debt, in far-flung regions of the developing world. They establish a vast duty to make good on harm that has been inflicted well within the moral statute of limitations I have defended (in fact, no further back in time than the lives of many living Americans). They are also a first step in the indictment for vast injustice in lethal violence that I will complete in the next chapter. Finally, because this destructive conduct constitutes an ongoing practice of widespread, deep intrusion by one government into the lives of people in the territory of other governments, it adds a great deal to a duty of trusteeship that has been growing in the course of this book.

Those who exercise exclusive ultimate control over a territory acquire a corresponding duty of trusteeship to serve as the ultimate care-givers for what deserves and requires care in the territory. In the assignment of responsibilities toward compatriots in Chapter 2, this connection between control and care was the most important basis for the duty to provide for helpless compatriots. In that context, it helped to explain the conviction that the mere existence of severely disabled people beyond the borders did not create the same duty of care as citizens must show to the severely disabled within the borders.

The imperial destruction that I am about to narrate is the most dramatically intrusive of the ways in which ultimate exclusive control by the local government is a fiction in most developing countries, over the long run and the full range of vital issues. Structural adjustment, the determination of governance by propping up client regimes, and the shaping of terms of participation in the world economy by threat influence are some others, previously described. This is not at all to say that these governments are powerless. Indeed, for many purposes, it is better for their leaders to act as if these governments exercised exclusive ultimate control, avoiding temptations to exchange demanding responsibilities for anti-imperialist complaints. But, by the same token, citizens of developed countries will evade responsibilities if they do not recognize the moral implications of shared control. A full account of which governments *together* ultimately exclusively control the terms of life in a developing country will generally include the governments of major developed countries and, above all, the United States.

The sharing of this control entails the sharing of the duty to take care—always with due regard for virtues of self-reliance but also with due regard for limited internal capacities to self-reliantly take care, for the shares of outside agents in collective control, and for the outside agents' resources. What follows is an enormous breach, through destruction, in local control. Over and above its specific impact on amends, it adds to a duty of transnational trusteeship that is the moral fate of Americans so long as the American empire endures.

## Histories of Destruction

The Persian Gulf region since the mid-twentieth century provides a striking initial illustration of how devastating, continuous and bipartisan the U.S. resort to destructive power has been. It is also an epitome of how diverse these uses of destructive power are and what a small fraction are recollected in respectable American political discourse at any given time.

In 1953, the United States organized a coup in Iran that overthrew a democratically elected, constitutionalist and secular nationalist regime, which, with pervasive popular support, had embarked on nationalization of the oil industry. The coup invested dictatorial power in Reza Pahlevi, who reorganized the oil industry on terms favorable to the United States, and used direct U.S. aid (over $1 billion in the decade following the coup[6]) and arms purchased in the United States (amounting to $9 billion from 1965 on, nearly half in the two years' overlap with the Carter administration[7]) to sustain control requiring brutal repression. In 1975, Amnesty International condemned this regime for "a history of torture beyond belief," noting that reports of the current number of political prisoners ranged upward from 25,000.[8] The main agency of this repression, the SAVAK, had been established in the late 1950s, after consultation with U.S. officials, largely through training by a CIA team.[9]

In 1972, the United States initiated a project in collaboration with Pahlevi, which, as Kissinger later put it, aimed to "keep Iraq occupied by supporting the Kurdish rebellion within Iraq."[10] By 1975, the rebellion was so far advanced that it threatened to succeed in establishing Kurdish autonomy that no local power in the region wanted. The United States cut off support, guaranteeing defeat of the insurgency it had stoked, an insurgency that resulted in about 20,000 deaths and the displacement of as many as 250,000 Kurds.[11]

Starting in 1980, U.S. efforts to prevent a decisive victory of either side in the Iraq–Iran War included the sharing of "deliberately distorted or inaccurate intelligence data . . . to prevent either Iraq or Iran from prevailing," according to a 1987 *New York Times* report.[12] Half a million died in that prolonged war, eight years of agony that exceeded the time-span of any other conventional war in the twentieth century. When the numerical superiority of Iran and a second Kurdish insurgency threatened to turn the tide, the United States facilitated Saddam Hussein's resort to weapons of mass destruction. As the *Washington Post* reported, over ten years later, "The administrations of Ronald Reagan and George H.W. Bush authorized the sale to Iraq of numerous items that had both military and civilian applications, including poisonous chemicals and deadly biological viruses, such as anthrax and bubonic plague"; for example, $1.5 million worth of chemicals useful for poison gas or pesticides were sold by Dow Chemical, with Import–Export Bank approval, in December 1988, in the midst of reports of Iraqi poison gas attacks on Kurds.[13]

In 1990, in a National Security Council meeting right after Saddam's invasion of Kuwait, there was much support for a strategy of public denunciation, diplomatic pressure and economic sanctions. At a second meeting the next day, the administration decided, instead, on readiness to force Iraq out by military means, to prevent Saddam's being (as the initial briefing put it) "in an inequitable position, since he would control the second- and third-largest proven oil reserves with the fourth-largest army in the world."[14] Five months later, when Saddam offered a basis for negotiation that held great promise of avoiding war through negotiated withdrawal, Secretary of State Baker and Armed Forces Chief of Staff Powell took this to be an adequate ending, but, according to Bob Woodward's reconstruction of the crucial exchange, Bush and National Security Advisor Scowcroft would not accept an outcome preserving Iraq's regional power. "Looking squarely at his advisers [Powell and Baker], the president said plainly, 'We have to have a war.' His words hung in the air as heavily as any he had ever spoken."[15]

In that war, precision-guided weapons destroyed the power stations on which refrigeration, water supply and sewage treatment depend and bombs destroyed the main Baghdad sewage treatment plant.[16] Planners of these attacks explained to a *Washington Post* reporter that they were a deliberate effort to strike "against 'all those things that allow a nation to sustain itself' . . . to let people know, 'Get rid of this guy and we'll be more than happy to assist in rebuilding.'"[17] Toward the end of this war, President Bush repeatedly appealed to "the Iraqi military and the Iraqi people to take matters into their own hands—to force Saddam Hussein the dictator to step aside."[18] But when Saddam's defeat was followed by a popular uprising rather than the desired military coup, the United States abandoned tens of thousands of rebellious Iraqis to a bloodbath for fear that they were too sympathetic to Iran or apt to provoke Turkey through excessive Kurdish independence. In the south, Iraqi helicopters organized the carnage with American aircraft flying above them, as U.S. forces prevented rebels from seizing Iraqi arms and ammunition stores.[19] The most extensive U.S. assessment of the human costs of the war to Iraqis, by a demographer at the U.S Census Bureau who was forced out after a leak of her report, estimated that the war, the suppression of the uprising at its end and the first year of suffering from destruction and economic sanctions resulted in the deaths of 158,000 Iraqis, of whom 40,000 were soldiers killed in combat and 32,000 were children.[20]

The subsequent relay from a Republican to a Democratic administration was flawless. Because of vigorous defense of sanctions on imports by the Clinton administration, which made it impossible to restore sanitation and health care in Iraq, the sanctions ultimately led to 100,000 or more excess deaths among Iraqi children under five.[21] After the next transition between the two political parties, an invasion and occupation, mobilizing overwhelming firepower to reduce American casualties, added to the toll. About 5,000 Iraqi soldiers were killed in the invasion.[22] Reports of civilian deaths during the invasion in major news sources added about 6,000.[23] Estimated through a careful application of standard epidemiological techniques in 2006, there were about half a million excess Iraqi deaths in the first forty months after the invasion, an assessment highly compatible with other surveys and tabulations.[24]

Once Saddam Hussein was overthrown, the obligation to make good damage to unwilling innocent victims of its destructive choices would have engaged the United States in prompt massive aid to Iraq and the quick conveyance of genuine independence regardless of whether subsequent Iraqi policies in trade, investment, ownership, oil and regional alignments would serve U.S. interests. An American government unwilling to do so would certainly have merited fear but would not have been worthy of trust. This was not the sequel to U.S. victory.

Extremely deadly, long-drawn-out destruction in bipartisan pursuit of American power, without commensurate projects of repair or compensation, has been the fate of every other region in the developing world. In Afghanistan, Zbigniew Brzezinski told an interviewer, "secret aid to the opponents of the pro-Soviet regime in Kabul" was approved by Jimmy Carter in light of Brzezinski's opinion that "this aid was going to induce a Soviet military intervention." "That secret operation," he boasted, "was an excellent idea. It had the effect of drawing the Russians into the Afghan trap and you want me to regret it?"[25] The death toll from that trap was over a million, mostly Afghan civilians. After the Soviet withdrawal, the United States continued funneling arms and subsidies through Pakistan to rigidly Islamicist warlords, hoping to restrict the influence of Iran. These warlords subjected the country to a reign of lawless terror in which, for example, 25,000 people, mostly civilians, died in factional fighting over control of Kabul in 1994.[26] In 2001, the United States combined its overwhelming firepower with the troops of a coalition of brutal and fanatic warlords to drive out the Taliban. Of the two extensive analyses of reports of civilian deaths from the first two months of U.S. bombing in Afghanistan, one estimates the toll at over three thousand,[27] the other at 1,000 to 1,300, a difference largely due to the severe numerical deflation of reported death tolls in the latter study.[28]

Even if the Cold War, containment of Iran and the rooting out of al-Qaida and the Taliban were all just causes for this violence, they were causes to which few innocent Afghan victims of the consequent devastation had committed their lives. The damage has not remotely been made good. Indeed, after the 2001 invasion, rather than repairing the damage of these decades of violence in its causes, the United States left most of Afghanistan to the brutal, fanatic warlords, disastrously compromised the perceived neutrality of long-established, effective nongovernmental agencies,[29] and provided little aid until, after two years, there was an urgent need to counter a resurgence of the Taliban.[30] In the 2007 *Afghanistan Human Development Report*, part of a global series sponsored by the United Nations Development Programme, a collaboration of Afghan, UNDP and other international researchers produced estimates for Afghanistan of the two main indices of over-all national wellbeing issued by the United Nations. The Human Development Index they assigned to Afghanistan in 2007 ranked it behind all but four countries (Burkina Faso, Mali, Sierra Leone and Niger) of the 177 with indices assigned by the UNDP itself, with a rating a third less than the next worst nearby country (Pakistan). Afghanistan's Human Poverty Index ranked even worse. Both estimates for 2007 were worse than estimates for 2004.[31]

In Central America, four decades of U.S.-inaugurated military rule in Guatemala led to the deaths of over 200,000 in civil violence, the vast majority of them noncombatant Mayan villagers killed by the Guatemalan military.[32] In recent years, U.S. development aid to Guatemala has generally been about one-quarter of the bilateral total, sometimes less than Japan's or the largest European donor's (for example less than Spain's and only slightly more than Japan's in 2005).[33] In Nicaragua, a decade of U.S. opposition to the Sandinista regime included sponsorship of an insurgency that led to about 30,000 deaths, the mining of Nicaraguan harbors, a total U.S. trade embargo, and the blocking of loans from the World Bank and the Inter-American Development Bank.[34] As this exercise of destructive power intensified, economic growth in the first four years of the regime—at a much faster pace than Central America's as a whole—was followed by the devastation of an already poor country.[35] Nicaragua is now the second poorest country (after Haiti) in the Western hemisphere, with an average income less than several sub-Saharan countries'. Its ratio of foreign aid to Gross National Income has been as high as 58% (in 1996). In recent years, the United States has usually contributed less than a fifth of total bilateral development assistance to Nicaragua. Indeed, in 2004, the U.S. contributed 8%, a quarter of the German contribution.[36]

In Indonesia, in late 1965 and early 1966, the United States vigorously promoted an operation, by the generals who eventually displaced the Sukarno regime, which the U.S. Ambassador in Jakarta celebrated for "moving relentlessly to exterminate PKI [the Indonesian Communist Party, the largest party in Indonesia] as far as it is possible to do so."[37] The United States aided the extermination with funds, equipment, and information, urging perseverance and making effective promises of material and political support for pressing on when inclinations to peace or national unity threatened to slacken the pace of the killing.[38] In six months, the anti-communist massacres killed about half a million people, while about 750,000 were imprisoned, many to be held in appalling prison camps for the rest of their lives.[39]

In Vietnam, the deployment of vastly destructive American airpower killed a large proportion of the 400,000 or more civilian war dead,[40] and devastated the whole industrial capacity of the North, civilian as well as military. The main U.S. contribution to Vietnamese reconstruction was vigorous opposition to post-war World Bank loans, continuing until 1980.[41] In 2003, U.S. aid to Vietnam amounted to 4 cents per Vietnamese, 4% of total bilateral aid, declining to 3% in 2006.[42] This level was a sharp increase above the previous norm.

## A New African Paradigm

The scramble for Africa inaugurated the climax of destruction in the last great age of literal empire. Weak indigenous governments, attractive natural resources and competitive anxieties among rival powers led to decades of conquest, repression and forcible appropriation, in which the Congo Free State was the paradigm of horrors. More recently in Africa, the United States has deployed resources for destruction to exercise domineering influence in response to the same triad of weakness, resources and competition. The favored process, the use of client regimes, has been crass and flagrant, without much pretence of respect for the will of people whose lives are at stake. The results have been brutally violent, on a wide scale, for decades. So Africa continues to provide exemplary narratives of the wages of empire. I will conclude this survey of destruction and intrusion with two lurid African narratives, from the Congo and Somalia, encompassing many lives and deaths, starting in the middle of the last century and extending through the start of this.

At the dawn of Congolese independence, declared on June 30, 1960, two pivotal facts were clear to all. First, the only political leader with a broad national following, a popularly based national party and the capacity and desire to motivate national support on a basis other than graft was Patrice Lumumba. Indeed, the Belgian Resident Minister reported that as independence approached the representatives of Western powers led him to understand "that 'there was no other card to play than the Lumumba card.' . . . The U.S. and British representatives . . . saw in M. Lumumba a man of authority essential to the governance of the Congo."[43]

The other great fact was the importance of mineral wealth mainly extracted in Katanga province, i.e., its importance both to external powers and to the economic viability of the new government. In 1956, Chester Bowles—who was to lead the planning of policy toward developing countries as Under Secretary of State at the start of the Kennedy administration—wrote: "If we should be denied access to the raw materials of Asia, we should be seriously handicapped, but we could still maintain our economic growth. But if we were also cut off from the apparently limitless natural resources of Africa, we would face formidable obstacles . . . within a decade . . . If . . . the tricky balance of forces in the Congo . . . [should] break down, our position in the nuclear jet age could be mortally threatened. . . . [P]ractical American policy . . . [must] extend beyond the arrival of the next shipload of cobalt, columbite or pitchblende . . . "[44] In 1959, the year before Congolese independence, the Congo produced 9% of the "Free World"'s copper, 69% of its industrial diamonds, 7% of its tin, and 49% of its cobalt (used, for example, in heat-resistant alloys for jet engines and gas turbines).[45] Three-quarters of Congolese mineral production was located in Katanga, a province providing half of the country's tax revenues and most of its foreign exchange.[46] This wealth was controlled by Belgian holding companies—in which the Belgian government had a financial stake that it eagerly transferred to Belgian investors as independence approached, while transferring an inflated colonial public debt to the new government.[47]

When the two great facts of Lumumba's nationalist leadership and Katanga's wealth collided, the United States replaced the Lumumba card. In Eisenhower's view "the determination of the peoples [of Africa] for self-rule, their own flag and their own vote in the United Nations resembled a torrent overrunning everything in its path, including, frequently, the best interests of those concerned."[48] In particular, in his assessment, Congolese independence "went badly from the start" when Lumumba showed himself to be "radical and unstable" at the ceremonies marking independence: "with Belgian King Baudouin present . . . Lumumba took the occasion to excoriate Belgium for afflicting 'atrocious sufferings' on the Congolese, although he promised that the Congo would remain on friendly terms with Belgium."[49] What quickly established insufficient reliability to the U.S. President was a measured expression of national dignity and independence in response to abysmal racist strutting by the Belgian king, beginning with his celebration of the owner of the Congo Free State whose barbaric depredations had caused the death of 8 million or more Congolese: "The independence of the Congo concludes the work conceived by the genius of King Leopold II, conducted by Him with tenacious courage and continued with perseverance by Belgium. . . . [King Leopold] presented himself to you not as conquerer but as civilizer." After the royal speech, full of further praise of Belgian colonizers as "the pioneers of African emancipation," Lumumba's acknowledgment of sovereignty began, "Men and women of the Congo, fighters for the independence that has been won today," continued in a narrative of past suffering and humiliation, at once noble, touching and precise, and went on, without bitterness, to proclaim tasks of independence, unity and prosperity, ending with an invitation to all Congolese citizens to "the hard work of creating a prosperous national economy which consecrates our economic independence."[50]

Two weeks later, on July 14, after a Kantagan politician aligned with Belgian mining interests declared the independence of the province, backed by Belgian troops, Lumumba called for Western and U.N. support for immediate Belgian military withdrawal, and noted that he might eventually call on the Soviets for aid, if necessary, as a last resort. His evident lack of full commitment to Western tutelage, confirmed by occasional similar gestures, which evoked no materially significant Soviet response, sealed his fate.

On July 19, the U.S. Ambassador to Belgium replied to a State Department inquiry with the cabled advice, "LUMUMBA GOVERNMENT THREATENS OUR VITAL INTERESTS IN CONGO . . . WE MUST FIND OR DEVELOP ANOTHER HORSE TO BACK."[51] On August 1, the Secretary of State cabled the Ambassador, "EVIDENCE EXISTS THAT HE [Lumumba] WILL NOT RPT [i.e., repeat] NOT PROVE SATISFACTORY. US WILL THEREFORE CONTINUE SEARCH FOR MORE TRUSTWORTHY ELEMENTS IN CONGO . . . "[52] According to the minutes of the National Security Council meeting of August 18, "the President stated that . . . we were talking of one man forcing us out of the Congo; of Lumumba supported by the Soviets." An NSC staff member present at the meeting subsequently recalled, in testimony to the Senate Intelligence Committee, "President Eisenhower said something . . . that came across to me as an order for the assassination of Lumumba."[53]

On August 26, the Director of the CIA cabled to the CIA station chief in Leopoldville that Lumumba's "removal must be an urgent and prime objective and under existing conditions this should be a high priority of our covert action."[54] According to the station chief's testimony to the Senate Intelligence Committee, a CIA scientist visited him in late September, to convey a poison for use in Lumumba's food or toothpaste, which would leave "normal traces found in people that die of certain diseases."[55] The station chief preferred other methods, responding to an October cable offering further assistance with a request for a "HIGH POWERED FOREIGN MAKE RIFLE WITH TELESCOPIC SIGHT AND SILENCER," to be sent by diplomatic pouch. "HUNTING GOOD HERE WHEN LIGHTS RIGHT."[56] As it happened, these measures were unnecessary. Lumumba was surrounded by the forces of Joseph Mobutu, the horse the United States decided to back, escaped, was captured by those forces and was flown to his worst enemy, the leader of secessionist Katanga, who had him killed and dissolved in acid by Belgian military and police officers, after a day's torture, on January 19. Learning of the death flight, the CIA station chief cabled his Katangan base chief, "THANKS FOR PATRICE. IF WE HAD KNOWN HE WAS COMING WE WOULD HAVE BAKED A SNAKE" (after a ditty of those times, "If I knew you were coming I'd have baked a cake").[57]

The coming to power of Joseph Mobutu as the Congolese guarantor of U.S. interests led to the eventual reintegration of Katanga, under the aegis of U.N. forces. The establishment of this guarantee began with what U.N. liaison officers reported as visits to Mobutu, the new head of the Congolese army, by Western military attachés carrying cash in "bulging brief-cases containing thick brown paper packets which they obligingly deposited on his table."[58] Its consolidation included CIA air and mercenary support against Lumumbist insurgents,[59] and army training missions from the U.S., Belgium, Israel and Italy (but not black African countries—"*Je ne veux pas ces nègres*," Mobutu is said to have replied, when the American embassy offered Senegalese trainers[60]). Indeed, the *New York Times* subsequently described Mobutu, along with his major allies, as "found" by the CIA, someone whose "eventual emergence as President of the country . . . proved a tribute to the Americans' judgment and tactics," tactics initially implemented with "money and shiny American automobiles furnished through the logistic wizardry of Langley [Virginia, the hometown of the agency]," later requiring "hastily supplied arms and planes, as well as dollars and cars."[61]

On May 19, 1963, four months after the Katanga secession ended, President Kennedy invited his visitor, General Mobutu, to a photograph session in the

White House Rose Garden, noting, "General, if it hadn't been for you, the whole thing would have collapsed and the Communists would have taken over." Mobutu graciously replied, "I do what I am able to do."[62] Once Mobutu was officially established as president, U.S. aid and multilateral loans, sometimes prompted by vast doomed construction projects, flowed into his regime. From 1970 through 1994, loans and aid to the regime by the World Bank, the IMF, and bilateral donors, mostly the United States, amounted to over $8.5 billion, continuing despite a 1978 IMF report that 40 percent of the government's revenues were being diverted to the bank accounts of the ruling elite.[63]

The sponsorship of a band of armed thieves was a cheap way for the United States to dominate a vast, strategic, naturally rich country, but the cost to the people of the Congo was devastating. At the start of the twenty-first century, the World Bank tabulated national trends in economic development from 1965, the year in which Mobutu's presidency was proclaimed, through 1999, two years after Mobutu's overthrow. In this period, the average annual change in per capita Gross Domestic Production in the Congo was minus 2.4% (compared to the troubling stagnation of minus 0.2% in sub-Saharan Africa as a whole).[64] At independence, the Congo had by far the largest wage-labor force in sub-Saharan Africa, about 40% of the adult male population.[65] Twenty years later, the average real wage had fallen by 90%.[66] In sub-Saharan Africa, where one in seven people dies before the age of five, measles was, during Mobutu's rule, the leading cause of death in childhood. At the end of Mobutu's reign, the immunization rate for measles in the Congo was the lowest in the world, one-fourth of the sub-Saharan average.[67]

The devastation wrought by sponsorship of Mobutu was by no means limited to the Congo. At U.S. urging and with U.S. aid, he joined the United States and South Africa in providing troops, weapons, refuge and funds in support of armed groups in Angola that challenged the MPLA regime.[68] When a Senate inquiry asked the director of the CIA to explain why the United States was supporting the warlord it favored, his explanation was, "Because the Soviets are backing the MPLA."[69] Half a million or more people died in that war, which lasted for over twenty years.[70]

The end of Mobutu in 1997 marked the start of even greater carnage, vastly increased by the extreme degradation of supports for life under his client regime and stoked by great powers' recourse to African client regimes, together with their tolerance of corporate exploitation. At the conclusion of the Rwandan genocide, France, the patron of the Hutu extremist regime, salvaged some of its threatened influence through an intervention that mainly served to protect the retreat of Hutu forces into the eastern Congo. The new Rwandan regime, allied with the United States, invaded to attack the Hutu camps, which combined genuine refugees and genocidal fighters. Then, with Laurent Kabila, a Katangan diamond smuggler and warlord in tow, as their appointed leader of a nominal Congolese rebellion, the Rwandan forces joined with forces of Uganda, which had become America's favorite African dictatorship, to easily overthrow the dying Mobutu's regime, a remnant so decrepit that it was useless to all foreign powers.[71]

In the twilight of the regime, a broad and coherent democracy movement had taken shape, based on articulate discussions in a politically engaged civil society, attached to a long-standing multiparty deliberative assembly, and centered on a national movement led by Étienne Tshisekedi. Given another choice between a prospect of Congolese leadership with independent popular support and the prospect of a client dependent on external aid fueling a network of graft, the United States responded in a familiar way. As the U.S. ambassador said to a *New York Times* reporter, in the usual language of gambling, "There is a growing consensus that we have to deal with Kabila. Tshisekedi is an obstacle, and we don't see him as a player anymore. I just don't see any reason why Kabila at this point should deal him into the game."[72] Assured of vitally needed support by the Clinton administration, Kabila began his presidency with an inaugural speech in which he declared, "Let's stop talking about democracy and elections."[73] Tshisekedi was put under house arrest, and then exiled to a remote village.[74]

A year later, Kabila decided that his Rwandan and Ugandan sponsors were exacting too great a reward in territorial control and natural resources. In the ensuing war, he inflamed anti-Tutsi sentiment, culminating in pogroms in the eastern Congo, and found new allies—mostly Zimbabwe and Angola, also Chad and the Central African Republic, French client regimes sustaining interests that France had once invested in the Rwandan Hutu regime.

The war in the resource-cursed eastern Congo was kept going for years by magnificent opportunities for theft, in which lucrative exports to foreign firms motivated and funded violent pillage of vast territories. The years of violent pillage included frequent massacres, widespread rape by armed forces with HIV rates far higher than the appalling Congolese norm, and repeated displacement, ruthless requisitioning, and forcible labor recruitment that wrecked the agricultural economy.[75] (In November 2002, for example, about one-fifth of the people of the eastern Congo suffered from acute malnutrition and over a million people who had fled their homes were currently displaced.[76]) In the first year of the Ugandan military presence, the re-export of gold taken from the Congo provided 12 percent of Ugandan export earnings.[77] In 2000–1, at the height of a boom in the price of coltan, a mineral used in cellphones and other electronic devices, the government of Rwanda, which contains no significant mineral resources, used control over coltan mining and sales in the eastern Congo to extract about $200 million a year from re-exports, equal to a tenth of Rwanda's Gross National Income.[78] The army of Zimbabwe became the dominant partner in the largest forest concession in the world, 125 square miles of hardwood, equal to the combined land area of the United Kingdom and the Republic of Ireland.[79] When a U.N. Panel of Experts presented a detailed report of how firms based in the United States and Europe had engaged in mineral extraction, trading and transportation that facilitated and inflamed the pillage, this excited some energy on the part of their governments, expended in criticizing the panel and insuring that the report had no significant impact. OECD panels in the United States and the United Kingdom declared themselves unwilling or unable to investigate the charges directed at major firms.[80]

Relying on a legacy of virtually nothing from the decades of Mobutu's U.S.-sponsored rule—no health system, bare traces of a transportation network, no state beyond cliques and armed bands organized for predation, only narrow ethnic networks of reliable affiliation—the people of the eastern Congo died by millions as incessant fighting, often for mineral plunder, cut off prospects of meager subsistence. By the time the warring governments accepted a peace accord in 2002, the war had been responsible for 3.3 million excess deaths, the vast majority from hunger and disease among civilians. Continued violence after the accords produced further hundreds of thousands of excess deaths, 600,000 just in the sixteen months beginning January 2003.[81]

In March 2005, while violence still blazed in the eastern Congo, leaders of the Group of Eight, the most important developed countries, held their annual meeting, convened at Gleneagles, Scotland, by Tony Blair. Bruised by an election in which his traditional electoral base showed deep disenchantment with his Iraq policy, Blair emphasized the plight of developing countries, above all sub-Saharan African countries. The conclusion of the Summit was marked by an unprecedented signing of the final communiqué by the participating political leaders and by Blair's description, as Summit host, of the significance of the program for Africa. "It is," Blair explained, "the definitive expression of our collective will to act in the face of poverty, death and conflict."[82] In their statement on Africa, the Group of Eight noted, "Peace is the first condition of successful development. We support Africa's efforts to build a stable and peaceful Africa."[83] The wisdom of their view of peace is reflected in Branko Milanovic's finding that the inferior average growth rate of the poorest developing countries as compared with other developing countries, from 1980 through 2002, can entirely be explained by greater frequency of war.[84] But

African peace and stability was about to be subordinated, again, to the interests of great powers, in an American initiative in Somalia that Pentagon officials would celebrate as a "relative success story."[85]

By 2006, the people of Somalia had suffered through fifteen years of anarchy in which murderous warlords and their armies competed in predation, with the capital, Mogadishu, the derelict focus of mayhem. Throughout these years of anarchy, death rates among Somali children were at a dreadful plateau much higher than the rest of the Horn of Africa, 225 per thousand dying before the age of five, in contrast to substantial declines in neighboring Ethiopia and Eritrea.[86]

In the face of this turmoil, the Union of Islamic Courts, a broad coalition of clan leaders, businessmen, and clerics, most moderate, some assertively Islamicist, successfully sought peace and order under Islamic law, culminating in the defeat of warlord militias in Mogadishu in June 2006.[87] Not surprisingly, Western reporters discovered that "the Islamist forces . . . seem to be very popular here, having defeated Mogadishu's warlords . . . to pacify one of the world's most murderous cities."[88] Somalis' appreciation of the new peace was accompanied by some disputes over local rigors in the application of Islamic law, leading to demonstrations and negotiations. A popularly rooted Islamic government, independent of the U.S., might have become established across a narrow sea from the Arabian peninsula and bordering Ethiopia, a U.S. ally with a population that is about half Muslim, kept in line by the largely Christian army of a regime centered on members of a small, Christian ethnic group. An Islamic Courts regime might have made it safer for perpetrators of terrorist bombings in the 1990s to remain at large, which the State Department said it feared. Or it might not have: there were unrequited efforts to conciliate the United States.[89] In any case, these terrorists had been at large for years.

As the Union of Islamic Courts spread through central and south Somalia, the United States invigorated civil disorder by distributing payments to its favored warlords, in order to reverse their dwindling fortunes.[90] Despite these efforts, by the end of November 2006, the military and political successes of the Courts had brought peace to much of the country, while the pro-U.S. regime only controlled one minor town near the Ethiopian border. This tiny foothold depended on the protection of 6,000 to 8,000 troops from Ethiopia, which had become the major U.S. client in the Horn of Africa.[91]

This mighty regional power was at the southern end of a chain of five countries anchored at the northeast by Jordan, guarding the global crossroads of the Middle East and vital oil reserves, and receiving three-quarters of U.S. foreign aid (a proportion rising to four-fifths if an Iraq link and Iraq reconstruction funds are added).[92] Abjectly poor, highly aid dependent, yet well-equipped for armed violence, Ethiopia provided an ideal test of the collective commitment declared at Gleneagles to support peace and stability in Africa.

In 2006, foreign aid amounted to 15% of Ethiopia's Gross National Income. With per capita Gross National Income of $630 at purchasing power parity (37% of the per capita GNI of sub-Saharan Africa as a whole), one in eight Ethiopians died before the age of five and health expenditures averaged about $6 per person. Military expenditures amounted to 22% of total government expenditures, 2.6% of GDP, and arms imports amounted to about a tenth of total manufactured imports.[93] While containment of an insurgency among ethnic Somalis and competition for regional power with Eritrea and Sudan provided reasons for Ethiopia to extend its armed might into Somalia, these reasons were as nothing compared with the need for the good will of the United States. For the U.S had become a vital sponsor of this ungainly combination of destitution, aid dependence and military commitment, through aid that mounted as evidence proliferated of the Ethiopian government's brutality in suppressing domestic opposition.[94] In 2004, 39% of bilateral development assistance came from the United States, with the next most generous contribution, 14%, from Britain.[95] In 2005, U.S. development assistance increased 55%, to a level six times its contribution in 2000, becoming 52% of the bilateral total.[96]

On December 4, 2006, General John Abizaid, chief of the U.S. Central Command, which extended through twenty-five countries from Sudan and Egypt through Pakistan and Kazakhstan, paid a visit to the Prime Minister of Ethiopia, "who had told American officials that he could cripple the Islamic forces 'in one or two weeks.'"[97] Far from asking for a reduction of the Ethiopian presence in Somalia, Abizaid responded positively to a request for the sharing of battlefield information based on U.S. satellites in case of an Ethiopian offensive.[98]

Two days later, the United States steered a resolution through the U.N. Security Council authorizing a military force of African states whose task would be to "protect members of the Transitional Federal Institutions and Government [the regime the U.S. supported] as well as their key infrastructure" and "maintain and monitor security in Baidoa [the one town they controlled]." An embargo on arms to Somalia was also to be lifted to admit arms "for the support of or use by" this force.[99] Within a week, the leader of the pro-U.S. regime declared that the "door to peace talks" was closed;[100] the leaders of the Islamic front organized wide, enthusiastic support for holy war against Ethiopian invasion;[101] and the Prime Minister of Ethiopia dismissed negotiations as "a ploy used to facilitate their [the Islamic front's] goal," while condemning reluctance to send in troops as "worse than fecklessness in the face of a challenge."[102]

With 15,000 to 20,000 troops now stationed in Somalia, Ethiopia launched its offensive on December 21.[103] Its well-trained soldiers, tanks, fighter planes and artillery killed over a thousand of the Islamic Courts' forces, mostly teenaged boys, in a series of triumphs leading to the taking of Mogadishu nine days later.[104] In addition to supplying battlefield intelligence, the United States pursued fleeing Islamic forces with airborne gunships and patrolled the Red Sea to cut off access to Yemen,[105] while the State Department endorsed the invasion as an expression of "legitimate security concerns."[106]

Almost immediately after this triumph, extortionate gunmen roamed the streets of Mogadishu again and set up checkpoints.[107] Tens of thousands fled their homes throughout the country, and cholera epidemics broke out due to displacement, flooding, and restricted access of medical personnel.[108] Then, in the face of a mounting anti-Ethiopian insurgency, Ethiopia launched relentless assaults on hostile areas of Mogadishu. From late March to late April over 1,400 were killed, mostly civilians.[109] Out of a population of a million, about 400,000 fled.[110] The displaced, according to a U.N. report, were "subject to looting, assault and rape. Many were forced to live in crowded camps where there was a lack of water, food, sanitation, basic health services and shelter."[111] Housing, for example, was often an inadequate patch of sheeting thrown over sticks, open to rain, and to snakes and hyenas that roamed the camps at night.[112] Reviewing the first four months after the overthrow of the Islamic Courts regime, a report published by the Royal Institute of International Affairs (London) noted that "this experience dramatically underlines the benefits of the brief period of 'Islamist' authority in southern Somalia which already begins to seem like a 'Golden Age.' "[113]

Despite the rigors of displacement, hundreds of thousands more subsequently fled their homes in response to continued fighting, in which over six thousand civilians were estimated to have been killed in the first year after the defeat of the Islamic Courts.[114] For example, nearly 200,000 fled Mogdishu in two weeks of fighting in mid-November 2007. By late November, in a country of about 8 million, over a million people were displaced.[115] Entire neighborhoods in the capital were emptied. Burdened by refugees and fighting as well as the usual environmental challenges, fertile rural regions suffered from malnutrition rates as high as 19% (compared to the standard food emergency threshold of 15% and 13% in the contemporary turmoil of Darfur).[116] A year later, around the second anniversary of the Ethiopian invasion, malnutrition had become even worse in Somalia, which had the highest levels in the world, with up to 300,000 children acutely malnourished in 2008.[117] Most of the country had come under the sway of a harshly repressive faction of the Islamic Courts coalition, in an insurgency that left the Ethiopian-backed regime the effective government of a few city blocks of Mogadishu along with its initial foothold in a small border town. The expert prognosis was that Somalia would be consumed for years to come by fighting among clans and factions, with much external support from governments competing for regional power.[118]

A week after the conquest of Mogadishu by Ethiopian forces, Jendayi Frazer, the U.S. Assistant Secretary of State for Africa, hoped to visit Somalia, but, for security reasons, had to be content with a meeting in Nairobi, Kenya (which was, in any case, the de facto seat of the U.S. supported government). She complimented the Somali people for "pushing uphill . . . to try to overcome their history." She explained that Somalia "is important to the United States because of its strategic location in the Horn of Africa where the Red Sea enters into the Indian Ocean," as well as on the account of the need to deny safe haven to terrorists. "Some people would like the United States to lead [in Somalia]," Frazer said. "I would prefer that we lead from behind."[119]

# 7

# Imperial Excess

So far, the moral assessment of the American empire has evaded two central questions: To what extent is its violence justifiable? How deeply rooted in enduring tendencies are the wrongs of empire? In this chapter, I will argue for condemnation on both counts: the normal interactions of American elites and the American electorate are bound to give rise to vast and morally unjustified harms, including vast harms of unjustified violence, so long as the American empire endures.

Agreement with this accusation should have a large impact on the moral outlook of a citizen of the United States. Her duty as a citizen is to make choices that promote justice on the part of her government. Unjust deadly violence on a large scale is the gravest injustice that a government can impose on people in another country. So, given the tendency toward unjust violence, opposition to initiatives that inflict such suffering ought to be her foremost concern. Admonitions to U.S. citizens that their government ought to do more to help the global poor risk distraction from the main issue, if they are not accompanied by fervent warnings that their government is doing too much by way of violent harm.

The truth of the indictment would also affect the kinds of activity through which an American citizen should discharge her political responsibilities. In what might be called the process of institutional governance in a constitutional democracy, a few have or strive for political authority or provide the strivers with influential advice or substantial support, and the electorate choose among options that emerge from this elite, responding to information from the major media within a framework of presuppositions that are entrenched in the public political culture and nurtured in public education. If the view of enduring tendencies which I will defend is right, institutional governance in the United States tends to be a prolific source of grave wrongs of violence and inequity inflicted on people in developing countries. To discharge her responsibility to promote justice on the part of her government, an American citizen should try to limit this immoral excess through initiatives originating outside of institutional governance, if this political endeavor is not especially costly to her and has some prospect of success. That there is such an option will be the argument of the last chapter, describing the promise of social movements, especially those that advance a community of outlook and affiliation that I will call "global social democracy." Thus, the description of deep tendencies to immoral excess in this chapter is the first part of an argument for a duty to devote attention, energy and time to the promotion of a social movement changing the public agenda and the strategic calculations to which political leaders respond.

## A Pattern of Excess

Previous chapters identified patterns of grave imperial injustice in shaping trade and development, meeting the greenhouse challenge and repairing the damage of imperial destruction. The narrative of destruction in the previous chapter described violent uses of American destructive power in many developing countries, resulting in the deaths of millions and leaving the lives of many millions more in shreds. But the question of the justice or injustice of this violence was postponed. It is time to consider whether these uses of destructive power had the powerful moral justifications that their foreseeable toll required.

When the United States sponsored the overthrow of popular, democratically chosen nationalists in Iran, Guatemala and the Congo, no informed person supposed that the people of those countries were being protected from domestic tyranny. Foreseeably, these exercises of destructive power inaugurated decades of violent oppression. Perhaps, opposition to Mossadegh, Arbenz and Lumumba that stopped short of their overthrow would have produced Soviet advances increasing tyranny worldwide. However, given the nationalism of those leaders, the sentiments of their peoples and the Soviets' severely limited capacity at the time to project their power, this was, at best, a speculative fear, insufficient to justify active American participation in installing and maintaining vicious client regimes. In any case, an alternative was available, namely, friendly relations with the nationalist regimes. As a consequence of their nationalist projects, firms based in the United States and its allies would have given up assets, plausibly regarded as unjustly obtained, with compensation that they would have found inadequate. These and other foreseeable losses of corporate wealth and income were not an adequate justification for the launching of those reigns of terror.

In Vietnam, the extension of the Hanoi regime to South Vietnam was accurately viewed as the triumph of a repressive government. But the Saigon regime was known to be both repressive and highly corrupt, and U.S. opposition to the elections prescribed by the Geneva Accords expressed an accurate estimate that the Hanoi regime was the most popular among major Vietnamese political forces. South Vietnam was one place to try to set up a bulwark against further Communist advances in Asia. But such astute anti-Communists as George Kennan, George Ball and Charles de Gaulle offered compelling arguments that this was unpromising terrain for such a project. The quick triumph of a nationalist, reasonably popular Vietnamese regime attached to an eclectic brand of Marxism-Leninism was virtually certain to lead to the victory of allied forces in Laos, and would have encouraged similar movements elsewhere. In response, accommodations of nationalist aspirations might have become the only way to reduce Soviet influence without inflicting vast violence. Avoiding the expense of those accommodations did not justify shedding oceans of blood.

Brzezinski's "excellent idea" of provoking a Soviet invasion of Afghanistan, followed by the launching of fanatic warlords against the Soviets and their client regime, produced hundreds of thousands of deaths and a post-Soviet reign of terror that made even the Taliban an improvement, in the eyes of many, perhaps most, Afghans.[1] The warlords were not an improvement on the pro-Soviet repressive modernizers that the U.S. sought to depose. Perhaps the Soviet intervention hastened the demise of the Soviet Union, or perhaps it prolonged the Soviet regime by strengthening the hand of its most authoritarian and aggressive factions. Speculation on the former prospect did not justify active U.S. participation in the devastation of a whole country and the killing of 14,000 Soviet troops, most of them conscripts.

The United States government caused the deaths of many hundreds of thousands by intentionally prolonging the Iraq–Iran War, decimating the Iraqi civilian infrastructure in the first Gulf War, insuring its further decay through the stringency of post-war sanctions, using massively destructive firepower in the overthrow of Saddam Hussein and imposing a prolonged occupation against the wishes of the majority of Iraqis.[2] These measures were not justifiable on grounds of national defense or as part of a larger struggle against Soviet tyranny. Neither were they justifiable on humanitarian grounds. Even in the case of the invasion to overthrow Saddam Hussein, there was never warranted confidence in the informed consent to the deadly operation of the vast majority of those who were to be saved from injustice or of likely benefit on balance to those affected whose interests had moral standing. Although largely justified by appeal to the threat of weapons of mass destruction, the invasion to overthrow Saddam was launched in the face of rich evidence that his arsenal of chemical and biological weapons was, at most, a tiny remnant meant for a last-ditch stand, despite the debunking of what little evidence there had been of significant progress toward nuclear weaponry, and in the midst of inspections that were confirming these assessments and could have laid the groundwork for reasonable security against a revived program of weapons of mass destruction.[3] The probable outcome of this invasion was not safety but danger: the invasion could be expected to quicken development of nuclear weaponry among regimes to which the U.S. was strongly opposed; it could also be expected to help recruitment to a world terrorist movement that would pay close attention to prospects of massive terrorism of global reach once the issue of Iraq was decided (as the same terrorist movement had before, when the end of armed jihad in Afghanistan generated al-Qaida).

Each of these deadly actions of the United States in the Persian Gulf region did weaken some local power independent of the United States in a strategic area. There was cause for concern on the part of the United States that strength and independence in Iraq and Iran might make oil supplies less steady or more expensive, slow economic growth, and lower the profits of oil firms. Avoidance of these changes (probably beneficent on balance, because of pressures toward fossil fuel conservation and lower greenhouse gas emissions) did not justify extremely active participation in this many deaths.

An extensive pattern has emerged of unjustified violent initiatives of the United States in developing countries, at least since the middle of the twentieth century, under the leadership of both political parties and all of their major factions. Discernment of underlying causes of this pattern might begin with inquiry into the decisionmaking that led to it.

## Imperial Decisionmaking

In the United States, as in all developed countries, the basic decisions in foreign policy are made by the elected leader of the national executive, aided and influenced by his appointed policy planners, with some need for acquiescence from the legislature. The pattern of violence suggests that decisionmaking at the highest level concerning the deployment of America's vast destructive power is guided by a lethal combination of interest and disinterest: goals of American world power are pursued in deliberations in which adverse consequences for foreigners, especially foreigners in developing countries, lack independent influence remotely matching their actual strength as moral reasons. The detailed evidence provided by memoirs, diaries, investigative reporting, interviews, covert tape recordings and internal documents confirms this assessment.

In the 2,899 closely printed pages of the published version of *The Pentagon Papers*, the detailed, deeply argued and contentious memoranda, records of deliberations, internal policy statements and rationales, and erudite narratives of decisionmaking only mention deaths of South Vietnamese as measures of success, in Vietcong body counts. The deaths of people in North Vietnam are only treated as reasons not to choose more lethal bombing options to the extent to which they increase opposition to U.S. policy in Europe and the United States, and figure as positive reasons to the extent to which they might demoralize the people of North Vietnam. As hopes for the survival of the Saigon regime faded, the reasons successfully advanced for adopting alternatives insuring large-scale death came mainly to consist of speculative psychological advantages in the preservation of U.S. power: insuring that deferential, weak regimes elsewhere would remain confident that the U.S. would shed much blood in their defense and maintaining fear of very heavy losses among groups seeking the overthrow of those regimes. As early as 1964, in a characteristic, successful case for heightened U.S. military action, Defense Secretary McNamara's most trusted advisor, Assistant Secretary of Defense John McNaughton, reasoned, "however badly SEA [Southeast Asia] may go over the next 1–3 years . . . [w]e must have kept promises, been tough, taken risks, gotten bloodied and hurt the enemy very badly. We must avoid appearances which will affect judgments . . . regarding how the U.S. will behave in future cases."[4] Successfully advocating sustained escalation of bombing of North Vietnam in February, 1965, National Security Advisor McGeorge Bundy noted, "We cannot assert that a policy of sustained reprisal [against North Vietnam] will succeed in changing the course of the contest in Vietnam . . . [But] even if it fails the policy will be worth it . . . a reprisal policy—to the extent that it demonstrates U.S. willingness to deploy this new norm in counter-insurgency—will set a higher price for the future upon all adventures of guerilla warfare, and it should therefore somewhat increase our ability to deter such adventures."[5]

The turning point in deliberations during the Johnson administration and the climax of *The Pentagon Papers* (which end with Johnson's announcement that he will not run for reelection) is the March 18, 1968 meeting of the Senior Advisory Group, the so-called "Wise Men," in which they shifted from nearly unanimous support for escalation of the U.S. war effort to nearly unanimous support for immediate deescalation and rapid disengagement. According to the detailed recollection of George Ball, who had joined the group as its lone dove after his resignation as Under Secretary of State, the Wise Men (with two exceptions) concluded that five or ten more years of fighting and bombing would be required to win the war. They rejected this alternative on the grounds that it would produce erosion of "support for the war on the homefront . . . bitterly dividing the country" as well as adversely affecting "our other problems and interests, including the dollar crisis." In contrast, the many hundreds of thousands of additional Vietnamese deaths implicit in their new assessment of the path to victory did not figure as reasons for taking a less lethal course.[6]

Because of access to many tapes of conversations between Nixon and his aides, we have abundant resources for determining the role of foreign deaths in the assessment of policy options in the Nixon administration. Despite the start of U.S. troop withdrawals early in the administration and a growing expectation that the Saigon regime would not survive, there were many discussions, usually inconclusive, of new and extremely lethal initiatives. A frequent theme is a vast expansion of bombing of North Vietnam, sometimes as a prod in negotiations, sometimes with (fading) hopes that the Saigon regime would be strengthened, but often, mainly, to end the war with a dramatic display of the costs of opposing the United States. "I put it quite bluntly," Nixon says, in a taped conversation with nearly all his major aides, Kissinger, John Haldeman, John Connally and Alexander Haig, on May 4, 1972, "now I'm being quite precise. South Vietnam may lose, but the United States cannot lose. It means that whatever happens in South Vietnam, we are going to cream North Vietnam. . . . for once we've got to use the maximum power of this country against a shit-asshole country to win the war. We can't use the word 'win.' Others can."[7]

In this vast record of deliberations, there are very few occasions (just two in Jeffrey Kimball's large assemblage of Vietnam War-related tape transcripts) on which Nixon and his top aides come close to assessing the moral significance of the large-scale killing of Vietnamese. In a taped conversation with Kissinger on April 25, 1975, describing "the attack on the North that we have in mind" (which he is not at all sure will "help in any way") Nixon says, "I still think we ought to take the dikes out now."

KISSINGER: I think—
NIXON: Will that drown people?
KISSINGER: That will drown about 200,000 people.
NIXON: Well, no, no, no, no, no. I'd rather use a nuclear bomb. Have you got that ready?
KISSINGER: Now that, I think, would just be, uh, too much, uh—
NIXON: A nuclear bomb, does that bother you?
KISSINGER: [unclear, reference to a military commander] he wouldn't do it anyway.
NIXON: I just want you to think big, Henry, for Christ's sake.[8]

A much more articulate discussion of Vietnamese deaths and their justification takes place in a conversation with Kissinger and Haldeman, on June 2,

1971, when Nixon, unsatisfied with his brief answer to a question about the morality of the war at a news conference, announces "I'd like to have for the first time a question planted at the next evening conference" so that with "this moral war thing, let 'em give me one more whack at it, I'm going to knock their brains out." Rehearsing his arguments, he says that "in a sense, we could all say that, one, the bombing of World War II was immoral, and, two, that war was immoral, but would it have been immoral to let Hitler conquer Europe and lead the world . . . [T]he bombing, the bombing which is, in in in South Vietnam. Yes! It's a tragedy . . . On the other hand, it is certainly immoral to send Americans abroad and not back them up with American power! . . . [W]ould it be moral to allow a communist takeover and . . . bloodbath . . . ?" Almost immediately, these reflections on how to answer moral criticisms of a war take a turn that is not familiar in discussions of war outside the highest governmental circles.

NIXON:   Well, let me say this, let me say this, because you, you don't think I mean what I'm saying. But I know this, that if we don't get any Soviet breakthrough, if we don't get the Chinese, if we don't get that ensemble, we can't get anything on Vietnam, the situation is deteriorating—about November of this year, I'm going to take a hard look at the hole card. As long as we've got the air force, as long as we've got the rest . . . [shouting and pounding his desk, as Kissinger tries to speak] I'm not talking about bombing passes, I'm, we're gonna take out the dikes, we're gonna take out the power plants, we're gonna level that goddamn country.

At this point, a future winner of the Nobel Peace Prize tries to interrupt.

KISSINGER:   Mr. President.
NIXON:   Now that makes me shout.
KISSINGER:   Mr. President, I think the American people will understand that.
NIXON:   . . . The point is, we're not gonna go out whimpering, and we're not gonna go out losing.
KISSINGER:   Mr. President, I will enthusiastically support that, and I think that's the right thing to do.[9]

Finally, the question of the civilian casualties is directly confronted in a conversation in May 1972, in which both the President and the future Nobel laureate clarify their views.

NIXON:   The only place where you and I disagree . . . is with regard to the bombing. . . . You're so goddamned concerned about the civilians and I don't give a damn. I don't care.

KISSINGER:    I'm concerned about the civilians because I don't want the world to be
mobilized against you as a butcher.[10]

Three decades later, the calmer deliberations of George H. W. Bush's
presidency also reflected an overriding interest in U.S. power as compared
with deaths of foreigners in developing countries. Critics of George W. Bush's
foreign policy often contrast it with his father's more thoughtful and restrained
pursuit of American interests. But (to revert to a narrative in Chapter 6) such
evidence as the George H. W. Bush—Brent Scowcroft memoirs and Bob
Woodward's interviews establish lethal limits to restraint in discussions of how
to respond to Iraq's invasion of Kuwait.

There were three main transitions to more lethal alternatives. In the second
National Security Council meeting after Saddam's invasion of Kuwait, when
the President and his closest advisors insisted on readiness to force Iraq out
by military means, their arguments did not address the consequences of war
for Iraqis. Rather, they appealed to a post-Cold War need to instill fear in
"people . . . who are not worried about the involvement of the superpowers"
and to the need to prevent Saddam's being "in an inequitable position, since
he would control the second- and third-largest proven oil reserves with the
fourth largest army in the world."[11]

Five months later, when Saddam offered a basis for negotiation that held
great promise of avoiding war through negotiated withdrawal, the President
said plainly, "We have to have a war."[12] In Bob Woodward's account of
this episode, the destruction of Saddam's army "so it would not be a threat
in the future" was the rationale for this insistence.[13] However, the diary
entries Bush presents in his joint memoir suggest that a broader advance in
imperial power was more important: insuring the fearsomeness of the threat
of American destruction, humiliating a potential leader of the resentful and
defiant and mobilizing the United States in support of future direct uses of
American firepower. "[February 25, 1991, in response to the latest Iraqi offers
to withdraw] It seems to me that we may get to a place where we have to
choose between solidarity at the UN and ending this thing definitively. I am
for the latter because our credibility is at stake. . . . We're not going to permit
a sloppy ending where this guy emerges saving face. . . . We may take some
hits for having our forces in Iraq to stop this; but far worse than that would
be if we lost credibility in some silly compromise. . . . [February 26, 1991, in
response to news of decisive military victories] The big news, of course, is this
high performance of our troops—the wonderful job they've done. . . . We're
doing something decent and we're doing something good; and Vietnam will
soon be behind us. . . . It's surprising how much I dwell on the end of the

Vietnam syndrome. . . . I remember the agony and the ugliness, and now it's together."[14] This theme dominates Bush and Scowcroft's positive assessment of the war, "American political credibility and influence had skyrocketed. We stood almost alone on the world stage in the Gulf crisis . . . Our military reputation grew as well. . . . The result was that we emerged from the Gulf conflict into a very different world from that prior to the attack on Kuwait."[15]

Bush's final decision was the most lethal. Determined to "break [Saddam's] hold on power"[16] but fearful of the consequences of using U.S. forces to overthrow him, he prescribed a bombing campaign in Iraq which, in the words of military leaders of the project, struck "against all those things that allow a nation to sustain itself" in order to provide "long term leverage," in combination with stringent sanctions, "to let people know, 'Get rid of this guy and we'll be more than happy to assist in rebuilding.' "[17] The Bush–Scowcroft memoirs and the Woodward narrative report some concern during this period for American lives lost in military action, one anxious inquiry as to the safety of the Kuwaiti royal family, and concern "over impressions being created in the press about 'the highway of death' from Kuwait City to Basra."[18] There is no indication that Iraqi deaths were treated as reasons that might make a use of lethal force excessive. Bush, whose background as a former CIA Director made him well equipped to foresee lethal consequences of his choices, is duly impressed by consequences for one Iraqi. Learning that a Scud missile has hit a barracks, killing twenty-eight U.S. soldiers, he reports "I was angry, but I knew Saddam was going to pay a terrible price."[19]

The Clinton administration's guidance of the sanctions regime reflected a similar trade-off of long-term leverage and human costs. On January 22, 1991, six days after war was launched against Iraq, U.S. military intelligence had reported, "Increased incidence of diseases will be attributable to degradation of normal preventive medicine, waste disposal, water purification/distribution, electricity, and decreased ability to control disease outbreaks. Any urban area in Iraq that has received infrastructural damage will have similar problems."[20] In 1999, a well-publicized UNICEF survey of childhood mortality in Iraq noted that there would have been 500,000 fewer deaths of children under five since the sanctions if pre-sanctions trends had continued.[21] A U.N. committee, deliberating in secret, in which each representative had veto power, controlled Iraqi imports under the sanctions regime. In a 2002 analysis of documents leaked by appalled U.N. staff, Joy Gordon found that the United States, "only occasionally seconded by Britain" had, since 1991, "blocked most purchases of materials necessary for Iraq to generate electricity, as well as equipment for radio, telephone and other communications . . . For example, Iraq was allowed to purchase a sewage-treatment plant but was blocked from buying the generator necessary to run it. . . . In September 2001 nearly one third of water and sanitation and one quarter of electricity and educational supply contracts were on hold. In early 2001, the United States had placed holds on $280 million in medical supplies, including vaccines to treat infant hepatitis, tetanus, and diphtheria, as well as incubators and cardiac equipment."[22]

Asked in a 1996 television interview whether gains from the sanctions were worth the price of the deaths of 500,000 children, Secretary of State Albright answered, "I think that is a very hard choice, but the price, we think, the price is worth it."[23] In a foreign policy address a year later, she clarified the objectives that were worth this price: "We do not agree with the nations who argue that if Iraq complies with its obligations concerning weapons of mass destruction, sanctions should be lifted. Our view, which is unshakable, is that Iraq must prove its peaceful intentions. . . . And the evidence is overwhelming that Saddam Hussein's intentions will never be peaceful. The United States looks forward, nevertheless, to the day when Iraq rejoins the family of nations . . . [B]ecause we are firmly committed to Iraq's territorial integrity, we would want to verify that the new Iraq [i.e., 'the successor regime' to Saddam's] would be independent, united and free from undue external influence, for example, from Iran."[24]

When the next administration set its framework for foreign policy delib-erations, emphasis shifted from long-term leverage to direct destruction, but otherwise there was basic continuity: a dominant interest in removal of Saddam was not accompanied by active concern for foreseeable costs to people in his country. According to George W. Bush's first Secretary of the Treasury, the first item on the agenda of the first meeting of the new National Security Council was introduced by the President's asking his National Security Advi-sor, "So, Condi, what are we going to talk about today?" "'How Iraq is destabilizing the region, Mr. President,' Rice said, in what several observers understood was a scripted exchange. She noted that Iraq might be the key to reshaping the entire region."[25]

In the moral assessment of imperial tendencies, imperial deliberations over war should be a central topic. The exercise of American destructive power has produced a vast toll. However, the impact on urgent material needs abroad of American policies concerning trade, finance and the global environment is also important. Here, the stubbornness of the United States in defending agricultural subsidies, extended worldwide drug patent rights, and "anti-dumping" measures ridiculed by economists of all persuasions, despite effects on needy people in developing countries, is strong evidence of the same insensitivity to severe costs to vulnerable people in developing countries. Foreign aid, which could, in principle, be the sphere in which the substantial independent force of concern for foreign needs is revealed, in fact yields further evidence of the dominant force of interests in American power and wealth. From 1965 to 1998, as competition with the Soviet Union for alliances with poor countries became less and less important and, finally, passed into history, the proportion of U.S. Gross Domestic Product devoted to overseas development assistance declined by 83% (from 0.58% to 0.10%, declining by 43% after 1988).[26] In the aid process that Chapter 5 began to scrutinize and Chapter 8 will investigate in more detail, the flow of aid is small, is badly allocated in terms of need, and advances interests in American wealth and power in ways that impose widely recognized, avoidable and debilitating losses in efficacy through volatile shifts in funding, promotion of dependency and bad coordination with other aid sources.

## The Imperial Political Process

The combination of guidance by the pursuit of American power and insensitivity to foreign costs of that pursuit has persisted for over fifty years despite variations in the political affiliations and personal temperaments of U.S. Presidents. This deliberative pattern reflects enduring features of normal interactions among American political and economic elites and the American electorate.

However powerfully they are affected by choices at the top of the country on top, foreigners do not get to vote in U.S elections, influence the opinions of only a tiny minority of those who do, and rarely participate in policymaking in U.S. elites. People in developing countries are especially uninfluential. So, lethal costs of the defense of imperial power for foreigners in developing countries will not, as such, significantly affect decisionmaking, if American political and economic elites have an overriding commitment to protect and promote American world power and if the beneficence of American world power is a very widely shared premise of the American electorate, as well as these elites. In fact, these mutually reinforcing commitments to American world power *are* entrenched and interact to shape U.S. foreign policy.

Leading American firms all now vitally depend on American world power for their growth and independence. They provide cadres (usually including Secretaries of the Treasury, often Secretaries of Defense) and interpersonal networks of information and influence essential to the management of government. Defeats of their corporate strivings reverberate throughout the economy, with adverse domestic consequences that cause discontent in the electorate.

Quite apart from influence of and dependence on economic elites, those who command levers of great political power over world affairs have never been spontaneously inclined to accept its weakening. The strength of this power seems to be part of their own vitality. As life goals do, theirs has a powerful impact on the moral framework of their reasoning: identifying with the goal of promoting their country's world power, they presuppose, in their deliberations, that what promotes this power is good, preserving this assumption from searching moral scrutiny.

That political leaders have this outlook is an outcome of the process of becoming a political leader. To succeed in politics, American politicians must accommodate economic elites and win elections shaped by the public political culture. In the public political culture, the premise that what strengthens American world power is good is the common property of both political parties and the standard presupposition of American schooling. This milieu reflects a long cultural history and a general tendency to gain a sense of vitality from collective success in national goals long pursued. It also reflects endeavors of established political leaders and leading firms. For example, it is constantly reinforced by the large and influential media of entertainment and information.

In particular, reporting of foreign affairs in the major media in the United States strengthens and reflects the presupposition that American power only harms through temporary departures from the prudent pursuit of its normal goals. This is an important constraint, meriting specific and detailed scrutiny, on efforts to change policies that originate outside of institutional governance, since those efforts depend on changing public opinion.

In major media coverage of foreign affairs, the basic framework for interpretation, attention and controversy is set by reports of what is said by government officials, by leading representatives of the party not holding presidential power and by U.S. allies in sites of conflict. When U.S. military forces are not directly engaged in violence, suffering due to U.S. actions in developing countries sustains little interest in the major media. Armed clashes are typically ascribed to ancient enmities or the excesses of radicals if they are reported at all. Mostly, the suffering merges into the background noise of wretchedness in the developing world. If U.S. military forces are involved, access to facts is strongly steered by the U.S. command, severely limited by dangers to American reporters in hostile territories, and powerfully restrained by reluctance to condemn important U.S. military endeavors when U.S. troops are in harm's way.

What reporting there is of American destructiveness of morally troubling kinds is dominated by isolated, specific episodes in conflict with U.S. victory, rather than the contributions of American strategies to massive destruction. Thus, the American audience was confronted with the My Lai massacre, but had little exposure to the routine and massive toll of U.S. bombing in the "free fire zones" of South Vietnam, in which hundreds of thousands were killed or maimed by bombs followed by leaflets bearing such advice as "Be sure to follow the example of 70,000 compatriots who have used the free-movement pass to . . . re-establish a comfortable life in peace; or stay to die in suffering and horrible danger."[27] In Daniel Hallin's survey of television news archives from 1965 through 1973, reporting of this lethal activity consists of a few interviews with U.S. pilots who express their concern to minimize civilian casualties. In the 779 broadcasts, there are, all-told, fifteen mentions of destruction of homes by forces of the U.S. or the Saigon government. In remarks on the general toll of civilian casualties, attribution to North Vietnamese and Vietcong forces dominated attribution to the U.S. and the Saigon government by two to one.[28]

Similarly, television and the front pages confronted the American audience with the indignities imposed by U.S. soldiers for some months in Abu Ghraib prison, but not with the deaths of over five thousand Iraqi civilians through use of massive firepower to protect U.S. lives in the invasion of Iraq or the civilian deaths from violence by U.S. forces of thousands more in subsequent years—a combined toll that may have reached tens of thousands.[29] Those who read the occasional mention of Iraq Body Count tabulations of reports of violent civilian deaths—routinely mischaracterized as estimates of the war's total Iraqi or Iraqi civilian toll—were not exposed to any mention of the role of violence by U.S. military forces. Yet Iraq Body Count found U.S. forces to be the most important killers of civilians in the first two years from the start of the invasion; as compared to anti-occupation forces, whose killings were the basic story of violent civilian death as told in major American media, Iraq Body Count attributed about four times as many deaths to U.S. forces in this period, and just as many deaths after April 30, 2003, the end of the invasion phase of the U.S. presence.[30]

After the destruction of the Golden Mosque of Samarra in February 2006, the growing carnage of sectarian violence became the dominant theme of American reporting from Iraq. The incidents were routinely framed with reports of opinions of American officials that the continued presence of U.S. troops was a vital safeguard against further explosive expansion of this violence. Yet in January an extensive poll had found that a large majority of Iraqis, including a majority of both Sunni Arabs and Shiites, believed that "day to day security for ordinary Iraqis" would increase and "the amount of inter-ethnic violence" would decrease "if US-led forces withdraw from Iraq in the next six months"; the finding was repeated in September, when horrific sectarian violence had become the basic story from Iraq. These (and similar) results were barely reported.[31]

Iraqi public opinion was responding to a long chain of realistic choices by the United States in Iraq that have contributed both to risks of carnage and to goals of power. Quick elections and early American withdrawal might soon have produced a reasonably peaceful Iraq, but would have given more scope to pro-Iranian groups and former Baathists than U.S. regional interests allowed. The dissolution of the Iraqi army and the extensive purge of Baath party members from government positions destroyed well-organized groups that might have led a reversion to anti-American nationalism in a successor regime, but also gave major impetus to Sunni insurgency, which soon consumed much of Iraq as counter-insurgency by occupation forces further inflamed anti-American fury. When, forced by huge demonstrations, the United States finally organized parliamentary elections, the chosen basis was voting for national lists, a format that lent itself to monitoring of candidates yet strongly favored lists based on religious or ethnic affiliation. Because of the recalcitrance of Sunni Arab soldiers and police, the "Iraqification" of counter-insurgency (including the massively destructive re-taking of Falluja) had to emphasize the deployment, against Sunni Arabs, of Shiite and Kurdish troops and police, including units renowned for brutality. The United States created and nurtured a political class with much to fear and little to gain from pursuit of the most promising national settlement, one premised on nationalist rejection of the U.S. presence and of U.S. guidance of Iraqi policies. Commenting on this class's avoidance of effective initiatives toward reconciliation while under U.S. protection, 68% of Shiites, 87% of Sunni Arabs, and 62% of Kurds in the January 2006 poll said that U.S. withdrawal in six months would increase the "willingness of factions in Parliament to cooperate."[32]

Inevitably, America in Iraq worked against terms of settlement that would constitute a flagrant American defeat and widely popular but anti-American leaders who could play an active role in sustaining this settlement (above all, Moqtada al-Sadr). Tellingly, the high point of armed opposition to the American presence, the combination, in 2004, of a Sunni insurgent center in Falluja and a Shiite uprising in Najaf, had been a moment of hope for most Iraqis concerned to avoid sectarian conflict. In a Coalition Provisional Authority poll including the Kurdish north, 64% had said that "recent events in Fallujah and the acts of Moqtada al-Sadr [the leader of the Najaf uprising] made Iraq more unified" (as opposed to 14% "more divided"). Small wonder, since opposition to Coalition forces as occupiers was already the great unifying stance, the position of 92%.[33] —Nonetheless, the frequent portrayals of the American presence as a bulwark against chaos were rarely accompanied by mention of the possibility that most Iraqis said was fact, that the American presence had helped to create growing, deadly disorder.

Granted, news of outrageous incidents on the front pages or on television does inspire concern. Evidence that policy makers have been overly ready to inflict violence to strengthen American power is accessible, especially in the back pages of quality newspapers, often long after the event. Very large anti-war demonstrations are reported and can change the public agenda. But these glimpses do not affect the framework for the ongoing narrative: any large excesses of unjustified violence in defense of American power are foolish blunders or tragic mistakes, occasional setbacks in a process of cultivating American power that coincides with the interests of humanity at large. The bases for success of major newspapers, television stations and journalists working for them provide strong incentives to respect this framework. The abundant provision of evidence that the advancement of American power often harms humanity would invite the scorn of both political parties, undermine the most important American corporations, and excite the anger and disbelief that accompany wounded patriotic pride.

Within this web of mutually reinforcing influences, specific emotional, social and electoral pressures at the peak of the executive branch, where the action is in setting foreign policy, detach policymaking from consideration of dire costs to foreigners in developing countries. Among makers of American foreign policy, moral anxiety about lethal consequences is always waiting in the wings, threatening a constant burden of turmoil and hesitation. Policy planners can avoid these emotional costs by endorsing Sherman's remark about war and hell (as Nixon does after proclaiming his willingness to "level the goddamned country") and bracketing further scrutiny of degrees of hellishness with the rejected option of pacifism. Avoidance of moral reasoning about foreign deaths also solves a severe problem of impoliteness: it is one thing to tell another (perhaps one's boss, the President of the United States) that one favors a different strategy as the best means of reaching shared goals, something else to propose that his conduct inflicts death on many innocent people without an adequate moral justification. In this milieu, an attachment to contrary moral considerations seems to be the love that dare not speak its name: George Ball's biographer notes, "Ball privately questioned the [Vietnam] war on moral grounds. He avoided discussing the conflict in these terms because his first priority was to change what he considered to be a flawed U.S. policy."[34] Finally, given the appreciation of American world power by economic elites and in the schools, the mass media and the national culture as a whole, hesitation about the advancement of American world power on the basis of adverse effects on foreigners is a source of political peril for a U.S. President or would-be U.S. President. "Makes America weaker," "puts the U.S. in retreat," "incompatible with U.S. victory," and "deserts our allies" are daunting charges which successful politicians do not rebut by stating that these losses would be gains for humanity.

In sum, the interlocking mechanisms of institutional governance of U.S. foreign policy insure that losses to foreigners in developing countries do not have substantial, independent force in restraining the pursuit of American wealth and power. Granted, what would best promote American wealth or power does not always have these costs. But it often does.

Previous chapters described non-violent costs to people in developing countries of American uses of domineering influence to advance American economic interests. Cheap access to natural resources, unrestricted flows of goods and investments, and exclusive property rights in advanced technologies are always of interest to the United States, but do not always serve the interests of people in developing countries. National control over local choices or the preservation of a national way of life from American influence are frequent deep aspirations, sources of corresponding loss if local policies are shaped by American interests. The further grave costs of violent destruction are bound to arise from conflicts over political control in the developing world—in which violent American initiatives often, in part, advance American economic interests. Inevitably, some regimes will seek to expand their independent regional power while protecting the commanding heights of their economies from the global market forces favored by the United States. Especially if the region is important (say, on account of strategic location or natural resources) and the regime is disreputable, changing or crippling the regime may advance American power despite grave harms to those living under it. In the face of discontent with the thrust of American foreign policy and challenges to American power, client regimes, relying on U.S. support to make up for lack of popular support, are a useful resource. Their predations when stable can be terrible. The cost of their tottering can be much worse: to be an effective source of domineering influence, support for a client regime must include reliable assurance of energetic defense by the patron, without squeamish reluctance to shed blood.

## A Crisis of Empire

Of course, projects of domination have costs for the United States, as well, due to resistance, disorder, and the need to propitiate greedy and parasitic client regimes. Recurrently, the hope is voiced that appreciation of American goods, technology, commercial skill and help in the tasks of development will provide as much access to and influence in developing countries as threats and destruction, without these costs. Because of a new harmony of perceived interests, American bullying of developing countries to acquiesce in economic arrangements will become obsolete and American violence in developing countries will be limited to welcomed rescues from brutal oppressors. A new era will begin in which destructive or negligent advancement of the American interest is replaced by Kennedyesque alliances for progress, benign commercial competition under the aegis of Nixonian détente, the promotion of human rights rather than power under Jimmy Carter, or global civility, based on globalization, in the wake of the Cold War's end. These hopes have always proved to be illusory. While global economic changes have changed the shape of America's interests in access to developing countries and shifts in power have created new alliances, the interests in access, strategic and economic, always conflict with powerful local interests in some significant parts of the developing world. So threats and destruction, taking advantage of weaknesses in developing countries, remain useful instruments of American power.

Still, given the importance of the claim that the harmful tendencies of empire endure, the general and historical arguments for this claim should be supplemented by a description of the current challenge to American power that makes reliance on threat-influence and destruction in developing countries an important strategic resource. This challenge combines declining U.S. economic advantages with intensifying competition for geopolitical influence and for stable transnational access to raw materials. It has at least four components: the challenge of Europe, the decline in American technological superiority, the ascent of the most important and successful developing countries, and tightening constraints on stable access to oil.

*1. The challenge of Europe.*    The European Union has begun to pose an important threat to American prerogatives. In 2007, the combined GDP of the European Union was 22% higher than the GDP of the United States.[35] (Those twenty seven countries had a smaller combined GDP until 2003.[36]) EU exports of goods to the rest of the world were 46% greater than U.S. exports, with a trade deficit only 30% of the U.S. deficit.[37] The combined GDP of the euro-using countries was 88% of U.S. GDP, while their exports of goods to the rest of the world exceeded U.S. exports by about two-thirds—export strength accompanied by a trade surplus.[38] In 2006, EU service exports to the rest of the world were 30% greater than U.S. service exports and grew at a faster rate, while euro-zone service exports were 28% greater.[39] The flow of foreign direct investment into countries of the euro-zone (which had quintupled since 1995) was more than twice as great as the flow into the United States (which had tripled since 1995).[40] This large and growing European role in the world economy has already begun to challenge the dollar in important spheres. In 2006, the euro overtook the dollar as a currency in which short-term international debt was issued.[41] In 2003, the euro overtook the dollar as a currency of issue for outstanding international bonds and notes.[42]

Nonetheless, the dollar continues to dominate in international trade, with more than twice as great a share in foreign exchange transactions and in governmental currency reserves.[43] The dollar is especially important as a means of payment in vital commodities such as oil. But this preeminence of the dollar is, as an IMF paper noted in 2007, testimony to "habit and inertia."[44] It reflects the advantages of continuing to use a preponderant global currency even when its preponderance no longer reflects fundamentals, a hold-over that sustained the pound sterling as the primary world currency well into the twentieth century. As the same example shows, currency dominance cannot be protected indefinitely from changes in comparative roles in the world economy. In particular, the global economic role of the EU, especially the partners in euro-use, may well, sooner or later, reduce the primacy of the dollar to the tipping point at which U.S. indebtedness can no longer be refinanced at current levels and the attractiveness of dollar investments no longer counterbalances a huge trade deficit. At this point, U.S. policy initiatives would face the same fiscal disciplines as everyone else's do now, while a large permanent depreciation of the dollar would reduce access to imported goods.

In addition, the rise of the EU puts in question future global prospects of a centrally important sector of the American economy, financial, insurance, and other business-related services. The most dynamic and contested aspect of globalization among developed countries is the international provision of services. From 1990 through 2006, as the U.S. trade deficit in goods multiplied 7.5 times, the trade surplus in services multiplied 2.5 times. Central to this growth was the expansion of financial, insurance, and other business-related services, with a surplus growing 4.5 times.[45] As Britain showed in the final stages of its hegemony, the extension of such services to other countries, including relatively prosperous developing countries, can be a major source of influence and profit in the face of declining superiority in the production of goods. But the competitive vigor of this sector in Europe has always been strong, and is, if anything, stronger with the revolution in information technology and European accommodation to the use of English as the world lingua franca. This growing strength is already a challenge to a crucial American economic sector and the centrally important economic elite in banking. An end of the dollar's role as the world reserve currency and of global preferences for U.S. equities and obligations as investments would be a terrible blow in this competition.

The first important document marking official movement toward the eventual assertive unilateral reliance on military force and threats of George W. Bush's administration was the draft of the 1992 "Defense Planning Guidance" prepared by Paul Wolfowitz's staff for presentation to Defense Secretary Cheney. It was notable for including Western European nations among sources of threat to U.S. power in the post-Cold War era—perhaps the leading sources. A primary declared objective was that "The U.S. must . . . establish and protect a new order that holds the promise of convincing potential competitors that they need not aspire to a greater role . . . In non-defense areas, we must account sufficiently for the interests of the advanced industrial nations to discourage them from challenging our leadership or seeking to overturn the established political and economic order."[46]

2. *Losing the cutting edge.* In a globalized economy, cutting-edge technology is increasingly attractive, but U.S. dominance of the cutting edge continues to decline. In 1961–5, 10% of the new patents issued by the U.S. Patent Office went to foreign residents. In 1980, 36% of the new patents were foreign-held, 44% in 1985, 47% in 1990, 48% in 2004.[47] From 1995 to 2004, the value of U.S. high technology exports increased only 2.6% in real terms; as a proportion of world gross domestic production, it declined by 20%. In 1998, the U.S. component of high technology exports from high income and upper middle income countries was 22%. It had declined to 17% six years later.[48] The loss of the leading edge threatens to accelerate as local standards are determined by non-American firms, further purchases accommodate to large fixed investments in non-American plant and infrastructure, and additional extra-American locales gain the interlocking skills and facilities needed for innovation.

3. *The challenge of development.* As transnational links in manufacturing, trade and finance between developed and developing countries have strengthened, increased openness to U.S. goods and investment flows in developing countries, extension of patent rights and reduction of the role of local governments in directing national development have become increasingly important goals of the United States. Yet globalization also provides developing countries with experience, expertise, coordinative networks, access to publicity and, in some cases, economic strength, lending force to resistance to this "neo-liberal" trend. In the Doha Round and in parts of Latin America, the trend has been slowed, even in some respects slightly reversed. If the growing economic power of developing countries with large internal markets such as China, Brazil and India were accompanied by leadership in a unified bloc in negotiations, the

United States would find it much harder to achieve its favored resolutions of questions in the world trade regime. So the continued use of threat influence to inhibit unity is an important strategic need.

Even if divergent interests get in the way of effective coordination by the leading developing countries, leadership by example pushes against the model of subordination to external market forces that benefits the United States. In *Global Trends 2025: A Transformed World* (2008), the U.S. National Intelligence Council, the central council of U.S. intelligence agencies, notes that "For the most part, China, India and Russia are not following the Western liberal model for self-development, but instead are using a different model, 'state capitalism' . . . Over the next 15-20 years, more developing countries may gravitate toward Beijing's state-centric model rather than the traditional Western model of development."[49]

The combination of economic growth in China with China's regional interests and energy needs is a further deep concern of the report: "US security and economic interests could face new challenges if China becomes a peer competitor that is militarily strong as well as economically dynamic and energy hungry."[50] Indeed, while otherwise bland and generic in characterizations of the U.S. global military role as "regional balancer," *Global Trends 2025* posits an imaginary U.S. attack on Chinese warships in one of its four literary exercises which dramatize future possibilities: writing to a former President of Brazil in 2021, the Brazilian Foreign Minister reports his efforts to contain a conflict over access to Central Asian oil and natural gas in which the Chinese navy has attacked Indian warships in the Gulf of Oman, which "triggered the US attack disabling the Chinese ships as they tried to withdraw from the area."[51]

*4. Scrambling for oil.* American movement of people, goods and weapons is virtually all fueled by oil. *National Energy Policy*, the report of Dick Cheney's National Energy Policy Development Group in 2001, noted that 52% of oil consumed in the United States was imported in 2000 and predicted that 64% would be imported by 2020.[52] In this period, U.S. oil production will decline (by 1.5 million barrels per day, according to the report), world oil production will probably reach its peak, because of limits to what there is underground,[53] and world consumption will become half again greater.[54] The increase in consumption will be led by China, an oil-deficient country whose imports, in the conservative *National Energy Policy* estimate, will grow "from approximately 1 million barrels of oil per day . . . to possibly 5 to 8 million."[55] (In the transition to the Obama administration, *Global Trends 2025* characterized trends driven by "energy hungry China" as part of "*An Accelerated Resource Grab*" for control of or access to energy resources on the part of "the new powers . . . through their state-run energy firms."[56])

The vast majority of the world's oil reserves are in the hands of governments of developing countries, or of Arabian petromonarchies whose alliance with the United States is internally or regionally contested. This is partly because of where the unextracted oil lies, partly because extractive industries are easy and lucrative targets for expropriation. In particular, Middle Eastern governments, whose countries provided a quarter of U.S. oil imports at the start of the twenty-first century, controlled about two-thirds of proven world oil reserves.[57] Unless they are converted to deferential clients through subjugation or threats or through support in the face of frightening internal opposition, the oil-related interests of governments controlling most reserves will not coincide with those of the United States. Slowing the depletion of national oil reserves while maintaining relatively high prices would best serve interests in development. The multinational corporations, mostly American, that control the best means of extraction and marketing compete with governments controlling oil for shares of the profit that can be derived from a naturally scarce commodity in wide demand. Countries or groups of countries whose decisions have an impact on global oil supply can use this power to pursue distinctive foreign policy objectives, as in the Arab oil embargo. While the maintenance of a long-term reserve capacity used to pump more oil to ease temporary shortages could in principle serve a common interest in stability, in the real world large reserve capacity opens a government to pressures to reduce prices over the long run. Yet spurts of production using reserve capacity are the only means of damping the volatility of crude oil prices. *National Energy Policy* treats an increase in average initial purchase price from $8.03 a barrel in December 1998 to $30.30 in November 2000 as a paradigm of this volatility.[58] Subsequently, prices surged from $90 to $140 a barrel from February to June 2008.[59]

The American empire's best means of coping with the danger of uppity governments in oil-rich countries has been sponsorship of deferential, coercive client regimes. The centerpiece of this strategy has been the guarantee of the rule of the family who control and live off of Saudi Arabia. They certainly do not strive for an oil policy that promotes domestic development at cost to foreign interests. As petrodollars flowed abroad, mostly to the United States, per capita Gross National Income in Saudi Arabia, at foreign exchange conversion to current dollars, dropped from $16,700 in 1981 to $8,460 in 2001.[60] From 1965 through 1999, the average annual change in Gross Domestic Product at constant dollars was negative, −0.1.[61] This clumsy mismanagement of national development has been accompanied by agile use of Saudi spare capacity, which constitutes 70 to 90 percent of global spare capacity, to increase production to damp down instability in oil prices. As the *National Energy Policy* report graciously acknowledges, "Saudi Arabia has pursued a policy of providing effective assurances that it will use its capacity to mitigate the impact of oil supply disruptions in any region."[62] An article in *Foreign Affairs* was more fervent: "Saudi spare capacity is the energy equivalent of nuclear weapons . . . the cornerstone of U.S. oil policy."[63] However, as the *New York Times* reports, "the country's oil fields are in decline . . . capacity will probably stall near current levels."[64] Meanwhile, discontent in Saudi Arabia has grown, along with worldwide demand for oil.

In the face of these various challenges, vigorous use of America's residual advantages in threat influence and destruction helps to promote American wealth and power. In contrast, exclusive reliance on the soft mixture of mere commercial striving, help with tasks of development on the basis of need, and rational persuasion on the basis of shared principles and interests would entail much less wealth and much less expansion (indeed, more frequent outright contraction) for leading American firms, and a severely diminished capacity of the United States government to get its way in international affairs.

As in the Doha Round, the United States can be expected to respond to the challenge of developing countries, the loss of its leading edge, and the loss of economic advantages within the developed world through vigorous uses of threat influence to sustain long-term patent regimes, mandates of openness to mobile foreign investments and foreign supplies for government procurement, and reductions of developing countries' tariffs and subsidies, even where there are important costs to the people of developing countries. Conflict with developing countries over the trade and finance framework of globalization lends added importance to the manipulation of aid and use of fear to promote favorable political forces in developing countries. Such territorial domineering influence also advances U.S. interests and helps to respond to the challenge of Europe when it produces governments that manage the borrowing of funds, the development of infrastructure and the exploitation of natural resources in ways that favor American firms. Client regimes are useful, here, despite their tendencies toward repression, corruption and provocation of disorder. Conversely, the weakening and isolation of regimes opposed to U.S. interests can help fend off challenges to U.S. global power, even at cost to the wellbeing of people in those countries or regional stability.

The challenge of development promotes harmful American negligence in response to global climate change. China, India and Brazil will not take on stringent emissions constraints, which would have severe costs for people desperate to escape from destitution. Given this refusal, the United States government will not take on emissions constraints that are needed for climate safety yet will hasten the time when America is overtaken.

Finally, one can expect the United States to use its only remaining qualitative superiority, its overwhelmingly superior command of means of deadly violence, to slow its decline. Used directly or through clients, the exercise of destructive power can defend threatened allies in important locales and depose especially threatening regimes opposed to American interests. As a special point of vulnerability, responsive to the nature of local regimes in developing countries, the challenge of oil will be a powerful stimulus to the violent defense of empire. The rise of China will create new contests over territorial influence, for example, in Southeast Asia and Africa. The strategic location of Central Asia, including Iran, and its role as source and pipeline site for natural gas and oil will increase competition for influence there among the United States, Russia, India and China as China's and India's international power and energy needs increase, a contest in the European Union will have an important stake, as well.[65]

In such struggles over territorial domination, the imperial use of destructive power to shore up, depose, destabilize or threaten sometimes fails to achieve its objectives or does so at too great a cost. But it often succeeds, as did sponsorship of Central American violence and Persian Gulf interventions prior to the overthrow of Saddam Hussein. Even failures have auxiliary benefits, by underlining the risk of devastation to those who might challenge American power.

Over the long run, imperial decline is inevitable. But the long-run inevitability of defeat by the challenges to empire has the irrelevance to the current practice of economic and political elites evoked by Keynes' quip, "In the long run, we are all dead." Passive acquiescence now would not serve the interests of members of U.S. elites in maintaining their current power for as long as possible. Acceptance of loss of power now in the interest of the long-term future, especially a future of lost preeminence, is a formula for failure in American electoral politics.

## Iraq: A Fallacy of Stupidity

Even if morally excessive violence will not be eliminated through strategic arguments about what advances American power, it is important to see how useful strategic advocacy will be in reducing its extent, as the response to the current crisis of empire unfolds. In the debates over what advances American world power that are a continuous feature of institutional governance, particular violent initiatives are often opposed or criticized on strategic grounds. The more such advocacy is apt to accomplish in reducing unjust violence, the less the moral importance of engaging in activities outside the channels of institutional governance. Indeed, public charges of inherent tendencies to grave injustice of the American empire might turn out to be morally self-indulgent, offending patriots whose enhanced strategic insight is the means of saving vulnerable people from harm.

Currently, the measurement of the humane potential of strategic advocacy centers on the assessment of the most destructive use of America's means of violence in the early twenty-first century, the invasion and occupation of Iraq. In the United States, this initiative came to be widely seen as a stupendous blunder. When a book appeared in 2006 with the single-word title "*Fiasco*", there was hardly a need for a subtitle linking it to Iraq.[66] This grim appraisal was often accompanied by a basically optimistic view of the inherent tendencies of U.S. foreign policy: vast destruction from the unilateral direct deployment of America's destructive power now requires foolishness in high places that can be cured and prevented through sober reflection on the strategic costs of the Iraq fiasco; a foreign policy that seeks agreement from European powers and Japan and confines direct uses of U.S. military power to responses to aggression would serve current American interests in global power without anything like the destructive toll of bold unilateralism.

The diagnosis is exaggerated and the prognosis is too optimistic. The invasion of Iraq was neither wise nor utterly foolish. Declining empires often lack good options. A propensity toward outbreaks of highly destructive direct use of America's uniquely superior capacity for violence, in the absence of prior aggression, can be expected to endure, as one plausible response to enduring challenges of empire. (Of course, the future deployment of this capacity will be accompanied by judgments that it was implemented incompetently in Iraq.) While the more multilateral, less bold strategy is also a plausible way to advance imperial power, it can be expected to exact a toll of destruction on about the same scale as the bolder strategy over the long run. These were not reasons not to try to prevent the Iraq war, opposing the most deadly foreign policy initiative of its time. But they are reasons to fear enduring dangerous propensities of the American empire, not to confine those fears to the bolder, more direct and unilateral stance, and not to take clear-sighted strategic advocacy as a highly effective way of reducing harms of empire.

Even if the decision to overthrow Saddam Hussein proved to be unwise, it responded to rational strategic anxieties that could not be assuaged by other means. The concerns about Iraq's "destabilizing the region" that dominated the first meeting of George W. Bush's National Security Council were strategically insightful. The sanctions regime was losing international support and effectiveness. Saddam was "selling underpriced oil to Jordan and Syria," seeking to create "a web of interdependency and support." In good time, Iraq might have had some success in acquiring the sort of arsenal that was the focus of Secretary of Defense Rumsfeld's anxieties in a contemporary memorandum: "advanced military capabilities . . . that cannot defeat our forces, but can deny access to critical areas of Europe, the Middle East and Asia." (The list that follows makes no reference to non-conventional weapons, but includes "advanced air defense."[67]) The importance of Middle Eastern oil, the fragility of the Saudi regime and the hostility (and European tilt) of Iran made these tempting arguments for ending the threat of Saddam's resurgence, a project in which the United States would have to rely on its own might.

Armed occupation is bound to incite nationalist rage. But it can also serve as a means of shaping a society to suit American interests. In a large, commercially and technologically sophisticated country, in a region in which entrenched if decrepit forms of state-directed development have been the norm, Paul Bremer, as chief of the Coalition Provisional Authority, intelligently pursued this project, in imposing, by dictatorial decree, laws "meant to transform the economy," suspending all tariffs, putting a 15 percent cap on all future taxes, and throwing open the doors to foreign investment.[68]

While unilateral action costs good will, it creates opportunities to advance distinctively American interests. One of Saddam Hussein's acts of defiance was to break with the international practice of selling oil for dollars, getting payment in euros. After his overthrow, the reign of the dollar was restored. In the wake of the American conquest of Iraq, neighboring regimes made it clear that they now sought to avoid the provocation of a tilt toward Europe. The *Le Monde* business section mournfully reported that French gains in Qatar had turned into an often unsuccessful fight to hold contested ground "especially in big 'political' contracts. . . . The ruling family are relatively weak. Even if they express a certain resentment of the all-powerful Americans, they respect their power." The Qatar minister of oil expressed this respect with sage advice, in explaining why the French firm Total should accept Qatar's granting Exxon Mobil a large share of the natural gas reserves that Total had started to develop: "*Je dis toujours, si tu ne peux pas battre quelqu'un, rejoins-le*" ("I always say, if you can't lick him, join him").[69] In the wake of American destruction of the Iraqi telephone system, Bahrain's telephone company quickly established an effective wireless network through a $5 million investment in European wireless equipment. Unappreciative of this entrepreneurship, the

U.S. occupation authorities shut the system down, announcing, some months later, a grant of licenses to firms based in Kuwait, Egypt and the north-Iraq Kurdish protectorate, using Motorola equipment.[70]

By the third year after the invasion of Iraq, after it and its sequels had probably cost over two hundred thousand lives, the invasion was widely seen as a strategic blunder, failing to give enough weight to foreseeable risks. Yet even if the widespread strategic critique was sound, the invasion, while underestimating risks, responded to needs and opportunities of kinds that will continue to be salient in the enduring crisis of empire. So one can expect the direct use of military power to figure in future American responses to pressing challenges, perhaps a challenge more directly linked to the crucial regional resource, the Saudi regime.

Once launched, such initiatives are long maintained. An empire must hold on to what it openly and directly seizes, or, in any case, exact terrible costs before letting go. This is how an empire maintains its capacity to induce Hobbesian awe of its power. Long after the thoughtful and articulate strategists whose work we know as *The Pentagon Papers* had concluded that America's Vietnam intervention had been unwise, they insisted that the U.S. must fight on to preserve its credibility. In 2004, when the President who directed the continuing carnage of the invasion and occupation of Iraq campaigned for reelection, his opponent tightly embraced this tradition of imperial strategizing. In the presidential debates, John Kerry repeatedly endorsed the necessity of perseverance. "Yes," he declared, "we have to be steadfast and resolved and I am. And I will succeed for those troops, now that we're there. We have to succeed. We can't leave a failed Iraq."[71] More aid from allies, better armor, more troops, and more training of Iraqi forces were his prescription for success. In the less public forum of the Council on Foreign Relations, Kerry went so far as to invite support with fearmongering about the resolve of George W. Bush; "I fear that in the run up to the 2004 election the Administration is considering what is tantamount to a cut and run strategy. Their sudden embrace of accelerated Iraqification and American troop withdrawal without adequate stability is an invitation to failure."[72] In 2006, when the probable toll of Iraqi deaths due to the war and its sequels had grown to about half a million, Barack Obama, the only star of the 2004 Democratic Convention whose luster was undimmed by the presidential defeat, publicly affirmed the rationale for a continued presence that had been pressed more confidentially in the Vietnam War, explaining that he "looks at the war in Iraq as a test of American credibility—which is why he doesn't support an immediate withdrawal, even though he believed that the original invasion was ill-conceived and badly executed."[73]

The difficulties of America in Iraq are often part of a comparison favoring an approach to the defense of American power that relies more on accommodation of European powers and Japan, less on direct and large-scale use of American military forces in the absence of prior aggression by another country. Given the need to use the sole American qualitative superiority to strengthen the deferential and weaken the defiant, one can expect this alternative approach to give rise to great violence, as well. Destruction in the less bold mode is easier to initiate and to sustain over long periods, since joint participation, covertness, use of surrogates, reliance on destructive tactics other than large-scale military attack, and appeals to the need to repel aggression reduce losses in American resources and American reputation. So the less bold, more multilateral strategy will not protect people in developing countries as the enduring crisis of empire unfolds. The less bold strategy has produced the vast majority of the deaths due to the maintenance of the empire since the end of the Vietnam War. The devastating use of American military power in the first Gulf War, responding to Iraqi aggression against Kuwait and supported by all great powers, combined with the subsequent sanctions regime to produce a death toll on the scale of George W. Bush's invasion and occupation.

## Uses of Empire

Should those who share the view of enduring imperial tendencies that I have defended wish for an end to the American empire? Of course, they will hope for a world, some day, in which the strongest powers do not get their way by threats and destruction. But there is nothing distinctive in this hope. U.S. Presidents as well as critics of empire accept that an ideal world will lack empires, even in the broad, metaphorical usage that I have specified. On the other hand, the desire for an end of the American empire that is a frequent, distinctive attitude among its moral critics need not involve support for violent rebellion or an expectation that the empire will end soon. Rather, they seek an end to empire in the same spirit as they seek an end to racism. Those who seek to end racism have no illusion that this will happen any time soon. And they may well think that there are anti-racist measures that ought to be avoided as excessively intrusive means of reaching their goal. Still, they fervently wish that racism would simply disappear now and judge activities by their contribution to this goal. They do not have the attitude toward racism that nonanarchists have toward government: beneficial in some ways, dangerous in others, a process whose unconstrained exertion *and* whose absence would be catastrophic.

This wish for an immediate end to the American empire is one plausible response to the condemnation of this power structure for imposing unjust burdens as long as it lasts while continually offending human dignity by depriving people and peoples of autonomy. But another response is plausible, corresponding to the nonanarchists' attitude. Rather than wishing for the immediate disappearance of the American empire, one can wish for the immediate strengthening of initiatives outside the corridors of power that hem in the empire by reducing its immoral excesses, but do not end it. These initiatives (which, I will subsequently argue, are effectively advanced by social movements) ought to stand to the American empire as freedom of the press stands to a government: they reduce injustices without abolishing their abiding source, whose abolition would be worse than its injustice.

This wish to hem in the American empire seems more defensible than the wish that it end. Suppose that tomorrow (or any year soon), the qualitative military superiority of the United States were to disappear, along with any special capacity to change the policies of other countries by economic threats. The United States becomes just one among several great powers. One consequence would be less inhibition of China's rise to future status as a superpower, posing a risk of war over Taiwan and hastening the coming of a global hegemony that promises no advantage over the current power structure. Meanwhile, the great powers of the new multipolar world would, no doubt, strive to assemble a global analogue of the old Concert of Europe. But such clubs tend to break up in violent quarrels. And in any case, they are clubs of the powerful, promoting stability by coordinating the exploitation of the weak.

The immediate disappearance of American imperial power would also jeopardize the export-driven growth that is the best hope for escaping dire poverty of most of the world's neediest. If the United States, the European Union, Japan and China competed on a level playing field in shaping the framework for commerce, it is not certain what the outcome would be. There are specific causes for concern, for example, the EU's stubbornness in maintaining the world's most harmful agricultural subsidies, Japan's proclivities for tariffs that harm developing countries, China's willingness to crowd out less well-equipped developing countries, and the inefficiencies of a currency regime in which no currency reigns supreme. There would also be new prospects of beneficent compromise. But what is certain is that the trajectory of the world economic framework would be much less certain if the American empire were to disappear. And markets hate uncertainty. The new caution and instability would harm the world's poor.

Admittedly, no one knows what Chinese hegemony would be like. If it advantages the people of China, it has the humane benefit of advantaging a fifth of humanity. Aid competition among great powers forced to compete more intensely for favors from lesser countries might produce improvements in health and subsistence. But a grimmer scenario is at least as likely: increased incidence of wars, oppressive client regimes, disruptive recessions and economic stagnation. The fervent wish that the American empire would disappear as soon as possible seems to underrate hard facts of power.

Mightn't the hemming in of the American empire similarly give rise to destructive disorder? After all (according to the argument of this chapter), the immoral excesses can be strategic resources in promoting American power. The proper response to this worry is not dismissal of the usefulness of empire, but modesty about everyone's control over the future trajectory of humanity. Trends toward greater equality of power, threatening consequent disorder, will occur, beyond the control of the greatest powers. China will grow in power. The largest developing countries will develop increasingly important internal markets and productive capacities. The supremacy of the United States on each dimension of domineering influence will be challenged and will someday end. No social movement can guarantee against calamity as the power structure, inevitably, changes. What it can do is use discussion, advocacy and action in a global movement in ways that make it more likely that inevitable shifts in power will inaugurate an era of reasonable compromise rather than destructive frenzy.

The duty to seek ways to hem in the immoral excesses of the American empire, including its propensity to vast unjust violence, should, then, be added to the political responsibilities of citizens of the United States and allied countries. The list of duties has become long and diverse. It is time to add up the accounts.

# 8

# Quasi-Cosmopolitanism

THE relationships generating political duties of people in developed countries to help people in developing countries have turned out to be diverse both in their nature and in the countries they connect. It is time to gather these different threads of transnational responsibility together, to respond to two leading questions about global justice: How great are the total benefits and demands of the unmet political duties to help? What goals for humanity as a whole are pursued in fulfilling them?

In answering the question about benefits and demands, one should not expect precision, but rather a broad gauge of prospects and sacrifices that helps in judging present efforts and in comparing what is owed to needy foreigners with what is owed to compatriots. My argument will be that the transnational duties, taken as a whole, extend to all developing countries, that meeting their unmet requirements would provide extensive, vitally important benefits to people in these countries, and that the fulfillment of these unmet responsibilities would impose significant demands on people in developed countries, including the disadvantaged. Standard assumptions of priority for compatriots' needs are overridden by transnational ties.

In answering the further question of over-all goals, one should not assume that the diverse, specific projects of help derive their moral importance from a single global standard of distributive justice. (I will ultimately reject such standards.) Still, global justice is advanced by a common standpoint for judging the relative importance of specific current endeavors and an inspiring long-term goal at which these efforts aim. Within present limits of political feasibility, efforts to reduce transnational irresponsibility will turn out properly to give priority to the needs of the worst-off, a priority further specified by choice behind a global veil of ignorance. The ultimate goal of global justice will turn out to combine provision for basic needs with respect for autonomy in an ideal best characterized as global civic friendship.

Thus, despite the valuing of relationships to compatriots and the limited duty of beneficence at the origins of the relational approach to global justice, it sustains demands, concerns and aspirations that are, broadly speaking, cosmopolitan. Emphasis on specific relationships rather than responsiveness to neediness as such might seem a way of permitting people in developed countries to be Scrooges in good conscience. In fact, it is a powerful means of establishing demanding duties toward the foreign poor.

## Back to Beneficence

Before embarking on this quest for sums and over-all goals of transnational political duties, a loose end must first be tied concerning beneficence, i.e., responsiveness to neediness as such regardless of special relationships to the needy. Chapter 1 established limits to the personal duty of beneficence, but did not address its political limits. Does a citizen of a developed country have a duty of beneficence to support measures by her government, including exercises of its power to tax, that reduce neediness in developing countries while imposing costs on her compatriots? The position, "No, not a penny in taxes merely to relieve abject destitution abroad," is so repugnant that it casts doubt on a moral perspective that compels this conclusion. But once beneficence toward the global poor is admitted as a political duty, it threatens to marginalize responsibilities to help due to special relationships. So the proper political role of beneficence has to be established, on the way to an over-all view of the political duty to help.

The burden of justifying forcing others to give up what they would not willingly part with on their own is especially heavy in the case of forced beneficence, because the underlying duties are so sensitive to personal concerns, goals and responsibilities. Without wrongdoing, a person may depart from the default position of giving that would do the most for those with the severest needs in order to honor the worthwhile causes closest to her heart. These will be a small selection from the vast diversity of worthwhile causes dear to some of her fellow citizens. "I prefer to give elsewhere" is a morally stupid response to arguments for political duties of concern based on coercively imposed disadvantage, civic loyalty, political trusteeship or on processes of exploitation, domination and destruction that span borders. But it is a relevant response to state-mandated beneficence—not decisive, but demanding an adequate reply.

In addition, Sympathy respects the demands of worthwhile special personal goals to which someone is securely, intelligently attached, including expensive goals, such as grace and aesthetic value in home furnishings or varied, edifying travel. Similarly, Sympathy's demands are limited by special personal responsibilities. Love of foreign travel or responsibilities to a wide circle of friends do not limit one's political duties of justice to disadvantaged fellow citizens or to foreign citizenries collaborating in the international trade regime, but they may limit one's duty of responsiveness to neediness as such. Yet such goals and responsibilities vary enormously from person to person.

Adjustment of publicly imposed burdens (say, taxes) to account for all of these variations is not feasible, and would, in any case, entail overly intrusive prying into private life. So public enforcement of beneficence has a special tendency to impose more on individuals than their individual circumstances warrant. This is not a decisive objection. Laws have to be tailored to what is typical. But the greater the prevalence of individual impositions which are not justifiable by the situation of the individual who is politically coerced, the stronger the case must be for engaging the state in enforcing an obligation rather than leaving this to the initiative of those bound by it.

To meet its burdens of justification, an argument for a duty to use laws, to some extent, to promote Sympathy must describe important ways in which some reliance on these public means would be superior to total privatization. Three important disadvantages of total privatization, relevant to the case for tax-financed help to the foreign poor, are difficulties in coordination, competitive loss through freelance giving and the risk of deadly negligence.

The more important it is that a goal be pursued through projects that are large scale, dependent on reliable support over long periods of time, interactive with other large and long-term projects, or in need of regulation through political deliberations, the stronger the case for government participation. Without coordination and assurance requiring the force of law, too few resources are apt to be provided, in the wrong patterns. For these reasons, such diverse endeavors of the people of a country as highway construction, banking and the protection of large tracts of wilderness do not go well unless government plays an active role. The same considerations extend to some important projects for helping needy people in developing countries. Voluntary individual choices of what to donate are not feasible or desirable alternatives to large scale, long-term, negotiated commitments of governments of developed countries to help governments of developing countries establish and maintain essential infrastructure (say, decent road networks in Africa) or to provide hard currency reserves to meet and forestall crises.

In the second place, the implementation of demands of beneficence by laws rather than private initiative protects responsible people from competitive defeat by those who do not live up to their own duties of beneficence.

For nearly everyone, large private contributions would impose a cost of disadvantage in competing with others who do not similarly contribute. Access to such centrally important goods as a nice house in a pleasant neighborhood with good local schools is mainly determined by the capacity to outbid others. So people resort to funding by taxation to avoid harming themselves by doing good, not just to force others to do good.

While these considerations are reasons to favor some reliance on the state as opposed to total privatization, their proper political role might be severely limited by the need to respect the diversity of causes that are close to benefactors' hearts. Political deliberations among citizens who care profoundly about their distinctive affiliations and conceptions of the good must respect the pursuit of a great many causes that are not best promoted by public provision. (In the United States, charitable contributions tend to express religious affiliations.) So the need to give people fair and adequate opportunities to honor their individual attachments to worthwhile causes could limit publicly funded beneficence toward the foreign poor to part of what Rawls calls "the exchange branch" of government, in which those for whom governmental provision of a good is preferable get such provision but are required to fully cover its cost.[1] Not much would be transferred abroad by this route, if actual beneficent concerns continue to favor causes within the borders.

What converts governmental help to the foreign poor by a developed country from a minor prerogative to a significant duty is the special connection of their needs with the default position in the project of Sympathy. For anyone who equally values everyone's life, the fact that a type of help would do more for a greater number of the neediest is a serious reason to favor it as part of the policies of giving that discharge her duty of Sympathy. A strong attachment to a worthwhile cause can justify some departure, but there is a need for such a special justification, which ought to leave some room for doing what most effectively helps those who are neediest. Unlike most worthy causes, this ought to be everyone's. Poor people in developing countries have the severest unmet needs and constitute the vast majority of those with serious unmet needs. So, if help for these people would be effective, citizens of a developed country ought to provide it as a significant proportion of the giving required by the duty of Sympathy.

Coordinative needs and the reduction of competitive loss provide reasons to use government, to some extent, to implement this obligation of all fellow-citizens. In addition, because this particular cause is both urgent and obligatory, another consideration comes into play, the duty to use political coercion to reduce the incidence of deadly negligence. Where the neediest who can be helped the most live abroad, local concerns are sure to get an excessive share of support, through backing by local resources that every responsible person regards as morally irrelevant. The class agent who calls every year for more money for alma mater is enough of an acquaintance to induce shame, or, in any case, to make it unseemly to abruptly end the conversation. The local poor threaten more frequent unappetizing spectacles than the foreign poor. Countering these irrelevancies, the use of the government of a developed country to help the poor of developing countries avoids negligence with dire consequences that would otherwise occur. In this last respect, the rationale for governmental help for the foreign poor is like the rationale for using state coercion to enforce the responsibilities of parents toward their children.

General beneficence has yielded a political duty of concern for the foreign poor. But its extent is still narrowed by the limitations of Sympathy, even in the most advanced developed countries. What worsens lives in developed countries is determined by secure attachments to relatively expensive personal goals, which tend to become more demanding in the course of history. Enduring commitments to local worthy causes reduce the mandate to help the foreign poor. Developed countries are the site of demanding special responsibilities, including political responsibilities to those who are disadvantaged among compatriots, even though they are much better off than the poor of developing countries.

This last constraint, of special political responsibility, might seem to end, not just to limit, political duties of foreign beneficence, if one takes the goal of basing one's political order on self-respectful loyalty to require priority for least advantaged compatriots. Following Rawls' lead, egalitarian political philosophers often express this political responsibility as a requirement "to make the worst-off as well-off as possible," i.e., to do what can be done to promote the life-prospects of a typical member of the most disadvantaged group among compatriots, then, the next-most-disadvantaged, and so on up. It is always understood that a goal of precise maximization of the worst-off situation is neither feasible nor desirable: its pursuit would disrupt the economy and interfere with civil liberties, privacy, secure expectations and civic trust. But there would be no such objection to a policy that eliminates one drain of resources from disadvantaged compatriots, namely, a ban on state-funded foreign beneficence. Why isn't this ban a dictate of political responsibility?

To create the required space for beneficence, one must accept that general beneficence is not a repellent practice; it has positive importance for nearly everyone, not just rich people and saints. Doing what Sympathy requires is, for nearly everyone, a way of escaping crabbed self-concern, overcoming alienation from humanity as a whole, and making one's life more valuable to oneself. If they are not utterly destitute, people want to help those worse off than themselves. By the same token, it is demeaning and depriving to treat disadvantaged compatriots in a developed country as people for whom responsiveness to the needy is a repellent burden. Telling them, "We won't use the least bit that might go to you to help the world's neediest" is not assurance that underpins their civic loyalty, but an insult that properly inspires their alienation. Yet the political duty of concern for disadvantaged compatriots is grounded on the pursuit of self-respectful loyalty. Thus, the ban on state-financed foreign beneficence would misinterpret the demands of egalitarian justice among compatriots. "Make the worst-off as well-off as possible" is a slogan that has to be interpreted in light of the considerations of loyalty, trust and respect that justify it in the first place.

Nonetheless, it is certainly the case that the more seriously disadvantaged a compatriot is, the weaker the tie between her integrity and purely beneficent concern for others. A political society that seeks the self-respectful loyalty of all its members cannot help needier foreigners out of sheer beneficence at the cost of significant reduction of life-prospects of seriously disadvantaged compatriots. The presence of disadvantaged compatriots may not abolish political duties of foreign beneficence. But it does further reduce their demands, which are, in any case, small for other reasons.

Because of the transnational responsibilities created by the actual network of transnational interactions, the small scope of the political duty of beneficence toward the foreign poor does not, remotely, establish the current limits of the political duty of people in developed countries to help the foreign poor. Still, one can imagine a different world. Suppose, for example, that developed countries were all in the Eastern Hemisphere and that, through a bizarre postponement of the intrusion of 1492, the lands of the Western Hemisphere were only just discovered by Easterners, mere curious travelers, who have found the West to be full of many poor people, typically much needier than the poor of any Eastern Hemisphere country. The political duty of a citizen of a developed country to give up advantages in the interest of Westerners would, then, be extremely undemanding on the scale of Western neediness. This seems an appropriate response to the Poor New World. If Columbus, Cortez and Pizarro had simply been highly adventurous tourists, Ferdinand and Isabella's duties to give up advantages in the interest of the New World poor would have been small.

It might seem that this assessment of the moral importance of relationships requires acceptance of disengagement from responsibilities that merits Robert

Goodin's disdainful label, "clubbish justice."[2] Suppose that governments, enterprises and people based in developed countries were to retreat from developing countries, avoiding activities in which they would take advantage of others if they abused their power. Once they have made good for past abuses, they confine help to those outside the rich countries' club to the limited demands of Sympathy, even though the poor nonmembers are much worse off than before the retreat, above all because of the end of vital commercial opportunities. How could the members of this rich countries' club be condemned to the extent that they should be, without relying on a principle of general beneficence more demanding than Sympathy?

Part of the condemnation might note that retreat is not as easy as it seems. Unintended cross-border processes such as releasing greenhouse gases into the global atmospheric sink will give rise to harmful effects in developing countries, whatever the desire for retreat. If borders are open to goods and people, there is a need to guard against immoral participation in exploitation. Departures from open borders must be justified as means of avoiding significant worsening inside. Disengagement can be part of an active process of disruptive betrayal, when it leaves vulnerable people saddled with arrangements formerly imposed, which were reasonably well-suited to old forms of engagement, but are now made dysfunctional by the unilateral divorce. However, these piecemeal criticisms of illusions of retreat do not seem to capture the basic irresponsibility of unilaterally ending all the forms of interaction that people in developing countries need.

The deeper condemnation would begin with the observation that the retreat would be profoundly irrational. Every process in which power is currently abused is of a kind that can be engaged in responsibly to the benefit of stronger parties, based in developed countries. For example, if an American firm's low wages in Thailand merely reflect difficulties in generating net revenue using Thai labor, then the firm can benefit while displaying full appreciation of the interests and autonomy of its Thai employees. The morally troubling question is whether the firm irresponsibly derives additional benefits from weak bargaining power due to desperate neediness. The use of threat influence to shape negotiations and steer the course of development and the use of violence to sustain or change regimes can be both responsible and beneficial to the strong and rich. The self-portrayals of great powers are broadly accurate portraits of how this could be done, however fantastic they may be as depictions of reality.

Because of its irrationality, the retreat into a rich countries' club would violate the commitment to do one's part in implementing the Principle of Sympathy, the same commitment as yielded the duty of nearby rescue. Without threatening to worsen the lives of affluent participants, a policy of continuing engagement in genuine cooperation with the needy sustains an effective division of labor in discharging Sympathy, counters tendencies to shirk and postpone, and combines concern for needs with a proper valuing of the self-reliance of the needy. Indeed, even in the absence of prior interaction, there is a limited duty to extend cooperation, rather than a cold shoulder, to the needy. If one's current activities (or activities toward which one is inclined and for which one is prepared) would readily, naturally extend to a group of needy people, in a process that benefits them and oneself as well, one should extend these activities to them, without taking advantage of them. This policy would not lead a typical doctor in Chicago to move her practice to a doctor-starved country or a firm with experiences and personal ties rooted in Toulouse to move operations to employment-starved locales in Chad. But large firms engaged in their restless pursuit of opportunities and great powers engaged in negotiations of international arrangements would violate this duty of cooperation if they held back from the borders of poor countries in need of their engagement.

The fact that responsible transnational engagement would benefit the strong does not make the duty to engage responsibly an undemanding duty. The shift from actual abuses of power to responsibility in relationships would deprive people in developed countries of resources by which they now pursue worthwhile goals they have come to care about, disrupting projects on which they have come to rely. If transnational conduct had always been responsible, people in developed countries might have formed less expensive goals in light of lesser resources, and responsibility now would not be disruptive. However, growing up as they actually do, they face different moral demands. Similarly, if there were only trivial departures from responsibility in transnational interactions, those seeking benefits to the global poor from fulfillment of unmet responsibilities would rightly look, primarily, to the duty of general beneficence. This is not our world.

Political duties of beneficence toward the foreign poor of developing countries, though genuine, are undemanding and yield little on the scale of current unmet needs. It is time to take account of the other political duties to help them, involving special relationships, in summing up benefits and demands of currently unmet responsibilities.

## Sums of Benefits and Demands

Each special relationship that generates a transnational responsibility is limited in geographic scope. But taken together, they cover virtually the whole developing world. Poor countries, such as China, whose course of development is not deeply shaped by external domineering influence tend to have strengths that make exploitation of their workers lucrative and are burdened by inequities in global trade arrangements. Transnational duties of fairness in coping with global climate change create important duties not to inhibit growth unduly within their borders. Countries not of much interest as sites of exploitation tend to be apt sites for client regimes or for exemplary projects of structural adjustment. Lacking large internal markets, they tend to be deeply affected by the shaping of global trade and finance. (In 2006, exports and imports of merchandise amounted to over a half of Malian GDP, four-fifths of Honduran GDP, but only a fifth of U.S. GDP.[3]) The prospects of people in poor agrarian economies are especially sensitive to global efforts to meet the greenhouse challenge. When countries are poor but endowed with rich natural resources or a strategic location, developed countries are especially energetic in shaping the local terms of life through rewards and threats that promote the local dominance of elites favoring their interests. Such countries are, disproportionately, the targets of violence, direct or sponsored, that advances the power or wealth of leading developed countries. If any isolated, destitute countries are unaffected by the network of exploitation, subordination and damage, these outliers are appropriate beneficiaries of the political duty of beneficence of citizens of developed countries. The Principle of Sympathy dictates provision for neediness as such in addition to fulfillment of special responsibilities. Counting a response dictated by a special relationship—whether parenthood or structural adjustment—as a beneficent response to neediness is bad moral bookkeeping.

How much would the fulfillment of currently unmet transnational responsibilities benefit people in developing countries? An adequate answer requires breaking a tempting fixation on foreign aid.

Currently, the flow of foreign aid—transfers of goods, services and funds (including below-market-rate credit) from the government of one country to the government or people of another, directly or via multilateral agencies—is meager. In 2006, it amounted to $115 per person in donor countries, 0.31% of their total Gross National Income,[4] and $21 per person in recipient countries.[5] Foreign aid is a simple and obvious means of discharging responsibilities to return benefits from exploitation, promote successful development, and compensate for past destruction. Large claims are made for an increase from the current, meager level, a change which is proclaimed the route to *The End of Poverty* in the title of a widely read book by a major economist.[6] So it is tempting to base the case for great benefits from the fulfillment of unmet responsibilities on the potential of increased aid.

This would be a mistake. Increases in foreign aid beyond the average seem, in current practice, to yield small though significant benefits, but with diminishing returns that tend to dwindle to nothing at the current upper level of aid-dependency.[7] Clearly, current practice is marred by irresponsibility in donors. But aid efficacy also seems to be seriously constrained by limited institutional and political capacities in recipient countries. Indeed, these capacities may, to some extent, be weakened by foreign-aid-based processes, when aid nourishes client networks of negligent regimes, diminishes local political accountability and enmeshes a hard-pressed local bureaucracy in interactions with external agents.[8]

Perhaps, nonetheless, the small scale of current aid is its major limitation: a scaling up of aid to sustain large and interdependent projects of improving infrastructure, education and public health would, with feasible improvements in management and monitoring, do enormous good. This is the gist of Jeffrey Sachs' resourceful, widely read case for scaling up aid in *The End of Poverty*. Or perhaps scathing critiques of this "Big Push," such as William Easterly's *The White Man's Burden*,[9] are, in essence, right: the multiplication of aid would distort and undermine local initiatives, pouring funds into vast projects with long gestation periods that cannot be adequately monitored, managed and adjusted to local needs. Current assessments of efficacy combine with current responsibilities to dictate some increase in the amount and improvement in the nature of foreign aid. But uncertainties about the impact of the scale of aid on recipients' and donors' actions and effectiveness make it unclear how much could be accomplished.

Rather than wrapping the question of benefit in these uncertainties, one should distinguish foreign aid from the many other ways in which people in developed countries could change their government's conduct in the interest of people in developing countries. I will speak of this broader category as one of "help" to distinguish it from the specific vehicle of foreign aid. Often, help that is not foreign aid involves a kind of transfer, giving up advantages in the interest of the disadvantaged. But unlike foreign aid, such transfers work by reducing developed countries' interference with the opportunities of individuals in developing countries.

Stopping the wrongful resort to violence as a means of domineering influence would avoid a vast toll of death, suffering and destruction. If an international trade regime that could be the outcome of responsible deliberations were to replace the current outcome of bullying, there would be large gains to needy people from enhanced economic opportunity. For example, appropriate responsiveness to degrees of need for transnational opportunities would lead to the adoption of something like Andrew Charlton's proposal that all members of the WTO commit themselves to abolishing all tariffs on goods from developing countries that are poorer (as measured by per capita GDP) and smaller (as measured by total GDP) than themselves.[10] In responsible deliberations over the framework for globalization, appropriate concern for openness to transnational movement of labor along with openness to goods and capital would lead to a substantial increase in developed countries of immigrants from developing countries, including the unskilled. (Even apart from trade negotiations, greater openness to goods and people from developing countries would implement developed countries' imperial responsibilities: powers steering the course of economic development, making it more dependent on world markets, ought to open their markets to those whose means of self-advancement they shape.) On evidence cited in Chapter 3, Charlton's proposal would bring benefits in the range of $100 billion a year to people now living in developing countries, and so would a modest increase in openness to immigration without bias against the unskilled. Finally, responsible deliberations over greenhouse gas reduction would save hundreds of millions of people in developing countries, especially those neediest to begin with, from burdens of hunger, disease and displacement, while minimizing the extent to which the pursuit of climate safety blocks escapes from destitution.

These benefits would result from a dramatic reduction of interference with people's efforts to advance themselves and their dependents. The local institutional limits on aid efficacy are by-passed. So the benefits to those helped might well far exceed what foreign aid could provide. Transnational responsibility dictates an effort to expand effective foreign aid, as well. This might provide further large gains. But if aid absorbency proves to be a hard constraint, this expands the duty to rely on other, highly productive means of helping, rather than limiting the duty to help.

So far, the over-all assessment of unmet transnational responsibilities has concerned benefits to people in developing countries who are owed more help. Since governments of developed countries act in basic concert in the activities generating transnational responsibilities and developed countries generally benefit from transnational exploitation, the unmet obligation is shared among the citizens of developed countries. Different citizenries' respective portions of this obligation depend on differences in initiative and resources, which allocate an especially large unmet responsibility to the United States.

The sum of foreign benefits from meeting these responsibilities has turned out to be great. But—to further explore the benefactors' side—would such fulfillment be genuinely demanding, imposing morally serious costs in some developed countries? Since the United States has both the lion's share of responsibilities and a significant minority of economically vulnerable citizens, it is the natural focus (though hardly the only site) for this investigation of the demands of transnational justice.

Here, too, concentration on foreign aid distorts assessment of transnational responsibility. Recognizing uncontroversial limits to aid absorbency, informed fervent advocates of increased foreign aid make no significant demands on people in developed countries. For example, when Jeffrey Sachs proposed, in 2005, that official development assistance immediately double and then increase to triple the 2005 flow in 2015, he noted that the tripled flow would amount to about 0.5 percent of donor countries' total Gross National Income.[11] In an average year from 1990 through 2006, the rate of increase in their Gross National Income was about five times as great.[12] Progressivity in taxation, protection of domestic social programs and sensible macroeconomic timing could limit the internal human costs of the outward flow of foreign aid so that people in developed countries suffer no significant loss.

However, it would be irresponsible just to take this path among the several ways to help. The limited efficacy of aid is one important reason to help by reducing interference with the opportunities of people in developing countries. The value of self-reliance is another. Everywhere, people properly prefer to get ahead by their own efforts and, if they need help, properly prefer it from those to whom they are bound by symmetrical ties of family or civic obligation. This preference should be reflected in the choice of means to help them. By the same token, transnational respect makes the removal of transnational constraints on opportunities, rather than compensatory aid, especially appropriate as a remedy for inequitable constraint. For example, in avoiding inequitable constraints on self-advancement in a trade, investment, property-rights or greenhouse gas regime, elimination of constraint rather than aid to its victims should be the first resort.

Once the various ways of helping by reducing interference with foreign opportunities, rather than giving foreign aid, have their proper place, transnational responsibility poses a significant risk of serious loss to vulnerable people in developed countries. For example, moral responsibility dictates stringent emissions reductions concentrated in developed countries. But, as we saw in Chapter 4, this equitable allocation of burdens is likely to disrupt the employment, lifetime economic trajectories and ways of life of a significant number of people in developed countries, especially the United States. No doubt, these countries can afford payments and facilities within their borders that soften the domestic blows. But, in developed as in developing countries, people rightly want to get ahead self-reliantly, continuing in the way of life with which they identify. Even if these aspirations are violated for good reason, they should be honored by taking their violation to be a morally serious cost.

Increased openness to goods, services and immigration from developing countries has a similar impact on the demands of global justice, masked by concentration on foreign aid. According to one influential estimate, about two-fifths of the decline in the relative wages of U.S. high school dropouts as compared with high school graduates from 1980 to 1995 was due to immigration while another 6–11% was due to imports using cheap labor in developing countries. High school graduates and those in the upper 80% of the wage distribution suffered no net burden.[13] But the unskilled are especially vulnerable and, hence, of special moral concern. In 2002, high school dropouts were 15% of the U.S. population over 25 but 37% of those over 25 who were below the official poverty line. They had a poverty rate of 23%, a two out of three probability of being poor for at least a year in their lives if white, a 98% chance if African-American.[14] The moral significance of the domestic costs of increased openness would be less than the significance of trapping people in China or Bangladesh in lives of fatigue, drudgery and ill-health. But these are significant costs, like other costs of trade equity such as the disruption of traditional rural ways of life in Europe and Japan, now protected at excessive cost to the rural poor of developing countries.

In sum, the vast benefits of meeting unmet transnational responsibilities would probably be accompanied by morally significant costs for people in developed countries. The evasion of those responsibilities on these grounds would dishonor ties to compatriots by using them as an excuse to neglect transnational ties that are also, independently, morally important. In response to the transnational demands, people in developed countries should express the proper valuing of ties to compatriots in another way. The total complex of modern relationships, which makes transnational justice demanding, should be taken to strengthen the demands of domestic justice, since the total complex requires extra help for disadvantaged compatriots to moderate the impact of transnational justice.

## Comparing Budgets

While clarity about the demands of transnational political responsibility requires broadening the topic beyond the use of government funds to help, one important prevalent conviction about those demands concerns aid in this narrow sense. It is a comparative judgment, noted in Chapter 2, which can now be assessed, in light of subsequent chapters. Countries which are among the best-off per capita contain many economically disadvantaged people. This is, paradigmatically, the circumstance of life in the United States. People in these countries generally believe that most of their government's spending on help to the disadvantaged should go to help disadvantaged compatriots, even if spending more to help disadvantaged foreigners than disadvantaged compatriots would do more to alleviate more serious needs. If one assumes that the only morally relevant fact about interactions across borders is the mere existence of commerce, then the strength of political responsibilities due to ties to compatriots and the weakness of transnational duties would support this comparative judgment, on the basis of arguments in the first two chapters of this book. But can this budgetary priority survive acceptance of the transnational political responsibilities created by the full range of actual transnational relationships?

An answer requires clearer accounting rules for identifying the sums that are compared. The difficulties in interpreting the comparative conviction should not be surprising, since the prevalent claim, "We owe more aid to disadvantaged people in our own country," rarely results from reflection on the relevant relationships, foreign and domestic.

The comparative belief will not be accurately represented if every use of public funds to help a needy compatriot is assigned to the patriotic budget. Often, these are payments from social insurance in the narrow sense: hedges against the frailties of old age or misfortune that people who are not currently disadvantaged have reason to fund through taxes in order to pool risks, minimize transaction costs or avoid future burdens of their own improvidence. What the *United States Statistical Abstract* lists as "Government Transfer Payments to Individuals" consists of funds mostly transferred to people currently in need. But the largest item is "Retirement and disability insurance benefits"; the second largest, "Medical payments," mostly goes to the elderly and disabled; the third largest, "Income maintenance," has supplements for the disabled or elderly as its leading component; and the fourth largest is "Unemployment insurance benefits." The three largest categories constitute over nine-tenths of total transfers. For those who are not born into great wealth, tax payments supporting these government transfers have an important function as insurance premiums, for themselves and, usually, as children who would otherwise risk a devastating clash of family obligations with nursing home costs. If the budgetary comparison paired total funds going to compatriots who are currently needy with total funds going to needy foreigners, the former might exceed the latter simply because of its insurance component. The prevalent conviction that compatriots should be put first surely requires more than this.

On the other hand, the prevalent conviction is not a comparison of domestic aid net of all indirect and long-term benefits to contributors with similarly uncompensated foreign aid. Some take nearly all domestic aid that justice requires, over and above social insurance, to yield correspondingly extensive indirect benefits, over the long run, in increased productivity, reduced crime, and increased social harmony. If they share the prevalent conviction about budgetary priority, they do not insist that the tiny unrecompensed residue be greater than the analogous residue in foreign aid. Rather, they are glad that proper loyalty to compatriots imposes such little sacrifice in the end. Others regard large claims of compensating benefits as speculation, even wishful thinking, while sharing the prevalent conviction of budgetary priority for compatriots. Like virtually all politically important matters of consensus, the conviction of budgetary priority is shared by fellow citizens with different views of social consequences. The common thought in the case at hand is that departure from a certain benchmark ought to prompt moral anxiety among fellow citizens, as an indication of neglect of domestic needs. In the benchmark comparison between foreign and domestic aid, expenditures are classified by immediate functions. If an expenditure on currently deprived compatriots results from insurance that currently undeprived compatriots are well-advised to choose as a hedge against those deprivations, this function removes it from the benchmark category of domestic aid. But otherwise, expenditures to help disadvantaged compatriots should be included. Foreign expenditures that serve to shore up allied regimes do not belong on the foreign side in the comparison of aid budgets if they would play no role in a commitment to relieve poverty. Otherwise, foreign economic assistance to developing countries should be counted. The common conviction is that if the latter sum comes to approach the former, citizens of a developed country with many disadvantaged people within the borders should take this as a sign of moral danger, evidence of injustice toward compatriots.

This shared benchmark of moral danger does not presuppose special limits to the efficacy of foreign aid. It is shared by people who take foreign aid to be a waste and by those who think that basic needs in developing countries could absorb vast quantities of aid with good effect. Even if a shift of funds from domestic to foreign aid would more effectively relieve more serious needs, the shift is held to be wrong

In light of the transnational responsibilities identified in previous chapters, this commitment to budgetary priority for compatriots is unjustified. If limits to the efficacy of foreign aid are put to one side, justice might well require such extensive reliance on foreign aid to fulfill responsibilities of dominion and repair, avoid wrongful exploitation, alleviate unjust burdens of trade liberalization, support adaptation to global climate change and compensate for recent inequities in the global trade and finance regime that it exceeds the requirements of just provision for disadvantaged compatriots. For example, in the United States in 2005, aid to disadvantaged compatriots was about $400 billion, over and above mere social insurance. If it came from taxes on the top 80 percent of the population by income, their contribution would be about $1,700 per person in that year. Even if the sum of domestic aid were significantly higher, a contribution at least as great in effective foreign aid to poor people in developing countries would not have been a sign of neglect of compatriots. — Certainly, a substantial shift of funds actually used to help disadvantaged compatriots to effective aid to the foreign poor would have reduced, rather than increasing, irresponsibility: U.S. development assistance amounted to $27 billion in that year, about 7 percent of domestic aid.[15]

Again, the web of transnational relationships has sustained a view of help to the global poor that is familiar from self-described cosmopolitan perspectives. However, one should not exaggerate the undermining of patriotic priority. The people of any developed country share their moral debt to the foreign poor with people in other developed countries and owe their part of the debt to poor foreigners who are vastly more numerous than their compatriots. So, in a developed country in which some people are disadvantaged, aid given to a typical disadvantaged compatriot would, presumably, be greater than aid given to a typical disadvantaged foreigner when all moral debts in aid are discharged.

## Political Feasibility and Cosmopolitan Priorities

What are the goals of the pursuit of justice that currently generates these benefits and demands? It might seem that the question has already been answered by the survey of unmet duties: a politically responsible person in a developed country should support measures returning gains from exploitation, a framework for trade that could result from responsible deliberations, and so forth. But to take this list as a full account of goals is to ignore two needs in moral reflection and political action.

First, the pursuit of international justice is advanced by a shared understanding of what is most important in the multiple tasks of reducing current international irresponsibility. Setting priorities according to the loudness of actual complaints means guidance by fashions and political resources that can produce a moral misallocation. While specialization has its uses, those pressing for international economic justice will want to have a common understanding of where their special causes fit into the current project of justice, so that they are allied as cooperators in a common task despite their inevitable competition for attention and funds.

Second, the pursuit of justice is furthered by connection with an inspiring positive goal. This is an especially urgent need of the relational perspective. The measures it requires would impose significant costs on deserving compatriots. Yet the current duties to which it appeals are largely duties to act responsibly in relationships of power that are, at best, regrettable. A world in which exploitation is responsibly managed, courses of development are imposed by domineering outside agents that take on their responsibility to make development work, and damage is inflicted by outside powers that compensate is not an ultimate aim apt to inspire efforts that make headway despite the opposition of currently irresponsible powers and the rational fears of vulnerable people in developed countries.

I will first describe priorities in overcoming current obstacles to global justice. Then, I will describe the ultimate aim that is implicit in the diverse current duties of global justice.

The complete fulfillment of all current transnational responsibilities would be a patchwork process, piecing together responsibilities with diverse distinctive emphases. The return of benefits of exploitation would be channeled abundantly toward China. Responsibilities due to imposed courses of development would be especially responsive to needs in sub-Saharan Africa and Latin America. Iraq would be a favored site for repair of imperial destruction. There is no reason to suppose that complete fulfillment would satisfy a global extrapolation of any familiar standard of domestic justice, or even that it would broadly conform to one type of standard of justice. Justice in a trade regime or a greenhouse gas regime is a matter of fair distribution in specific projects. Justice in fulfilling responsibilities in steering the course of development is a matter of provision for basic needs. Justice in imperial destruction is a matter of compensation. Because of this diversity in the standards regulating politically responsible choice in global processes, there is no such thing as "global distributive justice," in the sense of a single, determinate unifying standard concerned with material well-being throughout the world that regulates choice of particular arrangements.

If anything approaching a complete settling of moral accounts were a realistic prospect, then the absence of a regulative standard might be a troubling obstacle to effective coordination. But it is an appalling irony of the relational view that relations of transnational power that currently generate transnational responsibilities guarantee that transnational responsibilities will not, remotely, be met. An appreciation of how high the barriers are will make it clearer what standard of priority is appropriate to current endeavors.

The appalling irony reflects the nature of national decisionmaking in a world divided among governments of very unequal power. In part, the inevitable irresponsibility is due to inevitable self-absorption among electorates, in which anxieties of people in developed countries about their personal goals combine with the weak electoral force of foreign needs to drag the politics of developed countries from the track of justice. Apart from electoral self-absorption, the interests in economic power and domineering influence that shape the foreign policies of the major developed countries guarantee irresponsibility. Because of its leading role, I have emphasized ways in which interests in wealth and power in the United States depart from justice. But the other major developed countries share the same general interests and press in the same directions in shaping the institutional framework for trade and structuring the course of economic development, often allying with the United States in violent initiatives, as well.

In addition to guaranteeing harm, the interests shaping foreign policy in major developed countries guarantee that foreign aid, the remedy that is least threatening to the power of elites and the vulnerability of the disadvantaged in developed countries, will not do much good. To begin with, volatile change in the level of aid to a country severely reduces its usefulness in development. In a leading study, Ales Bulir and Javier Hamann assessed aid volatility from 1975 to 2003 in a large sample of developing countries receiving significant amounts of development aid. The ratio of aid to government revenue was, on average, 35%, and the volatility of aid was twelve times greater than the volatility of revenue. In 2000–3, it was 45 times greater, 56 times in the poorest countries. Aid tended to decline when government revenue declined, rather than compensating.[16] Far from having an interest in eliminating volatility, great powers, especially the United States, have an interest in using aid to cajole, support and threaten that guarantees volatility as challenges and opportunities change location over time.

The multiplicity of aid flows creates enduring problems of coordination, a notorious source of waste, missed opportunities and diversion of limited capacities of local bureaucracies. The multiplicity mostly results from the predominance of bilateral aid, which is about three-quarters of the total. Most donors, especially the two largest by far, the United States and Japan, openly proclaim a sufficient cause of this diversity, the use of aid to advance their distinctive national interests.

Similarly, over-reliance on "technical cooperation" is a never-ending scandal, sustained by an enduring rationale of power. Technical cooperation, i.e., the provision of experts from donor countries and scholarships for study there, is a gigantic presence, 29% of net bilateral official development assistance in 2006.[17] Despite the dedication and skill of individual foreign experts, statistical findings, anecdotal evidence and common sense all suggest that this much reliance on foreign expertise neglects local knowledge and local ties. The correlation of economic growth with reliance on technical cooperation is negative.[18] "Technical assistance has become part of the problem of institutional weakness [in Africa], not the solution," is the verdict of a former Deputy Administrator of USAID, Carol Lancaster.[19] Yet current reliance on "technical cooperation" is just right as a means of influencing poor countries. A continued high level of provision of foreign experts combined with scholarship programs nurtures an international network of relationships of acquaintance, certification, reliance, shared cultural cues and shared political assumptions dominated by people and institutions in developed countries.

The stringent limits of political feasibility make it unimportant in practice to find a general pattern in the full dues of responsibility. These dues will not, remotely, be paid. But within these limits, people seeking to make progress against injustice will benefit from a shared understanding of global priorities in their task. The right understanding is quasi-cosmopolitan. Over-all standards adapted from more cosmopolitan perspectives set the right priorities in the effort to make the world somewhat less unjust.

The web of unmet responsibilities has turned out to connect developed countries with all developing countries. Within entrenched limits of political feasibility, each major form of transnational irresponsibility will impose especially serious burdens on those who have great difficulty in general meeting urgent needs; so each creates widespread suffering, not just legitimate complaints of serious unfairness. When it is a daunting task, requiring much time and effort, to right injustice and negligence, priority ought to be given to helping those who suffer on account of irresponsibility, favoring measures that help those whose suffering is greatest, that help more sufferers and that afford more relief. Because of the correlation of suffering from transnational irresponsibility with general vulnerability, these priorities in rectification will be the priorities of beneficence, favoring measures that help those most in need, that help more people in serious need and that afford more important relief.[20] Concern for the needy should guide us in pursuit of responsibility in transnational relationships.

Though helpful in setting priorities, this borrowing from the standpoint of beneficence is itself troublingly fragmented. Very different policies may help the most people in serious need (often, people in China and India), help those who are neediest (disproportionately concentrated in sub-Saharan Africa) and do the most in helping needy beneficiaries (a topic of endless debates over efficacy). So it would be useful to have further guidance in judging these trade-offs. Here, those with a vision of economic justice grounded on relationships can adapt Rawls' original position.

In this adaptation, one asks which package of policies one would prefer behind a veil of ignorance of which country is one's home and of the specific content of one's life-goals, if one tried to advance one's interests while observing two highest-order interests: satisfaction of transnational responsibilities toward developing countries as a whole (an input here, not an outcome of the thought-experiment) and participation in self-advancement, individual and national, honoring values of self-reliance. Using this device, one balances gains and losses for all whose wellbeing is at stake in a way that respects all. For example, the weight of numbers will make a difference, since it increases the odds of being helped if the veil is lifted, but so will the degree of neediness and the amount of relief of those most helped, and so will the distinctive capacity for independent self-advancement of a large, poor, but effectively governed country, such as China. Relevant factors influence choice in a way that does not depend on investing any actual person's life with more importance than anyone else's.

Rawls' arguments that the domestic original position would lead to the choice of the difference principle, with its strict priority for the worst-off, rely on considerations that are not relevant here. Within a mobile society in which educational facilities and labor markets are shared, there is, he noted, a strong tendency of policies improving the situation of the better-off to be included in what maximizes the life-prospects of those worse-off.[21] The tendency is much weaker internationally. The type of acceptance that ought to be available domestically, Rawls argued, is deep allegiance by all—including the most disadvantaged—to a shared political order, in which a citizen identifies with the continuance of the shared institutions as central to her own good.[22] This is an overly demanding international requirement. In arguing against conceptions of justice supported by attention to probabilities behind the veil of ignorance, Rawls rejected gambles that take on avoidable risks of intolerable outcomes to improve on satisfactory circumstances.[23] No such gamble is in question in the relevant choices among politically feasible global alternatives, since every option consigns some to situations of desperate neediness.

The conflicts and connections among needs of different groups of the global poor are too diverse and changing to permit the choice of a single all-purpose enduring distributive standard for resolving trade-offs, an analogue of the difference principle, from the standpoint of this veil of ignorance. Still, when one chooses among alternative sets of changes in the global status quo on grounds of justice, one can better specify the right realistic aspirations in current circumstances by asking what one would choose, if one were governed by the general interests that I have described and chose in ignorance of one's nationality. This is an important truth in accounts of justice demanding globally impartial concern, even if none is valid as a whole.

## Global Civic Friendship as an Ultimate Aim

The appalling current limits to political feasibility make it all the more important to describe the sort of world that is the ultimate aim of the aspiration to global justice. The aim can both motivate resistance to those limits and help to locate future prospects of justice that they obscure.

The ultimate aim embodies the hope for the world implicit in a sincere commitment to fulfill transnational political responsibilities. When this goal is reached, bad things will still happen, due, for example, to disease and natural disasters. But transnational responsibility will not dictate a search for further large and enduring political measures to change the life-prospects of people in foreign countries.

Beneficence is an independent feature of transnational political obligation. A commitment to this aspect of transnational responsibility entails an aspiration to a world in which no country is so poor that its citizens, if responsible to one another, must hope for help from abroad (apart from expected aid in transient catastrophes) despite properly valuing self-reliance. So long as such poverty endures, responsible citizens of richer countries must be on the look-out for further means of enabling foreigners to meet their basic needs. They must implement these remedies now if the cost is not too great, and otherwise, in good faith, prepare for later implementation. If, at last, self-reliance is the proper basis, everywhere, for meeting basic needs, the people of some countries will still lack resources that people have elsewhere for attaining worthwhile life-goals. The advantaged foreigners may, admirably, help them to meet these goals. But these good deeds will not be a remedy for neediness that is dictated by political obligation.

However, dire, remediable poverty is hardly the only defect that transnational responsibility seeks to make good. Independently, the pursuit of international justice seeks to avoid and repair defects in interactions across borders. Indeed, this other aspect of the global aim might be seen as having greater practical importance, since current transnational responsibilities are, predominantly, duties to make global interactions better-ordered, beneficence to one side.

The various defects in current interactions have a shared feature: they involve taking advantage of people in foreign countries, using their weakness in ways that show inadequate regard for their interests and capacities for choice. The positive value that is honored in seeking to right these wrongs is cooperation, i.e., interaction based on deserved mutual trust, on terms that all participants can willingly, self-respectfully support. Now, international relations constantly give people in developing countries reason to resent governments, firms and people in developed countries, while people in developed countries merit this resentment if they do not pay the price of alienation from their governments and unease at their own prosperity. To a substantial extent, the transnational shaping of terms of self-advancement is based on the exploitation of fear, desperation and vulnerability rather than joint, self-respectful, informed acceptance. If these defects are overcome, transnational life will be a shared activity, based on self-respectful trust, in which people throughout the world affirm the importance of one another's lives and capacities for choice. Each government, while acting to fulfill political responsibilities among those in its territory, will act in ways, and insure that those under its authority act in ways, that merit the trust of the people of other countries. This aim of reliance on willing cooperation is a positive and inspiring goal for those seeking to make headway against wrongs that rely on fear.

When an ultimate aim has multiple aspects, one hopes that they are either ranked or interdependent. Otherwise, at best, the ideal prompts insistent questions of which aspect to pursue, while, at worst, it poses recurrent problems of trade-off while offering no solution. The two aspects of the ultimate aim of global justice are highly interdependent.

On the one hand, it would be naive to suppose that governments of developed countries would lift all burdens of dire need that properly self-reliant people in developing countries cannot lift for themselves, even though those governments, together with leading firms based in those countries, exploit weaknesses of those people without adequate regard for their interests and capacities for choice. Exploitation produces insensitivity to the neediness that facilitates it, insensitivity that is especially secure when those who benefit are insulated from the immediate reverberations of discontent among foreigners they exploit, with whom they share no strong ties of valued history or common culture.

Conversely, the aim of a world in which transnational interactions are based on mutual trust and willing, self-respectful assent entails ending the distinctive dire neediness of developing countries. The stark inequality guarantees that advantage will be taken. By making it hard for the destitute to hold out, easy for the well-endowed to benefit from their desperation, the economic differences create a constant temptation to exploit, to which the well-endowed will inevitably often succumb. Moreover, even if the citizenries of rich countries were constantly to strive to resist this temptation and frequently succeeded, they would show contempt for the autonomy of people in poor countries if they did not seek to end those foreigners' continuing distinctive dire neediness. For if one adequately values others' capacity for choice, meriting their trust, one seeks to end a situation in which they must depend, for their wellbeing, on one's benevolent inclination not to exploit their weakness.

This double rationale for reducing inequality is characteristic of relationships flawed by inequalities of power. Consider a Victorian marriage in which the husband benevolently seeks, of his own accord, not to make use of his opportunity to benefit from the marriage while ignoring his wife's views and independent needs, but makes no political effort to support changes that eliminate the lack of opportunities for independent self-advancement that forces wives to defer when husbands seek deference. He is doubly unworthy of her trust. In the first place, given partiality and restricted awareness that are inevitable among human beings, he is bound to take inadequate account of her views and needs if his continued enjoyment of their relationship is much less dependent on her satisfaction than her continued enjoyment is on his. In the second place, he shows that he cannot be trusted in his political activities to treat her capacity to shape her life through her own will as just as important as his own.

Similarly, to show an adequate valuing of willing cooperation, citizens must seek a world in which bullying is not a rational way for governments of better-off countries to set the terms of interaction with worse-off countries. Even a sincere commitment on the part of a rich country not to exercise the enduring capacity to bully a poor one would not yield adequate consideration of the views and interests of people who are geographically and culturally remote and who do not take part in domestic political processes. Symmetrical abilities to opt out and the consequent mutual need to attend to each other's views and interests are essential bases for adequate regard. Also, so long as they must depend on the generosity of foreigners to fulfill the basic functions of self-government, people in poor countries do not shape their own lives through their own endeavors and deliberations.[24]

Freedom from these indignities does not require economic equality. For example, Germany's reasons to seek Greece's willing acceptance of EU measures are strong enough, despite considerable economic inequality. But genuine cooperation is incompatible with the stark inequality between the basically prosperous and the desperately needy that separates developed from developing countries.

A combined commitment to help others and to respect their autonomy is characteristic of well-ordered relations in personal life as well as political interactions. Friends who live up to their responsibilities help in time of need and also cherish their friends' autonomy. (Jane Austen's Emma has to learn to let her friends make their own mistakes—learning, along the way, they are apt to know their interests better than she does, in any case. In this process, she learns how to be a good friend.) In the first and most penetrating investigation of the ethics of friendship, Aristotle emphasizes both the barrier that deep inequality poses to friendship and the analogy between genuine friendship and well-ordered political relationships: civic friendship holds a just polity together. International relations based on rational, enduring mutual trust in due regard for interests and respect for autonomy are, in a similar broad usage, a form of friendship. So one might characterize the ultimate aim of global justice as global civic friendship.

If and when this ultimate aim is reached, international political life will be attentive to considerations of distributive justice. For example, international deliberations will seek a fair distribution of the burdens of the joint pursuit of common goals. However, there is no reason to suppose that responsible political choice will be governed by a unified global standard of fairness used to judge inequalities in material prospects throughout the world. A global analogue of relationships among fellow citizens now would be required to sustain this extrapolation of standards of justice now appropriate within borders. But it is unlikely that a sufficiently centralized global authority with a sufficiently broad and deep impact on economic life would regulate global political cooperation based on mutually respectful trust.

Indeed, once current barriers to global civic friendship are overcome, it is apt to be even truer than it is now that the coercive imposition of terms of self-advancement occurs within borders, that differences in life prospects are determined by decisions among compatriots concerning shared laws and policies, and that the citizenry of a sovereign government have ultimate local control over life within the borders. Domineering influence will no longer shape foreigners' lives. The accountability of representatives and the resolution of important disagreements through appeals to shared convictions will be better sustained through national or regional than through global processes of political decisionmaking. Even with heightened global interdependence, the decisions with the greatest impact on people's prosperity will be decisions that they make with their compatriots (or fellow members of regional federations). For, in addition to creating local opportunities, these decisions determine how effectively people take advantage of global opportunities.

Of course, at the stage of global civic friendship, there will be important international arrangements of global scope. Would political responsibility within these institutions at least require adherence to a difference principle restricted to their impact, requiring that the worst-off countries enjoy the greatest benefits from these global arrangements? Perhaps not. In our current situation of stark inequality, responsible representatives of destitute countries cannot willingly accept arrangements that benefit countries that are well-off yet do not specially benefit their own desperately needy people. But when the worst-off are not separated from the best-off as developing countries are from developed countries today, responsible deliberations may take a different course. For example, if a proposed agreement would impose the same restrictions of prerogatives on each country (say, through reciprocal tariff reductions), each can provide for severely needy people within its borders, none is seriously burdened by the proposed arrangements and all would equally benefit, then it seems an evasion of responsibility for the worst-off country to insist, instead, on greater benefits.

If cosmopolitanism is understood to require a global extrapolation of principles of domestic justice, the ultimate aim of global civic friendship is not cosmopolitan. But in another sense, it is utterly cosmopolitan. Justice among fellow citizens expresses an aspiration to willing, self-respectful cooperation as a basis for mutual reliance. To adopt the ideal of global civic friendship is to affirm the same aspiration as a basis for global justice. The differences between domestic and global justice reflect the different forms that mutual reliance takes, but not a difference in the interpersonal good that is pursued.

## The Future of Global Injustice

A conception of an ultimate aim of global justice sets a long-term goal for current struggles, but also raises the question of how long the struggle can be expected to last. The sad answer seems to be: the reduction of severe international inequalities that global civic friendship requires will postpone its attainment for a long time.

When incomes are converted from local currencies to U.S. dollars at foreign exchange rates, international inequalities are stark. In 2006, 16% of the world's people lived in countries rated "high income" by the World Bank, with per capita Gross National Incomes of at least $11,1160; 72% lived in countries in the "low" and "lower middle income" categories, with an income ceiling of $3,595. The lower 72% had 13% of the total Gross National Income that year, the top 16% had 77%. Low and middle income countries, with 84% of population, had 23% of total GNI, just as, in 1980, at the start of globalization, low and middle income countries, with 82% of world population, had 23% of total GDP.[25] Over the decades, despite the growth of China and India, the share of the leading developed countries in these global totals has not changed much. In 2006, the 70% share of the combined GDPs of the United States, Canada, the countries of the European Union and Japan in Gross World Product was the same as it had been in 1970; the 5% decline since 1980 was almost entirely due to economic stagnation in Japan. China, with 20% of world population, had 5% of total GDP.[26]

Because it reflects the desirabilities of goods in world markets, the evaluation of national economies at foreign exchange rates yields important indicators of world economic power. But services and goods produced and sold within a developing country—for example, housing, housekeeping and foodstuffs raised for local consumption—tend to be very cheap relative to services and goods entering international trade, much more so than in developed countries. Another rate of exchange, equating local purchasing powers, is needed to assess standards of living.[27] At purchasing power parity, international inequalities are still stark. The low and lower middle income countries where 72% of the world's people live had combined Gross National Incomes in 2006 that were 26% of the global total at purchasing power parity.[28] This was inequality with poverty on one side. Per capita personal expenditures at purchasing power parity in those countries were about $1,700 in that year. In China, in 2005, they were $1,752, in India, $1,455, as compared to $31,995 in the United States.[29] In that year 36% of the people of China lived on less than $2.00 a day at purchasing power parity, 16% on less than $1.25, while 76% of Indians lived below $2.00 a day, 42% below $1.25. (In all, 42% of the world's people lived below $2.00 a day, 23% below $1.25 a day.[30])

International inequalities in per capita national income at purchasing power parity have grown rapidly since 1950, especially since 1980.[31] Suppose, as Branko Milanovic proposes in a powerful study of trends in global inequality, that we take the threshold for a country's entering the top economic tier to be the per capita GDP (at purchasing power parity) of the poorest country among the elite consisting of the Western European countries, the United States, Canada, Australia and New Zealand, the largest group of developed countries that have long been bound by cultural and political ties. We might label countries "economically inferior" if their per capita GDP is less than two-thirds of this cut-off, "far down" if it is below a third. (By these measures, Mexico and Malaysia are currently economically inferior but not far down, which is the status of poorer Guatemala and Jordan.) Milanovic shows that the proportion of inferior and of far down countries dramatically, steadily increased from 1960 until the end of the century, including the era of globalization. In 1960, 50% were inferior, 20% far down. In 1978, 62% were inferior, 44% far down. In 2000, 72% were inferior, 53% far down.[32]

There is one global measure on which international income inequality has diminished in recent decades. When contributions to the global distribution of average national incomes at purchasing power parity are weighted by population, the degree of international inequality has steadily decreased since around 1970.[33] But this is an effect of growth in one developing country, with distinctive interests, China. Once China is omitted, there is no population-weighted decline in inter-country inequality at purchasing power parity. Indeed, Milanovic found a significant increase in inequality after 1982 when the most common measure is applied to countries outside of China, and a steep increase when India is also excluded.[34] (Similarly, while the number of people living below the abysmal threshold of $1.25 a day declined in the world at large by 27% from 1981 to 2005, it increased by 11% outside of China. The below-$2.00 trends are an over-all increase of 2%, an extra-China increase of 35%.[35])

At the start of the U.S. civil rights movement, African-Americans were sometimes told that there was no need for disruption or political intervention: the routine interactions of people going about their business would ultimately dissolve burdens of racial prejudice. In response, they expressed an unwillingness to wait until they were long dead. Similarly, global trade and finance within the current institutional framework might ultimately work as an invisible hand wiping out differences between poor and prosperous countries that undermine global civic friendship, but there is no good evidence that this will happen until those now living are long dead. The interests and powers of the leading developed countries severely limit changes that would speed this process. So the quest for global justice will be a difficult struggle for a long time. Indeed, even if stark economic inequality were to end, competition for domineering influence might continue to inflict violence across borders. Perhaps the struggle for global justice will be a task for many generations.

The relational perspective is burdened with the irony that the processes generating demanding transnational responsibilities are daunting barriers to their fulfillment. If this were the whole story of global power and global justice, then understanding of the origins of demanding transnational responsibility would light the way to moral despair. But in fact, there is hope of improvement, not just as a side-effect of business as usual in global commerce and the rational pursuit of power by political elites, but also, in part, through morally motivated political activity outside of the corridors of power. Moreover, the arguments about justice and power in this book so far can make a distinctive contribution to moral progress, as public arguments and bases for political affiliation. This constructive use of arguments about unmet responsibilities will be the task of the next, final chapter.

# 9

# Global Social Democracy

So far, my arguments have been unconstructive. In my accounts of the exercise of transnational power, this power is, at once, a source of demanding duties to help people in developing countries and the vehicle of interests that tend to thwart these moral demands. There have been few indications of ways around this obstacle. The assessment of the demands of transnational responsibility and the sources of transnational irresponsibility has conflicted with arguments for helping the global poor that have broad currency in major developed countries, for example, arguments that what people in developing countries need would have no significant cost to people in developed countries, and that the foreign policies of the leading developed countries, especially the United States, would be much more morally responsible if they were more rational. Arguments for greater beneficence, whose scope I have diminished, appeal to a wish to help the global poor that is pervasive in developed countries, even if many take other interests and responsibilities to set strict limits to its pursuit. Alternative moral arguments have been developed, appealing to the need to make good defects of exploitation, inequity, domination and widespread violence. But even if sound, these arguments are bound to encounter widespread resistance in the countries that abuse power in these ways: people resist seeing themselves as taking part in the flawed transnational conduct that is presupposed, resistance that is encouraged by established institutions. So the arguments for unmet duties to help that have been presented in this book might be of little use in public persuasion.

In this last chapter, I will try to show that the view of international relations and transnational responsibility defended in this book has a productive role to play in seeking means to reduce the injustices it condemns. The underlying view of international relations provides reasons for people in developed countries to look to social movements as important initiators of change. By locating mechanisms by which such movements make a difference, this view helps to establish the special productive role of a movement that might otherwise seem marginal at best, a global version of social democracy. The distinctive contribution to global justice of global social democracy depends on moral opposition to transnational abuses of power which relies on arguments such as those of this book.

## Realism and Social Movements

In the current jargon of political science, the view of international relations that I have defended is realist, in its emphasis on the pursuit of power and wealth by nationally dominant elites as the driving force. More specifically, it is a left-wing version of this familiar, orthodox perspective. In this version, the interests of the governments of major developed countries in general, the U.S. in particular, in domineering influence and the economic power of their major firms override the demands of responsibility to people in developing countries, often imposing grave costs. The interests in power do not invariably conflict with imperatives of responsibility, but they always do to a significant extent in some developing countries with lots of people, because those interests do not fit local economic needs, the interests of the most vulnerable, or local aspirations to continuity, autonomy or peace. In the face of challenges to American power, recourse to violence, direct or sponsored, in some apparently crucial regions will have enduring strategic appeal and will, recurrently, carry the day in the making of foreign policy, often succeeding in promoting American power, often killing, maiming and destroying without adequate justification. The interaction of elites with the electorate in developed countries, structured by political, educational and economic institutions and the major media, will sustain these tendencies at least as long as a large gap in neediness separates a few rich countries from poor countries in which a vast majority of the world's people live.

This outlook does not foreclose improvements in global justice through the leadership by established authorities that I have labelled "institutional governance." Within each country, some have or strive for political authority or provide those making a political career with influential advice or substantial support, while most do their best to improve their lives and the lives of those they love in the frameworks for economic self-advancement maintained by the local elites, to which negotiations with foreign elites contribute. One hope for humanity is that these activities will advance the world toward the ultimate aim of global justice. I have emphasized limits to gains from institutional governance, especially limits due to interests and powers in leading developed countries. This is not at all to deny that institutional governance can yield benefits, sometimes extraordinary, to humanity at large. For example, industrialization in East Asia has done much to advance humanity toward the ultimate goal of justice, liberating hundreds of millions from dire poverty. Still, the repeated conclusion that institutional governance both creates unmet duties and prevents their fulfillment makes it urgent to see if other ways of advancing toward justice are currently available.

In the determination of political decisions with global reach, another sort of activity, outside of institutional governance, impinges on it: social movements in the broad sense of activities seeking to bring about change through moral advocacy which are non-electoral and are not led by major political parties. The broad tenets of left-wing realism suggest that social movements connecting global wrongs with the transnational conduct of leading developed countries might play a productive role. Since the international power of the United States is especially great and gravely departs from justice, this locale for activism is especially important. Unless otherwise indicated, the proposals in this chapter about ways forward through social movements will be addressed, in the first instance, to people in the sole superpower. But there will always be implications for activity promoting global justice in other developed countries, on account of analogous interests and internal political processes, as well as enduring alliances with the United States.

At a minimum, when strategic disagreements among foreign-policy-planners are reflected in alternative choices in elections, social movements might sometimes tip the electoral scales toward the side whose current tactic is less unjust. However, if the arguments of Chapter 7 are sound, both sides in strategic disagreements over the use of America's destructive power favor vastly lethal excesses. In matters of economic policy affecting people in developing countries, there is very little strategic disagreement in the highest circles of a major developed country over what advances its interests. In any case, during the life of a presidential administration, one approach to foreign policy will be ascendant.

Going beyond these limits, social movements might be able to change the course of foreign policy by creating new strategic considerations. At the start of his great catalog of sources of power, Hobbes sagely notes, "To have friends is Power; for they are strengths united."[1] Translated into the catalog governing foreign policy, this observation entails concern by those planning foreign policy over moral revulsion outside the corridors of power. Significant and growing moral revulsion makes it hard to inspire the willingness to sacrifice on which a great power depends for ready use of its armed forces. When these armed forces are committed, they will be less effective if revulsion at home and disgust at death and devastation for no good cause among those who do the fighting reinforce each other. The growth of moral opposition makes young people less likely to devote their creative talents and deep loyalties to careers in the planning and pursuit of their country's global power. Disenchantment moving beyond electoral support for candidates opposed to current policies threatens general crises of disorder. Moral revulsion abroad makes it harder to secure help from allies, makes a stance of defiance a basis for political success in developing countries and threatens the stability of client regimes. In these and other ways, moral revulsion might impose significant reputational costs, so that the concern to reduce or avoid it affects the calculus of power.

However, the description of these possible influences does not establish their importance in practice. The power of the governments whose decisions have global reach, the limits observed by electoral parties, the major media and formative educational institutions, and the urgency of the daunting challenges faced by the American empire might so restrict the influence of social movements that they make no significant difference to the course of global justice. To see whether they can have significant impact and what contributes to what force they have, we need to look at the actual historical record.

One good start is the greatest confrontation so far between social movements and U.S. foreign policy, opposition to the Vietnam War. The Vietnam War is the most important case in which the United States has reduced violence it had supported without achieving a central goal of its violent endeavor. This war also produced the most abundant documentation we are apt to have of policy discussions leading to the ending of violence by the United States. (Presumably, the fate of the Nixon tapes and *The Pentagon Papers* sounded enduring cautionary notes.) A look at this episode of opposition provides grounds for realistic hope in social movements, as well as important clues to the forms of effective activism now.

## The Vietnam War Revisited

Like all national leaders, Johnson and Nixon were concerned to have adequate public support for initiatives in which the nation's armed forces risked their lives. In the taped conversation in which McNamara conveyed what he regarded as "a bombshell," General Westmoreland's request, supported by the Joint Chiefs of Staff, for an increase in combat troops from 82,000 to 175,000, Johnson's immediate response was to explore the prospect of Eisenhower's going on television to defend whatever choice Johnson made. After asking McNamara, "Do you watch television?" (answer: "I see it sometimes"),

Johnson made his first decision in response to the bombshell, namely, to "make them get you [viz., McNamara] one of these sets in your office where you can turn them all three [networks] on."[2] In a conversation with Kissinger, Haldeman and Ehrlichman in 1971, discussing options ranging from rapid and complete withdrawal to a vast expansion of the war, Nixon goes so far as to insist, "you've gotta remember that everything is domestic politics from now on. And, uh . . . Everything's domestic politics."[3]

The further claim that the anti-war movement reduced the over-all toll of violence in Vietnam by undermining public support is more controversial. Throughout the war and in retrospect, some policy makers claimed that the reverse was true: if only massive increases in deadly force had adequate public support, this radical surgery would have ended the war quickly. Presumably, this is why Kissinger refers to the anti-war movement as "these bastards."[4] But detailed intelligence reports, deeply experienced advice and the consequences of actual escalations all indicated that further use of deadly force would not break the will of the enemy and end the decades-long insurgency without adding enormous devastation. Indeed, the dramatic expansions of violence that were considered but never launched—"Bomb 'em. You take out the dikes; you take out Haiphong; you take out the whole thing" in Nixon's neat formulation in 1971—were so apocalyptic in their short-term costs that they would hardly have reduced death over-all even if they had quickly turned the tide.[5]

Still, it is not obvious that extra-electoral activity morally opposed to the war played an important role in reducing violence. Doubts as to the chances of victory and sheer war-weariness certainly contributed to public pressure toward "deescalation." Quite apart from any new strategic reasons created by the anti-war movement, there were strategic reasons to doubt that South Vietnam was the right place to draw or hold the line. One has to look at the detailed record to decide whether and how criticisms of the war as morally wrong helped to reduce the killing. At the three great crossroads at which a much less lethal path was taken, there is strong evidence that attacks on the morality of the war did make a difference, and did so, in part, by inspiring doubts among Americans as to the goodness of the pursuit of American power.

The first great turning point was the shift of virtually all the "Wise Men" of Johnson's Senior Advisory Group to a recommendation of rapid deescalation and a negotiated settlement on terms that were likely to lead to the collapse of the Saigon regime. Their leading reasons not to try to stay the course for the five or ten more years required for victory were matters of domestic political morale. Cyrus Vance said that "the war was bitterly dividing the country," in announcing his conversion from his past support for the war effort. In George

Ball's climactic and most successful effort to make hawks into doves, he himself "emphasized, as I had done many times, that the war was demoralizing the country and that we had to get out."[6] In mournful retrospect, Ball was to describe this demoralization as "the poisoning of the minds of some Americans toward their own government."[7]

The "Wise Men" deliberated in the midst of a great wave of campus protests, with significant actions on 101 campuses in the first half of 1968, which followed a series of large and growing demonstrations, including a demonstration of a hundred thousand in Washington the previous October.[8] Having lived through a much more deadly war, those advisors were well aware that public support is not a matter of sheer energy or fatigue but a matter of moral commitment. Johnson had stated the point with characteristic pith at a meeting with his chief aides seven months before: "we have no songs, no parades, no bond drives . . . and we can't win the war otherwise."[9] At the first turning point, the anti-war movement had given Johnson's senior advisors more reason to fear moral revulsion than to expect this widespread moral support.

The second turning point was Nixon's abandonment of the option of dramatic reescalation that came to be known as "Operation Duck Hook," a projected series of operations against North Vietnam which, as a Joint Chiefs of Staff contingency plan put it, "will be designed to achieve maximum political, military, and psychological shock, while reducing North Vietnam's over-all war-making and economic capacity to the extent feasible."[10] In the late summer and fall of 1969, this option took shape, produced detailed contingency planning and then faded away. Although it would have led to losses among U.S. Air Force personnel, it would have been much less lethal to Americans than reescalation on the ground, and was supposed to end the war quickly by forcing Hanoi to come to terms. Yet the American public's resistance is a dominant theme in internal discussions. Morton Halperin suggested to Kissinger, in a memorandum in August, that the search for military victory must be "dismissed because: past experience has shown that this objective, if possible at all, will exact enormous costs at home and abroad." The enormous domestic cost he cited was the fact that "the American people would not support this course of action."[11] Commenting on a part of the evolving package of "Duck Hook" actions which, in Kissinger's opinion, would have drowned about 200,000 North Vietnamese, Tony Lake noted just one difficulty, in a memorandum to Kissinger in mid-September, "Bombing the dikes will raise particular problems here in the U.S."[12] This was a period of rapid advance in moral opposition to the war. The largest anti-war mobilization took place on October 15, comprising two hundred demonstrations nationwide, joined by millions.

(High school attendance in New York City was reduced to 10 percent.[13]) In the course of that fall, Operation Duck Hook was abandoned. Instead, Nixon emphasized phased withdrawal. In his memoirs, Nixon describes his intention in announcing withdrawal of 150,000 American troops in April of the following year as to "drop a bombshell on the gathering storm of antiwar protest."[14]

The final crossroads was reached in the summer of 1971, when the number of U.S. troops had been halved, and the Nixon administration had to plan for a future in which the Saigon regime was no longer propped up at all by U.S. troops. In these deliberations, a leading option was an air war against North Vietnam that would "level that goddamned country."[15] Sometimes, this option was supposed to help the Saigon regime survive by incapacitating the North, sometimes to force North Vietnam to offer more favorable terms, sometimes to create a decent interval between American withdrawal and Hanoi's triumph so that America would save face, and sometimes simply to create so much carnage that North Vietnam could not be seen as winning and no defiant regime or movement would want to follow its example. This is an especially nasty period in the Nixon tapes, during which Nixon says and demonstrates that the prospect of leveling North Vietnam is so exciting that it "makes me shout,"[16] and urges Kissinger to "think big, for Christ's sake" by taking more seriously a nuclear attack on North Vietnam.[17] In a conversation between Nixon, Kissinger and John Connally in May 1973, Connally is well received when he describes the strategic advantages of killing more civilians: "[T]his is one of the great weaknesses we have. . . . There's been no devastation. People in North Vietnam have been relatively free of the fear of retribution! [Nixon interrupts: 'Civilians—.'] Civilians. And fear of retribution is a powerful motivating force, and we let 'em go ten years without it."[18]

Operating in this morality-free zone, Nixon and his aides were also unconstrained by fears of Chinese or Soviet intervention, on account of discussions attending the movement toward recognition of the former and the establishment of détente with the latter. The havoc they contemplated would have been suffered by North Vietnamese, as American troops withdrew. What held these policymakers back? Presumably, they were held back, in significant measure, by memories of the moral outrage in response to the invasion of Cambodia in May 1971, when over 450 campuses were closed by anti-war protests and 75,000–100,000 people assembled at short notice in Washington. The moral disapproval of the war that this revulsion accelerated must have given them pause, since it now often embraced the majority. In May 1971, the view that "It is morally wrong for the U.S. to be fighting in Vietnam" was endorsed by 58% of respondents to a Harris poll—a proportion that later rose to 63%—while 71% agreed that involvement in the war had been a mistake.[19] Nixon's statement in June 1971 that "Domestic politics is everything" in the endgame of the war dictated the consequences as straightforwardly as the more measured cadences of the Wise Men. On January 27, 1973, after the limited if lethal spasm of Linebacker II, the "Christmas bombings," the peace treaty was signed.

At the three great crossroads, public moral opposition to the war, originating from outside established political institutions, played an important role in limiting violence directed against foreigners in a developing country. The growth of this opposition depended on highly visible organized actions by a small minority who were criticized as disloyal by most Americans (who were urged to disapprove by their Presidents) for most of the war. In November 1969, when Nixon asked the "great silent majority" to side with him against the anti-war movement, 65% of Harris poll respondents agreed that "protestors against the war are giving aid and comfort to the Communists." Yet, by a margin of 81% to 11%, they also agreed that "the protestors are raising real questions which ought to be discussed and answered."[20] In effect, this vast majority were expressing their appreciation of the protestors' interference with established powers' capacity to set the agenda of public discussion.

By re-shaping the agenda and insistently presenting facts that challenged the expectations of loyal compatriots, the activist minority eventually persuaded the majority that their government was doing wrong. They did not create a majority view that the U.S. government's promotion of its global power is, in general, dangerous to humanity. Even within the protesting minority, this was a minority position. And yet, the inroads made by this minority in the minority, making use of the new agenda and the new evidence produced by the war, were an important source of the retreat from violence at the highest levels. The "demoralization" that the "Wise Men" feared the most, "the poisoning of the minds of some Americans toward their own government," was a fearsome prospect even if only some were part of this significant and growing minority.[21]

Fears of electoral defeat and long-term concerns about loss of legitimacy were not the only vehicles by which opposition to the war influenced the exercise of destructive power. Nor was the organized movement the only context for influential yet unrespectable rejection of the war. Resistance by U.S. soldiers in South Vietnam disgusted with the war was also a major constraint on policy makers. It invigorated the organized anti-war movement, which, in turn, encouraged this resistance. At the start of large-scale American involvement, when all of the mass media, including the quality newspapers, narrated this involvement as an intrepid battle for freedom, morally disturbing reports often came from GIs—informally, when they returned home, and also conveyed by the most trenchant reporting in the larger journals of opinion. ("'You Can Tell 'Em Buddy,'" the urging of one of those soldiers, was the apt title of the most poignant dispatch by Bernard Fall, the most impressive journalist reporting from combat zones.[22]) As the anti-war movement grew, rebellious GIs converted more and more "search and destroy" missions in South Vietnam into "search and avoid" missions, sometimes resorting to "fragging," i.e., rolling live grenades into the tents of zealous platoon leaders, to discourage engagement with the enemy. The Department of Defense reported 96 fragging incidents in 1969, 209 in 1970, and 215 in the first eleven months of 1971, despite declining troop levels.[23] By 1970, enlisted men were often denied access to grenades and firearms when not on guard duty or patrol, and troops who had newly arrived were separated from experienced troops in segregated areas surrounded by barbed wire, before being sent into the field.[24]

Although certainly moved by the desire to preserve themselves, disobedient soldiers were also moved by the thought, freely conveyed to reporters, that "the war was not 'worth it' in terms of life, limb and disrupted youth."[25] This attitude was encouraged by the organized anti-war movement, which also provided growing approval at home of their disobedience. As the commander of Fort Benning, a leading embarkation point, put it, "In the long run, our Army cannot exist without the good will of the people. . . . They will come to it bitterly and with distaste, or with pride and willingness to perform—based upon the national attitude of the people as a whole."[26]

By the end of 1970, there were frequent reports of a "growing feeling among the Administration's policy makers that it might be a good idea to accelerate the rate of withdrawal," reflecting a concern "that discipline and morale in the American Army are deteriorating very seriously."[27] Returning, Vietnam veterans came to play a leading role in the organized anti-war movement, culminating in a week of protests in mid-April 1971, when veterans threw their medals over a fence at the Capitol—protests that consolidated moral disapproval just before the Nixon administration began to contemplate apocalyptic devastation as a fitting end to the war.

In sum, the movement against the Vietnam War provides evidence that moral revulsion promoted from outside of institutional governance can make a substantial difference, not just to electoral fortunes (in fact, throughout this period, pro-war presidential candidates won) but to strategic calculations in the corridors of power. This movement also included vital contributions to change by small minorities: they shifted the focus of attention of the broad public and raised the threat of serious losses of legitimacy by connecting widespread moral outrage to doubts about the basic goodness of American power.

## A Movement of Social Movements

In recent years, a cluster of movements in the United States and many other countries have tried to reduce every kind of injustice described in this book. Participants side with vulnerable people in developing countries, appeal to values of equity, democracy, and compassion, and treat major aspects of American foreign policy as negligent or worse. At the beginning of the twenty-first century, this cluster included international movements against the Iraq war and the subsequent U.S. military presence in Iraq, inequity in globalization, negligence in response to world poverty, and irresponsible failure to do enough to limit global climate change. Participation in these movements overlaps, and those strongly committed to one typically wish the other movements well and derive comfort and support from their successes. So the cluster is itself a movement composed of movements in specific causes.

The experience of this movement provides further grounds for hope that initiatives outside of institutional governance can reduce global injustice and further indications that a minority condemning deep tendencies of U.S. foreign policy can play a distinctive productive role. The processes nudging against injustice have taken diverse forms, including protest movements, focussed campaigns, and mere public argument. If just one type of process is considered, the prospects of the movement of social movements are radically underrated. For each type of process contributes to the others, magnifying the total consequences of any single endeavor.

*Protest movements.*    The processes that I will label "protest movements" have the following features, which were, previously, prominent in opposition to the Vietnam War. People are drawn by shared moral outrage to assemble in large numbers to proclaim the wrongness of what is being done by established institutions. Much leadership is shown by people and groups convinced of enduring tendencies toward injustice of those institutions, who openly proclaim this conviction. While there is a unifying sentiment of opposition to wrongs committed, there is no unifying commitment to get the target institution to adopt a specific, enduring reform. Political processes of this kind have played a leading role in opposition to the invasion and occupation of Iraq and to the shaping of development by the major developed countries through the trade and financial institutions that they steer.

The demonstrations of millions, in the United States and allied countries, that opposed the invasion of Iraq were led, disproportionately, by those who took the move toward war to be an effort to promote U.S. power, spending "blood for oil," as the posters put it. These demonstrations failed. But the moral revulsion promoted among many Americans, the moral doubts inspired in many more and the condemnation of the war and occupation by a large international movement including many Americans helped to deprive the Bush administration of means for the ambitious reshaping of the Middle East that was proposed. Despite the growing violence of the occupation and strenuous efforts to convince Americans that it was the main front of a Global War on Terror, conscription was unthinkable and recruitment an increasingly frantic project failing to meet centrally important goals.[28] In the months in which the invasion and occupation were widely viewed as a successful, if misleadingly promoted, initiative, moral activism laid the basis for public pressure for American withdrawal. The condemnation summed up in "No blood for oil" contributed to a legacy of Iraq very different from strategic criticisms and much more resistant to future violent injustice—a legacy of doubt about the moral rightness of what promotes American power and distrust of the violence of American foreign policy whether though unilateral or multilateral initiatives, through the direct use of American forces or through sponsored forces.

In contrast to a war, international loan conditions, intellectual property rights regimes, tariff reductions, fiscal policies and farm subsidies do not seem likely topics for moral revulsion beyond the circle of their immediate victims. But these were leading targets of the most active protests in the years before the invasion of Iraq, in which Americans joined with people from around the world in the "anti-globalization" movement.

Once the major media reported massive demonstrations at the WTO ministerial meeting in Seattle in 1999, large numbers of people in the United States and other developed countries became attentive to arguments that poor people in developing countries were victims of severe economic injustice imposed by great powers, not just sufferers worth considering for foreign aid. The series of "anti-globalization" protests, which included major demonstrations in Genoa and Washington, as well, made challenges to the Washington Consensus on development a more central topic in the major media and in universities. In the course of these controversies, disdainful attacks on the "anti-globalization" movement sometimes changed to affirmation of some of its central claims (as in the widely-read commentaries of Paul Krugman).[29] Critics of the Washington Consensus (such as Dani Rodrik) gained a broader audience and support. Even self-described defenses of globalization (such as Jagdish Bhagwati's) conceded profound flaws.[30] Joseph Stiglitz developed his doubts about the Washington Consensus into an incisive critique reaching well beyond universities through widely read books.

As Stiglitz noted at the start of the first of these books, "The protests at the Seattle meeting of the World Trade organization . . . were a shock. Since then the movement has grown stronger and the fury has spread. . . . Now sixteen-year-old kids from the suburbs have strong opinions on . . . GATT . . . and NAFTA. . . . It is clear to almost everyone that something has gone terribly wrong."[31] While the shift in opinion among experts and the global public did not make the Doha Round (supposedly, "the Development Round") an occasion for reversing inequities of the Uruguay Round, it did help to prevent uses of Doha that would have further increased the volatility of capital flows, the weakening of local political management of the course of development, and inequity in subsidies and trade barriers.

*Focussed campaigns.* The "anti-globalization" protest movement was notable for interaction with processes of a different sort, focussed campaigns. In these processes, a coalition of advocacy groups coordinates a campaign for a specific enduring change in policy in a government, multigovernmental institution or emblematic business firm. The reform is proposed as a feasible change that will be sustained by a commitment obtained from the target. The campaign is based on the cultivation of sympathetic insiders in the target, the accumulation of public endorsements from organizations and individuals held in wide esteem, and broad public support. Recruitment of this public support depends on vivid portrayal of actions to be stopped as shameful on the basis of precepts to which a great many people are already attached: the poor should not be burdened by interminable crushing debt to rich creditors; villagers should not be driven from their ancestral homes; children should not be at risk of being blown up by land mines or unexploded cluster bombs.[32]

Thus, the anti-globalization protest movement paralleled, lent some credence to and derived some credence from Jubilee 2000, a campaign focussed on the cancellation of debts owed to the World Bank and the IMF by heavily indebted poor countries with no prospect of repayment. The coordinated leadership of this campaign by advocacy organizations relied on lobbying of legislators and Bank and Fund bureaucrats, negotiations with the Bank and Fund to extend their own programs for debt relief, endorsement by religious groups of high stature, including the Catholic Church, and petition campaigns collecting vast numbers of signatures, for example, one-quarter of the population of Ireland.[33] Similarly, a focussed campaign for stricter and more open World Bank reviews of environmental impact, decrying such harms as the inundation of villages by planned hydroelectric projects in Nepal and India, contributed themes and participants to anti-globalization protests, protests which also strengthened the focussed campaign in negotiations directed at specific reforms.[34] Just as the campaigns for debt cancellation and environmental restraint shared aspirations of anti-globalization protestors while pursuing them by a different route, harms of concern to anti-war protestors have been addressed by focussed campaigns for treaties committing signatories not to lay landmines and not to use cluster bombs.

The victories of focussed campaigns have not, in themselves, been large. Assured that reform would be a triumph of moral common sense secured by a commitment from the target institution, the broad public base of a focussed campaign are not a source of effective pressure when an apparent victory falls short of the campaign's goal in actual practice. Usually, a reform within the complex decisionmaking of a powerful institution is easily contained. The debt forgiveness that Jubilee 2000 accepted as basic victory produced only a small reduction in debt service costs in poor countries while affording the World Bank and IMF new means of imposing their favored development prescriptions.[35] Similarly, the World Bank's environmental reviews somewhat reduced the incidence of damage from funded projects, especially in the first few years, but further change was well-contained by institutional pressures to keep funds flowing and by overlapping interests of recipient governments and major donors.[36]

When the reform pursued by a focussed campaign is a more specific and peremptory commitment, governments whose interests might be significantly affected will say, "No." Within a decade, 156 countries signed the 1997 Ottawa Treaty banning the use of land mines, most very soon, but the non-signatories were those with a significant interest in keeping this option, including the United States, China, Russia, Israel, India, and Pakistan. These and other countries with an interest in the use of cluster munitions took no part in the negotiation of the 2008 convention banning their use and were not expected to sign, while the convention left signatories allied with non-signers free to join them in military initiatives in which they continued to use cluster munitions. Justifying U.S. non-participation, a State Department spokesperson explained that "Cluster munitions have demonstrated military utility."[37]

Still, a focussed campaign can have long-term consequences beyond its own limited victories. In the process of recruitment, a great many people have been made more sensitive to harms to which the target institutions are prone. World Bank and IMF loan policies are more suspect than before. Their environmental probity is not assumed. Land mines and cluster bombs have moved closer to the taboo status of poison gas. (While the United States did not sign the 1997 land mine treaty, it has stopped using and producing land mines.) The reputational cost of future injustices can be substantially increased by a process that wins a small immediate victory.

*Public arguments and communities of outlook.* Protest movements and focussed campaigns interact productively with another process, the promotion of critical outlooks by authors, teachers, creative artists, religious figures and, in the recent movements, providers of information and argument on the internet. Sometimes, these persuaders are spokespersons for organizations dedicated to global causes, such as Oxfam or Human Rights Watch. Often, they are not. But regardless of organizational ties, their work should count as part of the growth of a social movement so long as they try to contribute to a community of outlook of like-minded people seeking change. By shifting the public agenda, protest movements can increase the audience for these persuaders. In turn, productive protest movements and focussed campaigns depend on them. Their work is sometimes in the forefront, as in the movement to press governments to respond to the challenge of global warming. Works of persuasion (Noam Chomsky's writings, for example) can express and promote a community of outlook that is a minority in protest movements and focussed campaigns yet strongly affects the course of activism and powerfully adds to the reputational costs of policies that are opposed.

## Hope at the Present Stage

On the basis of these processes, mechanisms of influence, and episodes of (limited) success, what is a realistic hope for the movement of social movements for global justice? At the current stage of global power, not ready for global civic friendship, the movement of social movements can be expected to make the bad somewhat less bad than it might have been.

Wars will be fought due to imperial needs. Still, it is a realistic hope that the deadly force employed will be limited, the wars will end sooner and life-giving "Vietnam syndromes" of reluctance to intervene will last longer, on account of moral opposition. Inequity in trade and finance will exact a heavy toll. But heightened reputational costs and shifts in the outlook and morale of economists and bureaucrats confronted by the movement will limit efforts to make matters worse, as in the Doha Round, and produce small concessions, as in the cancellation of some exceptionally heavy, unrepayable debt burdens. The shared commitment to continued U.S. dominance of both political parties in the United States and the interests of important U.S. corporations will combine with fears of economic displacement to insure that the challenge of greenhouse gases will not be met through the fair sharing of burdens of adequate containment. The consequent diplomatic maneuvering will be excruciating for the world's most vulnerable people. Still, the exposés and protests of an international movement including Americans can supplement and, to some extent, replace disasters in providing incentives to move forward.

Granted, no one in a social movement will have reason to believe that her individual actions will add much of anything to well-being or justice. But if the expectation of significant pay-off from one's own action were required for participation, no rational person would bother to vote in a national election. To give meaning to their lives, people want to identify with a large cause, in which they can join with others in collectively making some difference in their lifetimes. The aspiration to global justice pursued through the protests, campaigns and advocacy of social movements is an undeluded source of meaning of this kind.

Acceptance of the left-wing realist view of transnational power has turned out to support hope for a movement of social movements as a way around the limits of institutional governance. It remains to be seen how much a social movement consisting of a distinctive community of outlook based on opposition to the transnational abuse of power might, realistically, add to this promise of change.

## Global Social Democracy

People's reasons for supporting changes that would help vulnerable people in developing countries are extremely diverse. Compassion, national strategic interests, religious convictions, and the avoidance of costs to compatriots of dangerous foreign initiatives provide important reasons among those who are by no means convinced that widespread suffering results from wrongs of exploitation and irresponsible domination or that the domineering influence of the United States is an enduring obstacle to justice. Someone convinced of these propositions about wrongs and obstacles—recurrent themes in this book—need not regard them as useful bases for solidarity and public persuasion in a social movement. They could have the same standing as religious beliefs that lead someone to act in profound political solidarity with others without seeking to persuade them of her views. Assuming these convictions are valid, do they also have a useful public role to play as the basis for a constituent of the movement of movements?

There is already a community of outlook aiming at global change in which these views are the basis for solidarity and shared means of persuasion and recruitment. Like traditional social democracy, it combines a commitment to

relieve suffering with a commitment to end domination condemned as both
a source of suffering and an obstacle to cooperation based on mutual respect.
So it might be called "global social democracy." Global social democrats do
not just try to exert pressure on governments of developed countries to reduce
burdens of global poverty, mitigate transnational damage to the environment
and lower the global toll of violence. They take exercises of power through
which agents in developed countries take advantage of weakness in developing
countries to be major causes and constituents of global injustice. Viewing the
domineering influence of the United States as an especially powerful, enduring
source of injustice, they take the project of hemming in the American empire
to be an aspect of all their endeavors. Sometimes engaging in internationally
coordinated protests and focussed campaigns, sometimes acting nationally but
in felt alliance with protests and campaigns in other countries, they try to
cooperate globally in a way that prefigures the ultimate aim of a world
in which their movement is made obsolete by the willing cooperation of
citizenries acting through responsible governments.

   Global social democrats are a small minority of citizens of the United States.
Just how small is hard to say. Asked by the National Opinion Research
Center whether they were very proud, somewhat proud, not very proud
or not proud at all of America's influence in the world, 19% of Americans
in 2004 said "Not very proud," 3% "Not proud at all," proportions that
were essentially the same in 1996.[38] Asked by the Pew Global Attitudes
Project in 2005 whether it would be better if another country or group of
countries emerged as a rival to U.S. military power, 26% of Americans said,
"Yes."[39] Asked whether they had a very favorable, somewhat favorable or
very unfavorable opinion of the United States, 12% of U.S. respondents in a
2007 Pew survey said "Somewhat unfavorable," 5% "Very unfavorable," and
2% said they did not know or refused to answer.[40] Cutting down the image
of pervasive American satisfaction with American virtue, such findings suggest
a small minority of global social democrats with a substantial reservoir for
further recruitment. Small though their numbers currently are, global social
democrats in the United States can have a substantial impact on protests in
times of national decision. On February 15, 2003, when more than 7 million
people in 300 cities throughout the world marched against the imminent
launching of war in Iraq, a coalition of U.S. global social democrats organized
demonstrations of about 2.5 million people.[41] In a random sample of U.S.
demonstrators, 85% agreed that "the United States wants to invade Iraq to
secure national oil supply"[42] and 25% agreed with the statement, "For me,
this anti-war protest is another way to express my feelings against neoliberal
globalization."[43] After the horrors of September 11, 2001, a global social

democratic response to the attacks, Noam Chomsky's *9/11*, was a best-seller in the United States.

Someone who already has the factual beliefs, moral convictions and sentiments of affiliation constituting global democracy might or might not seek to persuade others of these attitudes and help them to become better persuaders, through the vast spectrum of media that includes both best-selling books and conversations at the breakfast table. If the decision to go public were fated to exclude all other bases among her compatriots for pursuing her political goals, then she should decide to keep her global social democracy to herself, at least if she is an American. Because of limitations of electoral politics, the formation of outlooks in education, and the presuppositions of the major media, strategic arguments about the foolishness of imperial adventures and appeals to compassion that do not impugn the interests steering American foreign policy are vitally important resources, which should not be destroyed. But the decision to go public has no such power to suppress alternative bases for participation in the movement of social movements. Rather, the question is whether global social democracy can make a distinctive contribution, along with other outlooks which will endure. Precisely because she is in a relatively small minority, this would be a compelling reason to go public. Assuming that its constituent beliefs are valid, global social democracy does make a distinctive contribution to global justice through the pattern of distrust and trust that it promotes.

By strengthening background distrust of the interests steering U.S. foreign policy, global social democracy increases the reputational costs of the use of American destructive power; these intrusions become evidence of underlying tendencies, not simply blunders or expressions of the special enthusiasms of foreign policy cliques. This distrust heightens attention to American sponsorship of violence by clients, whose devastation otherwise tends to be ignored or portrayed as the outcome of local hatred, fanaticism, or greed. It makes wars of empire harder to continue, once begun, by questioning the value of victory, the disvalue of a loss that reduces American power. When war is advocated, global social democracy provides a special framework for assessing its consequences: the question is not whether a war that attacks a defiant dictator or terrorist movement *could* do enough good to justify its carnage but whether this war *will* do enough good if it produces the carnage that the drive to preserve imperial power can be expected to unleash.

While global social democrats will certainly take part in focussed campaigns, their suspicions will make it less likely that apparent victories produce undue credit and dangerous reputational gains for the targetted institutions. While they will certainly engage in electoral action, they reduce excessive optimism in the difference between one candidate and another, combatting both undue tranquility in the wake of victory and undue discouragement when electoral victory proves inadequate.

The distinctive patterns of distrust also help to align efforts to help the global poor more closely to their actual needs. In times of economic expansion in developed countries, when increased foreign aid is often the focus of aspirations to help more, global social democrats are responsive to the limits to aid efficacy set by the interests of powers steering the aid process. They offer these grounds for distrust not as an argument against aid increases, but to warn against over-emphasis on aid, which obscures the need for strenuous efforts to reduce inequity in international trade, investment, property rights and environmental regimes and self-serving rigidity in imposed development policies. In times of economic contraction, the assumption that duties to help the foreign poor are duties of beneficence contributes to the sentiment that help for the foreign poor should be taken off the agenda, because of heightened domestic needs. Without denying that charity begins at home, global social democrats urge that help to the global poor was never largely an imperative of charity: within the new macroeconomic constraints, the imperatives to give up advantages in the interest of the foreign poor endure as just responses to the abuse of power. Facing up to possible domestic costs of global justice, they urge that vulnerable compatriots be helped, but without suspending transnational duties. In good and bad economic times, global social democrats try to keep the hope that great powers will do more to help from weakening the effort to get them to do less to dominate and destroy, in projects that are always advertised as helping the vulnerable.

In addition to this productive distrust, the transnational patterns of trust and reliance in global social democracy are also distinctively beneficial. Global social democrats treat people in developing countries as victims of transnational domination, not just transnational neglect, and often follow the lead of movements and protests in developing countries. This disposition encourages respect for the local knowledge of developing countries and opposition to the global, one-size-fits-all prescriptions that the leading developed countries recurrently seek to impose. Active co-participation and mutual learning within the global movement make the ultimate moral goal of global civic friendship more salient and inspiring in a world in which the machinations of governments are far removed from friendship and official talk of cooperation is often a cover for subordination. By helping to construct a global alliance attempting to hem in excesses of American power, American global social democrats promote affiliations that reduce the chances of violent conflict as the American empire declines. In particular, they reduce the chances that the overtaking of the United States by China will end in bloodshed, like every past end of empire.

These prospects of transnational trust presuppose that global social democrats in the United States are part of a worldwide community of outlook, linked by solidarity, mutual learning and coordinated activity. So reflection on the potential of global social democracy in the United States leads to consideration of the prospects and promise of participation in the rest of the world, both in developing countries and in other developed countries.

The indicators of receptivity in the United States to tenets of global social democracy are much stronger elsewhere. In the poll of sixteen countries in which 26% of Americans favored a military counterweight to the United States, majorities, usually vast, had this preference elsewhere—for example, 85% in France, 81% in India, 74% in China. The study indicated a substantial global majority supporting the position that "United States policies increase the gap between rich and poor countries" (the response of 61% in China and in Brazil, 68% in Bangladesh, 72% in Germany).[44] Of course, global social democracy is by no means the only basis for opposing American domineering influence outside of the United States. But there, someone who accepts the tenets of global social democracy will have distinctive reasons for promoting local ties to a mutually supportive worldwide movement, based on these tenets, which includes the United States.

In developing countries, opposition to excesses of the American empire and associated harms of globalization can contribute to traditionalist attacks on modern values worthy of support as liberating people and enriching their lives. It can divert blame from the predatory negligence of local elites, and divert energy from local tasks of national construction. A better balance, alert both to international injustice and to the central role of local initiative in making good and bad use of globalization, can be sustained in a global movement against imperial excesses, in solidarity with, but not in subordination to, fellow adherents in developed countries including the United States.

In developed countries other than the United States, opposition to excesses of the American empire can be part of exclusive and oppressive nationalisms (e.g., nationalisms that would oppress immigrants and their children) or distract from blame deserved by local political leaders who pose as defenders of weak countries yet insist on destructive agricultural subsidies or inflict dominion in a mini-empire. Attachment to a global movement for global social democracy, in which Americans and people in developing countries play an active role, is the best way to steer between submissiveness and self-righteous parochialism in response to the American empire.

The globalization whose excesses global social democrats oppose can be expected to strengthen the ties of transnational political community that they seek, in a process that has already begun. Already, with abundant use of e-mail, demonstrations are fluently coordinated worldwide (for example, the simultaneous demonstrations of millions in North America and Europe against invading Iraq). Individual demonstrations (for example, the major "anti-globalization" demonstrations) often have highly multinational participation due to internet organizing and cheap international travel. Focussed campaigns are advanced by fluent cooperation in networks of organizations and activists from many countries, including both mighty developed countries and developing countries that are home to the primary victims. Information is gathered from websites in many countries drawing on information and expertise in many countries in a cyberworld in which participants are relatively unconcerned with actual geographic origins. Travel, e-mail, work abroad and immigration create politically resonant interpersonal ties. For example, with much greater frequency than before, Americans mix with, get to know, become friends of foreigners with similar backgrounds and occupations who take it as a premise that American world power is excessive and abused. Isolated though they sometimes are from political community with compatriots, global social democrats take part in a precursor of global civic friendship.

## Is American Patriotism a Virtue?

The advice to embrace global social democracy raises a special question for a citizen of the United States. Should she take the further step of abandoning American patriotism? She should, if the personal cost of this loss of a love is not too great.

There would be no conflict between global social democracy and American patriotism if patriotism were simply acceptance of special political responsibilities toward needy compatriots, the topic of the first chapters of this book. There, I argued that ties among compatriots are appropriate independent reasons for special concern. Admittedly, transnational relationships turned out to create other morally demanding reasons for concern. Still, even in the United States, these transnational ties leave room for some special political responsibilities for needy compatriots. Because an American citizen's foreign political responsibilities are divided among billions in developing countries and shared with people in other developed countries, the measures that he is obliged to support do not demand as much to help a typical disadvantaged person in a developing country as to help a typical disadvantaged compatriot, even if the total foreign obligation turns out to be at least as great. His responsibilities toward the foreign poor are, on the whole, duties to help provide for basic needs. Seeking a basis for allegiance among his compatriots and acknowledging profound reliance on common provision through a shared government, he ought to recognize a deeper political duty to improve the life-prospects of his disadvantaged compatriots even if their basic needs are guaranteed. The case for global social democracy is quite compatible with these and other special responsibilities. Indeed, in current political circumstances, global social democracy provides an additional reason for an American to support measures to fulfill responsibilities to disadvantaged compatriots. If American policies were more responsive to disadvantages within the borders, then the vulnerabilities of compatriots would give Americans less cause for reluctance to give up benefits from taking advantage of foreigners. The countries closest to global social democracy are, after all, domestic social democracies.

These days, philosophers' discussions of the ethics of patriotism largely consist of debates over claims of special responsibility toward compatriots. But politicians are better at understanding "patriotism" than philosophers, even if they sometimes use the word in appalling causes. As politicians constantly remind us, patriotism is love of country. Love is not just acceptance of special responsibility. I have all sorts of special responsibilities toward the students taking my classes, but I do not love my classes.[45]

Even though patriotism is a matter of love, not mere special responsibility, it would be wrong to insist that every American who commits herself to global social democracy must seek to end her American patriotism, on pain of irrationality. A combination of global social democratic goals with American patriotism might be her best compromise. Our loves make our world valuable to us. Even if one recognizes that it would be better not to have a love, it may be so deep-rooted and central as a source of value that one is rational to preserve it while trying to guard against its dangers. In this spirit, white Southerners in the 1960s who sincerely opposed Southern racism sometimes said that they still loved a white Southern way of life whose gentility and grace were bred in slavery and depended on cheap African-American labor. However, even when it responded to genuine values in this way of life and was cognizant of the underlying horrors, this nostalgic attachment tugged attention and affection in directions that made it harder to honor the demands of the South's great moral crisis. American patriotism is similarly burdensome. One should try to get beyond it if the personal cost is not too great.

The importance of unlearning American patriotism is a tribute to the special powers of love. To love someone or something is to be lovingly engrossed in what is characteristic of the beloved. One is drawn to being preoccupied with the wellbeing of the beloved. One identifies with the beloved's success in life as part of one's own success, gladly making sacrifices for the beloved which would only constitute obedience to stern commands of duty toward others. One tenaciously enjoys or longs for reciprocation of this desire for merging. Since one seeks a kind of second self in one's beloved, lack of reciprocity threatens to turn love into a kind of self-rejection. Because one opens one's self to the beloved, a self-respecting person has to think—or, in any case, be powerfully drawn to thinking—that the beloved is (really, if fully appreciated) worthy of love. So the self-respecting lover is spontaneously, powerfully drawn to seeing misdeeds that betray love as departures from the beloved's true nature, interfering with a relationship that deserves to be restored.

These dispositions of attention and affection are characteristic of patriotic Americans who agree that immoral imperial excess has been part of America's presence in the world. Thus, they believe, or are strongly drawn to believe, that the currently most vivid imperial excesses depart from America's underlying tendencies, hijacking a basically sensible and humane disposition that makes the United States worthy of their love. In a recent episode of undeserved moral nostalgia, George W. Bush was demonized for his great departure from America's global decency, even though the Clintonian sanctions regime was a similarly lethal attack on Iraqi lives, the statesmanlike George H.'s war was more deadly for civilians and soldiers than his son's invasion and about as needless, and Afghan events under Carter and Reagan rivaled later events in Iraq as examples of the pursuit of American power regardless of costs in foreign lives.

While an American patriot can certainly count deaths of foreigners as a severe cost and strong dissuasive reason, her patriotism draws her toward preoccupation with American deaths. For example, she is spontaneously drawn to great relief at the very low mortality among U.S. troops in the invasion overthrowing Saddam Hussein (138 in all, 109 in combat) and not to anxious inquiries as to the Iraqi costs (which included 10,000 deaths, half civilian).

Finally, an American patriot is drawn to treating American political institutions, above all, electoral competition, as sufficient means of restoring the moral wellbeing of the country she loves. Acknowledging that the enduring process of decisionmaking for America that Americans nearly all embrace has a fundamental tendency to conflict with her deepest moral values would turn her love of country into a kind of self-rejection. Acknowledging the incapacity of this system to inhibit the excessive quest for imperial power would make it hard to maintain the view that imperial excess departs from the true nature of the United States. Perhaps there are countries in which patriotism is so focussed on culture or ethnicity that it can readily absorb such bitter political appraisals. The United States is not one of them. For an American patriot, pride in the historical achievement of American political institutions, attachment to their basic features and celebration of their virtues is central to her love of country. These institutions are part of what it is to be American, in her own eyes as in the world's. If the left-wing realism of global social democracy is right, American patriotism tends toward exaggeration of the difference between one American politician and another.

A love that must constantly be nursed along with amnesia and wishful thinking and that encourages inattention to morally urgent matters is not steadfast and deep but obsessive and stultifying. In the face of an enduring foreign policy establishment who really are steadfast in pursuit of American power, the amnesia, wishful thinking and inattention guarantee that opposition congeals only after great damage is done. (When learned liberals who supported the Iraq invasion regret their support, they sometimes confess to surprise at how the U.S. behaved post-invasion. Did they expect the U.S. to be willing to lay the groundwork for an independent, defiant OPEC power, committed to strongly state-guided development and steering a course with Iran, the EU and Russia on the basis of domestic Iraqi interests? If not, why be surprised that the attempt to impose control over this great and fractious nation would involve great bloodshed?)

These are powerful reasons for unlearning American patriotism. But a forlorn hope is better than no hope at all, and alienation from the love of country that unites most of one's compatriots is a burden of loneliness. In principle, it could be best to struggle with tendencies toward amnesia, delusion and inattention that often win out, in order to retain a bit of hope and a sense of comfort by keeping one's American patriotism intact. Here, global social democracy makes a difference, for all its limitations. It inspires realistic hope of progress, binds in solidarity with many others throughout the world and focusses attention at the morally right spots.

What makes our world valuable to us is, above all, love that is gladly embraced. If the American empire makes the glad acceptance of love of country incompatible with knowledge and responsibility, it imposes a grave loss on Americans as well as its foreign victims. For Americans, insightful and loving participation in their political institutions may have to await the higher stage, of global civic friendship, at which global social democracy aims. Meanwhile, their closest approach to clear-sighted reconciliation with their social world involves participation in the global movement that seeks that higher stage.

# Notes

## INTRODUCTION

1. See Shaohua Chen and Martin Ravallion, "China is Poorer than We Thought, But No Less Successful in the Fight against Poverty" (Washington: World Bank, 2008), p. 15; World Bank, *World Development Indicators 2008* (Washington: World Bank, 2008), tables 1.a, 2.1, 2.18, 2.21; World Bank, *World Development Indicators 2007* (Washington: World Bank, 2007), table 1.1. At purchasing power parity, the per capita Gross Domestic Product of China was one-tenth that of the United States. (See *World Development Indicators 2008*, table 1.a.)

## CHAPTER 1

1. See Peter Singer, "Famine, Affluence and Morality," *Philosophy & Public Affairs* 1 (1972), pp. 241, 235. Unadorned page numbers in this chapter will refer to this article. Singer quickly adds that "ought, morally" is meant to single out a dictate of moral duty, "not an act that it would be good to do, but not wrong not to do."

2. The qualification "for the sake of enjoyed consumption" provides an exemption for purchases that are essential to someone's most effective strategy for helping the needy—say, the purchase of a fancy suit in order to maximize donations through use of income earned at a dressy Wall Street law firm. Like Singer, I will usually leave this exemption implicit. Even when it is taken into account, the radical conclusion imposes an extremely strenuous demand on nearly everyone substantially above the threshold of poverty.

3. See p. 242 and Singer, "Reconsidering the Famine Relief Argument," in Peter Brown and Henry Shue, eds., *Food Policy* (New York: Free Press, 1977), p. 49.

4. See Peter Unger, *Living High and Letting Die* (New York: Oxford University Press, 1996), p. 148.

5. Among works allied with Singer's, Shelly Kagan, *The Limits of Morality* (New York: Oxford University Press, 1989), Peter Unger, *Living High and Letting*

*Die*, and Liam B. Murphy, *Moral Demands in Nonideal Theory* (New York: Oxford University Press, 2000) have been especially influential. The nature and extent of the alliance with Singer vary. Unger defends a stronger version of the principle of sacrifice (which Singer also endorses), requiring aid whenever the sacrifice is less morally important than the relief. Kagan attacks ordinary limits on the consequentialist imperative always to act so as to produce the best results overall, a doctrine that entails the stronger principle. Murphy, in contrast, thinks that there is one legitimate basis for limiting the demands on oneself of a duty of optimizing beneficence: on grounds of fairness, one need not do more for others than one would if everyone complied with such a duty. However, he acknowledges that Singer's and Unger's discussions of rescue are pressing challenges to this qualification (see pp. 127–33), and he emphasizes the stringency of his qualified duty of beneficence in current world conditions of poverty and inequality—stringency which might well sustain Singer's radical conclusion. Although Henry Shue, *Basic Rights* (Princeton: Princeton University Press, 1996 [original edition: 1980]) is concerned with a limited set of basic rights and the specific question of what institutions to support, he presents powerful arguments for an institutional version of Singer's radical conclusion, some of which only depend on the distribution of needs, resources and capacities to help.—My defense of a moderate principle of general beneficence is opposed to this whole coalition. I will leave implicit some responses to Murphy's and Unger's work that I spell out in "Beneficence, Duty and Distance," *Philosophy & Public Affairs* 32 (2004): 357–83, especially on pp. 365 f. and 379 f. (Murphy) and pp. 381–3 (Unger).

6. In *The Morality of Freedom* (Oxford: Oxford University Press, 1986), pp. 241–3, Joseph Raz presents similar examples as part of a case for the thesis, "When happiness is understood as a quality of a person's life or of periods of his life, the pursuit of happiness is . . . satiable [i.e., involves a goal that can be completely met]" (p. 241).

7. For trenchant descriptions of this process, the basis for conduct that express-es a coherent, autonomous personality, see, for example, Harry Frankfurt, "The Importance of What We Care About" [1982] in his *The Importance of What We Care About* (Cambridge: Cambridge University Press, 1988) and Michael Bratman, "Reflection, Planning, and Temporally Extended Agency," *Philosophical Review* 109 (2000): 35–61.

8. In these cases, a goal consists of doing well in certain activities. But in general, I intend "goal" broadly, to include the full range of ways of doing well, including doing well in relationships one values and in expressing traits one values. One worthwhile trait that virtually all of us value is relaxed openness to

occasional harmless indulgences that do not promote the goals that structure our lives as a whole by focussing our strivings. So sufficient success in "just this once" choices contributes to our sufficiently successful pursuit of our goals in the relevant broad sense, even though it departs from a narrower goal-directedness.

9. At the end of "International Aid and the Scope of Kindness," *Ethics* 105 (1994), pp. 126 f., Garrett Cullity offers a similar argument as the most powerful basis for insisting that a duty of kindness requires a "huge" sacrifice by the affluent in response to worldwide suffering. He says that this argument can be blocked, but not by any means as yet presented in the literature.

10. In Cullity's version of the "little bit more" argument, an extreme demand is generated by the reiterated claim that it is wrong not to make the small incremental sacrifice that would save an additional life. In the rebuttal that he eventually offers, toward the end of his probing and richly thoughtful book *The Moral Demands of Affluence* (Oxford: Oxford University Press, 2004), he says that the basis for defending one's unwillingness to make these sacrifices is: "I can legitimately constrain my willingness to contribute toward helping others by reference to my engagement with defensible life-enhancing goods. But having this engagement is incompatible with the iterative approach" (p. 191). These judgments are very much a part of my own account of beneficence. But it is not clear where his version of the "little bit more" argument goes wrong, in his view. He is willing to accept the ultimate moral authority, in matters of beneficence, of "a point of view of impartial concern," which might be the "Equal Weighing View," involving the evaluation of any action by impartial evaluation of its effects (pp. 122 f.) Why, then, isn't each refusal wrong in light of the interests at stake? Indeed, why isn't the total self-deprivation produced by all the little increases in giving morally required, given the many lives that would be saved? In response to the second question, Cullity claims that "it is absurd to deny" that certain worthwhile pursuits that would be substantially inhibited by the extreme demand can themselves "ground requirements on others to help you"; and he infers that no requirement of beneficence is violated when you engage in these pursuits (p. 157; see also p. 193). But the denial that someone ought to be helped in these pursuits when the alternative is to save innocent lives instead does not seem to be absurd. And this seems to be the denial to which Cullity's opponent is committed. When one asks whether a given increment may be refused, in light of the stakes for others, the denial that this would be too much to require is even further from absurdity. For these and other reasons, a more direct attack on the morality of impartial concern, giving priority to equal respect and the underlying concern

prescribed in Sympathy, is needed to avoid the extreme demand that Cullity rejects.—I should add that my account of the demands of beneficence is not just more permissive than the extreme demand that Cullity rejects but also more permissive than the requirements of beneficence he supports, which rule out "expensive purchases that are made purely for enjoyment," for example, "holiday travel as a form of enjoyment" rather than as a means to such ends as "personal development" (pp. 183 f.)

11. See, for example, Scheffler, "Relationships and Responsibilities," *Philosophy & Public Affairs* 26 (1997): 189–209.

12. See, for example, Singer, *One World* (New Haven: Yale University Press, 2002), pp. 154–67.

13. In support of a radical conclusion about donations to lessen the serious suffering of others ("a typical well-off person, like you and me, must give away most of her financial assets, and much of her income"), Peter Unger has appealed to a duty to rescue in an analogous case, involving sacrificed resources for retirement, the Case of Bob's Bugatti. See *Living High and Letting Die*, pp. 134–9.

14. See Kagan, *The Limits of Morality*, p. 14.

15. In "The Possibility of Special Duties," *Canadian Journal of Philosophy* 16 (1986): 651–76, Philip Pettit and Robert Goodin emphasize the coordinative benefits of widely shared norms allocating special responsibilities. However, they are not concerned with the moral status of closeness, and they deploy a rule-consequentialist framework which would yield Singer's radical conclusion in current global circumstances of neediness and inequality.

16. In T. M. Scanlon's highly influential contractualist view of moral wrongness, "an act is wrong if its performance under the circumstances would be disallowed by any set of principles for the general regulation of behavior that no one could reasonably reject as a basis for informed, unforced general agreement" (Scanlon, *What We Owe to Each Other* (Cambridge, Mass.: Harvard University Press, 1998), p. 153). If, as he intends, reasonableness is taken to be a moral notion, whose constraints must be specified through different determinations in different contexts, responsive to specific moral judgments (see pp. 242–7), his formula and the precept about respectful commitment to a moral code are coextensive. However, I think that judgments in terms of respect and closely allied notions are more compelling and decisive in the cases at hand.

17. "Nil," as opposed to "no more than trivial," would be an exaggeration. Some people, after all, are less vulnerable than most to catastrophes creating a need for rescue. So they have some net risk of serious loss, even from

an appropriate *ex ante* perspective. The existence of such people seems an insuperable obstacle to grounding Nearby Rescue on a morality of mutual benefit. As Liam Murphy notes, in criticizing efforts to base restricted principles of obligatory rescue on "a mutually beneficial ex ante bargain," " a well-guarded billionaire who never . . . takes personal risks . . . might well be called on in emergencies . . . while his chances of needing a stranger's assistance are close to zero" (Murphy, *Moral Demands in Nonideal Theory*, p. 158). However, in the morality of equal respect, the role of reflection on the *ex ante* net expected costs of Nearby Rescue is not to establish universal mutual benefit, but to show that someone who regards others' lives as no less valuable than his own would not regard Nearby Rescue as too demanding, given the triviality of the *ex ante* risks it imposes.

18. From 2003 through 2007, the average annual proportion was 4.36%. See Center on Philanthropy at Indiana University, *Giving USA 2008* (Indianapolis: AAFRC Trust for Philanthropy, 2008), pp. 212 f. *Giving USA 2007* reports that approximately 5% of U.S. households give to international causes (p. 181).

## CHAPTER 2

1. *World Development Indicators 2008* (Washington: World Bank, 2008), table 6.12. Direct government transfer payments to needy individual U.S. citizens were over thirty times greater, even when benefits from retirement, disability and unemployment insurance and veterans' benefits are put to one side. See U.S. Department of Commerce, *Statistical Abstract of the United States: 2008* (Washington: Government Printing Office, 2008), p. 346.

2. See Charles Beitz, "Justice and International Relations," *Philosophy & Public Affairs* 4 (1975): 360–89; Beitz, *Political Theory and International Relations* (Princeton: Princeton University Press, 1999 [original edition: 1979]), especially part III; Thomas Pogge, *Realizing Rawls* (Ithaca, NY: Cornell University Press, 1989), especially part III; Darrel Moellendorf, *Cosmopolitan Justice* (Boulder, Colo.: Westview, 2002), especially chs. 3 and 4. In his pioneering 1975 essay, Beitz emphasizes that "international economic cooperation creates a new basis for international morality. . . . Since boundaries are not coextensive with the scope of social cooperation, they do not mark the limits of social obligations. Thus, the parties to the original position cannot be assumed to know that they are members of a particular national society" (pp. 373, 376). Similarly, Moellendorf justifies his global extrapolation of Rawls' domestic theory of justice on the grounds that "duties of justice arise . . . when activities such as . . . commerce bring persons into association" (p. 32), while Pogge

took "significant global interdependence" to be the basis for bringing Rawls' "contractarian device to bear on the global plane" (p. 241).

3. See *World Development Indicators 2008*, tables 1.1, 4.8. Evaluation of output or consumption at purchasing power parity in U.S. dollars is (roughly) evaluation at prices for purchase in the United States. Because foreign exchange rates are determined by global supply and demand in international commerce, they result in very different evaluations, much lower in all poor countries. The $4,436 estimate of per capita GNI at purchasing power parity corresponds to $1,997 at foreign exchange rates. The consumption expenditures include the value of all goods and services purchased by individuals and households, including annual housing costs. "A World Without a Middle Class" is Branko Milanovic's apt title for the chapter describing the world income distribution in his rich and incisive study of global inequalities, *Worlds Apart* (Princeton: Princeton University Press, 2005).

4. See Shaohua Chen and Martin Ravallion, "The Developing World is Poorer than We Thought, but No Less Successful in the Fight against Poverty" (Washington: World Bank, 2008), pp. 5, 34, 35.

5. In his classic account of justice within a society, *A Theory of Justice* (Cambridge, Mass.: Harvard University Press, 1971), Rawls noted that the resolution of questions of international justice "may require different principles arrived at in a somewhat different way" (p. 8) and, late in the book, very briefly sketched an approach to justice among nations based on a significantly different version of the original position, in which "the principles chosen, would be, I think, familiar ones," such as familiar principles of non-aggression and national self-defense (p. 378). Returning to these questions late in life, in such works as *The Law of Peoples* (Cambridge, Mass.: Harvard University Press, 1999), Rawls confirmed his inclination to avoid the stringent demands of a global difference principle and the straightforward extrapolation of the domestic original position that would support it. The global extrapolators think this was a mistake. The implication of the arguments of this book will be that he was right not to take these further steps, even though his own account of international justice is severely incomplete as a basis for responding to the full range of transnational interactions.

6. Moellendorf, *Cosmopolitan Justice*, p. 79. Similarly, Simon Caney bases a global principle of equal opportunity on the consideration that "people should not be penalized because of the vagaries of happenstance, and their fortunes should not be set by factors like nationality and citizenship." He takes such reasoning to be at least implicit in nearly all defenses of a cosmopolitan conception of justice. See "Cosmopolitan Justice and Equalizing Opportunities," in Thomas Pogge, ed., *Global Justice* (Oxford: Blackwell, 2001), p. 125.

7. See Milton Friedman, *Capitalism and Freedom* (Chicago: University of Chicago Press, 1962), p. 165; Robert Nozick, *Anarchy, State and Utopia* (New York: Basic Books, 1974), p. 185.

8. The relevance to justice and desert of someone's making good use of undeserved advantages is incisively explored in David Schmidtz, "How to Deserve," *Political Theory* 30 (2002): 774–99.

9. At a number of points in *A Theory of Justice*, Rawls appeals to the fact that advantageous starting points are not deserved, in justifying the difference principle or establishing the moral importance of the original position. Although he offers these claims about what is not deserved in arguments through which fellow members of a political society would properly seek one another's allegiance to shared institutions and although his view of global justice is undemanding, some of these passages seem to presuppose a general moral aim of correcting "the arbitrariness of the world" in one's choices of moral principles (p. 141), an aim celebrated as "purity of heart" in the touching final paragraph of the book (p. 587). However, as the debate over *A Theory of Justice* unfolded and rival conceptions of fairness were pressed, Rawls came to emphasize, more and more strongly and explicitly, that the form of justification and the moral principles he sought to defend specifically concerned the joint political activity of fellow citizens in "society as a fair system of cooperation between citizens as free and equal" (*Justice as Fairness: A Restatement* (Cambridge, Mass.: Harvard University Press, 2001 [based on work in the 1980s]), p. 56). Making use of Rawls' post-*Theory* writings later in this chapter, I will describe why the difference principle might be favored as a standard of economic justice among those bound by this political, non-cosmopolitan tie. While the cosmopolitan extrapolation appropriates one plausible interpretation of some of Rawls' work, it does not reflect his considered judgment, arrived at for good reasons.

10. See Goodin, "What Is so Special about Our Fellow Countrymen?," *Ethics* 98 (1988): 663–86.

11. See *ibid.*, pp. 684–6.

12. See Dagger, "Rights, Boundaries and the Bonds of Community," *American Political Science Review* 79 (1985): 436–47.

13. See David Miller, *On Nationality* (Oxford: Oxford University Press, 1995), especially chs. 2 and 3.

14. Someone might object that the ethnic conception of Norwegian nationality is obsolete, because of evolution in the direction of the multi-ethnic nationality characteristic of the United States. But even if this shift did occur in the course of the twentieth century, it will not affect the larger issue. In the first

half of the twentieth century, there was an ethnically exclusive Norwegian nationality, in Miller's sense, yet in this period the scope of just provision for the disadvantaged within Norway was as broad as it is now.

15. In recent years, appreciation of the power of political ties among compatriots to generate special duties toward the disadvantaged has led to a variety of assessments of the distinctive moral significance of these ties. In "Cosmopolitan Respect and Patriotic Concern," *Philosophy & Public Affairs* 27 (1998): 202–24, I argued (as I will here) that a politically active citizen can only show respect for her compatriots while helping to coercively impose terms of self-advancement on them if she is especially concerned to improve the situation of those whose life-prospects are least. (See pp. 215–18.) I also argued, in terms that I have come to reformulate in precepts of loyalty, that special concern for disadvantaged compatriots is needed to fulfill a duty to make social trust the basis for civic cooperation. (See pp. 210–14.) These arguments were accompanied by an assessment of duties of general beneficence as demanding much less than these special responsibilities. Later, Michael Blake, in "Distributive Justice, Coercion and Autonomy," *Philosophy & Public Affairs* 30 (2002): 257–96, also described how respect for compatriots with inferior life-prospects creates special needs to address their disadvantages in justifying their coercion. In his view, the coercive network of law is a precondition of a concern with relative deprivation, while there is an obligation to remedy absolute deprivation, wherever found, regardless of any such precondition (see e.g. p. 294). The strong political duty of beneficence he asserts is one that I rejected in "Cosmopolitan Respect" and subsequent writings leading to this book. In "The Problem of Global Justice," *Philosophy & Public Affairs* 33 (2005): 113–47, Thomas Nagel described how respectful political coercion entails special concern for worst-off compatriots, and denied that any standard of distributive justice, for example, any standard of fairness, is properly applied beyond the borders of sovereign states; internationally, only minimal humanitarian concerns entailing no serious sacrifice are relevant. (See e.g. pp. 118 f., 120, 131. More precisely, Nagel presents arguments for this view, which he regards as "probably correct," p. 126.) Nagel claims that the international relationships with a bearing on material wellbeing constitute "mere economic interaction," "an inappropriate site for claims of justice" (pp. 137 f.). My claim, sketched in "Moral Closeness and World Community" (in Deen Chatterjee, ed. *The Ethics of Assistance* (Cambridge: Cambridge University Press, 2004)) and developed in the next four chapters of this book, is that current international relationships generate demanding duties, often duties of fairness, which are utterly different from our duties of

mere humanitarian assistance, though also different from the specific duties of economic justice among compatriots.

16. As T. M. Scanlon notes in his incisive criticism of teleological accounts of valuing. See *What We Owe to Each Other* (Cambridge, Mass.: Harvard University Press, 1998), p. 89.

17. An extended usage of "friendship" is an apt and well-established means of evoking interpersonal loyalty based on participation in shared political institutions. The connection between political activity and mutual concern among the citizens of a well-ordered state leads Aristotle to characterize them as bound by friendship, in the *Nichomachean Ethics* and elsewhere. Sibyl Schwarzenbach argues in trenchant detail that mutual concern on the model of friendship remains appropriate to modern citizenship in "On Civic Friendship," *Ethics* 107 (1996): 97–128. Rawls, too, saw mutual concern, expressed in political choices, as the fitting accompaniment of joint civic engagement, characterizing the well-ordered society that he sought as one in which "a shared conception of justice establishes the bonds of civic friendship" (*A Theory of Justice*, p. 5), describing the difference principle as corresponding to "a natural meaning of fraternity" among fellow members of a society (*ibid.*, p. 105), and noting that the right explication of the terms of political justification would "specify the nature of the political relation in a constitutional democratic regime as one of civic friendship" ("The Idea of Public Reason Revisited" [originally, 1997], Rawls, *Collected Papers* (Cambridge, Mass.: Harvard University Press, 1999), p. 579). In addition to evoking an important basis for political duties, the analogy with friendship helps to explain why people regard a political life in which these duties are pursued as part of their own good, not simply a constraint that they are obliged to endure.

18. See, for example, Raz, *The Morality of Freedom* (Oxford: Oxford University Press, 1986), pp. 369 f.

19. See Tom Hertz, "Riches and Race," p. 186 (finding that 36.6% growing up in the bottom decile were in the bottom as adults, while another 20.5% were one decile up); Bhashkar Mazumder, "The Apple Falls Even Closer to the Tree than We Thought," p. 96 (transmission of earnings differences from fathers to sons based on sixteen year earnings averages—the elasticity for six year averages is 40%); Samuel Bowles, Herbert Gintis and Melissa Osborne Groves, Introduction, p. 20; all in Bowles, Gintis and Groves, *Unequal Chances* (Princeton: Princeton University Press, 2005).

20. Here, I conflate two aspects of domestic economic justice, as Rawls describes it: the difference principle proper, which regulates lifetime expectations of income and wealth among typical members of groups ranked by advantage,

and the requirement of fair equality of opportunity, which has priority. Such nuances do not have much impact on the question of whether Rawls' theory deserves to be globalized, if it is right for a society considered in isolation.

21. Rawls, *Justice as Fairness*, p. 133. The effort to establish a social minimum instead of the difference principle that Rawls finds most challenging is Jeremy Waldron, "John Rawls and the Social Minimum," *Journal of Applied Philosophy* 3 (1986): 21–33. This powerful argument for a different standard is notable for sharing his assumption that the political duty to take account of disadvantage is based on the duty to sustain appropriate political commitments, not on a duty to impartially promote wellbeing.

22. Rawls, *Justice as Fairness*, p. 129.

23. *Ibid.*, p. 128.

24. *Ibid.*, pp. 128, 130.

25. *Ibid.*, p. 130.

26. See, for example, Rawls, *Political Liberalism* (New York: Columbia University Press, 1993), pp. 24 f., 35, 304 f. An alternative, complementary argument for favoring the difference principle, as the best expression of what citizens owe to one another in mitigating disadvantages, would establish especially good fit with secure convictions about what they owe to one another in the realm of civil and political liberties. This is Joshua Cohen's approach in "Democratic Equality," *Ethics* 99 (1989): 727–51, which Rawls singles out as accurately representing his views. (See *Justice as Fairness*, pp. 43, 100.) Again, the argument is based on a favored conception of ties within a political society.

27. See Shue, *Basic Rights* (Princeton: Princeton University Press, 1996 [original edition: 1980]), pp. 124–7.

28. See *ibid.*, pp. 114–19, 125. Shue does not think that extensive sacrifices, including substantial sacrifices of cultural enrichment, would, in fact, be required to fulfill all basic needs.

29. The benefits to poor foreigners of immigration are also limited by consequent changes in the labor market, such as John Roemer investigates in "The Global Welfare Economics of Immigration," *Social Choice and Welfare* 27 (2006): 311–25.

30. I am indebted to Daniel Koltonski for emphasizing the availability of moral criticisms of immigration restrictions even under this assumption.

## CHAPTER 3

1. World Bank, *World Development Indicators 2008* (Washington: World Bank, 2008), tables 1.1, 2.15, 2.21.

2. Comparing world poverty in 2005 with world poverty in 1981, Shaohua Chen and Martin Ravallion, the chief poverty researchers at the World Bank, estimate that there were 505 million fewer people living below $1.25 a day at 2005 purchasing power parity—their proposed revision, in light of improved purchasing power estimates, of the World Bank poverty threshold whose familiar, imprecise label is "a dollar a day." The decline in China was 627 million. There was a decline of 123 million in East Asia outside of China, 35 million in India, 12 million in the rest of South Asia, and 1 million in the Middle East and North Africa, accompanied by increases elsewhere, vast in sub-Saharan Africa (182 million). There was a worldwide increase of 56 million in the number living below $2.00 a day (the threshold corresponding to the median national poverty line among developing countries) from which China was a signal exception, with a decline of 499 million. See Chen and Ravallion, "The Developing World is Poorer than We Thought, but No Less Successful in the Fight against Poverty" (Washington: World Bank, 2008, pp. 34 f.)

3. Thomas Pogge, "A Global Resources Dividend" in David Crocker and Toby Linden, eds., *The Ethics of Consumption* (New York: Rowman and Littlefield, 1998), p. 502. See also Pogge, *World Poverty and Human Rights* (Cambridge: Polity Press, 2002), p. 197.

4. The turn toward the relational is also part of Pogge's orientation, and may be all that he intends. On the other hand, the content of our standards of responsibility is quite different. Here are some doubts about the soundness or scope of claims of irresponsibility advanced in Pogge's rich and resourceful discussions. His broadest basis for ascribing "misery to the existing global order and therefore ultimately to ourselves" is the fact that "there is a shared institutional order that is shaped by the better-off . . . implicated in the reproduction of radical inequality in that there is a feasible institutional alternative under which such severe and extensive poverty would not persist" (*World Poverty and Human Rights*, pp. 199, 201; see also "A Global Resources Dividend," pp. 504, 506). If, as Pogge is willing to concede, the existence of avoidable dire poverty does not, as such, entail a duty to eliminate it, it is not clear why its foreseeable persistence under current institutions entails a duty to eliminate it by institutional means. He also notes that current arrangements derive from a history of bloody conquests, include exclusive sovereign control of natural resources, and assign prerogatives to dispose of those natural resources which are incentives to tyrannical seizures of power. (See "A Global Resources Dividend," pp. 507–10, *World Poverty and Human Rights*, pp. 201–4, and "'Assisting' the Global Poor," in Deen Chatterjee,

ed., *The Ethics of Assistance* (Cambridge: Cambridge University Press, 2004), pp. 270–2.) But compensation for effects of bloody conquest in the past must be severely limited by the moral equivalent of a statute of limitations, so that people are not overly vulnerable to demands deriving from past wrongs over which they had no control. It is not clear why the current value of natural resources should be equally shared among people whose technologies and commercial activities make very different contributions to this value. A broad prohibition of purchases of natural resources from the territories of oppressive governments would be unduly burdensome to both people in those territories and people needing those resources elsewhere, since there would still be all-too-effective incentives to oppress. A narrow prohibition in extreme cases of ferocious tyranny might be useful, but the help to the global poor would be, correspondingly, limited.

5. See World Bank, *World Development Indicators 2002* (Washington: World Bank, 2002), tables 4.6, 6.3.

6. See World Bank, *World Development Indicators 2008*, tables 4.5, 6.4.

7. See World Bank, *World Development Indicators 2007* (Washington: World Bank, 2007), table 6.8.

8. See Paul Collier and David Dollar, *Globalization, Growth and Poverty* (Washington: World Bank, 2002), p. 45.

9. World Bank, *World Development Indicators 2006* (Washington: World Bank, 2006), table 2.6.

10. Quotation from Nicholas Kristof and Sheryl WuDunn, "Two Cheers for Sweatshops," *New York Times Magazine*, September 24, 2000, in Bhagwati, *In Defense of Globalization* (New York: Oxford University Press, 2004), p. 175.

11. *Ibid.*

12. In the United States in 2001, the top 20% of households owned 91% of net financial assets, the top 1% owned 40%, and the bottom 40% had less than zero net financial assets, on account of debt. The top 10% owned 77% of the worth of stocks, including indirect ownership through mutual funds and retirement accounts, the bottom 60% owned 3%. Of the bottom 60% of households ranked by income, two thirds owned no stocks, directly or indirectly, four-fifths owned less than $5,000 worth. See Edward N. Wolff, "Changes in Household Wealth in the 1980s and 1990s" in Edward N. Wolff, ed., *International Perspectives on Household Wealth* (Northampton: Edward Elgar, 2006), tables 2 and 13.

13. See T. M. Scanlon, *What We Owe to Each Other* (Cambridge, Mass.: Harvard University Press, 1998), pp. 164 f.

14. World Bank, *World Development Indicators 2008*, tables 1.1, 6.4, 6.12.

15. In connecting economic exploitation with taking advantage of others' bargaining weakness and in creating space for morally acceptable exploitation, my account parallels Allen Wood's illuminating discussion in "Exploitation," *Social Philosophy and Policy* 12 (1993): 135–58. There, Wood characterizes exploitation as one person's extracting a benefit from another by using her weakness or vulnerability in accordance with his plans (pp. 141–3). He takes this feature to be, in itself, a reason to criticize a relationship, but not a decisive one: other features can make exploitation morally acceptable all told. The main differences derive from the broader scope of the crucial benefiting-from-weakness in Wood's account and from his view that it generates an ineradicable taint of degradation. Wood says that the planned derivation of benefit from another's weakness or vulnerability, even "as doctors do when they treat patients," is, as such, degrading (p. 153). Although, as in the standard medical case, other aspects may make the interaction all right all told, the "inevitably exploitive side" should still occasion "profound moral ambivalence" (*ibid.*) These implausible assessments, which would give oncologists a (non-compelling) reason to be dealers in dispensable trinkets instead, result from putting people's difficulties in asserting their will in interaction with others on a par with difficulties that they overcome through interaction with others. Desperation can make it hard to hold out in bargaining or can be an expression of vulnerability to a need that one satisfies through bargaining. Only the former is an aspect of exploitation, on my view. Moreover, justifications deriving from burdens of avoiding exploitation sometimes reconcile it with respect for the other's capacity for choice, so that the morally well-ordered process of mere exploitation merits unambivalent acceptance. Bhagwati's unambivalent encomium to the leather goods factory may or may not fit the facts that shape the responsibilities in play, but it is not inherently misguided. (Some parts of Wood's rich essay are more receptive to these views.)

16. Jarrod Wiener, *Making Rules in the Uruguay Round of the GATT* (Aldershot: Dartmouth Publishing Company, 1995), p. 186.

17. Ernest Preeg, *Traders in a Brave New World* (Chicago: University of Chicago Press, 1995), p. 80. Preeg also notes similar threats to organize a "GATT for the like-minded" (U.S. Trade Representative Brock, p. 48) and "if insignificant progress is made . . . to explore regional and bilateral agreements with other nations" (President Reagan, p. 51) and describes the crucial role of threatened trade discrimination in advancing U.S. proposals on intellectual property rights ("[Recalcitrant] developing countries came to realize that a multilateral agreement in the GATT could be the lesser evil to unilateral U.S. demands

outside the GATT," p. 67). Preeg was a member of the U.S. delegation to the Uruguay Round. His history of the negotiations is accompanied, on the back cover, by praise from Carla Hills and from Arthur Dunkel, the director general of GATT for most of this period.

18. Robert Zoellick, "America Will Not Wait for the Won't-Do Countries," *Financial Times*, September 22, 2003, section 1, p. 23.

19. The section on the topic "Cooperative Organizations" in Rawls, *The Law of Peoples* (Cambridge, Mass.: Harvard University Press, 1999) involves three paragraphs of main text, one on an organization "framed to ensure free trade among peoples" (p. 42). Rawls says that reasonable deliberations would lead participants to "agree to fair standards of trade to keep the market free and competitive" and would correct "unjustified distributive effects between peoples" (p. 43), but does not attempt to describe how fairness and unjustified inequality would be determined, beyond noting that representatives must not rely on knowledge of the size of their economies.

20. This stand-off ended the WTO ministerial meeting in July 2008. See Alan Beattie, "Gamble Fails as Lamy Concedes Defeat," *Financial Times*, July 29, 2008. The proposed caps on rich countries' agricultural subsidies, which would also have been far above projected future expenditures in the European Union, would not have affected subsidies not tied to production, which are unconstrained in the current regime.

21. See Chen and Ravallion, "The Developing World is Poorer than We Thought, but No Less Successful in the Fight against Poverty," p. 34; World Bank, *World Development Indicators 2008*, tables 2.18, 2.15, 3.13.

22. See United Nations Development Programme, *Human Development Report 2005* (New York: United Nations, 2005), p. 127.

23. See United Nations Development Programme, *Human Development Report 1997* (New York: United Nations, 1997), p. 82.

24. As always, estimates are sensitive to assumptions in the underlying models. The models most commonly used to estimate the effects of alternative trade regimes make simplifying assumptions, known to be false, that the amount of employment in each country would be unaffected and that there would be no gains in productivity through economies of scale and learning by doing. The correction of such assumptions can greatly increase projected benefits. For example, Santiago Fernandez de Cordoba and David Vanzetti estimate that gains to developing countries under a proposal that would reduce tariffs on manufactures imposed by developed countries to an average of 0.8%, while reducing developing countries' tariffs to an average of 5.3%, would amount to $28 billion a year according to a standard model that assumes

fixed employment; the gains would amount to $87 billion on the plausible assumption that expanded production in developing countries could make use of a current large reserve of under-used unskilled labor. (See Fernandez de Cordoba and Vanzetti, "Now What? Search for a Solution to the WTO Industrial Tariff Negotiations," in Fernandez de Cordoba and Sam Laird, eds., *Coping with Trade Reforms* (Geneva: UNCTAD, 2005), pp. 30, 39 f.)

25. See OECD, *Agricultural Policies in OECD Countries at a Glance 2006* (Paris: OECD, 2006), p. 19; UNCTAD, *The Least Developed Countries Report 2006* (Geneva: UNCTAD, 2006), Annex: Basic Data on the Least Developed Countries, table 1.

26. See Oxfam, *Cultivating Poverty: The Impact of U.S. Cotton Subsidies on Africa* (2002), www.oxfam.org.uk/policy/papers/30cotton, pp. 2, 11. More precisely, the loss and subsidy figures are for the 2001–2 "marketing year."

27. See the discussion of Winters, Walmsley, Wang and Grynberg's 2002 study, along with other parallel findings, in Joseph Stiglitz and Andrew Charlton, *Fair Trade for All* (Oxford: Oxford University Press, 2005), pp. 250 f. Stiglitz and Charlton note that the somewhat lower estimate ($80 billion) in this study depends on neglect of the actual over-supply of unskilled labor in developing countries.

28. See Richard Adams and John Page, "Do International Migration and Remittances Reduce Poverty in Developing Countries?," *World Development* 33 (2005), pp. 1645, 1652 f.

29. See Cornia and Reddy, "The Impact of Adjustment-Related Social Funds on Income Distribution and Poverty," in Cornia, ed., *Inequality, Growth and Poverty in an Era of Liberalization and Globalization* (New York: Oxford University Press, 2004), pp. 275, 281.

30. See World Bank, *World Development Indicators 2003* (Washington: World Bank, 2003), table 4.13.

31. See Dani Rodrik, "The Global Governance of Trade as if Development Really Mattered" (New York: United Nations Development Programme, 2001) for a cogent account of these departures from free trade orthodoxy. Their use in the twentieth century—for example, in the great success stories of development in East Asia—paralleled earlier departures in the course of successful development in the United States, Germany and Japan.

32. See Branko Milanovic, *The Two Faces of Globalization* (Washington: World Bank, 2002), www.worldbank.org/research/inequality/pdf/naiveglob1.pdf, p. 14.

33. See Francisco Rodriguez and Dani Rodrik, "Trade Policy and Economic Growth: A Skeptic's Guide to the Cross-National Evidence" (Cambridge,

Mass.: National Bureau of Economic Research: 1999), www.nber.org/papers/w7081.

34. For a vivid account of the repeated past failures of the consensus among developed-country experts about the best path to development, see William Easterly, *The Elusive Search for Growth* (Cambridge, Mass.: MIT Press, 2001).

35. See Oxfam, *Rigged Rules and Double Standards* (2002), publications.oxfam.org.uk/what_we_do/issues/trade/downloads/trade_report.pdf. pp. 116 f.; "The Rigged Trade Game," *New York Times*, July 20, 2003, News of the Week in Review, p. 10.

36. See Joseph Stiglitz, *Globalization and its Discontents* (New York: Norton, 2002), pp. 200–13.

37. See Joseph Stiglitz, *Making Globalization Work* (New York: Norton, 2006), pp. 260–5; George Soros, *On Globalization* (New York: Public Affairs, 2002).

## CHAPTER 4

1. See European Union, "Strategy on Climate Change: Foundations of the Strategy" (2005) europa.eu/scadplus; Malte Meinshausen, "What Does a 2° Target Mean for Greenhouse Gas Concentrations?," in Hans Joachim Schnellnhuber *et al.*, eds., *Avoiding Dangerous Climate Change* (Cambridge: Cambridge University Press, 2006), p. 265. In practice, the average for 1861–90 has been treated as the pre-industrial benchmark.

2. See F. R. Rijsberman and R. Swart, eds., *Targets and Indicators of Climate Change: Report of Working Group II of the Advisory Group on Greenhouse Gases* (Stockholm: Stockholm Environmental Institute, 1990), pp. viii–ix.

3. See Climate Change Research Centre (University of New South Wales), "2007 Bali Climate Declaration by Scientists," www.climate.unsw.edu.au (December 2007).

4. George W. Bush, "Letter from the President to Senators Hagel, Helms, Craig, and Roberts," March 13, 2001, www.whitehouse.gov/news/releases/2001/03/2001.

5. See Meinshausen, "What Does a 2° Target Mean?," p. 270, ascribing respective probabilities of 54%, 28% and 71%.

6. See Terry Barker, Igor Bashmakov *et al.*, "Technical Summary," in IPCC, *Climate Change 2007: Mitigation* (Cambridge: Cambridge University Press 2007), p. 27.

7. See Susan Solomon, Dahe Qin *et al.*, "Technical Summary," in IPCC, *Climate Change 2007: The Physical Science Basis* (Cambridge: Cambridge University Press 2007), p. 36.

8. See Gerald Meehl, Thomas Stocker *et al.*, "Global Climate Projections," ch. 10, *ibid.*, p. 822; Gerald Meehl *et al.*, "How Much More Global Warming and Sea Level Rise?," *Science* 307 (2005), pp. 1769 f. Indeed, an immediate end of greenhouse gas emissions would have been followed by a delayed increase of about 0.2° over the next two decades. See Pierre Friedlingstein and Susan Solomon, "Contributions of Past and Present Generations to Committed Warming Caused by Carbon Dioxide," *Proceedings of the National Academy of Sciences of the United States* 102 (2005), p. 10834.

9. See Kenneth Denman, Guy Brasseur *et al.*, "Couplings between Changes in the Climate System and Biogeochemistry," ch. 7 of IPCC, *Climate Change 2007: The Physical Science Basis*, pp. 516 f.; H.-Holger Rogner, Dadi Zhou, *et al.*, "Introduction," IPCC, *Climate Change 2007: Mitigation*, p. 103.

10. See Meinshausen, "What Does a 2° Target Mean?," pp. 273 f.; Michel den Elzen and Malte Meinshausen, "Meeting the EU 2° C Climate Target: Global and Regional Emission Implications" (Bilthoven: Netherlands Environmental Assessment Agency, 2005), www.pbl.nl/publications, p. 17; Bert Metz, "Meeting a 2 Degree Target: Is It Possible?" (Bilthoven: Netherlands Assessment Agency, 2006), PowerPoint accessible at ips.ac.nz/events/completed-activities/Climate Change Symposium/Dr Bert Metz.pdf, p. 8.

11. See Detlef van Vuuren, Michel den Elzen *et al.*, "Stabilizing Greenhouse Gas Concentrations at Low Levels," *Climatic Change* 81 (2007), p. 123. Brian Fisher, Nebosja Nakicenovic *et al.*, "Issues Related to Mitigation in the Long Term Context," ch. 3 of IPCC, *Climate Change 2007: Mitigation,* pp. 198 f., acknowledge just six descriptions, in all, of emissions trajectories leading to stabilization as low as 445–90 ppm carbon dioxide equivalent. These included studies which, unlike FAIR's, did not assess the feasibility of widespread uses of low-emissions technologies on which they relied. Typically, non-FAIR studies also reduced estimates of costs by the positing of Business As Usual trajectories much more receptive to stringent targets than the median scenarios.

12. See den Elzen and Meinshausen, "Meeting the EU 2° C Climate Target," p. 18.

13. See van Vuuren, den Elzen *et al.*, "Stabilizing Greenhouse Gas Concentrations," pp. 127, 133.

14. *Ibid.*, pp. 135, 144.

15. See, for example, Christian Azar *et al.*, "Carbon Capture and Storage from Fossil Fuels and Biomass," *Climatic Change* 74 (2006): 47–79.

16. See van Vuuren, den Elzen *et al.*, "Stabilizing Greenhouse Gas Concentrations," p. 137.

17. See den Elzen and Meinshausen, "Meeting the EU 2° C Climate Target," pp. 22 f.

18. See Metz, "Meeting a 2 Degree Target," pp. 21 f.

19. See Jean-Charles Hourcade, Priyadashe Shukla *et al.* "Global Regional and National Costs and Ancillary Benefits of Mitigation," ch. 8 of IPCC, *Climate Change 2001: Mitigation* (Cambridge: Cambridge University Press, 2001), pp. 537–9. The processes of global exchange would mostly have involved reallocation through trade of permits reflecting the excessive emission budget offered to former Soviet Bloc countries as a bribe to ratify Kyoto together with assumed "ideal implementation . . . that can exploit all cost effective options" of the Clean Development Mechanism, by which developed countries get emissions credits for reductions due to measures they fund in developing countries.

20. David Victor, *The Collapse of the Kyoto Protocol* (Princeton: Princeton University Press, 2001) incisively describes liabilities of cap and trade. Michael Grubb and Karsten Neuhoff, "Allocation and Competitiveness in the EU Emissions Trading Scheme," *Climate Policy* 6 (2006): 7–30, note the impact on European practice of problems inherent in assignment of allocations under conditions of uncertainty, along with effects of specific policy choices that exacerbated these problems.

21. See William Nordhaus, *A Question of Balance* (New Haven: Yale University Press, 2008), p. 19, World Bank, *World Development Indicators 2008* (Washington: World Bank, 2008), table 3.8.

22. See Energy Information Administration, "International Energy Outlook 1999", www.eia.doe.gov, p. 137.

23. See Metz, "Meeting a 2 Degree Target," p. 21.

24. In Timothy Carter, Roger Jones and Xianfu Lu *et al.*, "New Assessment Methods and the Characterization of Future Conditions," ch. 2 of IPCC, *Climate Change 2007: Impacts, Adaptation and Vulnerability* (Cambridge: Cambridge University Press, 2007), A1B is characterized as "Intermediate case", B2 as "Intermediate/low case" (p. 160).

25. See van Vuuren, den Elzen *et al.*, "Stabilizing Greenhouse Gas Concentrations," p. 138.

26. In the United States in the second half of the twentieth century, tripling of per capita real income accompanied a downward trend in reports of being "very happy." See Robert Lane, *The Loss of Happiness in Market Democracies* (New Haven: Yale University Press, 2000), p. 5, drawing on work by Ed Diener. Robert Frank, *Luxury Fever* (Princeton: Princeton University Press, 1999), p. 73 presents a similar finding by Ruut Veenhoven concerning Japan, an unchanged average level of self-reported wellbeing between 1960 and 1987 as per capita income rose fourfold.

27. The most extensive data on economic displacement in the United States are the biennial Displaced Workers Surveys of the U.S Bureau of Labor Statistics. Analyzing recent surveys, Henry Farber notes that about 35% of job-losers in a typical three-year period have not found a job at the end of the period; among the reemployed, 13% of those losing a full-time job have only found a part-time job; full-time job losers who do find new full-time jobs earn 17% less on average than they would have if not displaced ("What Do We Know about Job Loss in the United States?," *Economic Perspectives* [Federal Reserve Bank of Chicago, www.chicagofed.org] 2005 (second quarter):13–27). Workers displaced after twenty years' tenure tend to find work at pay about a third less than their old job (Louis Jacobson, Robert LaLonde and Daniel Sullivan, "Is Retraining Displaced Workers a Good Investment?," *Economic Perspectives*, 2005 (second quarter), p. 48).

28. See Amit Dar and Indermit Gill, "Evaluating Retraining Programs in OECD Countries: Lessons Learned," *World Bank Research Observer* 13 (1998): 79–101.

29. Scenario B1. See Carter *et al.*, "New Assessment Methods," pp. 159 f.

30. In his resourceful discussion of bases for international cooperation in dealing with climate change, "Fair Chore Division for Climate Change," *Social Theory and Practice* 28 (2002): 101–34, Martino Traxler argues, instead, for allocation into equally burdensome shares. However, the harshest consequences are supposed to be modified to accommodate "rationally compelling" needs. In any case, Traxler's proposals are offered in response to a different sort of problem within a different moral framework from my own: they are meant to cope with practical problems of intergovernmental agreement and commitment in a way that advances general duties of non-maleficence and assistance.

31. See Shaohua Chen and Martin Ravallion, "The Developing World is Poorer than We Thought, but No Less Successful in the Fight against Poverty" (Washington: World Bank, 2008), p. 35; World Bank, *World Development Indicators 2007* (Washington: World Bank, 2007), table 1.1.

32. See Kevin Baumert and Jonathan Pershing, "Climate Data: Insights and Observations" (Pew Center on Global Climate Change, 2004), www.pewclimate. org, p. 22. In India, where energy intensity of GDP also declined, increased GDP per capita was also the largest contributor, twice as important as population growth, the next largest.

33. See, for example, Shue, "Subsistence Emissions and Luxury Emissions," *Law & Policy* 15/1 (1993): 39–51.

34. See Paul Baer, "Exploring the 2020 Global Emissions Mitigation Gap," December, 2008, www.globalclimatenetwork.info, pp. 6, 8. A similar projection is entailed by Michel den Elzen and Niklas Hoehne, "Reductions

of Greenhouse Gas Emissions in Annex I and non-Annex I Countries for Meeting Concentration Stabilisation Targets," *Climatic Change* 91 (2008): 249–74 (see especially pp. 261, 263). In this article, den Elzen and Hoehne present the rationale for estimates summarized in Sujata Gupta, Dennis Sirpak *et al.*, "Policies, Instruments and Co-operative Arrangements," ch. 13 of IPCC, *Climate Change 2007: Mitigation*, p. 776. The projections in Peter Sheehan, "The New Global Growth Path: Implications for Climate Change Analysis and Policy," *Climatic Change* 91 (2008): 211–31 imply that developing countries' business-as-usual emissions would equal the global greenhouse gas budget considerably earlier, around 2025. See especially p. 222.

35. Those who assert this responsibility based on the past can cancel any implication that the living are responsible for pollution by the dead by singling out the current bearers of the obligation as beneficiaries, not as perpetrators. Their claim is that those who presently benefit from fossil-fuel-based industrialization in the past should sacrifice in proportion to those benefits in order to stop or relieve its current harmful effects. See, for example, Henry Shue, "Global Environment and International Inequality," *International Affairs* 75 (1999), p. 536. But cancelling the implication does not answer the question of why one must sacrifice an advantage due to acts in earlier generations that were not inherently illegitimate and whose harmful side-effects could not have been foreseen. Even if the harmful side-effects are part of the reason why advantages of living in a developed country are undeserved, this does not block the prerogative to make good use of one's undeserved advantages. Indeed, even if the past activity were, quite implausibly, condemned as wrong, the present obligation would not be established. The fact that the residents of one town currently benefit from effects of an old embezzlement whose impact continues to drag down the economy of a neighboring town does not seem to generate a current duty of sacrifice. Simon Caney notes the difference between "Beneficiary of pollution pays" and "Polluter pays" strictly construed, while offering a revealing account of the liabilities of both in "Cosmopolitan Justice, Responsibility and Global Climate Change," *Leiden Journal of International Law* 18 (2005): 747–75 (also in Thom Brooks, ed., *The Global Justice Reader* (Oxford: Blackwell, 2008)).

36. For example, in a recent pamphlet on climate change, Oxfam identified equity with the principle that "each person on the planet has the right to an equal share of the atmosphere's resources, and so has an equal claim to producing greenhouse gases within the earth's capacity to avoid dangerous global warming." See Oxfam, *Adapting to Climate Change* (2007), www.oxfam.org, p. 24. Anil Agrawal and Sunita Narain, *Global Warming in an Unequal World: A Case*

*of Environmental Colonialism* (New Delhi: Centre for Science and Environment, 1991) is a powerful early defense of this standard of equity.

37. See World Bank, *World Development Indicators 2008*, table 3.8.

38. More precisely, the fair deal in terms of net benefit could only involve unequal net benefits if it is superior to more equal alternatives from the standpoint of those whose net benefits are less. Since it will not affect the most striking consequences or the most compelling criticisms of the standard of a fair deal, I will omit this complication.

39. See World Bank, *World Development Indicators 2008*, tables 3.1, 4.2.

40. See Rex Victor Cruz, Hideo Harasaw, Murari Lal, Shaohong Wu *et al.*, "Asia," ch. 10 of IPCC, *Climate Change 2007: Impacts*, p. 484; Robert Nicholls, Poh Poh Wong *et al.*, "Coastal Systems and Low-Lying Areas," ibid., ch. 6, pp. 333 f., 339; Carter *et al.*, "New Assessment Methods," p. 159; Robert Nicholls and Jason Lowe, "Climate Stabilisation and Impacts of Sea-Level Rise" in Schnellhuber *et al.*, *Avoiding Dangerous Climate Change*, p. 200; Martin Parry, Nigel Arnell, Tony McMichael *et al.*, "Millions at Risk: Defining Critical Climate Change Threats and Targets," *Global Environmental Change* 11 (2001), p. 182.

41. NGOs in developing countries that press demands of equity in response to climate change are an especially rich source of exposes of the Clean Development Mechanism. See, for example, Patrick Bond and Rehana Dada, eds., *Trouble in the Air* (Durban Natal: Centre for Civil Society, 2005); Ritu Gupta, Shams Kazi and Julian Cheatle, "Newest Biggest Deal," *Down to Earth* [New Delhi: Centre for Science and the Environment], 14/12 (2005).

42. Of course, duties of cooperation and due care govern personal choices as well. Reflection on these personal obligations can confirm and further specify the demands of trust in climate policies.

43. See Michael Walzer, *Just and Unjust Wars* (New York: Basic Books, 1977), p. 152.

44. In Schnellnhuber *et al.*, *Avoiding Dangerous Climate Change*, Richard Tol and Gary Yohe emphasize the possible human costs of economic losses due to emissions cuts in "Of Dangerous Climate Change and Dangerous Emissions Reduction," pp. 291–8, while Terry Barker, Haoran Pan *et al.* argue for the optimistic scenario in "Avoiding Dangerous Climate Change by Inducing Technological Progress," pp. 361–71.

45. By "relevantly similar countries," I mean countries singled out by general rules based on characteristics appropriately connected to the goals of the global regime. Arbitrary burdening would be incompatible with the cooperative duty to seek self-respectful participation, which always helps to determine greenhouse obligations.

46. The direct abatement costs of mitigation in the FAIR team's estimates peak at 0.5% of business-as-usual Gross World Product for the stabilization target of 650 ppm, 1.2% for 550, 2% for 450, peaking about a decade earlier with each increase in stringency. See van Vuuren et al., "Stabilizing Greenhouse Gas Concentrations," p. 137. The Stern Review warns, "[C]arbon-energy models found very significant costs associated with moving below 450 ppm, as the number of affordable mitigation options was quickly exhausted. . . . **In general model comparisons find that the cost of stabilising emissions at 500–550 CO$_2$ eq would be around a third of doing so at 450–500 CO$_2$ eq.** The lesson here is to avoid doing too much too fast and to pace the flow of mitigation properly." See Nicholas Stern et. al., The Stern Review: The Economics of Climate Change (London: HM Treasury, 2006), www.hm-treasury.gov.uk, p. 247; bold face in original.

47. Even according to the business-as-usual scenarios of the IPCC, which do not fit the recent rapid growth of China and India, stringent targets combine with risks of industrial shutdown in developed countries to force reductions in emissive activity in developing countries that might otherwise serve important needs. In a projection based on the average outcome of these scenarios, if developed countries were to make a steep cut of 30% below their 1990 emissions by 2020, current developing countries would still have to accept a 19% reduction below business as usual in a greenhouse regime succeeding Kyoto that aims for stabilization at 450 ppm. In contrast, in a 550 ppm regime, a 30% cut below 1990 in developed countries would entail a 4% reduction below business as usual in developing countries, while in a 650 ppm regime, a 20% cut would require require no reduction at all. By 2050, even if developed countries were to eliminate greenhouse gas emissions entirely from their energy production, current developing countries would have to reduce 70% below business as usual in a 450 ppm regime, 50% in a 550 ppm regime, while in a 650 ppm regime a 40% reduction below 1990 in current developed countries would be compatible with 40% reduction below baseline in developing countries. More plausible estimates of business as usual in current developing countries, accounting for recent rapid growth in China and India, would make the impact of lower global targets more severe. For example, a 450 ppm regime in which developed countries cut to 30% below 1990 by 2020 would require current developing countries to reduce to 25% below their business-as-usual emissions. See den Elzen and Hoehne, "Reductions of Greenhouse Gas Emissions in Annex I and non-Annex-I Countries for Meeting Concentration Stabilisation Targets," pp. 264, 266.

48. See van Vuuren, den Elzen *et al.*, "Stabilizing Greenhouse Gas Concentrations," p. 149; Metz, "Meeting a 2 Degree Target," p. 16. Note that these particular estimates are correlated with simple carbon dioxide concentrations, not the carbon dioxide-equivalent concentrations, taking account of other greenhouse gases as well, that characterize targets in the rest of the FAIR team's work and in this chapter. Metz, "Meeting a 2 Degree Target," p. 15, permits a direct comparison. See also van Vuuren, den Elzen *et al.*, "Stabilizing Greenhouse Gas Concentrations," p. 147.

49. See Carter *et al.*, "New Assessment Methods," pp. 159 f.

50. See Metz, "Meeting a 2 Degree Target," p. 8; van Vuuren *et al.*, "Stabilizing Greenhouse Gas Concentrations," pp. 137, 141.

51. See Nicholls *et al.*, "Coastal Systems and Low-Lying Areas," pp. 323, 334; Carter *et al.*, "New Assessment Methods," pp. 159 f.

52. See, for example, Stern *et al.*, *The Stern Review*, p. 159.

53. See *ibid.*, pp. 299, 195; William Nordhaus, *A Question of Balance* (New Haven: Yale University Press, 2008), pp. 86 f., 106 f.

54. See Denman *et al.*, "Couplings between Changes in the Climate System and Biogeochemistry," p. 538, drawing on P. Friedlingstein, P. Cox *et al.*, "Climate–Carbon Cycle Feedback Analysis," *Journal of Climate* 19 (2006): 3337–53 (see especially pp. 3344, 3347).

55. See Peter Thornton *et al.*, "Influence of Carbon–Nitrogen Cycle Coupling on Land Model Response to $CO_2$ Fertilization and Climate Variability," *Global Biogeochemical Cycles* 21 (2007), GB4018, p. 13.

56. See Christopher Field *et al.*, "Feedbacks of Terrestrial Ecosystems to Climate Change," *Annual Review of Environment and Resources* 32 (2007), p. 9.

57. See Edward Schuur *et al.*, "Vulnerability of Permafrost Carbon to Climate Change," *BioScience* 50 (2008), p. 711. See also Meehl *et al.*, "Global Climate Projections," pp. 829–31; Andreas Fischlin, huy Midgley *et al.*, "Ecosystems, their Properties, Goods and Services," ch. 4 of IPCC, *Climate Change 2007: Impacts*, p. 231.

58. See Gary Yohe, Rodel Lasco *et al.*, "Perspectives on Climate Change and Vulnerability, ch. 20 of IPCC, *Climate Change 2007: Impacts*, p. 828; William Easterling, Pramod Aggarwal *et al.*, "Food, Fibre and Forest Products," *ibid.* ch. 5, p. 286.

59. Christopher Thomas *et al.*, "Extinction Risk from Climate Change," *Nature* 427 (2004): 145–8. See also Fischlin, Midgley *et al.*, "Ecosystems, their Properties, Goods and Services," p. 244; IPCC, *Climate Change 2007: Synthesis Report* (www.ipcc.ch), p. 10.

60. See, for example, Peter Cox *et al.*, "Acceleration of Global Warming due to Carbon Cycle Feedbacks in a Coupled Climate Model," *Nature* 408 (2000): 184–7.

61. See Jonathan Overpeck *et al.*, "Paleoclimatic Evidence for Future Ice-Sheet Instability and Rapid Sea-Level Rise," *Science* 311 (2006): 1747–50; Anders Carlson *et al.*, "Rapid Early Holocene Degalaciation of the Laurentide Ice Sheet," *Nature Geoscience* 1 (2008): 620–4.

62. See Nicholls *et al.*, "Coastal Systems and Low-Lying Areas," p. 334.

63. See Meehl *et al.* "Global Climate Projections," pp. 829–32; Schneider *et al.*, "Assessing Key Vulnerabilities," pp. 793 f.

64. See David Archer and Andrey Ganopolski, "A Movable Trigger: Fossil Fuel $CO_2$ and the Onset of the Next Glaciation," *Geochemistry Geophysics Geosystems* 6 (2005) Q05003; David Archer, *The Long Thaw* (Princeton: Princeton University Press, 2009), ch. 12. *The Long Thaw* is a fervent, richly informed plea for stringent emission reduction to contain global warming. Commenting on his work on the triggering of ice ages, Archer writes, "I would not put this forecast forward . . . in favor of $CO_2$ emissions, however. The potential dangers of warming are immediate, while the potential next ice age in a natural world was not due for thousands of years" (pp. 156 f.)

## CHAPTER 5

1. See United Nations Statistics Division, National Accounts Main Aggregates Database, unstats.un.org.

2. See Stockholm International Peace Research Institute, "The Fifteen Major Spender Countries in 2008," www.sipri.org, accessed June 2008. These are expenditures converted into dollars at foreign exchange rates. At purchasing power parity (which reflects the domestic buying power of Chinese currency over Chinese goods and services as a whole, rice, houses and haircuts as well as tanks), the U.S. military budget is four times China's.

3. For example, shortly after September 11, 2001, the distinguished historian Niall Ferguson called for "expanding the American empire—even if it were to mean a great many little wars like the one currently under way [in Afghanistan]. . . . [T]he United States should be devoting a larger percentage of its vast resources to making the world safe for capitalism and democracy. . . . The proper role of an imperial American is to establish these institutions where they are lacking" ("Clashing Civilizations or Mad Mullahs: The United States between Formal and Informal Empire," in Strobe Talbott

and Nayan Chanda, eds., *The Age of Terror* (New York: Basic Books, 2001), pp. 126, 140).

4. See Richard Caves, Jeffrey Frankel and Ronald Jones, *World Trade and Payments* (Boston: Addison-Wesley, 2002), p. 431; Ewe-Ghee Lim, "The Euro's Challenge to the Dollar," IMF Working Paper (Washington: IMF, 2006), p. 25.

5. See IMF, "Currency Composition of Official Foreign Exchange Reserves," www.imf.org, accessed June 2008; Menzie Chinn and Jeffrey Frankel, "Will the Euro Eventually Surpass the Dollar as Leading International Reserve Currency?" (Cambridge, Mass.: National Bureau of Economic Research, 2006), www.nber.org/papers/w11510, p. 50.

6. See Edmund Andrews, Michael de la Merced and Mary Walsh, "Fed's $85 Billion Loan Rescues Insurer," *New York Times*, September 17, 2008.

7. See Niall Ferguson, "True Cost of Hegemony: Huge Debt," *New York Times*, News of the Week in Review, April 20, 2003, p. 1.

8. *Statistical Abstract of the United States 2008* (Washington: U.S. Census Bureau, 2008), pp. 429, 789.

9. See Sergio Schmukler and Pablo Zoido-Lobaton, "Financial Globalization: Opportunities and Challenges for Developing Countries" (Washington: World Bank, 2001), p. 37. John Perkins, *Confessions of an Economic Hit Man* (San Francisco: Berrett-Koehler, 2004) is an appropriately lurid first-hand account of this era of development huckstering.

10. See Robert Gilpin, *Global Political Economy* (Princeton: Princeton University Press, 2001), pp. 313 f.; Joseph Stiglitz, *Globalization and Its Discontents* (New York: Norton, 2002), p. 239.

11. See Susan George, *A Fate Worse than Debt* (London: Penguin, 1988), p. 73.

12. See Branko Milanovic, *The Two Faces of Globalization* (Washington: World Bank, 2002), www.worldbank.org/research/inequality/pdf/naiveglob1.pdf., p. 14.

13. See Gilpin, *Global Political Economy*, p. 247; Stiglitz, *Globalization and Its Discontents*, ch. 4.

14. The major exception was the imposition of trade sanctions against Brazil, largely for nonobservance of U.S. patents and copyrights in the Brazilian computer industry.

15. Michael Doyle, *Empires* (Ithaca, NY: Cornell University Press, 1986), pp. 43 f. In the last sentence of the book, Doyle acknowledges that "empire," used in his extended sense, might be applied to the United States, but takes no stand (p. 372).

16. Thus, at the start of his book comparing "British and American imperialism," Tony Smith specifies that in his usage, "Imperialism may be defined as the effective domination by a relatively strong state over a weaker people" (*The Pattern of Imperialism* (Cambridge: Cambridge University Press, 1981), p. 6). In the same spirit, while acknowledging that some have defined "empire" more broadly, Michael Doyle proposes to limit the term to "relationships of political control imposed by the political societies over the effective sovereignty of other political societies," adding that "informal domination" counts as political control (*Empires*, pp. 19, 20).

17. In distinguishing the relationship of empire from other relationships of power, Doyle associates it with enduring "foreign penetration" by a stronger state, exercising "asymmetrical influence and power" and deeply affecting "both foreign and domestic policy." (See *Empires* pp. 34, 38, 40.) Similarly, in Gallagher and Robinson's influential argument that nineteenth-century European empires were based on the precept "informal control if possible, formal rule if necessary," the cogency of their broad use of "empire," including informal control, depends on the role of European powers, above all Britain, in using vastly asymmetrical domineering influence to shape the internal trajectory of development of weaker but politically independent countries. Tony Smith emphasizes this domestic impact of informal manipulation from outside in defending their perspective. See John Gallagher and Ronald Robinson, "The Imperialism of Free Trade," *Economic History Review* 6 (1953), p. 13; Smith, *Pattern of Imperialism*, pp. 21–6 (centered on the crucial case of Argentina).

18. Walzer, "Is There an American Empire?," *Dissent*, Fall 2003, www.dissent magazine.org, pp. 1 f.

19. See, for example, Robert Craig Brown and Ramsay Cook, *Canada 1896–1921: A Nation Transformed* (Toronto: McClelland and Stewart, 1974), pp. 39 f.

20. See, for example, P. J. Cain and A. G. Hopkins, *British Imperialism 1688–2000* (London: Longman, 2002), ch. 8 (on Canada, Australia and New Zealand, 1850–1914), especially pp. 212 f., 235 f.; and (on India), pp. 296 f.

21. See, for example, H. C. G. Matthew, *Gladstone* (Oxford: Oxford University Press, 1997), pp. 394 f.

22. See Cain and Hopkins, *British Imperialism*, p. 246. Cain and Hopkins describe Latin America's shares of British exports and British imports between 1850 and 1913 as "larger than those of any other continent or country within the empire, apart from India" (p. 249).

23. See Yoshiko Kojo, "Burden-Sharing under U.S. Leadership: The Case of Quota Increases of the IMF since the 1970s," in H. Bienen, ed., *Power, Economics and Security* (Boulder, Colo.: Westview, 1992), pp. 296–8.

24. See International Monetary Fund, "IMF Members' Quotas and Voting Power, and IMF Board of Governors," www.imf.org/external, accessed September 29, 2008.

25. See Catherine Gwin, *U.S. Relations with the World Bank, 1945–92* (Washington: Brookings Institution, 1994), pp. 56, 75 f. The description of the warning is from a Bank memorandum of the conversation. Gwin's monograph is also ch. 6 of Devesh Kapur, John Lewis and Richard Webb, *The World Bank: Its First Half Century* (Washington: Brookings Institution, 1997), ii: *Perspectives.*

26. Gwin, *U.S. Relations*, p. 64.

27. Kapur *et al.*, *The World Bank*, i: *History*, p. 155.

28. *Ibid.*, p. 1150.

29. Gwin, *U.S. Relations*, p. 59.

30. David E. Sanger, "A Fund of Trouble: As Economies Fail, the I.M.F. Is Rife with Recriminations," *New York Times*, October 2, 1998, Archive p. 5.

31. Joseph Kahn, "Argentina Gets $8 Billion Dollar Aid from the I.M.F.", *New York Times*, August 22, 2001.

32. Excerpts, "Rough Notes of Staff Loan Committee Meetings" in Kapur *et al.*, *The World Bank*, i: *History*, pp. 167 f.

33. See Keith Horsefield *et al.*, *The International Monetary Fund 1945–65* (Washington: International Monetary Fund, 1969), i, p. 65.

34. See Mark Harmon, *The British Labour Government and the 1976 IMF Crisis* (London: Macmillan, 1997), pp. 21–6. As the U.S. representative in the crucial meetings of the Executive Board reminisced, "the US voice in the Fund was decisive. . . . The practical question in those years, in any prospective large use of Fund resources, was whether the United States would agree—and the answer was obtained by direct inquiry"; see Frank Southard, *The Evolution of the International Monetary Fund* (Princeton: Princeton Economics Dept, 1979), pp. 19 f.

35. Gwin, *U.S. Relations*, p. 40.

36. Kapur *et al.*, *The World Bank*, i: *History*, p. 338.

37. Gwin, *U.S. Relations*, p. 45, citing an interview with Volcker in 1992.

38. *Ibid.*, pp. 40–8.

39. See Adam Przeworski and James Raymond Vreeland, "The Effect of IMF Programs on Economic Growth," *Journal of Development Economics* 62 (2000), p. 388.

40. See Giovanni Andrea Cornia and Sanjay Reddy, "The Impact of Adjustment-Related Social Funds on Income Distribution and Poverty," in Cornia, ed., *Inequality, Growth, and Poverty in an Era of Liberalization and Globalization* (Oxford: Oxford University Press, 2004), p. 272.

41. See Joseph Stiglitz, *Globalization and Its Discontents*, ch. 4; Stiglitz, "What I Learned at the World Economic Crisis," *New Republic*, April 17, 2000; testimony of U.S. Trade Representative Charlene Barshefsky, Ways and Means Committee, U.S. House of Representatives, February 24, 1998, www.waysandmeans.house.gov/Legacy, pp. 3–5; Nicholas Kristof, "Worsening Financial Flu in Asia Lowers Immunity to U.S. Business," *New York Times*, February 1, 1998.

42. See Harold Bedoya, "Conditionality and Country Performance," in Stefan Koeberle, Harold Bedoya, Peter Silarsky and Gero Verheyen, eds., *Conditionality Revisited* (Washington: World Bank, 2005), pp. 187, 192.

43. See Eric Neumayer, *The Pattern of Giving* (London: Routledge, 2003), p. 69.

44. See IMF Policy Development and Review Department, "Review of the 2002 Conditionality Guidelines" (Washington: IMF, 2002), p. 16.

45. See Jeremy Gould, "Poverty, Politics and States of Ownership" and Gould and Julia Ojanen, "Tanzania: Merging in the Circle" in Gould, ed., *The New Conditionality* (London: Zed, 2005), pp. 3, 25.

46. See Cornia and Reddy, "Social Funds," p. 280. In the World Bank's generally defensive report on its own work, Vittorio Corbo, Stanley Fischer and Steven Webb, eds., *Adjustment Lending Revisited* (Washington: World Bank, 1992), Anne Maasland and Jacques van der Gaag, "World Bank-Supported Adjustment Programs and Living Conditions" express concern at the decline in the proportion of GDP devoted to health and education among countries subjected to extensive structural adjustment in the course of the 1980s, a period in which the proportion increased among the non-adjusted developing countries in their sample (pp. 52 f.).

47. Przeworski and Vreeland, "IMF programs," pp. 297, 399–402.

48. See Axel Dreher, "IMF and Economic Growth," *World Development* 34 (2006), p. 779.

49. William Easterly, "The Effect of International Monetary Fund and World Bank Programs on Poverty," Policy Research Working Paper 2517 (Washington: World Bank, 2001), p. 5.

50. See John Walton and David Seddon, *Free Markets and Food Riots* (Cambridge, Mass.: Blackwell, 1994), pp. 40–2.

51. David Beim, "Rescuing the LDCs," *Foreign Affairs* 55 (1977), p. 725.

52. U.S. Department of the Treasury, *Assessment of U.S. Participation in Multilateral Development Banks in the 1980s* (Washington: U.S. Government Printing Office, 1981), p. D-14.

53. Joseph Stiglitz, "Globalization and the Logic of International Collective Action," in Deepak Nayyar, ed., *Governing Globalization* (New York: Oxford University Press, 2002), p. 244.

54. Alfred Prados, "Saudi Arabia: Post-War Issues and U.S. Relations," Congressional Research Service Report (Washington: Library of Congress, 2001), www.ncseonline.org/nle/crsreports/international/inter-74.cfm. pp. 5 f.

55. U.S. Department of State, "Background Note: Saudi Arabia," (2003), www.state.gov, p. 7.

56. U.S. Dept. of Commerce, *Statistical Abstract of the United States 2001*, "U.S. Foreign Military Aid by Major Recipient Countries" and analogous tabulations in 1981, 1991, 1995.

57. U.S. Dept. of Commerce, *Statistical Abstract of the United States 2008*, p. 798. In the proposed budget for foreign aid for 2008, 35% of the aid in the "Peace and Security" category was to go to Israel, 19% to Egypt. See U.S. Department of State, *Congressional Budget Justification: Foreign Operations*, fiscal year 2008, www.state.gov, pp. 760–2.

58. U.S. Central Intelligence Agency, *World Factbook* (www.cia.gov, accessed September 2008), entries for "Israel," "West Bank," "Gaza," entailing an Arab majority of about 51%.

59. See Madawi al-Rasheed, *A History of Saudi Arabia* (Cambridge: Cambridge University Press, 2002), pp. 136–9.

60. See *Statistical Abstract of the United States*, 2001, 2004, 2006, tables on "U.S. Foreign Economic Aid by Major Recipient Countries" and World Bank, *World Development Indicators 2001* (Washington: World Bank, 2001), table 6.11; 2005, table 1.1.

61. See World Bank, *World Development Indicators 2008* (Washington: World Bank, 2008), tables 1.1, 6.12, 6.15.

62. The 70% ratio was reported for 1998, when the ratio for other donors was about 20%. See World Bank, *World Development Indicators 2003* (Washington: World Bank, 2003), table 6.9. Since 1998, the United States has become the only major donor not to report the proportion of its aid that is "tied." According to United Nations Development Program, *Human Development Report 2005* (New York, United Nations: 2005), p. 102, 83% of U.S. aid to the poorest countries was tied, on average, from 1999 through 2001.

63. World Bank, *World Development Indicators* (1997–2004), tables 6.10, 6.11; U.S. State Dept., Bureau of International Information, "USAID official reaffirms U.S. commitment to helping Haiti," www. state.gov, January 20, 2004.

64. Ginger Thompson, "Candidate of Haiti's Poor Leads in Early Tally," *New York Times*, February 10, 2006, p. A10.

65. *Statistical Abstract of the United States 2008*, table 1278; *World Development Indicators 2008*, tables 1.1, 6.11.

66. World Bank, *World Development Indicators 2007* (Washington: World Bank, 2007), tables 1.1, 6.11, 6.12; *Statistical Abstract of the United States 2007*, table 1288.

67. Joel Brinkley, "U.S. Threatens to Shun Nicaraguan Business if President Is Ousted," *New York Times*, October 6, 2005. p. A13.

## CHAPTER 6

1. For a trenchant account of the role of food aid in the 1950s and 1960s in shaping development, see Harriet Friedmann, "The Political Economy of Food: The Rise and Fall of the Postwar International Food Order," *American Journal of Sociology* 88 (Supplement 1982, "Marxist Inquiries"): S448–S286.

2. See, for example, Tony Smith, *The Pattern of Imperialism* (Cambridge: Cambridge University Press, 1981), pp. 21–32; P. J. Cain and A. G. Hopkins, *British Imperialism: 1688–2000* (London: Longman, 2002), ch. 22.

3. See Joseph Raz, *The Morality of Freedom* (Oxford: Oxford University Press, 1986), pp. 374 f.

4. See World Bank, *World Development Indicators 2008*, tables 4.2, 5.7; U.S. Dept. of Commerce, *United States Statistical Abstract 2008*, table 1271.

5. Kok-Chor Tan notes the role of reparations in restoring trust in an illuminating argument for reparations for colonial injustice, "Colonialism, Reparations and Global Justice," in Jon Miller and Rahul Kumar, eds., *Reparations* (Oxford: Oxford University Press, 2007). Even if the value of trust is not a basis for a duty reaching as far back in time as he proposes, it certainly precludes neglect of relatively recent damage from ongoing practices.

6. See Stephen Kinzer, *All the Shah's Men* (New York: John Wiley, 2003), p. 202. Mark Gasiorowski, *U.S. Foreign Policy and the Shah* (Ithaca, NY: Cornell University Press, 1991), p. 94, reports a flow of nearly $1 billion in U.S. foreign aid, about equally divided between economic and military purposes, from 1954 to 1961, at an average annual rate five times that from 1949 to 1953.

7. See Gasiorowski, *U.S. Foreign Policy and the Shah*, p. 112. Both military sales and foreign aid figures are in then-current dollars.

8. Amnesty International, *Annual Report 1974/75* (London: Amnesty International Publications, 1975), pp. 8, 129.

9. See Gasiorowski, *U.S. Foreign Policy and the Shah*, pp. 116–18.

10. Henry Kissinger, *Years of Upheaval* (Boston: Little, Brown, 1982), p. 675.

11. See Christine Helms, *Iraq* (Washington: Brookings Institution, 1984), p. 148; William Cleveland, *A History of the Modern Middle East* (Boulder, Colo.: Westview, 2004), p. 411.

12. Stephen Engelberg, "Iran and Iraq Got 'Doctored' Data, U.S. Officials Say," *New York Times*, January 12, 1987, p. A1.

13. Michael Dobbs, "U.S. Had Key Role in Iraq Buildup," *Washington Post*, December 30, 2002, p. A01.

14. CIA Director Webster's words in a presentation starting the meeting, which, Brent Scowcroft reports, Scowcroft and Bush stage managed to create "solidarity" in favor of the more aggressive response. See Bush and Scowcroft, *A World Transformed* (New York: Alfred Knopf, 1998), p. 322.

15. Bob Woodward, *Shadow* (New York: Simon & Schuster, 1999), p. 185.

16. Andrew Cockburn and Patrick Cockburn, *Out of the Ashes* (New York: HarperCollins, 1999), pp. 4, 131.

17. Descriptions of the objective by a senior airforce officer "who played a central role in the air campaign but declined to be named" and an unnamed "Air Force planner," reported in Barton Gellman, "Allied Air War Struck Broadly in Iraq," *Washington Post*, June 23, 1991, p. A1. Gellman attributes similar characterizations of this goal of "long-term leverage," in less pithy formulations, to Colonel John A. Warden III, deputy director of strategy, doctrine and plans for the Air Force.

18. Bush's words in two widely reported speeches of February 15, 1991. See Cockburn and Cockburn, *Out of the Ashes*, p. 38

19. *Ibid.*, pp. 23, 39; Nora Boustany, "Violence Reported Spreading in Iraq; Army Units Clash," *Washington Post*, March 6, 1991, p. A26; Boustany, "U.S. Troops Witness Iraqi Attack on Town in Horror, Frustration," *Washington Post*, March 31, 1991, p. A20.

20. Thomas Ginsberg, "War's Toll: 158,000 Iraqis and a Researcher's Position," *Philadephia Inquirer*, January 5, 2003, p. A05, reporting a 1991 study by Beth Osbourne Daponte.

21. The 1999 UNICEF survey of childhood mortality in Iraq concluded that if the 1980s trend of reduced under-five mortality had continued through the 1990s, there would have been 500,000 fewer deaths than occurred from the start of the sanctions through 1998. See G. Jones, "Iraq: Under-Five Mortality" (UNICEF, 1999), www.unicef.org/reseval/pdfs/irqu5est/pdf, p. 1. In a reanalysis, Ali, Blacker and Jones consider the conservative assumption that under-five mortality rates would have remained the same in the absence of the sanctions and derive an excess deaths estimate of 400,000 on this basis. See Mohamed Ali, John Blacker and Gareth Jones, "Annual Mortality Rates and

Excess Deaths of Children under Five in Iraq, 1991–98," *Population Studies* 57 (2003): 217–26. In another widely cited study, "Morbidity and Mortality among Iraqi Children from 1990 through 1998" (Campaign against Sanctions on Iraq, 1999), www.casi.org.uk, Richard Garfield defended 227,000 as the most likely estimate based on all available data, with 106,000 as the outcome of quite conservative assumptions.

22. While the records which once would have provided a death toll of Iraqi soldiers have been destroyed, the U.S. military estimated that at least 2,320 Iraqis were killed in one operation, the attack on troops near Baghdad preliminary to the taking of the city. See "Special Analysis: Iraq has Fallen," *Independent* (London), April 16, 2003, p. 7. Reuters reports "unofficial think-tank estimates" of 4,895 to 6,370 Iraqi military deaths in the invasion ("Table of Military Deaths in Iraq," April 7, 2004, www.reuters.com).

23. Tabulations of deaths reported by at least two major news sources in Iraq Body Count, "A Dossier of Civilian Casualties 2003–2005" (www.iraqbodycount.net, 2005) include 5,232 to 6,882 deaths of civilians killed by U.S.-led forces during the invasion (see Fact Sheets 2 and 3). On June 11, 2003, the Associated Press Baghdad bureau reported a "fragmentary" count of civilian deaths during the month of war against Saddam, based solely on deaths recorded by 60 of Iraq's 124 hospitals. They further excluded records that did not distinguish between civilian and military deaths, a precaution which they took to exclude "hundreds, possibly thousands" of civilian victims. This death tally was 3,240. See Niko Price, "AP Tallies 3,240 Civilian Deaths in Iraq," www.rr.com/v5/1/my/news/story/0,2050,9000_430693,00.html.

24. Gilbert Burnham, Riyadh Lafta, Shannon Doocy and Les Roberts, "Mortality after the 2003 Invasion of Iraq," *The Lancet* 368 (2006): 1421–8 estimate the excess of deaths after the invasion over what would be expected on the basis of death rates in the three months immediately before (a baseline which itself reflected elevated death rates due to the sanctions regime). Their survey employed standard means of random selection of households and interviewed 1,849 households with 12,801 people. The results imply a 95% confidence interval of between 392,979 and 942,636 excess deaths, i.e., if their methods singled out a genuinely random sample it is 95% probable that the death toll they found reflected an Iraqi total in this range. The vast majority of the excess were violent deaths, steeply increasing over time. Coalition forces were the largest known cause of violent death in this period (31%). The interviewers asked for death certificates in response to 87% of the reports of deaths, which were presented 92% of the time. In the media, the most frequently cited figures concerning Iraqi deaths were not estimates but tabulations, by Iraq

Body Count, of reports by at least two well-established news sources of violent deaths of civilians, i.e., civilian deaths in military actions and from terrorist attacks, and deaths from criminal violence in excess of what would be expected from the (tiny) rate of such deaths under Saddam. Burnham *et al.* note that these reports involved from 43,491 to 88,283 deaths in the period of their survey. They also note the severe incompleteness of such tabulations, which generally provide a tenth or less of the toll in well-grounded epidemiological surveys in areas of prolonged violent conflict. Subsequently, Amir Alkhuzai *et al.*, "Violence-Related Mortality in Iraq from 2002 to 2006," *New England Journal of Medicine* 2008 (358): 484–93 presented estimates for the same period based on a survey of 9,345 households with 61,636 members, in which an extensive health questionnaire was administered to heads of households by employees of the Iraqi Ministry of Health. They note substantial evidence of severe underreporting of deaths, and a special problem concerning reports of violent deaths: 10% of the households in their initial sample could not be surveyed because of problems with security. Their solution was to extrapolate to these dangerous areas on the basis of the provincial distribution in Iraq Body Count's tabulations of reports of violent deaths. But in these dangerous areas, a higher proportion of violent deaths go unreported. Alkuzai *et al.* estimate 151,000 violent deaths in the forty months after the invasion. Their further estimates imply about 400,000 excess deaths. These two surveys only extended through the start of the fourth and by far the most violent year after the invasion, in which reported violent civilian deaths were 42% of Iraq Body Count's tabulation for the first four years. Shortly after the end of the fourth year, a British polling firm, Opinion Research Business, asked a representative sample of 2,414 Iraqis, "How many members of your household, if any, have died as a result of the conflict in Iraq since 2003 (i.e., as a result of violence rather than a natural cause such as old age)?" The answers implied about a million such deaths ("New Analysis 'Confirms' 1 Million+ Iraq Casualties," January 28, 2008, www.opinion.co.uk). Burnham *et al.*'s results for the first year after the invasion agree with the earlier study by their team, Les Roberts, Riyadh Lafta *et al.*, "Mortality before and after the 2003 Invasion of Iraq: Cluster Sample Survey," *The Lancet* 364 (2004): 1857–64. The other extensive study of post-invasion Iraqi deaths was part of the *Iraqi Living Conditions Survey 2004* (www.iq.undp.org/ILCS), a collaboration between the U.N. Development Programme and the Iraqi Ministry of Planning, which covered the first year after the invasion, and surveyed 21,688 households with about 140,000 people. The half-page on "war-related deaths . . . in the aftermath of the 2003 invasion" buried late in the report in a section on

"Maternal Mortality" (ii, p. 54) excludes soldiers living on military bases and only includes deaths in episodes of war, such as combat operations, shelling, and the setting off of explosive devices (see the survey questionnaire, www.fafo.no/ILCS/). Since interviewees were asked to name the victims in their household, by representatives of the Iraqi Ministry of Planning, dead insurgents were, presumably, severely undercounted. The ILCS estimates 24,000 deaths in episodes of war from the start of the invasion until April/May 2004, about one year later.

25. For the whole interview, see "How Jimmy Carter and I Started the Mujahideen," *Counterpunch*, October 8, 2001, www.counterpunch.org/brzez inski/html. This interview originally appeared in *Le Nouvel Observateur*, January 15–21, 1998, p. 76, but not in the shorter edition sent to the United States. John Cooley presents some excerpts in *Unholy Wars* (London: Pluto, 2000), pp. 19 f.

26. See Human Rights Watch, "Military Assistance to the Afghan Opposition," October, 2001, www.hrw.org/backgrounder/asia/afghan-bck1005.htm, p. 4.

27. Marc Herold, "A Dossier on Civilian Victims of United States' Aerial Bombing of Afghanistan" (2002), www.cursor.org/stores/civilian_deaths.htm, with tolls typically corresponding to those in news dispatches from reporters from British, French, or American newspapers.

28. See Carl Conetta, "Operation Enduring Freedom: Why a Higher Rate of Civilian Bombing Casualties" (Cambridge, Mass.: Commonwealth Institute, 2002), Project on Defense Alternatives, www.comw.org/pda/0201oef.html. By his severer standard, refugees' reports of "some deaths" are treated as indicating one, "a dozen or more," three or four, "dozens," eight to ten, "hundreds," forty to sixty.

29. For example, when Doctors Without Borders explained their withdrawal from Afghanistan in 2004, they associated the murders of aid workers with such efforts to "co-opt humanitarian aid" as U.S.-issued leaflets telling people in southern Afghanistan that "providing information about the Taliban and al Qaeda was necessary if they wanted the delivery of aid to continue." See Médecins Sans Frontières, "MSF Pulls Out of Afghanistan," July 28, 2004, www.msf.org.

30. In 2003, the United States provided less than half of total bilateral development assistance to Afghanistan. Its development assistance to that country was 27% less than it provided to Colombia, about half of what it provided to tiny, strategic Jordan, and only slightly more than it provided to Israel, a high income country. See World Bank, *World Development Indicators 2005* (Washington: World Bank, 2005), table 6.11.

31. [Kabul] Center for Policy and Human Development, *Afghanistan Human Development Report 2007* (New York and Kabul: United Nations Development Programme and Kabul University, 2007), pp. 18 f. While presenting no pre-2004 estimates of the indices, the report does note specific gains when 2005 is compared with 2002 or 2003. On grounds of insufficient data, the UNDP itself had no official estimates of the HDI or HPI for Afghanistan (or Iraq), although the 177 countries officially rated include countries as burdened, tumultuous and hard to survey as the Democratic Republic of the Congo. In a nationwide survey of Afghans taken by a U.S. firm in 2005, 57% said that the availability of jobs and economic opportunities was either the same as or worse than under the Taliban. See Charney Research for ABC News, "Despite Deep Challenges in Daily Life, Afghans Express a Positive Outlook," December 2005, www.charney.org, p. 11.

32. See the 1999 report of the Guatemala's official Commission for Historical Clarification, established under the peace accords, *Guatemala: Memory of Silence*, Conclusions, http://hrdata.aaas.org/ceh/report/english/concl.html, pp. 1, 6. The Commission estimates that 3% of human rights violations were committed by insurgent groups (p. 5).

33. See World Bank, *World Development Indicators 2007*, table 6.12.

34. See Thomas Walker, *Nicaragua: Living in the Shadow of the Eagle* (Boulder, Colo.: Westview, 2003), pp. 47, 49, 54, 56; Catherine Gwin, *U.S. Relations with the World Bank 1945–92* (Washington: Brookings Institution 1994), p. 71; Mary McGrory, "Knowing When to Let Go," *Washington Post*, February 6, 1990, p. A2.

35. At constant dollars, Nicaraguan GDP was 9% higher in 1983 than in 1980, the first year of the regime, 14% higher than in 1979. The increases for Central America as a whole were 3% for 1983 as compared to 1980, 11% as compared to 1979. In the last six years of the regime, GDP declined by 19%. See United Nations Statistical Division (unstats.un.org), National Accounts. See also Walker, *Nicaragua*, pp. 55, 93–8.

36. See World Bank, *World Development Indicators 2006* (Washington: World Bank, 2006), table 6.11. After the Sandinista regime, U.S. aid was channeled to anti-Sandinista mayors, whose authority was strengthened by decentralization measures. This aid fueled the rise to power of the spectacularly corrupt Arnoldo Alemán, the Mayor of Managua who went on to loot the country as President from 1997 through 2001.

37. Office of the Historian, U.S. Department of State [Edward Keefer, ed.], *Foreign Relations of the United States, 1964–68*, xxvi: *Indonesia; Malaysia-Singapore; Philippines* (Washington: U.S. Government Printing Office, 2001), p. 346.

A compilation of declassified memoranda, interspersed with editorial notes including acknowledgment of refusals to declassify (p. vii), this volume was briefly available in Government Printing Office bookstores, but then withdrawn. It is available online through the National Security Archive, George Washington University, www.nsarchive.org.

38. The events leading to the mass killings began on September 30, 1965, with an attempted coup, an almost immediate failure, in which six Army generals were captured and killed. The announced aim of the mid-level officers leading the attempt was to forestall an anti-Sukarno coup and to end the corruption of generals "living in luxury over the sufferings of their troops" (broadcast statement; see Harold Crouch, *The Army and Politics in Indonesia* (Ithaca, NY: Cornell University Press, 1988), p. 97). In April 1965, the U.S. Ambassador in Jakarta had reported to the State Department that he was "privy to plans for a coup here [against Sukarno, led by "important civil and military elements"] . . . to play safe, I informed my contact that the U.S. government can in no way participate . . . I nevertheless conveyed clearly my own sympathy with his objective" (*Foreign Relations of the United States, 1964–68*, xxvi, p. 254. In the rest of this note, this volume will be cited through unadorned page numbers). In the CIA's assessment at the time, the September 30 coup did not have the endorsement of the PKI leadership, who would have opposed it had they known of it, though "young militants chafing against the peaceful united front tactics espoused by top Communist leaders . . . probably impetuous, zealous and none too clear in their thinking" played a role and "possibly a few militant members of the Central Committee approved the plan" (intelligence memorandum, October 6, p. 315). Led by Suharto, a group of Army generals totally suppressed the coup in two days and began to establish their independent power as they moved against the PKI. On October 5, the U.S. Ambassador proposed that the U.S. response "covertly . . . indicate clearly to key people in Army our desire to be of assistance where we can . . . Spread the story of PKI's guilt, treachery and brutality (. . . most needed immediate assistance we can give . . .)" (p. 307). In reply, the State Department strongly endorsed his guidelines and emphasized that the main danger was that Sukarno might succeed in "submerging Army's vengeful hostility toward PKI in a closing of ranks to preserve national unity" (p. 309). In telegrams of October 20 and 23, the Ambassador expressed alarm that "Indonesia's political crisis seems to be moving toward a 'political settlement'" (p. 323) while noting "Army has nevertheless been working hard at destroying PKI and I, for one, have increasing respect for its determination . . . in carrying out this crucial assignment" (p. 330). "By the end of October," the State Department history

notes, "the Embassy began to receive reports of killings and atrocities against PKI members" (p. 338). On October 30, an interagency working group was formed in Washington to develop "a covert plan of assistance [to the Indonesian Army] in which DOD [the Department of Defense] would work to insure the minimum risk of exposure" (p. 344). On November 1, the Ambassador reported "major gains from our viewpoint. Nasution in tandem with Suharto and other deeply motivated military leaders is moving relentlessly to exterminate PKI as far as it is possible to do so" (p. 346). In early November, the Indonesia Working Group and the U.S. Embassy discussed a request from the generals for tactical communications equipment, small arms and medical supplies, noting that "U.S. Government covert assistance in obtaining communications equipment and small arms" was intended "to arm Muslim and nationalist youths in Central Java [the most zealous killers in current reports] for use against the PKI" (p. 360). The Working Group's minutes note, "DOD and White House staff believe that the USG should not attach conditions initially because they feel it is important to assure the Army of our full support of its efforts to crush the PKI" (p. 352). On November 16, a telegram sent directly to the State Department as well as to the Jakarta embassy from a U.S. consulate in Sumatra reported, with some anguish, that "bloodthirsty" leaders of the anti-PKI campaign "told Consulate officers that their organization intends kill every PKI member they can catch" and reported evidence of "something like real reign of terror against PKI . . . [including] ordinary PKI members with no ideological bond to the party . . . the army plans to put many thousands in concentration camps" (p. 367). On November 19, the Senior Interdepartmental Group "for the direction and coordination of counter-insurgency activities overseas" (p. xxxvii) approved provision of the military aid the generals had requested, which was conveyed by December 17 (p. 371). On December 2, the Ambassador telegrammed Assistant Secretary of State Bundy to "confirm my earlier concurrence" that funds be given to the "Kap-Gestapu [Action Front to Crush the Thirtieth of September] Movement . . . This army-inspired but civilian staffed action group is still carrying burden of current repressive efforts targetted against PKI" (p. 379). Later that month, the Embassy provided Indonesian authorities with lists of PKI leaders' names, party positions and "present whereabouts . . . based on limited information available" (p. 387). In the face of the massacres, Sukarno had called for national unity and an end to the killings, appealing in one notable speech to Lincoln, quoted as saying "A nation divided against itself cannot stand," as well as Islam ("I wept to God, asked God, Allah, Robi, how can this happen?"). (See Crouch, *The Army and Politics in Indonesia*,

p. 136.) By February, the Ambassador expressed concern to the Secretary of State that Sukarno had convinced the army to buy "unity at the expense of further action" (p. 400). The main recourse chosen to promote more forceful assertiveness by the generals was encouragement of their hopes for an eventual large emergency shipment of rice, provided that they consolidated their power. Once Sukarno was marginalized, the shipments began (p. 427).

39. "Approximately half a million . . . killed" is the estimate of Robert Cribb, a leading scholar of the massacres. See "The Indonesian Massacres" in Samuel Tutten, William Parsons and Israel Charney, eds., *Century of Genocide* (Routledge: New York, 2004), p. 233. The head of Indonesia state security estimated the toll as between 450,000 and 500,000. See Crouch, *The Army and Politics in Indonesia,* p. 155. In an airgram on April 15, 1966, at the end of the massacres, the U.S. Embassy in Jakarta reported to the State Department, "We frankly do not know whether the real figure is closer to 100,000 or 1,000,000 but believe it wiser to err on the size of the lower estimate, especially when questioned by the press." A background paper distributed to the National Security Council in August reported, "While the exact figure will never be known, an estimated 300,000 were killed." See *Foreign Relations of the United States, 1964–68,* xxvi, pp. 339, 450. Martin Ennals, Secretary General of Amnesty International, attributes an estimate of 750,000 arrested and detained for political reasons to the Indonesian chief of state security in "What Happened in Indonesia? An Exchange," *New York Review of Books,* February 9, 1978.

40. See James William Gibson, *The Perfect War* (Boston: Atlantic Monthly Press, 1986), pp. 229 f.; Guenter Lewy, *America in Vietnam* (New York: Oxford University Press, 1978), pp. 442–53 (where the estimate on p. 452 should be added to that on p. 444).

41. See Jonathan Sanford, *U.S. Foreign Policy and Multilateral Development Banks* (Boulder, Colo.: Westview, 1982), pp. 215 f.

42. World Bank, *World Development Indicators 2005,* tables 1.1, 6.11; World Bank, *World Development Indicators 2008,* table 6.15.

43. W. J. Ganshof van der Meersch, *Fin de la souveraineté belge au Congo* (Brussels: Institut Royal des Relations Internationales, 1963), p. 250; my translation.

44. Chester Bowles, *Africa's Challenge to America* (Berkeley: University of California Press, 1956), pp. 56, 100.

45. See Stephen Weissman, *American Foreign Policy in the Congo 1960–64* (Ithaca, NY: Cornell University Press, 1974), p. 28.

46. *Ibid.,* p. 24.

47. See Shafik-Georges Saïd, *De Léopoldville à Kinshasa* (Brussels: Centre National d'Étude des Problèmes Sociaux d'Industrialisation en Afrique Noire, 1969), especially pp. 187–97, 211–31.

48. Dwight D. Eisenhower, *Waging Peace* (Garden City, NY: Doubleday, 1965), p. 572.

49. *Ibid.*, p. 573.

50. See Ganshof van der Meersch, *Fin de la souveraineté belge*, pp. 325 f., 332–4. Adam Hochschild, *King Leopold's Ghost* (Boston: Houghton Mifflin, 1998) offers an estimate of 10 million deaths due to colonial brutality.

51. See Madeline Kalb, *The Congo Cables* (New York: Macmillan, 1982), p. 27.

52. *Ibid.*, p. 38.

53. *Ibid.*, p. 54.

54. *Ibid.*, pp. 64 f.

55. *Ibid.*, p. 129.

56. *Ibid.*, p. 133.

57. *Ibid.*, p. 192.

58. See Rajeshwar Dayal, *Mission for Hammarskjold* (Princeton: Princeton University Press, 1976), p. 66.

59. See Stephen Weissman, "The CIA and U.S. Policy in Zaire and Angola," in René Lemarchand, ed., *American Policy in Southern Africa* (Washington: University Press of America, 1978), pp. 391–3.

60. See Weissmann, *American Foreign Policy in the Congo 1960–64* (Ithaca, NY: Cornell University Press, 1974), pp. 213 f.

61. Tom Wicker, John Finley, Max Frankel, E. W. Kenworthy *et al.*, "How C.I.A. Put 'Instant Air Force' into Congo," *New York Times*, April 26, 1966, pp. 1, 30.

62. See Kalb, *Congo Cables*, p. 372.

63. See Kevin Dunn, "A Survival Guide to Kinshasa," in John F. Clark., ed., *The African Stakes of the Congo War* (New York: Palgrave Macmillan, 2002), p. 60; Kalb, *Congo Cables*, p. 381.

64. World Bank, *World Development Indicators 2001*, pp. 24, 26.

65. See Georges Nzongola-Ntalaja, *The Congo from Leopold to Kabila* (London: Zed Books, 2002), p. 71.

66. Kalb, *Congo Cables*, p. 387.

67. World Bank, *World Development Indicators 2001*, pp. 102, 104.

68. See Crawford Young, "The Zairian Crisis and American Foreign Policy," in Gerald Bender *et al.*, *African Crisis Areas and U.S. Foreign Policy* (Berkeley: University of California Press, 1985), p. 218; Thomas Turner, "Angola's Role in the Congo War," in Clark, *The Congo War*, pp. 78 f.

69. See Philip Agee, ed., *The Pike Report* (London: Spokesman Books, 1977), p. 218.

70. Lynne Duke, "Angola's Peace Withers Again under Fire," *Washington Post*, December 15, 1998, presents estimates of a toll of 650,000 to 800,000.

71. For mutually supportive accounts of this and subsequent phases of the Congo wars, see Clark, ed., *The Congo War*, especially Dunn, "A Survival Guide to Kinshasa" and Timothy Longman, "The Complex Reasons for Rwanda's Engagement in Congo"; Nzongola-Ntalaja, *The Congo from Leopold to Kabila*, ch. 7; Thomas Turner, *The Congo Wars* (London: Zed Books, 2007); Howard French, *A Continent for the Taking* (New York: Alfred Knopf, 2004), especially chs. 7, 10 and 11.

72. See French, *A Continent*, p. 199.

73. See Tom Cohen, "Kabila Sworn in, Assuming Sweeping Powers to Rule Congo," Associated Press, May 29, 1997.

74. See French, *A Continent*, pp. 233, 249.

75. See International Crisis Group, "The Kivus: The Forgotten Crucible of the Congo Conflict," *ICG Africa Report* 56 (2003); Tony Barnett and Alan Whiteside, *AIDS in the Twenty-First Century* (Houndmills: Palgrave Macmillian, 2002), p. 145, reporting estimates of HIV infection rates of 40–60% in the Angolan and Congolese armies, as high as 80% in the Zimbabwean army; World Bank, *World Development Indicators 2001*, table 2.18, estimating adult prevalence of HIV at 5% in Congo during 1999.

76. International Crisis Group, "The Kivus," pp. 13 f., reporting United Nations estimates.

77. See John F. Clark, "Museveni's Adventure in the Congo War," in Clark, *The Congo War*, p. 152. Virtually no gold is mined within Uganda.

78. See Stephen Jackson, "Making a Killing: Criminality and Coping in the Kivu War Economy," *Review of African Political Economy* 29 (2002), pp. 525–7; World Bank, *World Development Indicators 2002* (Washington: World Bank, 2002), table 1.1.

79. See Global Witness, *Branching Out: Zimbabwe's Resource Colonialism in Democratic Republic of Congo* (London: Global Witness, 2002).

80. See High Level Panel on the Illegal Exploitation of Natural Resources and Other Wealth in the Democratic Republic of the Congo, *Third Report* (2002) and Rights and Accountability in Development (London), "Unanswered Questions: Companies, Conflict and the DR Congo" (2004); both accessible via www.raid-uk.org.

81. See Benjamin Coghlan *et al.*, "Mortality in the Democratic Republic of Congo: A Nationwide Survey," *The Lancet* 367 (2006): 44–51.

82. Philip Thornton, "G8 Summit Agrees $50bn Aid Rise but Critics Attack Delay," *Independent*, July 9, 2005.

83. *The Gleneagles Communiqué*, "Africa," paragraph 8, www.g8.gov.uk.

84. See Milanovic, "Why Did the Poorest Countries Fail to Catch Up?" (Washington: Carnegie Endowment for International Peace, 2005), www.carnegieendowment.org, especially p. 26.

85. Michael Gordon and Mark Mazzetti, "U.S. Used Bases in Ethiopia to Hunt Al Qaeda in Africa," *New York Times*, February 23, 2007, p. A10.

86. See World Bank, *World Development Indicators 2007*, table 2.20.

87. This characterization of the Union of Islamic Courts was unanimous among reasonably independent informed commentators. See, for example, Cedric Barnes and Harun Hassan, "The Rise and Fall of Mogadishu's Islamic Courts" (London: Chatham House [Royal Institute of International Affairs], 2007); International Crisis Group, "Somalia: The Tough Part is Ahead," Africa Briefing 45 (International Crisis Group: Nairobi/Brussels, January 2007); Jeffrey Gettleman and Mark Mazzetti, "Somalia's Islamists and Ethiopia Gird for War," *New York Times*, December 14, 2006, p. A1; Kenneth Menkhaus, "Seven Questions: War in Somalia," *Foreign Policy* (on-line), December 2006; and, on the main precursor to the Islamic Courts movement, Menkhaus, "Political Islam in Somalia," *Middle East Policy* 9/1 (2002): 109–23. All observers also agreed that the position of the more rigidly Islamicist minority was greatly strengthened by increasingly strident U.S. opposition to the Courts and material assistance to their opponents. "Moderates, he [the Courts' foreign minister] said, were backed into a corner by an American campaign to discredit and isolate the Islamic administration," Gettleman and Mazzetti, "Somalia's Islamists and Ethiopia Gird for War," p. A26.

88. Gettleman and Mazzetti, "Somalia's Islamists and Ethiopia Gird for War," p. A1.

89. See, for example, the report by a prominent International Crisis Group analyst of early December 2006 discussions between the Union of Islamic Courts and a grouping of east African governments favored by the United States, in Matt Bryden, "Washington's Self-Defeating Somalia Policy," Africa Policy Forum (Washington: Center for Strategic and International Studies), forums.csis.org, December 2006.

90. See David Morgan, "Experts say US Funding Somali Warlords," Reuters, June 5, 2006; "Fall of Mogadishu Leaves US Policy in Ruins," *Mail and Guardian* [South Africa], June 10, 2006.

91. See Associated Press, "U.N. Authorizes Regional Force to Protect Somalia's Weak Government," *International Herald Tribune*, December 6, 2006, citing "a confidential U.N. report."

92. From 2003 through 2005, Ethiopia received $950 million in U.S. foreign aid, 14% more than the next highest country in sub-Saharan Africa, Sudan, where

the U.S. aid commitment was to the southern region controlled by former rebels against Khartoum. The chain to the north of Ethiopia consisted of Jordan, Israel, Egypt and Sudan; Kenya and Uganda were other significant southern links. In 2003, Ethiopia received $5 million in U.S. military aid, as compared to $3 million going to the next highest in sub-Saharan Africa (Kenya and Mozambique). From mid-2005 through 2006, Ethiopia received $11 million in U.S. military aid. See Congressional Research Service, *Foreign Aid: An Introductory Overview* [2004] (Washington: Library of Congress, 2004), p. 13; Congressional Research Service, *Foreign Aid: An Introductory Overview* [2005] (Washington: Library of Congress, 2005), p. 15; Dept. of Commerce *Statistical Abstract of the United States: 2006* (Washington: Government Printing Office, 2006), p. 831; USAID, *Congressional Budget Justification 2006*, "Sudan", www.usaid.gov, accessed December 2006; Shashank Bengali, "Hunt for al-Qaida Overshadows Repression in Ethiopia, Some Fear," *Mercury News* [San Jose, Calif.; McClatchy Newspapers News Bureau], February 19, 2007.

93. See World Bank, *World Development Indicators 2008*, tables 6.14, 1.1, 2.21, 5.7, 2.15; World Bank, *World Development Indicators 2006*, tables 4.5, 5.7; United Nations Statistical Division, National Accounts (unstats.un.org.), Ethiopia, GDP by Type of Expenditure; Stockholm International Peace Research Institute (the main source of *World Development Indicators* military data), Arms Transfers Project (www.sipri.org), Importer/Exporter Tables and Financial Value of the Arms Trade.

94. According to Human Rights Watch, the subjection of "thousands of Oromo [the largest Ethiopian ethnic group] to detention, torture and harassment for voicing their political opinions" included the imprisonment of 25,000 in 2001, acknowledged by the President of Ethiopia upon his retirement. See Human Rights Watch, *Suppressing Dissent: Human Rights Abuses and Political Repression in Ethiopia's Oromia Region* (2005), www.hrw.org, pp. 1, 12. Starting in 2003, the Ethiopian Army "committed numerous human rights violations against Anuak communities in the Gambella region," where large oil reserves had started to be exploited, beginning with a massacre in which over 400 Anuak were killed and over 400 Anuak homes destroyed. See Human Rights Watch, *Targeting the Anuak* (2005), www.hrw.org, pp. 1, 19 f. Amnesty International noted that "opposition candidates and supporters were arrested, beaten and intimidated in the run-up to elections" in 2005, after which dozens of people were killed when demonstrations against election fraud were fired upon and over 10,000 opposition supporters and demonstrators were detained. See Amnesty International, *Annual Report, 2006*, "Ethiopia," www.amnesty.org, p. 1. The Ethiopian armed presence in Somalia in 2006

partly expressed concerns to reduce transborder support for further opposition, including an insurgency, among ethnic Somalis in the adjacent Ethiopian province of Ogaden. After a surreptitious journey through this sparsely settled desert region, a *New York Times* reporter conveyed descriptions, which he encountered "in village after village," of "a widespread and longstanding reign of terror, with Ethiopian soldiers gang-raping women, burning down huts and killing civilians at will." See Jeffrey Gettleman, "In Ethiopian Desert, Fear and Cries of Army Brutality," *New York Times*, June 18, 2007, p. A8.

95. See World Bank, *World Development Indicators 2006*, table 6.12.

96. World Bank, *World Development Indicators 2007*, table 6.12; *World Development Indicators 2002*, table 6.11.

97. Gettleman and Mazzetti, "Somalia's Islamists and Ethiopia Gird for War," p. A26.

98. See *ibid.* and Gordon and Mazzetti, "U.S. Used Bases in Ethiopia to Hunt Al Qaeda in Africa," p. A10.

99. Security Council, Resolution 1725, December 6, 2006, sections 3 and 5, www.un.org.

100. Anthony Mitchell (Associated Press), "Somalia's President Says Door to Peace Talks Closed" *[Toronto] Globe and Mail*, December 15, 2006.

101. See Gettleman and Mazzetti, "Somalia's Islamists and Ethiopia Gird for War"; BBC News, "Islamist Warning for Somali Force," December 7, 2006.

102. Stephanie McRummen, "Interview with Meles Zenawi," *Washington Post*, December 14, 2006.

103. See Hassan Yare, "Somali Islamists 'at War' with Ethiopia," Reuters, December 21, 2006.

104. See Jeffrey Gettleman, "Somali Forces Retake Capital from Islamists," *New York Times*, December 29, 2006, p. A12.

105. See Gordon and Mazzetti, "U.S. Used Bases in Ethiopia to Hunt Al Qaeda in Africa," p. A10.

106. See Caren Bohan, "U.S. Signals Support for Ethiopia in Somalia" Reuters, December 27, 2006.

107. See, for example, Shashank Bengali and Mahad Elmi, "Fear and Guns Still Constant Companions in Somalia," *Minneapolis Star Tribune* [McClatchy Newspapers News Bureau], January 4, 2007; Elizabeth Kennedy, "Some in Somalia Fear Ex-Warlord Is Back," Associated Press, *Washington Post*, December 31, 2006.

108. See Ibrahim Mohamed, "Suspected Cholera Outbreak Kills Scores in Somalia," Reuters, February 1, 2007; "Access Restrictions Hamper Aid Delivery in Somalia," U.N. Office for the Coordination of Humanitarian Affairs, January 19, 2007, www.reliefweb.int.

109. See Sahal Abdulle, "Death Toll from Mogadishu Clashes Tops 1,000," Reuters, April 10, 2007; Abdulle, "Somali PM Declares Gains in Mogadishu War," Reuters, April 26, 2007.

110. See Office of the United Nations High Commissioner for Refugees, "Head of UNHCR Operations Division Shocked by Condition of Somali Displaced," May 4, 2007, www.unhcr.org.

111. Report of the Independent Expert on the Situation of Human Rights in Somalia, U.N. Human Rights Council, "Human Rights Council Takes up Situation of Human Rights in Cambodia, Haiti and Somalia," June 12, 2007, www.reliefweb.int, p. 8. In the "Interactive Dialogue on the Situation of Human Rights in Somalia" that followed, the United States representative "said . . . [t]he United States wished to see a stable national government to promote security and stability on the ground" (p. 9).

112. See UNHCR, "Head of Division Shocked."

113. See Cedric Barnes and Harun Hassan, "The Rise and Fall of Mogadishu's Islamic Courts" (London: Chatham House [Royal Institute of International Affairs], 2007), p. 6.

114. See Reuters, "Somalia PM Wants Dialogue; 6,000 Dead this Year," December 2, 2007.

115. See UNHCR, "Somalia: Number of Displaced Rises to one Million," UNHCR Briefing Notes, November 20, 2007, www.unhcr.org.

116. See Jeffrey Gettleman, "As Somali Crisis Grows, Experts See a Void in Aid," New York Times, November 20, 2007, p. A6.

117. "Somalia: Highest Levels of Malnutrition in the World," U.N. Office for the Coordination of Humanitarian Affairs, December 5, 2008, www.irinnews.org.

118. Jeffrey Gettleman, "Situation in Somalia Seems About to Get Worse," New York Times, December 7, 2008, p. 6.

119. Chris Tomlinson, "Envoy Says Somalia Must Find Solutions," Guardian (U.K.), Associated Press, January 6, 2007.

## CHAPTER 7

1. See Ahmed Rashid, The Taliban (New Haven, Yale University Press, 2001), p. 213; William Vollmann, "Across the Divide," New Yorker, May 15, 2000 (a report of extensive travels in Taliban-ruled Afghanistan reaching the conclusion, "The Western notion that the Taliban imposed themselves by force on an unwilling population is less than half true . . . Many people I spoke with expressed contentment with the Taliban. Why? Quite simply because they could not forget how bad it had been before").

2. According to a poll sponsored by the British Ministry of Defence, reported in the *Daily Telegraph* on October 23, 2005, 82% of Iraqis were "'strongly opposed' to the presence of coalition troops'" (Sean Rayment, "Secret MoD Poll: Iraqis Support Attacks on British Troops"). This underestimated opposition of those on whom coalition forces are imposed, since the military presence in the Kurdish north consisted of militias of a Kurdish political leadership that had controlled this territory under a U.N. protectorate before the overthrow of Saddam. Kurds are the only segment of the Iraqi population who have mostly supported the U.S.–British presence. In a large poll one year after the invasion, when Iraqis were asked, "Should US/British forces leave immediately (next few months) or stay longer?," the majority, 57% said, "Immediately," the response of 65% of non-Kurds ("Key Findings: Nationwide Survey of 3,500 Iraqis," *USA Today*, April 28, 2003, www.usatoday.com/news/world/iraq/2004-04-28-gallup-iraq-findings.htm, pp. 1 f., 6 f.; Cesar Soriano and Steven Komarow, "Poll: Iraqis Out of Patience," *USA Today*, April 4, 2004, www.usatoday.com/news/world/iraq/2004-04-28-poll-cover_x.htm, p. 1). Nine months later, on the eve of Iraqi elections, another extensive survey asked "When should U.S. forces leave Iraq?" Offered "When safety and security are restored" and "After an Iraqi army is in place" as other options, 66% (approximately 72% of non-Kurds) either responded "Now" (37% of all, 41% of non-Kurds) or "After elected government is in place" (29% of all, 31% of non-Kurds) (Zogby International, "Elections in Iraq" (January–February 2005), www.zogby.com, pp. 4, 18).

3. On the state of the evidence prior to the dire warnings that led to the final, aborted U.N. inspections, see "The Case for Iraq's Qualitative Disarmament," *Arms Control Today* 30/5 (June 2000): 8–14, by Scott Ritter, a major in the U.S. Marines who had recently been chief of the weapons detection unit of the U.N. inspection program for Iraq. The detailed narrative of Ritter's *Iraq Confidential* (New York: Nation Books, 2005) describes both the accumulation of evidence of qualitative disarmament in the late 1990s and entrenched resistance to this assessment by U.S. officials as the evidence grew.

4. See U.S. Department of Defense, *The Pentagon Papers: The Senator Gravel Edition* (Beacon Press: Boston, n.d.), iii, p. 582. The assessment of McNaughton's standing is, for example, George Ball's in *The Past Has Another Pattern* (New York: Norton, 1982), p. 385.

5. Memorandum of February 7, 1965, *The Pentagon Papers*, iii, p. 690.

6. See Ball, *The Past Has Another Pattern*, pp. 407–9. There is a similar, somewhat less detailed account of these deliberations in *The Pentagon Papers*, iv, pp. 591–3.

7. See Jeffrey Kimball, *The Vietnam War Files* (Lawrence: University of Kansas Press, 2004), pp. 220 f.
8. *Ibid.*, p. 217.
9. *Ibid.*, pp. 161–3.
10. Associated Press, "Tapes: Nixon Wanted to Use Nuke Bomb," *New York Times*, February 28, 2002.
11. From presentations by Deputy Secretary of State Lawrence Eagleburger and CIA Director William Webster, which, Bush and Scowcroft explain, were part of a sequence they organized in advance to achieve solidarity in favor of military force. See Bush and Scowcroft, *A World Transformed* (New York: Alfred A. Knopf, 1998), pp. 322 f.
12. Bob Woodward, *Shadow* (New York: Simon & Schuster, 1999), p. 185.
13. *Ibid.*
14. Bush and Scowcroft, *A World Transformed*, pp. 482–4.
15. *Ibid.*, p. 491.
16. *Ibid.*, p. 489.
17. Barton Gellman, "Allied Air War Struck Broadly in Iraq," *Washington Post*, June 23, 1991, p. A1.
18. Bush and Scowcroft, *A World Transformed*, pp. 321, 485.
19. *Ibid.*, p. 481.
20. Armed Forces Medical Intelligence Center, "Disease Information," www.gulflink.osd.mil/declassdocs/dia/19950901/950901_0504rept_91.html.
21. G. Jones, "Iraq: Under-Five Mortality" (UNICEF, 1999), www.unicef.org/reseval/pdfs/irqu5est/pdf; UNICEF, "Child and Maternal Mortality Survey" (1999), www.unicef.org/reseval/iraqr/html.
22. Joy Gordon, "Cool War," *Harper's Magazine*, November 2002, www.harpers.org/CoolWar.html, pp. 4, 2, 8. Kenneth Pollack was director for Persian Gulf affairs at the National Security Council from 1995 to 1996 and from 1999 to 2001, where, according to the biographical sketch in the rear flap of the book-jacket on his case for war on Iraq, *The Threatening Storm* (New York: Random House, 2002), "he was the principal working-level official responsible for the implementation of U.S. policy toward Iraq." His exculpatory investigation of the effects of the sanctions in that book begins, "First, it is important to keep the scale of suffering in Iraq in perspective. Although numerous groups and personages have constantly issued dire warnings, there has been no mass starvation such as that which wiped out 50 percent of Somalia's children in the single year of 1992, that killed one million Ethiopians in 1984–85, or that has killed as many as 2.8 million North Koreans since 1995" (p. 126). Perhaps this passage offers some insight into means by which officials avoid disturbance by excessive sensitivity to foreign deaths. Eventually, Pollack posits about

200,000 excess deaths in the first seven years after the war, all constituting "slaughter . . . of his people" by Saddam Hussein (p. 140; see also p. 139).

23. See Madeleine Albright, *Madam Secretary* (New York: Miramax, 2003), pp. 274 f.

24. See "SecState Albright Policy Speech on Iraq, March 26 [1997]" text of a speech at Georgetown University, Federation of American Scientists, www.fas.org/news/iraq/1997. In addition to verifying the "territorial" situation of the successor regime, Albright described a second goal, requiring "improvements in behavior. Is there cooperation with UNSCOM and compliance with UN resolutions? . . . respect for human rights . . . ? . . . a convincing repudiation of terrorism? Are its military ambitions limited to those of reasonable defense?" Until a successor regime had satisfied the United States on all counts, "We will insist," she declared, "with all of the diplomatic tools at our command, that the UN sanctions remain in place."

25. See Ron Suskind, *The Price of Loyalty* (New York: Simon & Schuster, 2004), p. 72.

26. Judith Randel *et al.*, eds., *The Reality of Aid 2000* (London: Earthscan, 2000), p. 80.

27. For the leaflet text and casualty estimates, see James William Gibson, *The Perfect War* (Boston: Atlantic Monthly Press, 1986), pp. 229 f.

28. Hallin, *The "Uncensored War"* (New York: Oxford University Press, 1986), pp. 111, 137, 153.

29. The epidemiological survey reported in Gilbert Burnham *et al.*, "Mortality after the 2003 Invasion of Iraq," *The Lancet* 368 (2006): 1421–8 entails a midpoint estimate of about 76,000 violent deaths attributable to Coalition forces among Iraqi males younger than fifteen or older than forty-four and Iraqi women in the forty months after the invasion (see pp. 1421, 1425).

30. The most extensively reported study by Iraq Body Count was a tabulation and analysis of reports of violent civilian deaths by morgues and other established news sources in the two years after the invasion. It was presented (as an over-all estimate) in some newspapers as a minor accompaniment to stories about the cumulative two-year toll among American troops, without any mention of the role of U.S. forces in those Iraqi civilian deaths, See, for example, Sabrina Tavernise, "Rising Civilian Toll Is the Iraq War's Silent, Sinister Pulse," *New York Times*, October 26, 2005, p. A12; Jim Krane, "Iraq Death Toll Estimated at 30K," Associated Press, October 26, 2005 (e.g., *Ithaca [N.Y.] Journal*, p. 3A). In fact, in findings announced in bold-faced "bullets" at the start of a section vividly entitled, "WHO WERE THE KILLERS?" Iraq Body Count had reported that "US-led forces were the sole killers

of 37% of the civilian victims. Criminals killed 36% of all civilians. Anti-occupation forces were sole killers of 9% of civilian victims. US military forces accounted for 98.5% of 'Coalition' killings." Below these statements, a highlighted table began by attributing 9,270 civilians killed to "U.S.-led forces alone." In the tabulations presented in the report as a whole, 13% of the reported post-April 30, 2003 civilian deaths are attributed to U.S-led forces alone, 12% to anti-occupation forces alone, 1% to terrorist attacks not directed at occupation-related targets. See Iraq Body Count, "A Dossier of Civilian Casualties 2003–2005," www.iraqbodycount.org, especially Fact Sheets 1, 2 and 3.

31. See Program on International Policy Attitudes, University of Maryland, "What the Iraqi Public Wants" (from data collected January 2–5, 2006) and "The Iraq Public on the US Presence and the Future of Iraq" (September 1–4, 2006), www.worldpublicopinion.org. In January, 61% of Shiites and 83% of Sunni Arabs responded that the departure of US-led forces would increase day-to-day security; in September, this was the response of 57% of Shiites (another 5% of whom thought there would be no effect either way) and 78% of Sunni Arabs. The view that American withdrawal would decrease interethnic violence was endorsed by 61% of Shiites and 81% of Sunni Arabs in January, 57% of Shiites (with 5% seeing no effect either way) and 72% of Sunni Arabs in September. There was some coverage of a further finding in September: 61% of Shiites and 92% of Sunni Arabs expressed approval of "attacks on US-led forces in Iraq." See "Iraqi Public on US Presence," "Questionnaire and Methodology," pp. 3, 9. Broadly similar views of the impact of U.S. forces had predominated in a British Ministry of Defence poll reported in late October, 2005, in which less than 1% of Iraqis assessed coalition forces as responsible for any improvement in security (Sean Rayment, "Secret MoD Poll: Iraqis Support Attacks on British Troops," *Daily Telegraph*, October 23, 2005). In November 2005, in a poll by Oxford Research International, of those who thought security had improved in recent months, 5.5% mentioned the American or Coalition forces among the two main causes. Of those who thought the situation had worsened, 34.5% mentioned them among the two main causes (Oxford Research Institute, "National Survey of Iraq November 2005," www.oxfordresearch.com, pp. 24 f.) General Iraqi dissent from assumptions of beneficence in American media did not end with the 2007 surge of U.S. forces, directed primarily at improving security in Baghdad. In a poll conducted in February and March 2008, only 28% of Baghdadis judged that the surge had been "very successful" (4%) or "fairly successful" (24%) "in reducing the level of violence in Baghdad," while 55% of Baghdadis

judged it either "not very successful" (24%) or "not at all successful" (31%). See Opinion Research Business, "Public Attitudes in Iraq: Fifth Anniversary Poll," Final Tables, March 2008, www.opinion.co.uk, p. 61. In a poll a year later, asked, "How do you feel about the way in which the United States and other coalition forces have carried out their responsibilities in Iraq?" 69% of Iraqis chose either "Quite a bad job" (30%) or "A very bad job" (39%). This negative verdict, shared by about three-quarters of non-Kurds, was more common than when the same question had been posed before the great outbreak of sectarian violence. Asked whether the United States was "over-all . . . playing a positive, neutral or negative role now," 64% chose "Negative" (17% "Neutral", 18% "Positive"), a negative view shared by about three-quarters of non-Kurds. See ABC, "Dramatic Advances Sweep Iraq, Boosting Support for Democracy," abcnews.go.com/PollingUnit, March 19, 2009, pp. 9, 34, 47.

32. See Program on International Policy Attitudes, "What the Iraqi Public Wants," p. 8. The question was not asked in September.

33. In the same poll 86% said that Coalition forces should leave soon, either immediately (41%) or after a permanent government was elected (45%); 55% said that immediate departure would make them "feel more safe" (32% "less safe"). Coalition Provisional Authority, "Public Opinion in Iraq" (June 15, 2004), wid.ap.org/documents/iraq/cpafiles, slides 28, 35, 36, 37.

34. James Bill, *George Ball: Behind the Scenes in U.S. Foreign Policy* (New Haven: Yale University Press, 1997), p. 174.

35. IMF, *World Economic Outlook Data Base*, www.imf.org.

36. Eurostat, *Eurostat Yearbook 2008* (European Commission: Luxembourg, 2008), ch. 2, table 1.

37. Eurostat, "International Trade of the European Union in 2007," 2008, epp.eurostat.ec.europa.eu, pp. 1 f.

38. IMF, *World Economic Outlook Data Base*; Eurostat, *Eurostat Yearbook 2008*, ch. 8, table 4; Eurostat, *Panorama of EU Trade* (European Commission: Luxembourg, 2007), p. 50.

39. *Eurostat Yearbook 2008,* ch. 8, table 2.

40. World Bank, *World Development Indicators 2008* (Washington: World Bank, 2008), table 6.10.

41. European Commission, *Annual Report on the Euro Area—2007* (ec.europa.eu), p. 41.

42. Axel Bertuch-Samuels and Parmeshwar Ramlogan, "The Euro: Ever More Global," *Finance & Development: A Quarterly Magazine of the IMF* 44 (2007), p. 3.

43. European Commission, *Annual Report—2007*, pp. 40 f.

44. Bertuch-Samuels and Ramlogan, "The Euro," p. 6.

45. U.S. Department of Commerce, *Statistical Abstract of the United States 2008* (Washington: Government Printing Office, 2008), pp. 787 f.

46. Patrick Tyler, "Pentagon Drops Goal of Blocking New Superpowers," *New York Times*, May 24, 1992, p. A14.

47. U.S. Department of Commerce, *Statistical Abstract of the United States 1985* (Washington: Government Printing Office, 1985), p. 536; *Statistical Abstract 1990*, p. 535; *Statistical Abstract 2006*, p. 521.

48. See World Bank, *World Development Indicators 1997* (Washington: World Bank, 1997), tables 2.1, 5.13; *World Development Indicators* 2000, table 5.12; *World Development Indicators 2006*, tables 4.2, 5.11; *Statistical Abstract of the United States 2006*, table 705 (producer prices).

49. National Intelligence Council, *Global Trends 2025: A Transformed World* (Washington: National Intelligence Council, 2008), www.dni.gov/nic/ NIC_2025_project.html, pp. vii, 14.

50. *Ibid.*, p. 29.

51. *Ibid.*, p. 77.

52. National Energy Policy Development Group, *National Energy Policy* (2001), www.ne.doe.gov/pdfFiles/nationalEnergyPolicy.pdf, Overview, p. x, ch. 1, p. 13.

53. In an influential study at the National Energy Technological Laboratory of the U.S. Department of Energy, "Peaking of World Oil Production" (Washington: Department of Energy, 2005), www.netl.doe.gov/ publications/others/pdf/Oil_Peaking_NETL.pdf., Robert Hirsch, Roger Bezdek and Robert Wendling note a strong expert consensus that oil production will pass its peak before 2020, and support an Energy Information Administration scenario in which the peak is reached in 2016. See pp. 19, 69 f.

54. See International Energy Agency, *World Energy Outlook 2007: China and India* (Paris: International Energy Agency, 2007), p. 80; Energy Information Administration, U.S. Department of Energy, "International Energy Outlook 2008," www.eia.doe.gov, figure 2.

55. *National Energy Policy*, ch. 8, pp. 14, 16. International Energy Agency, *World Energy Outlook 2007*, p. 168, presents a mid-range estimate of growth from 3.5 million barrels per day in net Chinese imports in 2006 to 7.1 million in 2015 and 13.1 million in 2030.

56. National Intelligence Council, *Global Trends 2025*, pp. 29, 12.

57. *National Energy Policy*, ch. 8, p. 4. In estimates of proved oil reserves tabulated by the U.S. Energy Information Agency in 2008, the proportion of Middle Eastern reserves averaged 60%, while Africa accounted for about 10% more,

as did Russia and the Caucasian republics. See Energy Information Agency, "World Proved Reserves of Oil and Natural Gas, Most Recent Estimates," www.eia.gov/emeu/reserves.html, posted August 27, 2008.

58. *Ibid.*, ch. 1, p. 11.

59. International Energy Agency, *Oil Market Report*, July 10, 2008, p. 36.

60. World Bank, "Railroad Data for Saudi Arabia," www.worldbank.org/transport/rail/rdb/raildata/saudi.xls; World Bank, *World Development Indicators 2003* (Washington: World Bank, 2003), p. 16.

61. World Bank, *World Development Indicators 2001* (Washington: World Bank, 2001), p. 26.

62. *Ibid.*, ch. 8, p. 5.

63. Edward Morse and James Richard, "The Battle for Energy Dominance," *Foreign Affairs* 81/2 (2002), p. 20.

64. Jeff Gerth, "Forecast of Rising Oil Demand Challenges Tired Saudi Fields," *New York Times*, February 25, 2004.

65. Proven reserves of natural gas, a relatively clean energy source projected to grow in use more rapidly than oil, are even more concentrated than oil reserves: 55% are in three countries, Russia, Iran and Qatar, 70% in Russia, the Caucasian republics and the Middle East. See International Energy Agency, *World Energy Outlook 2007*, p. 74; Energy Information Agency, "World Proved Reserves of Oil and Natural Gas."

66. Thomas E. Ricks, *Fiasco: The American Military Adventure in Iraq* (New York: Penguin, 2006).

67. See the report of the National Security Council meeting by Treasury Secretary O'Neill and the text of the memorandum in Ron Suskind, *The Price of Loyalty*, pp. 72, 74, 77. The quoted remarks from the meeting are, respectively, by National Security Advisor Rice and CIA Director Tenet.

68. Daphne Eviatar, "Free-Market Iraq? Not So Fast," *New York Times*, News of the Week in Review, January 10, 2004. The "Not So Fast" refers to impotent doubts about the compatibility of such measures with Hague and Geneva conventions. The changes were largely promulgated as "Orders" of the Coalition Provisional Authority on September 19, 2003.

69. Laure Belot, "Les groupes americains menacent les positions français au Qatar," *Le Monde*, May 10, 2003, pp. 2 f.

70. See Tarek al-Issawi, "Iraq Awards Mobile Telephone Contracts," *Independent*, October 7, 2003, p. 2; Edward Wong, "The Struggle for Iraq," *New York Times*, December 23, 2003.

71. Commission on Presidential Debates, *First Bush–Kerry Presidential Debate* (2004), www.debates.org, p. 7.

72. John Kerry, "Making America Secure Again," address to the Council on Foreign Relations, December 3, 2003, www.johnkerry.com, p. 3.

73. Jeffrey Goldberg, "Letter from Washington: Central Casting," *New Yorker*, May 29, 2006, p. 68.

## CHAPTER 8

1. See Rawls, *A Theory of Justice* (Cambridge, Mass.: Harvard University Press, 1971), pp. 282–4.

2. See Goodin, "Clubbish Justice," *Politics, Philosophy and Economics* 7 (2008): 233–7. I am indebted to him for raising this question at a panel at the 2009 Pacific Division meeting of the American Philosophical Association.

3. World Bank, *World Development Indicators 2008* (Washington: World Bank, 2008), table 6.1.

4. See World Bank, *World Development Indicators 2008*, table 6.12. More precisely, these were the net disbursements of official development assistance from members of the Development Assistance Committee of the OECD, which provide 95% of such assistance. See also Development Co-operation Directorate-Development Assistance Committee (DCD-DAC), *Statistical Annex to the 2007 Development Co-operation Report* (Paris: OECD, 2007), table 33.

5. See World Bank, *World Development Indicators 2008*, table 6.14.

6. Jeffrey Sachs, *The End of Poverty: Economic Possibilities for Our Time* (New York: Penguin, 2005).

7. This is the outcome of the vast majority of statistical analyses employing multilinear regressions on large data bases that estimate the independent impact of aid on growth and allow for diminishing returns. Henrik Hansen and Finn Tarp, "Aid Effectiveness Disputed" in Tarp, ed., *Foreign Aid and Development* (London: Routledge, 2000), pp. 103–28 and Michael Clemens, Steven Radelet and Rikhil Bhavnani, "Counting Chickens When They Hatch: The Short Term Effect of Aid on Growth" (Washington: Center for Global Development, 2004), www.cgdev.org/contents/publications/detail/2744, present findings of the authors along these lines and survey the extensive literature on aid and growth. In a rare attempt to identify the relationship between foreign aid and a direct measure of the quality of life, Stephen Kosack took rate of increase in the Human Development Index, an annual rating by the United Nations Development Program, as the desired quantity. He found no positive independent contribution of aid. However, he sought a linear association, not the quadratic relationship that typically reveals small positive diminishing returns in growth

studies. See Kosack, "Effective Aid: How Democracy Allows Development Aid to Improve the Quality of Life," *World Development* 31 (2003): 1–22, especially tables 2 and 5.

8. The study of mechanisms by which large aid flows relative to the size of an economy can exacerbate weaknesses in governance has focussed on sub-Saharan Africa, recipient of two-fifths of official development assistance and primary target of leading proposals for a large increase in the scale of aid. In "Foreign Aid, Institutions, and Governance in Aid," *Economic Development and Cultural Change* 52 (2004): 255–85, Deborah Brautigam and Stephen Knack describe mechanisms by which the political distortions might occur, note specific cases in which they seem to have occurred, and offer these mechanisms as part of the explanation of their finding that aid/GNP and aid/government expenditure in sub-Saharan Africa are negatively correlated with the quality of government and with tax-collection efforts, controlling for other relevant factors. (Alberto Alesina and Beatrice Weder, "Do Corrupt Governments Receive Less Foreign Aid?," *American Economic Review* 92 (2002): 1126–37, report a positive independent correlation of aid with corruption among aid-receiving countries in general.) Other studies of recent African political processes describing significant negative political impacts of large aid inflows include Ravi Kanbur, "Conditionality and Debt in Africa," in Tarp, *Foreign Aid and Development*; Nicolas van de Walle's wide-ranging study *African Economies and the Politics of Permanent Crisis, 1979–1999* (Cambridge: Cambridge University Press, 2001); Marc Wuyts, "Foreign Aid, Structural Adjustment, and Public Management: The Mozambican Experience," *Development and Change* 27 (1996): 717–49; Joseph Hanlon, "Do Donors Promote Corruption?: The Case of Mozambique," *Third World Quarterly* 25 (2004): 747–62; Tony Hodges, *Angola: Anatomy of an Oil State* (Bloomington: Indiana University Press, 2004); and Todd Moss, Gunilla Pettersson and Nicolas van de Walle, "An Aid-Institutions Paradox? A Review Essay on Aid Dependency and State Building in sub-Saharan Africa" (Washington: Center for Global Development, 2006), www.cgdev.org/contents/publications/detail/5646. The tendency of increased channeling of aid through NGOs to weaken governmental capacities that are important for development is a significant theme in recent studies.

9. Easterly, *The White Man's Burden* (New York: Penguin, 2006).

10. See Joseph Stiglitz and Andrew Charlton, *Fair Trade for All* (Oxford: Oxford University Press, 2005), pp. 94–102.

11. See Sachs, *The End of Poverty*, p. 299.

12. *World Development Indicators 2008*, table 4.1.

13. See George Borjas, Richard Freeman and Lawrence Katz, "How Much Do Immigration and Trade Affect Labor Market Outcomes?," *Brookings Papers on Economic Activity* 1 (1997), pp. 2, 62. Such estimates are inevitably controversial, since many other relevant changes occur as a national economy evolves over the years. Studies of individual locales reveal no substantial negative effect on the local poor. For example, the Mariel boat-lift was not followed by a decline in wages for unskilled people in Miami. But Borjas *et al.* identify causal factors, such as changed residence patterns of native-born workers, that would diffuse the negative impact throughout the whole economy. What one can say is that past experience combined with economic theory is a basis for informed anxiety about the impact on unskilled workers already in the United States of large increases of immigration by unskilled and semi-skilled people.

14. See Mark Rank, *One Nation, Underprivileged* (Oxford: Oxford University Press, 2004), pp. 31, 99.

15. See U.S. Department of Commerce, *Statistical Abstract of the United States: 2008* (Washington: Government Printing Office, 2008), tables 140, 523; World Bank, *World Development Indicators 2007* (Washington: World Bank, 2007), tables 1.1, 6.9.

16. See Bulir and Hamann, "Volatility of Development Aid" (Washington: IMF, 2006), pp. 10, 12, 13, 27. The study as a whole analyzes volatility in 76 countries in which per capita GDP was less than $3,000, aid constituted more than 1% of GDP, and population was greater than 500,000 (eliminating the special aid problems of high overhead and volatility of very small countries). The results specific to the poorest countries concern the countries in their sample classified as Heavily Indebted Poor Countries for purposes of debt relief. The cited volatility ratios involve aid and revenues as percentages of GDP, all valued at foreign exchange rates. While other measures yield smaller volatility ratios, all fit the title of Bulir and Hamann's final table, "Aid Is Volatile: Never Mind the Definitions and Smoothing Techniques" (p. 30).

17. See OECD, DCD-DAC, *Statistical Annex 2007*, table 2.

18. See OECD, DCD-DAC, *2005 Development Cooperation Report* (Paris: OECD, 2005), ch. 5, "Technical Co-operation," p. 120. This thoughtful, critical and richly informed chapter is, at once, evidence of the informed commitment of the DAC Statistics and Monitoring Division, headed by Brian Hammond, and evidence that ignorance or theoretical controversy do not explain the persistence of high levels of "technical cooperation."

19. Lancaster, *Aid to Africa* (Chicago: University of Chicago Press, 1999), p. 57.

20. For cogent further discussion of these priorities, introducing further nuances, see Richard Arneson in "Luck Egalitarianism and Prioritarianism," *Ethics*

110 (2000): 339–49. See also Derek Parfit, *Equality or Priority?* (Lawrence: University of Kansas Press, 1995).

21.  See, for example, Rawls, *A Theory of Justice*, pp. 157 f.

22.  See Rawls, *Justice as Fairness* (Cambridge, Mass.: Harvard University Press, 2001), pp. 128–30, further specifying the strains of commitment to which Rawls appeals in *A Theory of Justice*, pp. 176 f.

23.  See *A Theory of Justice*, pp. 154–6, 206 f.; *Justice as Fairness*, pp. 98–102.

24.  In *Republicanism* (Oxford: Oxford University Press, 1997) and other writings, Philip Pettit has emphasized that relationships are tainted by domination when one party has the capacity to influence another's life regardless of her interests and views, even if the stronger party benevolently abstains from using the power to interfere. His work is full of cogent insights into the conflict between human dignity and subordination to others' benevolence and into historical tendencies to replace nondomination with other ideals of freedom in response to workers' and women's protests against subordination.

25.  See *World Development Indicators 2008*, table 1.1; World Bank, *World Development Report 1990* (Washington: World Bank, 1990), p. 160.

26.  Commission on Growth and Development, *The Growth Report* (Washington: World Bank, 2008), p. 117; *World Development Indicators 2008*, tables 1.1, 4.2.

27.  The World Bank's way of establishing this purchasing power parity, reflected in the figures that follow, is, roughly, to compare the cost in the local currency of a physical unit of each physical component of national output with its cost if purchased in the United States, evaluate the whole output in dollars on this basis, and adopt the ratio of this value to the value in the local currency as the purchasing power parity in dollars of the local currency.

28.  See *World Development Indicators 2008*, table 1.1.

29.  See World Bank, *2005 International Comparison Program* (Washington: World Bank, 2007), table 6; *World Development Indicators 2008*, tables 1.1, 4.8. These figures reflect a thorough restudy by the World Bank of the old, often badly grounded purchasing power parities on which it had relied. They turned out to have greatly overestimated purchasing power parities in the developing countries of East and South Asia, where the vast majority of the world's poor live.

30.  See Shaohua Chen and Martin Ravallion, "The Developing World is Poorer than We Thought, but No Less Successful in the Fight against Poverty," pp. 32–5; *World Development Indicators 2008*, table 1.1.

31.  See Branko Milanovic, *Worlds Apart* (Princeton: Princeton University Press, 2005), p. 39, using the most common measure of over-all inequality, the Gini coefficient. Using another measure, Xavier Sala-i-Martin reports a stark and steady rise from 1970 through 1998 in "The Disturbing 'Rise' of Global Income

Inequality" (Cambridge, Mass.: National Bureau of Economic Research, 2002), www.nber.org/papers/w8904, pp. 44 f. Sala-i-Martin's title is meant to be deeply ironic. These economists are at opposite ends of controversies over globalization and inequality.

32. See Milanovic, *Worlds Apart*, pp. 61–71; Milanovic, "Worlds Apart" (Washington: World Bank, 2002), www.worldbank.org/research/inequality, pp. 50–62.

33. See Milanovic, *Worlds Apart*, p. 87; Xavier Sala-i-Martin, "The Disturbing 'Rise' of Global Income Inequality," p. 45.

34. See Milanovic, *Worlds Apart*, p. 87. Using a different measure, Sala-i-Martin, "The Disturbing 'Rise' " finds constant over-all inequality in this period when China is excluded (p. 58).

35. See Shaohua Chen and Martin Ravallion, "The Developing World is Poorer than We Thought, but No Less Successful in the Fight against Poverty" (Washington: World Bank, 2008), pp. 34 f.

## CHAPTER 9

1. Thomas Hobbes, *Leviathan*, ed. Richard Tuck (Cambridge: Cambridge University Press, 1996), bk. II, ch. 10, p. 62.

2. Michael Beschloss, ed., *Reaching for Glory: Lyndon Johnson's Secret White House Tapes, 1964–65* (New York: Simon & Schuster, 2002), p. 349. Johnson employed a hidden tape recorder, under his control, for secretly recording conversations. The much more extensive taping of Nixon's conversations was due to Nixon's clumsiness, which dictated more automatic methods.

3. Jeffrey Kimball, *The Vietnam War Files* (Lawrence: University of Kansas Press, 2004), p. 168.

4. See, for example, *ibid.*, pp. 156, 164.

5. *Ibid.*, p. 169. Kissinger replies, approvingly, "I have always believed that rather than get bled to death, that that's the better way of doing it."

6. Ball, *The Past Has Another Pattern* (New York: Norton, 1982), p. 409.

7. *Ibid.*, p. 433.

8. See Melvin Small, *Johnson, Nixon and the Doves* (New Brunswick, NJ: Rutgers University Press, 1988), pp. 113, 127.

9. *Ibid.*, p. 108, relying on notes taken at the meeting.

10. Kimball, *The Vietnam War Files*, p. 103.

11. *Ibid.*, p. 91.

12. *Ibid.*, p. 103.

13. See Small, *Johnson, Nixon and the Doves*, p. 184.

14. Richard Nixon, *RN: The Memoirs of Richard Nixon* (New York: Warner, 1978), p. 448.

15. Nixon on tape in Kimball, *The Vietnam War Files*, p. 163.

16. *Ibid.*

17. *Ibid.*, p. 217.

18. *Ibid.*, p. 222.

19. See Louis Harris, *The Anguish of Change* (New York: Norton, 1973), pp. 3, 73; Small, *Nixon, Johnson and the Doves*, p. 220.

20. See Harris, *The Anguish of Change*, p. 67.

21. See Ball, *The Past Has Another Pattern*, p. 433.

22. Originally in *The New Republic*, 1967, reprinted in Fall, *Last Reflections on a War* (Garden City, NY: Doubleday, 1967), pp. 237–46. The title excerpts a GI's suggestion to Fall about reportage: " 'Home,' says a voice in the truck cab. 'We done made it again . . . And you can tell 'em buddy. War is shit.' "

23. See David Cortright, *Soldiers in Revolt* (Garden City, NY: Doubleday, 1975), p. 44.

24. See Fred Gardner, "War and G.I. Morale," *New York Times*, November 21, 1971, p. 30; Cortright, *Soldiers in Revolt*, p. 47.

25. Gardner, "War and G.I. Morale."

26. " 'Young People Know This War Is Wrong'," *Washington Post*, September 15, 1971, p. A8.

27. Stewart Alsop in *Newsweek*, December 7, 1970, p. 104, presented in Cortright, *Soldiers in Revolt*, pp. 48 f., with similar 1971 reports from *Time*, the *Washington Post*, and the *San Francisco Examiner*.

28. In the fiscal year ending October 2005, despite an increase in recruiters from 9,000 to 12,000 and an addition of $130 million to its advertising budget, the U.S. Army fell 8% below its recruitment goal, the largest gap, in proportions and absolute numbers, since 1979. In the consequent lowering of recruitment standards, the percentage of those with a high school diploma, the Army's most important predictor of success in military training, decreased from 83.5% in 2005 (compared to a goal of 90%) to 70.7% in 2007. See Ann Scott Tyson, "Recruiting Shortfall Delays Army Expansion Plans," *Washington Post*, October 4, 2005, p. A–07; Associated Press, "Army's Recruiting Lowest in Years," www.military.com/NewsContent/0,13319,77951,00.html, September 30, 2005; National Priorities Project (presenting Department of Defense data), "Military Recruiting 2007: Army Misses Benchmarks by Greater Margin," www.nationalpriorities.org/militaryrecruiting2007, table 3.

29. Krugman's initial response to the Seattle demonstrations was characteristic of his discussions of globalization in the first years of his influential *New York*

*Times* column: "[I]t is a sad irony that the cause that has finally awakened the long-dormant American left is that of—yes!—denying opportunity to third-world workers" (Op-ed column, January 2, 2000). As the public controversy developed, he began to emphasize truths in a movement that had initially prompted his disdain. "First and foremost, the promise of export-led growth has failed in too many places . . . Latin nations have liberalized, privatized and deregulated, with results ranging from disappointing (Mexico) to catastrophic (Argentina). Open world markets, it seems, offer the possibility of economic development—but not an easy, universal recipe" (Op-ed column, November 28, 2003).

30. See Jagdish Bhagwati, *In Defense of Globalization* (New York: Oxford University Press, 2004), chs. 13 and 14.

31. Stiglitz, *Globalization and Its Discontents* (New York: Norton, 2002), pp. 3 f.

32. Focussed campaigns require sustained coordinated planning and leadership, increasingly provided by the transnational networks of advocacy groups whose workings were powerfully described by Margaret Keck and Kathryn Sikkink, *Activists beyond Borders* (Ithaca, NY: Cornell University Press, 1998) and have been much studied since. Studies that give prominence to protest movements, such as Sidney Tarrow, *The New Transnational Activism* (Cambridge: Cambridge University Press, 2005) and Charles Tilly, *Social Movements, 1768–2004* (Boulder, Colo.: Paradigm, 2004) often describe a more diffuse process.

33. Elizabeth Donnelly, "Proclaiming Jubilee: The Debt and Structural Adjustment Network," in Sanjeev Khagram, James Riker and Kathryn Sikkink, eds., *Restructuring World Politics* (Minneapolis: University of Minnesota Press, 2002), pp. 155–80, and Carole Collins, Zie Gariya and Tony Burdon, "Jubilee 2000: Citizen Action across the North–South Border," in Michael Edwards and John Gaventa, eds., *Global Citizen Action* (Boulder, Colo.: Lynne Riener, 2001), pp. 135–48, are detailed narratives of the campaign.

34. On the environmental campaigns, see Robert O'Brien, Anne Marie Goetz, Jaan Aart Scholte and Marc Williams, *Contesting Global Governance* (Cambridge: Cambridge University Press, 2000), pp. 109–58; Sanjeev Khagram, "Restructuring the Global Politics of Development" in Khagram *et al.*, *Restructuring World Politics*, pp. 206–30.

35. The central outcome of the debt cancellation campaign was the Multilateral Debt Relief Initiative, largely negotiated in connection with the 2005 Gleneagles G-8 Summit. It is directed at cancelling debts owed to the World Bank, African Development Bank, Inter-American Development Bank and IMF by the poorest of debt-burdened countries, provided that they are certified, through the Heavily Indebted Poor Country program which began in 1996, as

fulfilling the policy and governance prescriptions of the World Bank and IMF. A year after Gleneagles, 19 of 40 sufficiently burdened countries had been approved for debt-cancellation. But the actual gain to debtor countries was small. The decline in debt service of those 19 countries amounted to 5.5% of their total foreign aid. Moreover, current savings in cancelled debt service to the World Bank and the two regional development banks are to be deducted from their future loans under the terms of the MDRI. In effect, the MDRI process is a cheap substitute for traditional structural adjustment among poor and debt-burdened countries. See International Development Association and International Monetary Fund, "Heavily Indebted Poor Countries (HIPC) and Multilateral Debt Relief Initiative (MDRI)—Status of Implementation," (Washington: World Bank, 2006), pp. 5, 65; OECD, Development Co-operation Directorate–Development Assistance Committee, *Statistical Annex of the 2007 Development Co-operation Report* (Paris: OECD, 2007), table 25.

36. A 2001 review by the Bank's internal evaluation unit noted that in a recent sample of 150 projects 20% took inadequate measures to mitigate and monitor adverse environmental impacts. A 2007 review by the Bank's Quality Assurance Group estimated that 32% of projects in 2005–6 did not deserve an over-all rating of Satisfactory or better in "environmental due diligence." The advisory panel to a comprehensive environmental review in 2007 singled out the hard obstacle to focussed campaigns: "[The World Bank] continues to give low de facto priority to the goal of enhancing the environmental sustainability of development. . . . [It] has too often failed to translate its environment agenda effectively from upstream analytic work through to its downstream lending operations." See Operation Evaluation Department, "OED Review of the Bank's Performance on the Environment" (Washington: World Bank, 2007); Quality Assurance Group, "Quality of Supervision in FY 05–06," Annexes (Washington: World Bank, 2007), p. 36; Independent Evaluation Group, *Environmental Sustainability* (Washington: World Bank, 2007), p. xxv.

37. John F. Burns, "Britain Joins a Draft Treaty on Cluster Munitions," *New York Times*, May 29, 2008.

38. National Opinion Research Center, General Social Surveys, 1972–2006, publicdata.norc.org, PROUDPOL.

39. Pew Global Attitudes Project, "U.S. Image Up Slightly but Still Negative [16-Nation Pew Global Attitudes Survey]," June 24, 2005, pewglobal.org, IV. p. 2.

40. Pew Global Attitudes Project, "Global Unease with Major World Powers: 47-Nation Pew Global Attitudes Survey," June 27, 2007, pewglobal.org, p. 88.

41. See Stefaan Walgrave and Joris Verhulst, "The February 15 Worldwide Protests against a War in Iraq," International Peace Protest Survey, Media, Movements and Politics Program, University of Antwerp, www.m2p.be/IPPS (2003), pp. 1 and 11.

42. See Joris Verhulst and Stefaan Walgrave, "Protests and Protestors in Advanced Industrial Democracies: The Case of the 15 February Global Anti-War Demonstrations," in Derrick Purdue, Civil Societies and Social Movements (London: Routledge, 2007), p. 134.

43. From the data base of Stefaan Walgrave, Dieter Rucht et al., International Peace Protest Survey 2003, Media, Movements and Politics Program, University of Antwerp, www.m2p.be/IPPS; provided by Dieter Rucht. The IPPS findings on the February 15 demonstrations are to be presented and analyzed, as a whole, in Stefaan Walgrave and Dieter Rucht, eds., The World Says "No" to War: Demonstrations against the War in Iraq (Minneapolis: University of Minnesota Press, 2010).

44. Pew Global Attitudes Project, "Global Unease with Major World Powers," pp. 88, 98.

45. As Anthony Appiah cogently notes, arguments for special responsibilities to compatriots, even if sound, do not capture patriotism's "evaluative affect," any more than nutritional arguments for eating chocolate describe why people eat it. See The Ethics of Identity (Princeton: Princeton University Press, 2005), p. 330.

# Bibliography

ABC News, "Dramatic Advances Sweep Iraq, Boosting Support for Democracy," abcnews.go.com/PollingUnit, March 19, 2009.

Adams, Joseph, and John Page, "Do International Migration and Remittances Reduce Poverty in Developing Countries?," *World Development* 33 (2005): 1645–69.

Agee, Philip, ed., *The Pike Report* (London: Spokesman Books, 1977).

Agrawal, Anil, and Sunita Narain, *Global Warming in an Unequal World: A Case of Environmental Colonialism* (New Delhi: Centre for Science and Environment, 1991).

Albright, Madeleine, "SecState Albright Policy Speech on Iraq, March 26, [1997]," Federation of American Scientists, www.fas.org/news/iraq/1997.

—— *Madam Secretary* (New York: Miramax, 2003).

Alesina, Alberto, and Beatrice Weder, "Do Corrupt Governments Receive Less Foreign Aid?," *American Economic Review* 92 (2002): 1126–37.

Ali, Mohamed, John Blacker and Gareth Jones, "Annual Mortality Rates and Excess Deaths of Children under Five in Iraq, 1991–98," *Population Studies* 57 (2003): 217–26.

Alkhuzai, Amir, *et al.*, "Violence-Related Mortality in Iraq from 2002 to 2006," *New England Journal of Medicine* 358 (2008): 484–93.

al-Rasheed, Madawi, *A History of Saudi Arabia* (Cambridge: Cambridge University Press, 2002).

Amnesty International, *Annual Report, 2006*, "Ethiopia," www.amnesty.org.

Appiah, Anthony, *The Ethics of Identity* (Princeton: Princeton University Press, 2005).

Archer, David, *The Long Thaw* (Princeton: Princeton University Press, 2009).

—— and Andrey Ganopolski, "A Movable Trigger: Fossil Fuel $CO_2$ and the Onset of the Next Glaciation," *Geochemistry Geophysics Geosystems* 6 (2005), Q05003.

Arneson, Richard, "Luck Egalitarianism and Prioritarianism," *Ethics* 110 (2000): 339–49.

Azar, Christian, *et al.*, "Carbon Capture and Storage from Fossil Fuels and Biomass," *Climatic Change* 74 (2006): 47–79.

Baer, Paul, "Exploring the 2020 Global Emissions Mitigation Gap," December 2008, www.globalclimatenetwork.info.

Ball, George, *The Past Has Another Pattern* (New York: Norton, 1982).

Barker, Terry, Haoran Pan, *et al.*, "Avoiding Dangerous Climate Change by Inducing Technological Progress," in Schnellnhuber *et al.*, *Avoiding Dangerous Climate Change*.

Barnes, Cedric, and Harun Hassan, "The Rise and Fall of Mogadishu's Islamic Courts" (London: Chatham House [Royal Institute of International Affairs], 2007).

Barnett, Tony, and Alan Whiteside, *AIDS in the Twenty-First Century* (Houndmills: Palgrave Macmillian, 2002).

Baumert, Kevin, and Jonathan Pershing, "Climate Data: Insights and Observations" (Pew Center on Global Climate Change, 2004), www.pewclimate.org.

Bedoya, Harold, "Conditionality and Country Performance," in Stefan Koeberle, Harold Bedoya, Peter Silarsky, and Gero Verheyen, eds., *Conditionality Revisited* (Washington: World Bank, 2005).

Beim, David, "Rescuing the LDCs," *Foreign Affairs* 55 (1977): 717–31.

Beitz, Charles, "Justice and International Relations," *Philosophy & Public Affairs* 4 (1975): 360–89.

—— *Political Theory and International Relations* (Princeton: Princeton University Press, 1999 [original edition: 1979]).

Bertuch-Samuels, Axel, and Parmeshwar Ramlogan, "The Euro: Ever More Global," *Finance & Development: A Quarterly Magazine of the IMF* 44 (2007).

Beschloss, Michael, ed., *Reaching for Glory: Lyndon Johnson's Secret White House Tapes, 1964–65* (New York: Simon & Schuster, 2002).

Bhagwati, Jagdish, *In Defense of Globalization* (New York: Oxford University Press, 2004).

Bill, James, *George Ball: Behind the Scenes in U.S. Foreign Policy* (New Haven: Yale University Press, 1997).

Blake, Michael, "Distributive Justice, Coercion and Autonomy," *Philosophy & Public Affairs* 30 (2002): 257–96.

Bond, Patrick, and Rehana Dada, eds., *Trouble in the Air* (Durban, Natal: Centre for Civil Society, 2005).

Borjas, George, Richard Freeman and Lawrence Katz, "How Much Do Immigration and Trade Affect Labor Market Outcomes?," *Brookings Papers on Economic Activity* 1 (1997): 1–90.

Bowles, Chester, *Africa's Challenge to America* (Berkeley: University of California Press, 1956).

Bowles, Samuel, Herbert Gintis and Melissa Osborne Groves, eds., *Unequal Chances* (Princeton: Princeton University Press, 2005).

Bratman, Michael, "Reflection, Planning, and Temporally Extended Agency," *Philosophical Review* 109 (2000): 35–61.

Brautigam, Deborah, and Stephen Knack, "Foreign Aid, Institutions, and Governance in Aid," *Economic Development and Cultural Change* 52 (2004): 255–85.

Brown, Robert Craig, and Ramsay Cook, *Canada 1896–1921: A Nation Transformed* (Toronto: McClelland and Stewart, 1974).

Bryden, Matt. "Washington's Self-Defeating Somalia Policy," Africa Policy Forum, (Washington: Center for Strategic and International Studies), forums.csis.org, December 2006.

Brzezinski, Zbigniew, "How Jimmy Carter and I Started the Mujahideen" [1998 interview with *Le Nouvel Observateur*], *Counterpunch*, October 8, 2001, www.counterpunch.org/brzezinski/html.

Bulir, Ales, and Javier Hamann, "Volatility of Development Aid" (Washington: IMF, 2006).

Burnham, Gilbert, Riyadh Lafta, Shannon Doocy and Les Roberts, "Mortality after the 2003 Invasion of Iraq," *The Lancet* 368 (2006): 1421–8.

Bush, George H. W., and Brent Scowcroft, *A World Transformed* (New York: Alfred Knopf, 1998).

Bush, George W., "Letter from the President to Senators Hagel, Helms, Craig, and Roberts," March 13, 2001, www.whitehouse.gov/news/releases/2001/03/2001.

Cain, P. J., and A. G. Hopkins, *British Imperialism 1688–2000* (London: Longman, 2002).

Caney, Simon, "Cosmopolitan Justice and Equalizing Opportunities," in Thomas Pogge, ed., *Global Justice* (Oxford: Blackwell, 2001).

——"Cosmopolitan Justice, Responsibility and Global Climate Change," *Leiden Journal of International Law* 18 (2005): 747–75; (also in Thom Brooks, ed., *The Global Justice Reader* (Oxford: Blackwell, 2008)).

Carlson, Anders, *et al.*, "Rapid Early Holocene Degalaciation of the Laurentide Ice Sheet," *Nature Geoscience* 1 (2008): 620–4.

Caves, Richard, Jeffrey Frankel and Ronald Jones, *World Trade and Payments* (Boston: Addison-Wesley, 2002).

Center for Policy and Human Development [Kabul], *Afghanistan Human Development Report 2007* (New York and Kabul: United Nations Development Programme and Kabul University, 2007).

Center on Philanthropy at Indiana University, *Giving USA 2008* (Indianapolis: AAFRC Trust for Philanthropy, 2008).

Chen, Shaohua, and Martin Ravallion, "China is Poorer than We Thought, but No Less Successful in the Fight against Poverty" (Washington: World Bank, 2008).

——"The Developing World is Poorer than We Thought, but No Less Successful in the Fight against Poverty" (Washington: World Bank, 2008).

Chinn, Menzie, and Jeffrey Frankel, "Will the Euro Eventually Surpass the Dollar as Leading International Reserve Currency?" (Cambridge, Mass.: National Bureau of Economic Research, 2006), www.nber.org/papers/w11510.

Clark, John F., "Museveni's Adventure in the Congo War," in Clark, *The Congo War*.

——ed., *The African Stakes of the Congo War* (New York: Palgrave Macmillan, 2002).

Clemens, Michael, Steven Radelet and Rikhil Bhavnani, "Counting Chickens When They Hatch: The Short Term Effect of Aid on Growth" (Washington: Center for Global Development, 2004), www.cgdev.org/contents/publications/detail/2744.

Cleveland, William, *A History of the Modern Middle East* (Boulder, Colo.: Westview, 2004).

Coalition Provisional Authority, "Public Opinion in Iraq" (June 15, 2004), wid.ap.org/documents/iraq/cpa_files.

Cockburn, Andrew, and Patrick Cockburn, *Out of the Ashes* (New York: HarperCollins, 1999).

Coghlan, Benjamin, *et al.*, "Mortality in the Democratic Republic of Congo: A Nationwide Survey," *The Lancet* 367 (2006): 44–51.

Cohen, Joshua, "Democratic Equality," *Ethics* 99 (1989): 727–51.

Collier, Paul, and David Dollar, *Globalization, Growth and Poverty* (Washington: World Bank, 2002).

Collins, Carole, Zie Gariya and Tony Burdon, "Jubilee 2000: Citizen Action across the North–South Border," in Michael Edwards and John Gaventa, eds., *Global Citizen Action* (Boulder, Colo.: Lynne Riener, 2001).

Commission for Historical Clarification [Guatemala], *Guatemala: Memory of Silence*, http://hrdata.aaas.org/ceh/report/english/concl.html.

Commission on Growth and Development, *The Growth Report* (Washington: World Bank, 2008).

Commission on Presidential Debates, *First Bush–Kerry Presidential Debate* (www. debates.org, 2004).

Conetta, Carl, "Operation Enduring Freedom: Why a Higher Rate of Civilian Bombing Casualties," (Cambridge, Mass.: Commonwealth Institute, 2002), Project on Defense Alternatives, www.comw.org/pda/0201oef.html.

Congressional Research Service, *Foreign Aid: An Introductory Overview* [2004] (Washington: Library of Congress, 2004).

—— *Foreign Aid: An Introductory Overview* [2005] (Washington: Library of Congress, 2005).

Cooley, John, *Unholy Wars* (London: Pluto, 2000).

Cornia, Giovanni Andrea, and Sanjay Reddy, "The Impact of Adjustment-Related Social Funds on Income Distribution and Poverty," in Cornia, ed., *Inequality, Growth and Poverty in an Era of Liberalization and Globalization* (Oxford: Oxford University Press, 2004).

Cortright, David, *Soldiers in Revolt* (Garden City, NY: Doubleday, 1975).

Cox, Peter, *et al.*, "Acceleration of Global Warming due to Carbon Cycle Feedbacks in a Coupled Climate Model," *Nature* 408 (2000): 184–7.

Cribb, Robert, "The Indonesian Massacres," in Samuel Tutten, William Parsons and Israel Charney, eds., *Century of Genocide* (Routledge: New York, 2004).

Crouch, Harold, *The Army and Politics in Indonesia* (Ithaca, NY: Cornell University Press, 1988).

Cullity, Garrett, "International Aid and the Scope of Kindness," *Ethics* 105 (1994): 99–127.

—— *The Moral Demands of Affluence* (Oxford: Oxford University Press, 2004).

Dagger, Richard, "Rights, Boundaries and the Bonds of Community," *American Political Science Review* 79 (1985): 436–47.

Dar, Amit, and Indermit Gill, "Evaluating Retraining Programs in OECD Countries: Lessons Learned," *World Bank Research Observer* 13 (1998): 79–101.

Dayal, Rajeshwar, *Mission for Hammarskjold* (Princeton: Princeton University Press, 1976).

den Elzen, Michel, and Niklas Hoehne, "Reductions of Greenhouse Gas Emissions in Annex I and non-Annex I Countries for Meeting Concentration Stabilisation Targets," *Climatic Change* 91 (2008): 249–74.

———and Malte Meinshausen, "Meeting the EU 2° C Climate Target: Global and Regional Emission Implications" (Bilthoven: Netherlands Environmental Assessment Agency, 2005); www.pbb.nl/publications.

Donnelly, Elizabeth, "Proclaiming Jubilee: The Debt and Structural Adjustment Network," in Sanjeev Khagram, James Riker and Kathryn Sikkink, eds., *Restructuring World Politics* (Minneapolis: University of Minnesota Press, 2002).

Doyle, Michael, *Empires* (Ithaca, NY: Cornell University Press, 1986).

Dreher, Axel "IMF and Economic Growth," *World Development* 34 (2006): 769–88.

Dunn, Kevin "A Survival Guide to Kinshasa," in Clark, *The Congo War.*

Easterly, William, "The Effect of International Monetary Fund and World Bank Programs on Poverty," Policy Research Working Paper 2517 (Washington: World Bank, 2001).

———*The Elusive Search for Growth* (Cambridge, Mass.: MIT Press, 2001).

———*The White Man's Burden* (New York: Penguin, 2006).

Eisenhower, Dwight D., *Waging Peace* (Garden City, NY: Doubleday, 1965).

Energy Information Administration, U.S. Department of Energy, "International Energy Outlook 2008," www.eia.doe.gov.

Energy Information Agency, U.S. Department of Energy, "World Proved Reserves of Oil and Natural Gas, Most Recent Estimates," www.eia.gov/emeu/reserves.html, posted August 27, 2008.

European Commission, *Annual Report on the Euro Area—2007*, ec.europa.eu.

European Union, "Strategy on Climate Change: Foundations of the Strategy" (2005), europa.eu/scadplus.

Eurostat, *Eurostat Yearbook 2008* (European Commission: Luxembourg, 2008).

Fall, Bernard, *Last Reflections on a War* (Garden City, NY: Doubleday, 1967).

Farber, Henry, "What Do We Know about Job Loss in the United States?," *Economic Perspectives* [Federal Reserve Bank of Chicago, www.chicagofed.org] 2005 (second quarter): 13–27.

Ferguson, Niall, "Clashing Civilizations or Mad Mullahs: The United States between Formal and Informal Empire," in Strobe Talbott and Nayan Chanda, eds., *The Age of Terror* (New York: Basic Books, 2001).

Fernandez de Cordoba, Santiago, and David Vanzetti, "Now What? Search for a Solution to the WTO Industrial Tariff Negotiations," in Fernandez de Cordoba and Sam Laird, eds., *Coping with Trade Reforms* (Geneva: UNCTAD, 2005).

Field, Christopher *et al.*, "Feedbacks of Terrestrial Ecosystems to Climate Change," *Annual Review of Environment and Resources* 32 (2007): 1–29.

Frank, Robert, *Luxury Fever* (Princeton: Princeton University Press, 1999).

Frankfurt, Harry, "The Importance of What We Care About" [1982], in Frankfurt, *The Importance of What We Care About* (Cambridge: Cambridge University Press, 1988).

French, Howard, *A Continent for the Taking* (New York: Alfred Knopf, 2004).

Friedlingstein, Pierre, Peter Cox, *et al.*, "Climate–Carbon Cycle Feedback Analysis," *Journal of Climate* 19 (2006): 3337–53.

Friedlingstein, Pierre, and Susan Solomon, "Contributions of Past and Present Generations to Committed Warming Caused by Carbon Dioxide," *Proceedings of the National Academy of Sciences of the United States* 102 (2005): 10832–6.

Friedman, Milton, *Capitalism and Freedom* (Chicago: University of Chicago Press, 1962).

Friedmann, Harriet, "The Political Economy of Food: The Rise and Fall of the Postwar International Food Order," *American Journal of Sociology* 88 (Supplement 1982, "Marxist Inquiries"): S448–S286.

Gallagher, John, and Ronald Robinson, "The Imperialism of Free Trade," *Economic History Review* 6 (1953): 1–15.

Ganshof van der Meersch, W. J., *Fin de la souveraineté belge au Congo* (Brussels: Institut Royal des Relations Internationales, 1963).

Garfield, Richard, "Morbidity and Mortality among Iraqi Children from 1990 through 1998," Campaign against Sanctions on Iraq (1999), www.casi.org.uk/info/garfield/dr-garfield.html.

Gasiorowski, Mark *U.S. Foreign Policy and the Shah* (Ithaca, NY: Cornell University Press, 1991).

George, Susan, *A Fate Worse than Debt* (London: Penguin, 1988).

Gibson, James William, *The Perfect War* (Boston: Atlantic Monthly Press, 1986).

Gilpin, Robert, *Global Political Economy* (Princeton: Princeton University Press, 2001).

Global Witness, *Branching Out: Zimbabwe's Resource Colonialism in Democratic Republic of Congo* (London: Global Witness, 2002).

Goldberg, Jeffrey, "Letter from Washington: Central Casting," *New Yorker*, May 29, 2006.

Goodin, Robert, "What Is so Special about Our Fellow Countrymen?," *Ethics* 98 (1988): 663–86.

—— "Clubbish Justice," *Politics, Philosophy and Economics* 7 (2008): 233–7.

Gordon, Joy, "Cool War," *Harper's Magazine*, November 2002, www.harpers.org/CoolWar.html.

Gould, Jeremy, "Poverty, Politics and States of Ownership" and Gould and Julia Ojanen, "Tanzania: Merging in the Circle," in Gould, ed., *The New Conditionality* (London: Zed, 2005).

Grubb, Michael, and Karsten Neuhoff, "Allocation and Competitiveness in the EU Emissions Trading Scheme," *Climate Policy* 6 (2006): 7–30.

Gupta, Ritu, Shams Kazi and Julian Cheatle, "Newest Biggest Deal," *Down to Earth* [New Delhi: Centre for Science and the Environment], 14/12 (2005).

Gwin, Catherine, *U.S. Relations with the World Bank, 1945–92* (Washington: Brookings Institution, 1994); also ch. 6 of Kapur, Lewis and Webb, *The World Bank: Its First Half Century*, vol. ii.

Hallin, Daniel, *The "Uncensored War"* (New York: Oxford University Press, 1986).

Hanlon, Joseph, "Do Donors Promote Corruption? The Case of Mozambique," *Third World Quarterly* 25 (2004): 747–62.

Hansen, Henrik, and Finn Tarp, "Aid Effectiveness Disputed," in Tarp, *Foreign Aid and Development*.

Harmon, Mark, *The British Labour Government and the 1976 IMF Crisis* (London: Macmillan, 1997).

Harris, Louis, *The Anguish of Change* (New York: Norton, 1973).

Helms, Christine, *Iraq* (Washington: Brookings Institution, 1984).

Herold, Marc, "A Dossier on Civilian Victims of United States' Aerial Bombing of Afghanistan" (2002), www.cursor.org/stores/civilian_deaths.htm.

Hertz, Tom, "Riches and Race," in Bowles, Gintis and Groves, *Unequal Chances*.

Hirsch, Robert, Roger Bezdek and Robert Wendling, "Peaking of World Oil Production" (Washington: Department of Energy, 2005), www.netl.doe.gov/publications/others/pdf/Oil_Peaking_NETL.pdf.

Hobbes, Thomas, *Leviathan*, ed. Richard Tuck (Cambridge: Cambridge University Press, 1996).

Hochschild, Adam, *King Leopold's Ghost* (Boston: Houghton Mifflin, 1998).

Hodges, Tony, *Angola: Anatomy of an Oil State* (Bloomington: Indiana University Press, 2004).

Horsefield, Keith, *et al.*, *The International Monetary Fund 1945–65* (Washington: International Monetary Fund, 1969).

Human Rights Watch, "Military Assistance to the Afghan Opposition," October 2001, www.hrw.org/backgrounder/asia/afghan-bck1005.htm.

—— *Suppressing Dissent: Human Rights Abuses and Political Repression in Ethiopia's Oromia Region* (2005), www.hrw.org.

—— *Targeting the Anuak* (2005), www.hrw.org.

Independent Evaluation Group, *Environmental Sustainability* (Washington: World Bank, 2007).

Intergovernmental Panel on Climate Change, *Climate Change 2001: Mitigation* (Cambridge: Cambridge University Press, 2001).

—— *Climate Change 2007: Mitigation* (Cambridge: Cambridge University Press 2007).

—— *Climate Change 2007: The Physical Science Basis* (Cambridge: Cambridge University Press 2007).

—— *Climate Change 2007: Synthesis Report*, www.ipcc.ch.

International Crisis Group, "Somalia: The Tough Part is Ahead," *Africa Briefing* 45 (International Crisis Group: Nairobi/Brussels, January 2007).

—— "The Kivus: The Forgotten Crucible of the Congo Conflict," *ICG Africa Report* 56 (2003).

International Energy Agency, *World Energy Outlook 2007: China and India* (Paris: International Energy Agency, 2007).

International Monetary Fund, "Currency Composition of Official Foreign Exchange Reserves," www.imf.org, accessed June 2008.

—— "IMF Members' Quotas and Voting Power, and IMF Board of Governors," www.imf.org/external, accessed September 29, 2008.

International Monetary Fund, Policy Development and Review Department, "Review of the 2002 Conditionality Guidelines" (Washington: IMF, 2002).

—— World Economic Outlook Data Base, www.imf.org.

Iraq Body Count, "A Dossier of Civilian Casualties 2003–2005" (2005), www.iraqbodycount.org.

Jackson, Stephen, "Making a Killing: Criminality and Coping in the Kivu War Economy," Review of African Political Economy 29 (2002): 525–7.

Jacobson, Louis, Robert LaLonde and Daniel Sullivan, "Is Retraining Displaced Workers a Good Investment?," Economic Perspectives [Federal Reserve Bank of Chicago, www.chicagofed.org], 2005 (second quarter): 47–66.

Jones, G., "Iraq: Under-Five Mortality" (UNICEF, 1999), www.unicef.org/reseval/pdfs/irqu5est/pdf.

Kagan, Shelly, The Limits of Morality (New York: Oxford University Press, 1989).

Kalb, Madeline, The Congo Cables (New York: Macmillan, 1982).

Kanbur, Ravi, "Conditionality and Debt in Africa," in Tarp, Foreign Aid and Development.

Kapur, Devesh, John Lewis and Richard Webb, The World Bank: Its First Half Century, 2 vols. (Washington: Brookings Institution, 1997).

Keck, Margaret, and Kathryn Sikkink, Activists beyond Borders (Ithaca, NY: Cornell University Press, 1998).

Kimball, Jeffrey, The Vietnam War Files (Lawrence: University of Kansas Press, 2004).

Kinzer, Stephen, All the Shah's Men (New York: John Wiley, 2003).

Kissinger, Henry, Years of Upheaval (Boston: Little, Brown, 1982).

Kojo, Yoshiko, "Burden-Sharing under U.S. Leadership: The Case of Quota Increases of the IMF since the 1970s," in H. Bienen, ed., Power, Economics and Security (Boulder, Colo.: Westview, 1992).

Kosack, Stephen, "Effective Aid: How Democracy Allows Development Aid to Improve the Quality of Life," World Development 31 (2003): 1–22.

Kristof, Nicholas, and Sheryl WuDunn, "Two Cheers for Sweatshops," New York Times Magazine, September 24, 2000.

Lancaster, Carol, Aid to Africa (Chicago: University of Chicago Press, 1999).

Lane, Robert, The Loss of Happiness in Market Democracies (New Haven: Yale University Press, 2000).

Lewy, Guenter, America in Vietnam (New York: Oxford University Press, 1978).

Lim, Ewe-Ghee, "The Euro's Challenge to the Dollar," IMF Working Paper, (Washington: International Monetary Fund, 2006).

Longman, Timothy, "The Complex Reasons for Rwanda's Engagement in Congo," in Clark, The Congo War.

Maasland, Anne, and Jacques van der Gaag, "World Bank-Supported Adjustment Programs and Living Conditions," in Vittorio Corbo, Stanley Fischer and Steven Webb, eds., Adjustment Lending Revisited (Washington: World Bank, 1992).

Matthew, H. C. G., Gladstone (Oxford: Oxford University Press, 1997).

Mazumder, Bhashkar, "The Apple Falls Even Closer to the Tree than We Thought," in Bowles, Gintis and Groves, *Unequal Chances*.

Meehl, Gerald *et al.*, "How Much More Global Warming and Sea Level Rise?," *Science* 307 (2005): 1769–72.

Meinshausen, Malte, "What Does a 2° Target Mean for Greenhouse Gas Concentrations?" in Schnellnhuber *et al.*, *Avoiding Dangerous Climate Change*.

Menkhaus, Kenneth, "Political Islam in Somalia," *Middle East Policy* 9/1 (2002): 109–23.

—— "Seven Questions: War in Somalia," *Foreign Policy* on-line, December 2006.

Metz, Bert, "Meeting a 2 Degree Target: Is It Possible?" (Bilthoven: Netherlands Assessment Agency, 2006), PowerPoint accessible at ips.ac.nz/events/completed-activities/Climate Change Symposium/Dr Bert Metz.pdf,

Milanovic, Branko, *The Two Faces of Globalization* (Washington: World Bank, 2002), www.worldbank.org/research/inequality/pdf/naiveglob1.pdf.

—— "Worlds Apart" (Washington: World Bank, 2002), www.worldbank.org/research/inequality.

—— "Why Did the Poorest Countries Fail to Catch Up?" (Washington, Carnegie Endowment for International Peace, 2005), www.carnegiendowment.org.

—— *Worlds Apart* (Princeton: Princeton University Press, 2005).

Miller, David, *On Nationality* (Oxford: Oxford University Press, 1995).

Miller, Richard W., "Cosmopolitan Respect and Patriotic Concern," *Philosophy & Public Affairs* 27 (1998): 202–24.

—— "Beneficence, Duty and Distance," *Philosophy & Public Affairs* 32 (2004): 357–83.

—— "Moral Closeness and World Community," in Deen Chatterjee, ed. *The Ethics of Assistance* (Cambridge: Cambridge University Press, 2004).

Moellendorf, Darrel, *Cosmopolitan Justice* (Boulder, Colo.: Westview, 2002).

Morse, Edward, and James Richard, "The Battle for Energy Dominance," *Foreign Affairs* 81/2 (2002): 16–31.

Moss, Todd, Gunilla Pettersson and Nicolas van de Walle, "An Aid-Institutions Paradox? A Review Essay on Aid Dependency and State Building in sub-Saharan Africa" (Washington: Center for Global Development, 2006), www.cgdev.org/contents/publications/detail/5646.

Murphy, Liam B., *Moral Demands in Nonideal Theory* (New York: Oxford University Press, 2000).

Nagel, Thomas, "The Problem of Global Justice," *Philosophy & Public Affairs* 33 (2005): 113–47.

National Energy Policy Development Group, *National Energy Policy* (2001), www.ne.doe.gov/pdfFiles/nationalEnergyPolicy.pdf.

National Intelligence Council, *Global Trends 2025: A Transformed World* (Washington: National Intelligence Council, 2008), www.dni.gov/nic/NIC_2025_project.html.

National Opinion Research Center, General Social Surveys, 1972–2006, publicdata.norc.org.

Neumayer, Eric, *The Pattern of Giving* (London: Routledge, 2003).

Nicholls, Robert, and Jason Lowe, "Climate Stabilisation and Impacts of Sea-Level Rise," in Schnellhuber *et al.*, *Avoiding Dangerous Climate Change*.

Nixon, Richard, *RN: The Memoirs of Richard Nixon* (New York: Warner, 1978).

Nordhaus, William, *A Question of Balance* (New Haven: Yale University Press, 2008).

Nozick, Robert, *Anarchy, State and Utopia* (New York: Basic Books, 1974).

Nzongola-Ntalaja, Georges, *The Congo from Leopold to Kabila* (London: Zed Books, 2002).

O'Brien, Robert, Anne Marie Goetz, Jaan Aart Scholte and Marc Williams, *Contesting Global Governance* (Cambridge: Cambridge University Press, 2000).

OECD, *Agricultural Policies in OECD Countries at a Glance 2006* (Paris: OECD, 2006.)

—— DCD-DAC, *2005 Development Cooperation Report*, ch. 5, "Technical Co-operation" (Paris: OECD, 2006).

—— DCD-DAC, *Statistical Annex to the 2007 Development Co-operation Report* (Paris: OECD, 2007).

Opinion Research Business, "New Analysis 'Confirms' 1 Million+ Iraq Casualties," January 28, 2008, www.opinion.co.uk.

—— "Public Attitudes in Iraq: Fifth Anniversary Poll," Final Tables, March 2008, www.opinion.co.uk.

Overpeck, Jonathan, *et al.*, "Paleoclimatic Evidence for Future Ice-Sheet Instability and Rapid Sea-Level Rise," *Science* 311 (2006): 1747–50.

Oxfam, *Cultivating Poverty: The Impact of U.S. Cotton Subsidies on Africa* (2002), www.oxfam.org.uk/policy/papers/30cotton.

—— *Rigged Rules and Double Standards* (2002), publications.oxfam.org.uk/what_we_do/issues/trade/downloads/trade_report.pdf.

—— *Adapting to Climate Change* (2007), www.oxfam.org/en/policy/briefingpapers/bp104_climate_change_0705.

Oxford Research Institute, "National Survey of Iraq, November 2005," www.oxfordresearch.com.

Parfit, Derek, *Equality or Priority?* (Lawrence: University of Kansas Press, 1995).

Parry, Martin, Nigel Arnell, Tony McMichael *et al.*, "Millions at Risk: Defining Critical Climate Change Threats and Targets," *Global Environmental Change* 11 (2001): 181–3.

Perkins, John, *Confessions of an Economic Hit Man* (San Francisco: Berrett-Koehler, 2004).

Pettit, Philip, *Republicanism* (Oxford: Oxford University Press, 1997).

—— and Robert Goodin, "The Possibility of Special Duties," *Canadian Journal of Philosophy* 16 (1986): 651–76.

Pew Global Attitudes Project, "Global Unease with Major World Powers: 47-Nation Pew Global Attitudes Survey," pewglobal.org, June 27, 2007.

—— "U.S. Image Up Slightly but Still Negative [16-Nation Pew Global Attitudes Survey]," pewglobal.org, June 24, 2005.

Pogge, Thomas, *Realizing Rawls* (Ithaca, NY: Cornell University Press, 1989).

—— "A Global Resources Dividend," in David Crocker and Toby Linden, eds., *The Ethics of Consumption* (New York: Rowman and Littlefield, 1998).

—— *World Poverty and Human Rights* (Cambridge: Polity Press, 2002).

—— "'Assisting' the Global Poor," in Deen Chatterjee, ed., *The Ethics of Assistance* (Cambridge: Cambridge University Press, 2004).

Pollack, Kenneth, *The Threatening Storm* (New York: Random House, 2002).

Prados, Alfred, "Saudi Arabia: Post-War Issues and U.S. Relations," Congressional Research Service Report (Washington: Library of Congress, 2001), www.ncseonline.org/nle/crsreports/international/inter-74.cfm.

Preeg, Ernest, *Traders in a Brave New World* (Chicago: University of Chicago Press, 1995).

Program on International Policy Attitudes, University of Maryland, "What the Iraqi Public Wants" (from data collected January 2–5, 2006), and "The Iraq Public on the US Presence and the Future of Iraq" (September 1–4, 2006), www.worldpublicopinion.org.

Przeworski, Adam, and James Raymond Vreeland, "The Effect of IMF Programs on Economic Growth," *Journal of Development Economics* 62 (2000): 385–421.

Randel, Judith, *et al.*, eds., *The Reality of Aid 2000* (London: Earthscan, 2000).

Rank, Mark, *One Nation, Underprivileged* (Oxford: Oxford University Press, 2004).

Rashid, Ahmed, *The Taliban* (New Haven: Yale University Press, 2001).

Rawls, John, *A Theory of Justice* (Cambridge, Mass.: Harvard University Press, 1971).

—— *Political Liberalism* (New York: Columbia University Press, 1993).

—— "The Idea of Public Reason Revisited" [originally, 1997], in Rawls, *Collected Papers* (Cambridge, Mass.: Harvard University Press, 1999).

—— *The Law of Peoples* (Cambridge, Mass.: Harvard University Press, 1999).

—— *Justice as Fairness: A Restatement* (Cambridge, Mass.: Harvard University Press, 2001).

Raz, Joseph, *The Morality of Freedom* (Oxford: Oxford University Press, 1986).

Ricks, Thomas E., *Fiasco: The American Military Adventure in Iraq* (New York: Penguin, 2006).

Rights and Accountability in Development (London), "Unanswered Questions: Companies, Conflict and the DR Congo" (2004), www.raid-uk.org.

Rijsberman, F. R., and R. Swart, eds., *Targets and Indicators of Climate Change: Report of Working Group II of the Advisory Group on Greenhouse Gases* (Stockholm: Stockholm Environmental Institute, 1990).

Ritter, Scott, "The Case for Iraq's Qualitative Disarmament," *Arms Control Today*, 30/5 (June 2000): 8–14.

—— *Iraq Confidential* (New York: Nation Books, 2005).

Roberts, Les, Riyadh Lafta, *et al.*, "Mortality Before and After the 2003 Invasion of Iraq: Cluster Sample Survey," *The Lancet* 364 (2004): 1857–64.

Rodriguez, Francisco, and Dani Rodrik, "Trade Policy and Economic Growth: A Skeptic's Guide to the Cross-National Evidence" (Cambridge, Mass.: National Bureau of Economic Research, 1999), www.nber.org/papers/w7081.

Rodrik, Dani, "The Global Governance of Trade as if Development Really Mattered" (New York: United Nations Development Programme, 2001).

Roemer, John, "The Global Welfare Economics of Immigration," *Social Choice and Welfare* 27 (2006): 311–25.

Sachs, Jeffrey, *The End of Poverty: Economic Possibilities for Our Time* (New York: Penguin, 2005).

Saïd, Shafik-Georges, *De Léopoldville à Kinshasa* (Brussels: Centre National d'Étude des Problèmes Sociaux d'Industrialisation en Afrique Noire, 1969).

Sala-i-Martin, Xavier, "The Disturbing 'Rise' of Global Income Inequality" (Cambridge, Mass.: National Bureau of Economic Research, 2002), www.nber.org/papers/w8904.

Sanford, Jonathan., *U.S. Foreign Policy and Multilateral Development Banks* (Boulder, Colo.: Westview, 1982.)

Scanlon, T. M., *What We Owe to Each Other* (Cambridge, Mass.: Harvard University Press, 1998).

Scheffler, Samuel, "Relationships and Responsibilities," *Philosophy & Public Affairs* 26 (1997): 189–209.

Schellnhuber, Hans Joachim, *et al.*, eds., *Avoiding Dangerous Climate Change* (Cambridge: Cambridge University Press, 2006).

Schmidtz, David, "How to Deserve," *Political Theory* 30 (2002): 774–99.

Schmukler, Sergio, and Pablo Zoido-Lobaton, "Financial Globalization: Opportunities and Challenges for Developing Countries" (Washington: World Bank, 2001).

Schuur, Edward *et al.*, "Vulnerability of Permafrost Carbon to Climate Change," *BioScience* 50 (2008): 701–17.

Schwarzenbach, Sibyl, "On Civic Friendship," *Ethics* 107 (1996): 97–128.

Sheehan, Peter, "The New Global Growth Path: Implications for Climate Change Analysis and Policy," *Climatic Change* 91 (2008): 211–31.

Shue, Henry, "Subsistence Emissions and Luxury Emissions," *Law & Policy* 15/1 (1993): 39–51.

—— *Basic Rights* (Princeton: Princeton University Press, 1996 [original edition: 1980]).

—— "Global Environment and International Inequality," *International Affairs* 75 (1999): 531–45.

Singer, Peter, "Famine, Affluence and Morality," *Philosophy & Public Affairs* 1 (1972): 229–43.

—— "Reconsidering the Famine Relief Argument," in Peter Brown and Henry Shue, eds., *Food Policy* (New York: Free Press, 1977).

—— *One World* (New Haven: Yale University Press, 2002).

Small, Melvin, *Johnson, Nixon and the Doves* (New Brunswick, NY: Rutgers University Press, 1988).

Smith, Tony, *The Pattern of Imperialism* (Cambridge: Cambridge University Press, 1981).

Soros, George, *On Globalization* (New York: Public Affairs, 2002).

Southard, Frank, *The Evolution of the International Monetary Fund* (Princeton: Princeton Economics Dept, 1979).

Stern, Nicholas *et al.*, *The Stern Review: The Economics of Climate Change* (London: HM Treasury, 2006), www.hm-treasury.gov.uk.

Stiglitz, Joseph, "What I Learned at the World Economic Crisis," *New Republic*, April 17, 2000.

—— *Globalization and Its Discontents* (New York: Norton, 2002).

—— "Globalization and the Logic of International Collective Action," in Deepak Nayyar, ed., *Governing Globalization* (New York: Oxford University Press, 2002).

—— *Making Globalization Work* (New York: Norton, 2006).

—— and Andrew Charlton, *Fair Trade for All* (Oxford: Oxford University Press, 2005).

Stockholm International Peace Research Institute, "The Fifteen Major Spender Countries in 2008," www.sipri.org.

Suskind, Ron, *The Price of Loyalty* (New York: Simon & Schuster, 2004).

Tan, Kok-Chor, "Colonialism, Reparations and Global Justice," in Jon Miller and Rahul Kumar, eds., *Reparations* (Oxford: Oxford University Press, 2007).

Tarp, Finn, ed., *Foreign Aid and Development* (London: Routledge, 2000).

Tarrow, Sidney, *The New Transnational Activism* (Cambridge: Cambridge University Press, 2005).

Thomas, Christopher *et al.*, "Extinction Risk from Climate Change," *Nature* 427 (2004): 145–8.

Thornton, Peter *et al.*, "Influence of Carbon-Nitrogen Cycle Coupling on Land Model Response to $CO_2$ Fertilization and Climate Variability," *Global Biogeochemical Cycles* 21 (2007), GB4018.

Tilly, Charles, *Social Movements, 1768–2004* (Boulder, Colo.: Paradigm, 2004).

Tol, Richard, and Gary Yohe, "Of Dangerous Climate Change and Dangerous Emissions Reduction," in Schnellnhuber *et al.*, *Avoiding Dangerous Climate Change*.

Traxler, Martino, "Fair Chore Division for Climate Change," *Social Theory and Practice* 28 (2002): 101–34.

Turner, Thomas, "Angola's Role in the Congo War," in Clark, *The Congo War*.

—— *The Congo Wars* (London: Zed Books, 2007).

UNCTAD, *The Least Developed Countries Report 2006* (New York: United Nations, 2006).

Unger, Peter, *Living High and Letting Die* (New York: Oxford University Press, 1996).

UNICEF, "Child and Maternal Mortality Survey" (1999), www.unicef.org/reseval/iraqr/html.

United Nations Development Programme, *Human Development Report* (New York: United Nations, various years).

United Nations Development Programme and the Iraqi Ministry of Planning, *Iraqi Living Conditions Survey 2004* (www.iq.undp.org/ILCS, 2004).

United Nations Statistics Division, National Accounts Main Aggregates Database, unstats.un.org.

United Nations, High Level Panel on the Illegal Exploitation of Natural Resources and Other Wealth in the Democratic Republic of the Congo, *Third Report* (2002) accessible via www.raid-uk.org.

U.S. Central Intelligence Agency, *World Factbook* (www.cia.gov).

U.S. Department of Commerce, *Statistical Abstract of the United States* (Washington: Government Printing Office, various years).

U.S. Department of Defense, *The Pentagon Papers: The Senator Gravel Edition* (Beacon Press: Boston, n.d.).

U.S. Department of State, "Background Note: Saudi Arabia" (2003), www.state.gov.

—— *Congressional Budget Justification: Foreign Operations, Fiscal Year 2008* (2008), www.state.gov.

—— Office of the Historian [Edward Keefer, ed.] *Foreign Relations of the United States, 1964–68*, Vol. xxvi: *Indonesia; Malaysia-Singapore; Philippines* (Washington: U.S. Government Printing Office, 2001).

U.S. Department of the Treasury, *Assessment of U.S. Participation in Multilateral Development Banks in the 1980s* (Washington: Government Printing Office, 1981).

U.S. Energy Information Administration, *International Energy Outlook 1999* (Washington: Department of Energy, 1999).

van de Walle, Nicolas, *African Economies and the Politics of Permanent Crisis, 1979–1999* (Cambridge: Cambridge University Press, 2001).

van Vuuren, Detlef, Michel den Elzen *et al.*, "Stabilizing Greenhouse Gas Concentrations at Low Levels," *Climatic Change* 81 (2007): 119–59.

Verhulst, Joris, and Stefaan Walgrave, "Protests and Protestors in Advanced Industrial Democracies: The Case of the 15 February Global Anti-war Demonstrations," in Derrick Purdue, *Civil Societies and Social Movements* (London: Routledge, 2007).

Victor, David, *The Collapse of the Kyoto Protocol* (Princeton: Princeton University Press, 2001).

Vollmann, William, "Across the Divide," *New Yorker*, May 15, 2000.

Waldron, Jeremy, "John Rawls and the Social Minimum," *Journal of Applied Philosophy* 3 (1986): 21–33.

Walgrave, Stefaan, and Dieter Rucht, eds., *The World Says "No" to War: Demonstrations against the War in Iraq* (Minneapolis: University of Minnesota Press, 2010).

—— and Joris Verhulst, "The February 15 Worldwide Protests against a War in Iraq," International Peace Protest Survey, Media, Movements and Politics Program, University of Antwerp, www.m2p.be/IPPS (2003).

Walker, Thomas, *Nicaragua: Living in the Shadow of the Eagle* (Boulder, Colo.: Westview, 2003).

Walton, John, and David Seddon, *Free Markets and Food Riots* (Cambridge, Mass.: Blackwell, 1994).

Walzer, Michael *Just and Unjust Wars* (New York: Basic Books, 1977).

—— "Is There an American Empire?," *Dissent* (Fall 2003).

Weissman, Stephen, *American Foreign Policy in the Congo 1960–64* (Ithaca, NY: Cornell University Press, 1974).

—— "The CIA and U.S. Policy in Zaire and Angola," in René Lemarchand, ed., *American Policy in Southern Africa* (Washington: University Press of America, 1978).

Wiener, Jarrod, *Making Rules in the Uruguay Round of the GATT* (Aldershot: Dartmouth Publishing Company, 1995).

Wolff, Edward N., "Changes in Household Wealth in the 1980s and 1990s," in Wolff, ed., *International Perspectives on Household Wealth* (Northampton: Edward Elgar, 2006).

Wood, Allen, "Exploitation," *Social Philosophy and Policy* 12 (1993): 135–58.

Woodward, Bob, *Shadow* (New York: Simon & Schuster, 1999).

World Bank, *World Development Indicators* (Washington: World Bank, various years).

Wuyts, Marc, "Foreign Aid, Structural Adjustment, and Public Management: The Mozambican Experience," *Development and Change* 27 (1996): 717–49.

Young, Crawford, "The Zairian Crisis and American Foreign Policy," in Gerald Bender *et al.*, *African Crisis Areas and U.S. Foreign Policy* (Berkeley: University of California Press, 1985).

Zogby International, "Elections in Iraq" (January–February, 2005), www.zogby.com.

# Index

Abizaid, John 178
advantage, taking, *see* taking advantage
Afghanistan 127, 142, 168−70
agricultural subsidies 78
Albright, Madeleine 190
Alkhuzai, Amir 292 n. 24
American empire, *see* empire, American
Amnesty International 166, 297 n. 39
Angola 174
"anti-globalization" protests 248−9
anti-war movements
    Iraq War 247−8, 253−4
    Vietnam War 241−6
Appiah, Anthony 320 n. 5
Archer, David 284 n. 64
Argentina 132, 136
Aristide, Jean-Bertrand 144f.
Aristotle 233, 269 n. 17
Arneson, Richard 314 n.20
Austen, Jane 233
autonomy:
    cultural 156
    personal 49, 60, 65, 231−3
    political 56, 152, 160

Baker, James 70, 167
Ball, George 183, 185−6, 195, 242−3
Bangladesh 97, 99
basic needs 151−2, 155−6
Bedoya, Harold 138
Beim, David 140
Beitz, Charles 31
Belgium 121−2
beneficence 2, 23−5, 29, 230
    neediest, special status of 24, 29
    political duty of 211−16
    *see also* Singer, Peter; Sympathy, Principle
        of
Bhagwati, Jagdish 65, 248
biofuels 89, 108
Blair, Tony 176
Blake, Michael 268 n. 15
Borjas, George 313 n. 13
Bowles, Chester 171
Bratman, Michael 262 n. 7
Brazil 132, 199, 256, 285 n. 14

Bremer, Paul 205
British Empire 125−6, 131−2, 141, 150, 161
Brzezinski, Zbigniew 168, 183
Bulir, Ales 227
Bundy, McGeorge 185
Burnham, Gilbert 292 n. 24
Bush, George H. W. 167, 188−9, 259
Bush, George W. 190, 199, 205, 206, 259

campaigns, focussed 249−51, 254
Canada 131, 132
Caney, Simon 266 n. 6, 280 n.35
cap and trade 90, 97
Carter, Jimmy 166, 168
carbon tax 90, 97
charity 29, 213
    *see also* beneficence
Charlton, Andrew 219−20, 275 n. 27
Chen, Shaohua 271 n. 2
Cheney, Dick 199, 200
China 7, 65, 74, 76, 93−4, 97, 116, 199−200,
    203, 208−9, 235−6, 250, 255, 256
choice, capacity for, *see* autonomy, personal
Chomsky, Noam 251, 254
civil rights movement, U.S. 236, 258
Clean Development mechanism 102, 278 n.
    19
client regimes 159−61
climate change:
    adaptation 86, 102
    adequacy of regimes 85−6, 103−7,
        111−12, 115−16
    costs of climate change 91−2, 98−9,
        101−2, 110−11
    costs of mitigation 89−92, 97, 103−7,
        108−9, 113−14
    equity of regimes 85, 87−8, 94−5, 100−2,
        115−16
    mitigation, 86, 89, 101−3
    temperature increase 101, 109−11, 114
Clinton, Bill 168, 189
cluster munitions treaty 250
Coalition Provisional Authority (Iraq) 205−6
coercion 39f., 52−54, 159
Cohen, Joshua 270 n. 26
communities of outlook 251, 252−3

compatriots, priority of 33–36, 39, 45–6, 48,
    52, 54–55, 69, 214–5, 223–5, 257–8
concern, special 18–21
    for self 17–18, 21
    parental 18–19, 20–1
    see also compatriots, priority of
Congo 127, 136, 144, 171–6, 182
Connally, John 244
Contract and Converge 98
cooperation 45, 100–1, 103–4, 217, 231,
    234
coordination prerogatives 123
Cornia, Giovanni 79, 287 n. 40, 288 n. 46
cosmopolitanism 17, 234
cosmopolitan justice 31–3, 229–30, 234
Cullity, Garrett 16–17, 263 n. 9, 263 n. 10

Dagger, Richard 36
death tolls:
    Afghanistan 168–9
    Angola 174
    Congo 176
    Guatemala 169
    Indonesia 170
    Iran 167–8
    Iraq 166–8, 193
    Vietnam 170
debt relief 249–50
developing countries 7, 32, 196, 199–200,
    235–36
    and climate change 88, 90, 84, 98–9,
        102–3, 104, 106, 107, 108, 282 n. 47
difference principle 32–3, 50–2, 214, 229
disadvantage, social 48–53
displacement, economic:
    in developed countries 75–6, 91, 94, 222
    in developing countries 79–80, 140
distance, significance of 25–6
default policy, see beneficence: neediest,
    special status of
development assistance, see foreign aid
Doha Round 73, 199, 249
dollar, U.S. 121–22, 128, 129, 198
domineering influence 120, 128, 147–8
Dominican Republic 126, 130, 143
Doocy, Shannon 292 n. 24
Doyle, Michael 126, 286 n. 17
Dreher, Axel 139
due care 84–5, 104–7, 113, 150–1

East Asian financial crisis 122, 136, 138
Easterly, William 139, 219, 276 n. 34

Ecuador 136
Egypt 130, 131, 132, 142, 144, 160–1
Eisenhower, Dwight 171–3
emissions of greenhouse gases:
    emissions rights 96–7
    growth 88–9, 94, 282 n. 47
    per capita 97
    subsistence emissions 94
    see also climate change: costs of mitigation,
        mitigation
empire, American:
    crisis of 197–203
    decisionmaking in 184–92, 195–6
    definition 119–20, 126–7, 128–9, 132–3
    destruction by 161–2, 207
    destructive power 126–8, 141–3
    end of 207–9
    excess violence 182–4
    financial rule, indirect 134–41
    media in 192–4
    prerogatives 119–22
    responsibilities 119–23
    territorial 128–33
    threat power 124–6
    trade, role of 145–6
enclaves 56
equality 17, 23–4, 232
    see also inequality
Ethiopia 177–9
European Union 86, 125, 197–9, 208
ex ante deliberations 27
exploitation 63–8, 231–2

FAIR, at Netherlands Environmental
    Assessment Agency 89–91, 108, 109,
    114, 281 n. 46
fair provision 46–8
    see also government, functions of
Fall, Bernard 246
farmers' republic 39–40, 45
Federal Reserve, U.S. 122, 137
Ferguson, Niall 284 n. 3, 285 n. 7
Fernandez de Cordoba, Santiago 274 n. 24
financial services, U.S. 121, 122, 198
foreign aid 102–3, 218–19, 221, 227–8
    U.S. 31, 143–5, 149–50, 160–1, 190–1
    450 ppm limit 88–9, 281 n. 46, 282 n. 47
France 129, 130, 156–7, 174, 256
Frankfurt, Harry 262 n. 7
Frazer, Jendayi 180
Freeman, Richard 313 n. 13
Friedman, Milton 35

Friedmann, Harriet 289 n. 1
friendship:
  civic 43–5, 233
  duties of 43, 69
  interpersonal 43–4, 46, 69, 232–3
  see also global civic friendship
future generations, duties to 112–3

Gallagher, John 286 n. 17
global civic friendship 232–4, 255,
  260
global extrapolation 31–4, 50
globalization 59, 62–3, 256–7
global justice:
  distributive 226, 229, 233–4
  goal of 255
  see also cosmopolitan justice;
    quasi-cosmopolitanism
global social democracy 252–7
global warming, see climate change
Goodin, Robert 36, 216, 264 n. 15
Gordon, Joy 189–90
government:
  functions of 40–43
  global 233
Guatemala 126, 169, 182
Gwin, Catherine 135

Haiti 144–5
Hallin, Daniel 193
Halperin, Morton 243
Hamann, Javier 227
happiness, and GDP 91
harm 59, 84–5, 104–7
  see also due care
Hills, Carla 70
Hobbes, Thomas 41, 124, 240
hope 251–2
Human Rights Watch 251, 302 n. 94
Hussein, Saddam 167, 183, 188–9, 190,
  204–5, 259

ice ages 115
ice sheets 111, 114, 115
IMF 71, 77, 82, 128, 130, 134, 136, 137,
  138–9, 141, 156–7, 174, 249–50
immigration 53–4, 79, 220
India 125, 199–200, 235–6, 250, 256
Indonesia 170
indirect rule 125–6, 141
inequality:
  domestic 49, 68
  global 32, 58, 231–2, 236

institutional governance 181–2, 239–40
IPCC 87, 88, 109, 110–11
IQ 49
Iran 127, 166–7
Iraq:
  First Gulf War 167–8, 183, 188–9
  invasion of 2003 and sequel 127, 168,
    183–4, 190, 193–4, 203–6, 247–8,
    253–4, 259–60
  sanctions against 168, 183, 189–90
Islamic Courts (Somalia) 177–9
Israel 142, 144, 250

Japan 122, 134
Johnson, Lyndon B. 185, 241–2
Jordan 144, 177
Jubilee 2000 249–50

Kabila, Laurent 175
Kagan, Shelly 24, 261 n. 5
Katz, Lawrence 313 n. 13
Keck, Margaret 318 n. 32
Kennedy, John F. 173–4
Kerry, John 206
Keynes, John Maynard 137, 203
Kimball, Jeffrey 186
Kissinger, Henry 166, 186–8, 242–4
Kristof, Nicholas 272 n. 10
Krugman, Paul 248
Kurds 38, 166, 168
Kyoto Protocol 87, 90, 102

labor standards 67–68
Lafta, Riyadh 292 n. 24
Lake, Tony 243
Lancaster, Carol 228
landmines treaty 250
liberalization, trade 76, 79–80, 81
libertarianism 42
loyalty 43–5, 51, 55–6
Lumumba, Patrice 171–2, 182

McNamara, Robert 135, 185, 241–2
McNaughton, John 185
Malawi 7
manufacturing, transnational 63–4, 69
methane hydrate 114
Mexico 132, 157
Milanovic, Branko 176, 235–6, 266 n. 3, 275
  n. 32, 285 n. 12
military sponsorship 141–3
  see also client regimes
Miller, David 37–8

minimum, decent 50–2
   *see also* basic needs
Mobutu, Joseph 127, 173–4, 176
Moellendorf, Darrel 31, 34
Montreal Accord 71
Mubarak, Hosni 160–1
multinational institutions 130, 140, 233–4
   *see also* IMF, World Bank, WTO
Murphy, Liam 262 n. 5, 265 n. 17
mutual benefit, *see* reciprocity

Nagel, Thomas 268 n. 15
National Intelligence Council (U.S.) 200–1
nationality 37–8
natural gas 203
negative responsibilities 59
Neumayer, Eric 138
Nicaragua 126, 136, 146, 169–70
nitrogen limitation 110
Nixon, Richard M. 186–7, 195, 242–5
Nordhaus, William 109, 278 n. 21
Nozick, Robert 35

Obama, Barack 206
oil 200–202
original position 33, 52, 229
   *see also* veil of ignorance
Oxfam 251, 276 n. 35, 280 n. 76

Pahlevi, Reza 166
Pakistan 168, 250
Parfit, Derek 314 n. 20
partiality, *see* concern, special
patriotism 258–9
   American 257–60
*Pentagon Papers* 143, 185–6, 206, 241
permafrost 110
Pettit, Philip 264 n. 15, 314 n. 24
Philippines 81
Pogge Thomas 31, 59
political liberalism 71
Pollack, Kenneth 306 n. 22
"polluter pays" principle 95–98
poverty 7, 32, 59, 74–5, 93–4, 235–6
   *see also* basic needs
Powell, Colin 167
Preeg, Ernest 273 n. 17
property rights 41, 52
protest movements 247–9
Przeworski, Adam 139
public goods 42
purchasing power parity 235

Qatar 205
quasi-cosmopolitanism 217–18, 228–35
   benefits to developing countries 218–20
   costs in developed countries 220–2
   *see also* global civic friendship

radical conclusion 10, 16–17, 21–2
Ravallion, Martin 271 n. 2
Rawls, John 32–3, 50–2, 71, 214, 229, 267 n. 9, 269 n. 17
   *see also* difference principle, original position
Raz, Joseph 49, 155, 262 n. 6
Reagan, Ronald 137
realism, left-wing 239–40, 260
reasonable deliberations, in trade regimes 71–7, 81
reciprocity 36–7, 72, 78–9, 82, 155
Reddy, Sanjay 79, 287 n. 40, 288 n. 46
relationships, special 1–2, 18–21, 59
repair, duty of 81–2, 116, 161–5
   temporal limit 162–4
rescue, duty of 23–9
respect, equal 17–18, 26, 49
responsibilities, transnational, *see* quasi-cosmopolitanism
responsibilities to compatriots, *see* compatriots, priority of
Rice, Condoleezza 190
Ritter, Scott 305 n. 3
Robinson, Ronald 286 n. 17
Roberts, Les 292 n. 24
Rodriguez, Francisco 80
Rodrik, Dani 80, 248
Roemer, John 270 n. 29
Rumsfeld, Donald 205
Russia 200, 250
   *see also* Soviet Union
Rwanda 174–6

Sachs, Jeffrey 218, 221
Sacrifice, Principle of 10, 21–2
Saudi Arabia 142, 143, 201–2
SAVAK 166
Scanlon, T. M. 69, 264 n. 16, 269 n. 16
Scheffler, Samuel 18
Schmidtz, David 267 n. 8
Schwarzenbach, Sybil 269 n. 17
Scowcroft, Brent 167, 290 n. 14, 305 n. 11
self-reliance 49, 155, 158, 221
self-respect 52, 155, 231
Senegal 130
Shue, Henry 52–3, 94, 262 n. 5, 280 n. 35

Sikkink, Kathryn 318 n. 32
Singer, Peter 9–12, 18, 23
Smith, Tony 285 n. 16, 286 n. 17, 290 n. 2
social insurance 223
social movements 240–1, 247, 251–2
    *see also* campaigns, focussed; communities
        of outlook; protest movements; global
        social democracy
Somalia 177–80
Soros, George 276 n. 37
South Korea 125, 136, 138
sovereignty 39, 56, 101
Soviet Union 126, 168, 182–3
Spain 130, 162
statutes of limitation 163–4
Stern, Nicholas 109, 282 n. 46
Stiglitz, Joseph 141, 248–9, 275 n. 27, 276 n.
    36, 276, n.37
structural adjustment 136–41, 149–59
Sympathy, Principle of 13–17, 21–2, 23–8,
    211–13, 216–17


taking advantage 60–2, 81, 154–5, 230–1
    *see also* exploitation
Taliban 169, 183
Tan, Kok-Chor 290 n. 5
Tarrow, Sidney 318 n. 32
teamwork, model of 92–3, 94, 96–7
technical cooperation 227–8
Thailand 125, 138
Tilly, Charles 318 n. 32
Traxler, Martino 279 n. 30
Treasury Department, U.S. 135–7
trust 84, 100–1, 103–7, 112–13, 115, 163,
    231, 254–6

trusteeship 56–7, 101, 165
Tshisekedi, Etienne 175
Two Degree limit 86, 88–9, 91–2, 101,
    107–112, 114


Uganda 175–6
Unger, Peter 11, 261 n. 5, 264 n. 13
Uruguay Round 70, 73, 78, 80, 124–5
utilitarianism 9, 19, 50, 52


Vance, Cyrus 242
Vanzetti, David 274 n. 24
veil of ignorance 27, 74, 93, 105, 229
    *see also* original position
Vietnam 135, 136, 170, 182–3, 185–8, 192–3
    War, opposition to 241–6
Volcker, Paul 137
Vreeland, James 139


Waldron, Jeremy 270 n. 21
Walzer, Michael 105, 131, 132
Westmoreland, William 241
Wolfowitz, Paul 199
Wood, Allen 273 n. 15
Woodward, Bob 167, 188
World Bank 130, 134–6, 137–8, 156–7, 174,
    249–50
WTO 70, 76, 77–80, 130, 220, 248–9
WuDunn, Sheryl 272 n. 10


Zaire, *see* Congo
Zimbabwe 176
Zoellick, Robert 70, 146